ISBN 978-1-333-01419-3
PIBN 10451067

This book is a reproduction of an important historical work. Forgotten Books uses
state-of-the-art technology to digitally reconstruct the work, preserving the original format
whilst repairing imperfections present in the aged copy. In rare cases, an imperfection in
the original, such as a blemish or missing page, may be replicated in our edition. We do,
however, repair the vast majority of imperfections successfully; any imperfections that
remain are intentionally left to preserve the state of such historical works.

1 MONTH OF
FREE
READING

at

www.ForgottenBooks.com

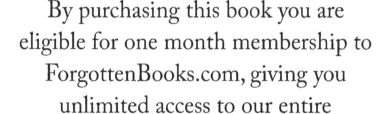

By purchasing this book you are eligible for one month membership to ForgottenBooks.com, giving you unlimited access to our entire collection of over 1,000,000 titles via our web site and mobile apps.

To claim your free month visit:

www.forgottenbooks.com/free451067

English
Français
Deutsche
Italiano
Español
Português

www.forgottenbooks.com

Mythology Photography **Fiction**
Fishing Christianity **Art** Cooking
Essays Buddhism Freemasonry
Medicine **Biology** Music **Ancient
Egypt** Evolution Carpentry Physics
Dance Geology **Mathematics** Fitness
Shakespeare **Folklore** Yoga Marketing
Confidence Immortality Biographies
Poetry **Psychology** Witchcraft
Electronics Chemistry History **Law**
Accounting **Philosophy** Anthropology
Alchemy Drama Quantum Mechanics
Atheism Sexual Health **Ancient History**
Entrepreneurship Languages Sport
Paleontology Needlework Islam
Metaphysics Investment Archaeology
Parenting Statistics Criminology
Motivational

THE

ENGLISH AND FOREIGN
PHILOSOPHICAL LIBRARY.

———◆———

EXTRA SERIES.

VOLUME VII.

AN ACCOUNT

OF

THE POLYNESIAN RACE

ITS ORIGIN AND MIGRATIONS

AND THE

ANCIENT HISTORY OF THE HAWAIIAN PEOPLE
TO THE TIMES OF KAMEHAMEHA I.

VOL. III.

COMPARATIVE VOCABULARY

OF THE

POLYNESIAN AND INDO-EUROPEAN LANGUAGES.

BY

ABRAHAM FORNANDER,

CIRCUIT JUDGE OF THE ISLAND OF MAUI, H.I.
KNIGHT COMPANION OF THE ROYAL ORDER OF KALAKAUA.

WITH A PREFACE BY

PROFESSOR W. D. ALEXANDER,

OF PUNAHOU COLLEGE, HONOLULU.

LONDON:

TRÜBNER & CO., LUDGATE HILL.

1885.

𝔅𝔞𝔩𝔩𝔞𝔫𝔱𝔶𝔫𝔢 𝔓𝔯𝔢𝔰𝔰
BALLANTYNE, HANSON AND CO.
EDINBURGH AND LONDON

PREFACE.

HAVING been invited by Hon. A. Fornander to contribute a few introductory remarks to this third volume of his work on the Polynesian race, although feeling myself unworthy of such a compliment, I can at least bespeak for his work a fair hearing and an impartial verdict. It is a truly monumental work, and gives ample proof of the indefatigable industry and critical acumen of the author.

Probably there is no race upon earth which, in proportion to its numbers, has been the subject of so much interest and of such minute investigation as the Polynesian. This is owing not only to the interesting character of the race, but also to the mystery, as yet unsolved, which shrouds their origin, and to their extreme isolation. The evidence both of language and tradition points unmistakably to the East Indian Archipelago as at least a stage in their eastward migration. Few, if any, will accept Dr. Lesson's theory that they are autochthons of New Zealand.

And yet the intervening region of Melanesia is occupied by races entirely dissimilar, which separate them by thousands of miles from their nearest congeners, the brown tribes of the Moluccas.

It is, however, generally admitted that the great work of Wilhelm von Humboldt, " Ueber die Kawi Sprache," has established on an impregnable basis the fundamental relationship between the Malagasy, East Indian, and Polynesian groups of languages, to which we can now add the Micronesian.

Still it was certainly an unfortunate mistake to apply the term " Malayan" to this vast family of languages, in view of the fact that the West Malayan tribes are comparatively late invaders of the Archipelago, having been previously largely Mongolised by mixture with the Indo-Chinese races, to a greater degree than their language alone would indicate. The Malagasy in like manner has acquired many African and some Arabian elements in its distant home.

Undoubtedly the Polynesian, as it is the most remote, is the purest and most typical representative of the family.

Many considerations combine to prove the great antiquity of the epoch when the Polynesians left the East Indian Archipelago.

Humboldt observed a large class of Sanskrit words existing in the Malay proper, the Javanese, and the Bughis, but wanting in the other languages of this stock. Hence it is evident that such words must have been introduced *after* the separation of the Malagasy and the Polynesian group from the other branches of the Oceanic family. But this period must have been very remote, since these Sanskrit words are pure and genuine in form, and free from the corruptions which the modern Indian languages present. Now the Sanskrit was a dead language 300 B.C. The Javanese mythology, and the style and decorations of the magnificent ruins of the Javanese temples, all prove the great antiquity of the Indian civilisation of Java, of which the Polynesians show little if any trace.

But besides the comparatively late infusion of Sanskrit words just mentioned, Humboldt held that there was a second class of Sanskrit words extending to remote dialects, such as the Tagala, Polynesian, and Malagasy. The wide diffusion of these words he attributed to an older form of the Sanskrit, or a " pre-Sanskrit" language.

This idea was taken up by the illustrious Professor Bopp, who published his views on the subject in 1841. His hypothesis was that the Polynesian is but the degraded remains of a once highly organised language like the Sanskrit.

As the modern languages of the South of Europe grew up out of the ruins of the Latin language, whose grammatical structure had crumbled to pieces, so he imagined that this great family of languages had arisen out of the wreck of the Sanskrit. But the dissolution of the grammatical structure of the Sanskrit in the Oceanic languages had been much more thorough than that of the Latin in its daughters, which preserve much of the old system of conjugation, and have wholly abandoned it only in their treatment of the nouns. These Oceanic dialects, he said, "have entirely forsaken the path in which their Sanskrit mother moved; they have taken off the old garment and

put on a new one, or appear, as in the islands of the
Pacific, in complete nudity."

On the other hand, M. Gaussin has clearly shown from
internal evidence the extremely primitive character of
the Polynesian language. He has shown that most of
its words express sensations or images, while most abstract terms are wanting. He demonstrates the primitive
character of its grammar, and proves that some of the
formative particles have even yet hardly ceased to be independent words. Everything about this language shows
that it is in its childhood, so to speak, and that instead of
having lost its inflections, it has never had any to lose.
Having been at a very early period separated from the
rest of the human race, destitute of metals or beasts of
burden, and deprived of nearly all the materials and
incentives which develop civilisation, the Polynesians
seem to have remained nearly stationary, and their language to be still in its infancy as regards its degree of
development.

Judge Fornander has taken up the question again from
a different point of view. Assuming that the monosyllabic,
agglutinative, and inflected systems of grammar are three
successive stages of development, through which all inflected languages have passed, he concludes, with Professor
Sayce, that there must have been once a time when the
supposed ancestor of the Aryan languages was in the
same stage of grammatical development as the Polynesian
of to-day. It was at that distant period "in the night of

time" that the ancestors of the Oceanic race separated from the Aryan stock somewhere in Central Asia.

As in Iceland the old Norse tongue has been preserved with little change, so, according to his view, the Oceanic languages have remained in a state of arrested development as a survival of the primeval language of the Aryans; as, in fact, a "living specimen" of that ancient form of speech.

His extensive knowledge of Polynesian languages has given him a great advantage over Professor Bopp in the treatment of this subject.

It must be admitted by his opponents that he has fairly stated the objections made by leading philologists to his method of comparing languages of widely differing morphological structure by means of their roots.

It must also be admitted that he has made out a strong case for the existence of an Aryan element in Polynesian, whether inherited or obtained by mutual intercourse.

Among the more striking coincidences may be mentioned the first four numerals, the pronouns, and a number of common nouns, such as *ra*, the sun = Sanskrit *ravi*, and the Assyrian and Egyptian god Ra; *kuri*, a dog = *Kuri*, an Aryan dialect of the Hindu Kush; *vai*, water = Sanskrit *vari*; *afi*, fire = Sanskrit *agni*, &c.

It may be supposed that, at that immensely remote epoch to which our author refers, the distinctions between the principal races were just beginning to be formed, and the Aryan tribes just assuming a distinct character from the other Turanian communities.

If we believe, with Quatrefages, in the original unity of the human species, then all distinctions of race are simply comparative, and merely signify a greater or less degree of consanguinity.

This much will probably be conceded by most ethnologists, that the Oceanic family, and its Polynesian branch in particular, stands in a much nearer relation to the Aryan family, both in respect to language and physical traits, than any of the Mongoloid races, or even the Dravidians. ,

At the same time we find all South-Eastern Asia occupied at present by Mongoloid races, speaking monosyllabic, tonic languages, and all traces of preceding populations are well-nigh obliterated.

It is certain, however, even from historical records, that the present occupants of Farther India are not the first settlers of those countries, but have for many centuries been moving southward, absorbing or driving out the aborigines. In like manner the Aryans or Sanskrit-speaking race had previously descended into Hindostan from the north-west, and subdued the original inhabitants.

According to Mr. Hodgson and the late Mr. Logan of Singapore, South-Eastern Asia was originally occupied by brown races allied to the Bhotiya tribes of Northern India and the Karens of Burmah. Displaced by the pressure of the Mongoloid tribes from the north, they emigrated into the Malaysian Archipelago, where in their turn they drove the black aborigines into the interior of some of the islands and peninsulas, and entirely expelled them from others.

The foremost wave of this migration of the brown race was probably composed of Polynesians, who in the opinion of our author were to a certain extent allied to the Aryan races both in blood and language.

Mr. A. H. Keane imagined that he had found a remnant of the Polynesian race in the Khmers of Central Cambodia; but, as Judge Fornander has ascertained, there is not the slightest resemblance between their languages.

He has examined the Dravidian languages of Southern India with no better success.

Messrs. Logan and Hodgson discovered remarkable, and, as they believe, conclusive analogies between the languages and customs of the Bhotiya races and those of South-Eastern Malaysia and Polynesia.

The researches of our author, however, as he believes, have tracked the footsteps of the first Polynesian emigrants still farther to the highlands of South-Western Asia, and revealed the impress of the ancient Cushite civilisation in their religion and customs.

To conclude, it is to be hoped that the discussion of this subject may serve to throw new light on certain disputed questions relating to the history of language, viz., whether languages in their historical development proceed from the simple to the complex, from monosyllables to polysyllables, and from an analytical to a synthetic grammatical structure, or the contrary; and whether, beginning with few and simple sounds, they tend to acquire new consonants, to enlarge their alphabet, and become harsher as they grow older; and finally, whether languages of radically different types necessarily pass through the same order of development or not.

W. D. ALEXANDER.

HONOLULU, *Sept.* 8, 1884.

ORIGIN AND MIGRATIONS

OF

THE POLYNESIAN RACE.

—◆—

COMPARATIVE VOCABULARY OF THE POLYNESIAN AND INDO-EUROPEAN LANGUAGES.

INTRODUCTION.

IN the first volume of my work, " An Account of the Polynesian Race, its Origin and Migrations," I have, among
other suggestions, referring to an Aryan origin of the
Polynesian family, advanced the proposition that the
Polynesian language was fundamentally a branch of the
great Aryan family of languages, and, so far as yet is
known, probably the oldest still surviving. That proposition has been denied, ridiculed, and scoffed at by some,
and treated with, I venture to say, unmerited silence by
others, whose good opinion and co-operation in elucidat-
ing this subject it would have been my highest ambition
to obtain. But, bearing in mind what Professor A. H.
Sayce so wisely says, that[1] " all new things are sure to
be objected to by those who have to unlearn the old,"
I have endeavoured to work out my problem alone, with
the satisfaction, however, of knowing that, if it fails, no
one else is inculpated in its failure.

[1] Introduction to the Science of Language," ii. 267.

To Franz Bopp, of world-wide philological fame, I am indebted for the first idea of comparing the Polynesian and Aryan languages with a view of establishing their common origin. In his "Ueber die Verwandtschaft der Malayisch-Polynesischen Sprachen mit den Indisch-Europäischen" (Berlin, 1841), he endeavoured to establish the proposition which I have now resumed. With that marvellous intuition which characterised Bopp's genius, he perceived that there was a connection between the Polynesian and the Indo-European, but he failed to demonstrate it ; not so much from disregard of his own method of proceeding with other languages, as some writers advance (A. H. Sayce, B. Delbrück), as from the fact, as I believe, that he started from incorrect premises. Bopp assumed, what almost all literary men of his day admitted as a fact, and which John Crawford alone denied—and was treated as an ethnological heretic—viz., that the Polynesians were the descendants, the degenerate and brutalised *rejetons*, of the Malay race or family. Having found a large number of Sanskrit words, in a more or less well-preserved condition, in the Malay and Javanese, and having found the same and other Sanskrit words in the Polynesian, in, as he thought, a less well-preserved condition, Bopp argued that the Malay was a corrupted daughter of the Sanskrit, and the Polynesian a still worse corrupted grand-daughter. Bopp intuitively recognised the true ring of the Aryan metal in both Malay and Polynesian, but he failed to discriminate between younger and older, and failed to detect, what in the course of this work I hope to establish, that the Aryan element in the latter—the Polynesian—was genuine and inborn, and in the former—the Malay—was adventitious and imported.

Let us glance for a moment at the appreciation which Bopp has received from those who now lead the van in philological and ethnological studies.

Professor A. H. Sayce, in his "Introduction to the Science of Language," vol. i. p. 49 (London, 1880), says :

" But even Homer nods at times ; and, as if to warn us against following too implicitly any leader, however illustrious, Bopp sought to include the Polynesian dialects in his Indo-European family, and thereby violated the very method that he had himself inaugurated."

B. Delbrück in his " Einleitung in das Sprach-Studium," p. 23 (Leipzig, 1880), speaking of Bopp's attempt to compare the Malayo-Polynesian with the Indo-European, says : " Es wird jetzt, so viel ich weiss, von den Kennern durchweg angenommen, dass diese Sprachen mit den Sanskritischen Sprachen nichts zu thun haben. Bopp aber empfing den Eindruck, dass sie zum Sanskrit in einem töchterlichen Verhältniss stünden, und suchte die Verwandtschaft in derselben Weise zu erhärten, wie die der indo-germanischen Sprachen in seiner Vgl. Gr., so weit der Charakter dieser Sprachen, welche eine totale Auflösung ihres Urbaues erfahren haben, es gestattet."

Professor W. D. Whitney, in his " Language and the Study of Language" (3d ed., 1870), p. 245, says : " Even those who are most familiar with its " (Comp. Philol.) " methods may make lamentable failures when they come to apply them to a language of which they have only superficial knowledge, or which they compare directly with some distant tongue, regardless of its relations in its own family, and of its history as determined by comparison with these." And in a note to this the Professor says : " Thus, as a striking example and warning, hardly a more utter caricature of the comparative method is to be met with than that given by Bopp, the great founder and author of the method himself, in the papers in which he attempts to prove the Malay-Polynesian and the Caucasian languages entitled to a place in the Indo-European family." On the next page the Professor says : " No man is qualified to compare fruitfully two languages or groups who is not deeply grounded in the knowledge of both ; " and that " no language can be fruitfully compared with others which stand, or are presumed to stand, in a more distant relationship with it, until it has been first compared with its own next of kin."

Thus the leaders, while souls of lesser note have taken up the slogan. But without arrogating to myself either deeper knowledge or clearer ideas of the requirements of comparative philology, I may be permitted to add to Professor Whitney's maxim above quoted, that "no man is qualified to *criticise* fruitfully" a comparison of two languages or groups "who is not deeply grounded in the knowledge of both."

Granted that Bopp's knowledge of the Malayo-Polynesian was greatly inferior to his knowledge of the Indo-European; that it was "lamentably," though perhaps excusably, insufficient to establish what he proposed; and that, however correct his perception of a relation between the two groups, yet his performance was a failure;—granted all this, are his critics who condemn him better qualified than he was, by being "deeply grounded in the knowledge" of both groups of languages? I think that few Polynesian scholars will hesitate to say that they are not, and thus, by Professor Whitney's own formula, are disqualified to pass judgment on Bopp, or rather the cause he advocated.

As between Bopp and his critics, the "tu quoque" retort might suffice, if not to justify himself, at least to silence their strictures until the last word has been spoken. But for my part, I am too conscious of my own shortcomings, defects, and possible mistakes to seek to avoid my responsibility by impeaching the jurisdiction of the tribunal. The judges are too much my masters in other things, if not in Polynesian lore, and I have too much need of their evidence in numerous details, that I could forego their good opinion; for my effort shall be to induce them eventually to acknowledge that Bopp was right in the main point, though his method of showing it might have been better.

Ethnologists of all shades of opinion are now beginning

to agree, with better data in their hands and after a
more thorough study of the subject, that the Polynesians
are not descendants of the Malays; and not a few,
among whom I notice such men as De Quatrefages, A. H.
Keane, A. R. Wallace, Dr. A. Lesson—however widely
differing on other points—positively deny any relationship, either proximate or ultimate, between the Malay
and the Eastern Polynesians. There are a few who still
maintain a sort of middle-ground of thought, and hold that
if the Polynesians are not the descendants of the Malays,
they are at least descended from the same proximate
ancestor, and are, in fact, either brothers or cousins to the
Malays. I differ from these, and think that, tested by
every ethnological, and even linguistic method, the Polynesians have no inheritance and no kindred in the
Malayo-Javanese race or culture.

That a very large number of Polynesian vocables may
be found in the Malay language I believe no one now
will deny. But, so far from proving the derivation of
the former from the latter, the very reverse is now considered to be the fact; and to any one conversant with
both languages, it is evident that almost all such words,
in their process of adoption by the Malays, have been
loaded with terminations and modes of pronunciation
entirely foreign to the idiom and genius of the Polynesian
language. Mr. A. H. Keane, in his excellent little treatise " On the Relations of the Indo-Chinese and Inter-
Oceanic Races and Languages," [1] has shown how in all
probability this adoption and adaptation of Polynesian
words by the Malays came about; and the absence of
Malay words in the Polynesian is a proof that the latter
had left the Indian Archipelago before the former had
invaded it, or before they had become so far the dominant
race as to affect the language of those Polynesian tribes
who still remained in the Archipelago, whether in a free
or a subject condition, and from whom, through mutual

[1] "Journal of Anthrop. Instit. Great Britain and Ireland," Feb. 1880.

intercourse, hostile or peaceful, the Malays obtained the Polynesian vocables which for so long have misled philologists and ethnologists.

As to the words in both languages referring themselves to an Aryan origin, I think the critical and candid inquirer will find that the Malayo-Javanese words of that character refer themselves almost exclusively to Sanskrit and Sanskritoid sources, whereas the Polynesian words of similar character refer themselves to a pre-Vedic period of Aryan speech, before the terminations and casus-endings of nouns or the inflections of verbs had been yet fully developed or finally established.

That the Polynesian is an agglutinative, and the Indo-European an inflectional language, is admitted; and that, for that very reason, there is apparently a great gulf between them, which no philological *tour de main* can bridge over, is also admitted. The Indo-European stands on the hither side of that gulf, in all the conscious, even if at times arrogant, pride of its flowers and fruits, its development and its flections.[1] The Polynesian still remains on the other side of that gulf, in a semi-nude condition, and with progress and development arrested by

[1] How some philologists of deep research and of growing fame look upon the so much boasted-of inflections in speech may be gathered from "Språkels makt öfver tanken" ("The Power of Language over Thought"), by Professor Esaias Tegnér, Stockholm, 1880, who says, p 49, "In the inflectional languages, in so far as they are inflectional, is the fusion of the elements of flection and the stem complete, so that they cannot be separated from each other. But in place of calling the fusion 'organic'—an expression to which we are wont to attach the idea of something of higher standing—it may just as well be called 'amalgamation,' a muddle, or such like. We might then see the conditions from another point of view, and the flections would then appear to us as a decay and a falling down from a purer and more perfect form of speech. . . . The Danish *vindue*, the English *window*, do not give us the impression of something more 'organic' than our old Northern *vind-òga*, but rather the contrary. Why then, for instance, should the obscuration of suffixed pronouns, through which the Indo-European verbal flections are thought to have arisen, be set forth as being especially praiseworthy? . . . And if flections, as a higher form of speech, stand in any connection with a higher civilisation, how explain the case that all the principal cultivated languages at present show a decided tendency to replace flections with turns of expressions which rather belong to the class of isolated or agglutinated languages?"

separation and isolation. Yet both these languages once stood together on that farther Aryan plateau, and well-known calls from the Indo-European camp received well-known answers from the Polynesian.

But although it seems the fashion for Indo-European savants to look upon the Polynesian, not as a chip of the same block, as a member of the same family left behind in the race, but as an alien and a stranger, whom, for the convenience of classification, it has been the custom these last hundred years to stick into the Malay pocket, yet, for all that, to use a familiar saying, " blood will tell," and the day will come when the kindred will be recognised.

To aid in the accomplishment of that event, to assist in clearing the jungle which hides the stepping-stones by which the Indo-European Aryans passed from yonder side the gulf to this, will be the object of this work. I offer no excuse for the boldness of my undertaking. The consciousness that I am right will be my answer and my apology. But though it is in vain, and alas! too late, yet it is human to wish that to my acquaintance with Polynesian subjects could have been added the advice and co-operation of those master-minds in Europe and America who are the ornaments of this age, and will be the rulers and guides of future ages in scientific research.

In retracing the steps of the Indo-European languages, the first question arises, have they always been inflectional, in contradistinction from the so-called agglutinative ? From the days of Franz Bopp and W. von Schlegel, I believe that question, though not without certain demurrers, has been answered in the negative, and the majority of distinguished philologists now concede that there was, and must have been, a time when the Indo-European branches of the Aryan were still in an agglutinative condition, when the casus- and verbum-endings, and other now fossilised forms of accretion to roots and stems, were still independent, living, sense-bearing words, agglutinated to others for the purpose of greater emphasis and precision, and to distinguish the relation of the various members of a sentence. That such is the *resumé* in fewest words, and the final decision of modern research, I gather from the "Introduction to the Science of Language," by A. H. Sayce, *passim*, and more especially in vol. ii. p. 149, and from "Einleitung in das Sprach-Studium," by B. Delbrück.[1] With the history of the flectional developments within the Indo-European branches, I, of course, have no concern in this treatise. But it is to the period of Aryan speech, when, as Professor Sayce informs us, "the cases were not as yet sharply defined," and "when as yet an Aryan verb did not exist," when the relations of nouns were indifferently expressed by prefixes or suffixes, when people said "love-I," instead of I love, *ama-yo*, contracted *amo*, φη-μι, "speak-I," &c., as the Polynesians express themselves to this day: *lofa-áu*, "love-I," *fai-áu*, "say-I," *fai-ma*, "say-we," &c., that I wish to call the reader's constant attention in the following pages.

As I have referred to Professor Sayce's "Introduction to the Science of Language," and every well-informed student has probably read the work, I feel in candour bound to state the explicit condemnation which Professor Sayce puts upon just such an attempt at comparison as I am now undertaking. The Professor says (vol. i. p. 136, &c.):—

"Unless inscribed monuments are hereafter brought to light, or comparison with the Malayan dialects results in

---

[1] P. 75: "In unendlicher Ferne hinter aller Ueberlieferung liegt die Zeit, in welcher die indo-germanische Flexion noch nicht existierte, in welcher man, sagen wir, *da* gebrauchte, um geben, Geber, u. s. w. auszudrucken. Als dann etwa *dami* ich gebe, *datar* der Geber, u. s. w. entstand, war damit die Wurzel *dā*, als solche aus der Sprache entschwunden" And on p. 98 : "Schon bei der Erörterung des Begriffes Wurzel hat sich herausgestellt, dass wir in der Geschichte des indogermanischen zwei Perioden zu unterscheiden haben, namlich : die vorflexivische oder die Wurzelperiode und die flexivische. . . . Aber auch die Flexion kann sich nicht auf einen Schlag vollzogen haben, sondern muss in verschiedenen Akten vor sich gegangen sein, so dass die flexivische Periode wieder in Unterabtheilungen zerfallen muss."

the recovery of a common parent-speech, the condition of the Polynesian languages a thousand years ago must remain unknown.   Much, no doubt, may be effected by comparing the scattered relics of these languages together, by showing that a sibilant, for instance, has been preserved in Samoan which has become a simple aspirate elsewhere, or that a guttural is retained between two vowels in Maori which has been dropped in most of the other Polynesian settlements ; but to assert that some thousand years back they resembled another language to which they bear little similarity at present, would be to argue without data, and to violate the fundamental principles of comparative philology."   And again, vol. ii. pp. 31–32, the Professor says : " The genealogical classification of languages, that which divides them into families and sub-families, each mounting up, as it were, to a single parent-speech, is based on the evidence of grammar and roots. Unless the grammar agrees, no amount of similarity between the roots of two languages could warrant us in comparing them together and referring them to the same stock."

Unfortunately no " inscribed monuments," in Polynesia or elsewhere, have been discovered to attest the condition of the Polynesian language a thousand years ago ; and " a comparison with the Malayan dialects " would be worse than useless, seeing that the latter, in so far as they resemble the Polynesian, are of comparatively younger date, and would thus only mislead, as they misled Bopp. Failing these aids, however, some traces of a former condition of Polynesian speech may be recovered by comparing the various dialects of the Polynesian itself, and by critically examining its ancient chants and prayers, which have been handed down—orally, it is true, but with wonderful correctness—and which are now historically, though approximately, estimated to be some six to seven hundred years old—many doubtless much older.   We thus find that, substantially, the Polynesian language was at that time the same as it is now, that its structure and grammar, its stunted development and half-accomplished flections, were the same then as now; and there is no reason to believe, no evidence to show, that such as it was seven hundred years ago, it may not have been three, five, or seven times seven hundred years ago.

This comparison, in the line that Professor Sayce intimates—the dropping of the gutturals in some and the changing of sibilants in others of the Polynesian dialects— I am constrained to say does not bear on the question of age at all. That the Hawaiians, Tahitians, Tongans, and others employ the aspirate *h* instead of the Samoan *s*, is no proof that the Samoan is the older form of a word. On the other hand, that the Samoans, Hawaiians, Tahitians, and others frequently drop the guttural, which is retained in the New Zealand and other dialects, is no proof that the latter is older than the former. In fact, these and some other differences of pronunciation must be referred back to a period immeasurably anterior to the arrival of the Polynesians in the Pacific, probably to the time before their separation from the other members of the Aryan stock, with whom these differences were apparently as much *en règle* at that time as they are this day in Polynesia, and with remarkable resemblance in detail. For instance, the Polynesian dialectical use of *h* in some and *s* in others, has its parallel in the conversion of the Sanskrit, Latin, Gothic *s* into the Iranian, Greek, and Old Welsh aspirate. The conversion of *k* and *p* within the Polynesian area has its parallel in the Greek and Latin, the Zend and Sanskrit. The interchange of *l* with *r* and sometimes *n*, so common within the Polynesian circle, finds its counterpart in the Sanskrit, Greek, and Latin. The conversion of Greek and Latin gutturals into Gothic aspirate and Slavonic sibilant is not unknown to, and finds examples within, the Polynesian dialects. The conversion of the Sanskrit, Zend, Latin, and other nasal *ng* into the Slave *n* has its counterpart in the

Samoan, New Zealand, and other *ng*, and the Hawaiian, Tahitian, and other *n.* Even the hardening of this *ng* into the guttural Greek γ shows itself in the Marquesan conversion of *ng* into *k.* The change of the Sanskrit and Zend *v* into the Greek F, and the Old Irish *f* has its parallel in the Hawaiian *w*, the New Zealand *wh* becoming in the Samoan, Tongan, Tahitian, and others *f.* No one now claims that the Indo-European languages are descended from the Sanskrit ; and I hope that hereafter none will claim that the principal Polynesian dialects are descended one from the other. If, according to Professor Sayce, the retention of the sibilant in the Samoan would indicate that it is the older branch of the Polynesian, the dropping of the guttural would indicate that it is the younger. It cannot be both at the same time ; and thus the Professor's criterion for determining the relative age of Polynesian dialects cannot be the correct one. Professor Sayce would hardly advance that the conversion of the Sanskrit, Latin, Gothic *s* into Zend, Greek, Old Welsh aspirates, is an evidence that the former were the older, more genuine, modes of utterance, and the latter were younger corruptions. So far as the alphabets of the Indo-European and Polynesian dialects will admit of a comparison, the phonetic changes in both are remarkably similar, and would seem to indicate a common starting-point.

If we now pass from sound to sense, it will be seen that in the majority of the Indo-European and Polynesian words which I have compared together the primary archaic sense has been better preserved in the latter than in the former, the material, underlying, sense retained in the one, and frequently lost in the other.[1]

[1] Professor W. D. Whitney, in his "Language and the Study of Language," p. 111, says on this subject : "Among the examples already given, not a few have illustrated the transfer of a word from a physical to a spiritual significance. This method of change is one of such prominent importance in the development of language, that it requires at our hands a more special treatment. By it has been generated the whole body of our intellectual, moral, and abstract vocabu-

But we are told by Professor Sayce, and doubtless correctly, that "no amount of similarity between the roots of two languages" (in sound and sense) "could warrant us in comparing them together—unless the grammar agrees."[1] Where, then, is the grammar of the ancient pre-Vedic Aryan language to be found? the grammar of the period, "when the flections had not yet been evolved, and when the relations of grammar were expressed by the close amalgamation of flectionless stems in a single sentence-word;"[2] when "there was as yet no distinction between noun and verb," and "the accusative and genitive relations of after-days did not yet exist;"[3] when "the cases were not as yet sharply defined, when the stem could be furnished with a number of unmeaning suffixes, and when these suffixes could be used indifferently to express the various relations of the sentence;"[4] "when as yet an Aryan verb did not exist, when, in fact, the primitive Aryan conception of the sentence was much the same as that of the modern Dyak;"[5] when, "apart from the imperative, the verb of the undivided Aryan community possessed no other tenses or moods;"[6] when "the Aryan language, or rather the ancestor of that hypothetical speech which we term the Parent-Aryan, was once itself without any signs of gender;"[7] when, in short, the ancestor of the Indo-European languages stood in the same semi-nude, undeveloped condition as the Polynesian of to-day still stands.

There was then, apparently, a time when the Indo-European languages,—or the dialects of a common parent-speech from which they developed themselves,—were

---

lary; every word and phrase of which this is composed, if we are able to trace its history back to the beginning, can be shown to have signified originally something concrete and apprehensible by the senses : its present use is the result of a figurative transfer, founded on the recognition of an analogy be-

tween a physical and mental act or product."
[1] *Loc. cit.* vol. ii. p. 31. |
[2] *Loc. cit.* vol. i. p. 301.
[3] *Loc. cit.* vol. i. p. 431.
[4] *Loc. cit.* vol. ii. p. 150.
[5] Ibid.
[6] *Loc. cit.* vol. ii. p. 156.
[7] Vol. i. p. 405.

not possessed of a system of inflections, and when their
grammatical relations were expressed by separate particles and "the close amalgamation of flectionless stems,"
or, in other words, they were an agglutinative language
making its first steps towards becoming inflectional. It
is to that period of the Indo-European languages, it is
with the Aryan speech of that time, that I wish to refer
and compare the Polynesian.

August Schleicher thought that that primitive Aryan
speech ("Indo-Germanische Ursprache") might be recovered by comparison and analysis. The procedure was
probably correct, but the result failed to be demonstrated,
because there were no ancient historical remains, no
accessible living specimen—that philologists then were
aware of—of that ancient Aryan speech, wherewith to
compare it. His efforts, therefore, became simply tenta-
tive and the result hypothetical, and has been treated as
such by later philologists.

With reverent hands I now take up the thread which
slipped from the hands of Bopp and eluded the grasp of
Schleicher, and propose the Polynesian as a living specimen of that ancient Aryan speech, that "Indo-Germanische Ursprache," as one of the doubtless many dialects
into which Aryan speech had already began to diverge
ere the flections had been definitely developed or generally
adopted, and while that speech was still substantially
agglutinative.

Professor Sayce tell us [1] that "we may catch glimpses,
indeed, of a time when the cases were not as yet sharply
defined," &c. Let us follow those glimpses, and see how
the probable Aryan of that period and the Polynesian
would agree.

What was the alphabet of that early Aryan speech?
What letters, and how many, served them to express
those colloquial words which were common to all their
branches before their adoption of inflections, and before

[1] See p. 12 *supra.*

their still later separation ? What was the nature and
extent of their alphabet while yet they were agglutinative
and stood on a par with the Polynesians ? No "inscribed
monuments" remain to tell. But it is well known that
most, if not all, the Indo-European languages, when first
reduced to writing, had fewer letters in their alphabets
than they have at present. How many or how few
letters served their purpose at that time may perhaps
never be known. Professor Whitney tells us that the
"earliest Indo-European language" contained only three
vowels and twelve consonants : *a, i, u,* vowels ; *l, r,* semi-
vowels ; *n, m,* nasals ; *h,* aspirate ; *s,* sibilant ; *g, d, b, k,
t, p,* mutes ; "all others are of later origin." [1] From the
inter-convertibility of several of those consonants it may
reasonably be inferred that at a still earlier period than
that referred to by Professor Whitney even fewer consonants served the purposes of colloquial intercourse.
The best developed Polynesian alphabet, the Samoan,
contains fifteen letters, ten consonants, and five vowels ;
the New Zealand and Easter Island, fourteen letters ;
the Tahitian and Marquesan, thirteen letters ; the
Hawaiian, twelve letters. To the peculiar converti-
bility of different letters common to the Indo-European
and the Polynesian dialects I have already referred on
page 10.

In regard to the Polynesian vowels,—not feeling competent to solve the question which occupied the attention of men like Bopp, Grimm, Schleicher, Pott, and
others, who, arguing from Sanskrit and Gothic, held that
the primitive Aryan had only three vowel sounds, *a, i, u,*
or whether, conformably to Greek, Latin, and others, it
contained five vowels, *a, e, i, o, u,*—it is sufficient to state
that the Polynesian, like the latter, possessed the same
five vowels. The latter may be a development of the
primitive three, but if so, it must be very ancient indeed,
and with the Polynesians they are of the very substance

---

[1] "Language and the Study of Language," p. 265.

of the language. Consonants, through dialectical pecu-
liarities above referred to, may change or be elided, but,
except in very rare and comparatively modern instances,
the vowels are permanent. The *a* of immemorial time
is the *a* of the present day, in whatever stem or root
occurring, throughout the purely Polynesian dialects.
And so with *e, i, o, u*. Hence I think it will be found,
on future inquiry and comparison, that the Polynesian
pronunciation of a word that can be fairly assumed to be
of Aryan origin will be a valuable guide in determining
the earlier, if not original, pronunciation of that word
within the unbroken Aryan circle, before the flections
began to affect the vowel sounds, the modulation of the
voice.

In regard to the morphology of the Polynesian and
Indo-European languages, their construction of sentences,
there are several points of contact and comparison which
invite the attention of the philologist.

The article, whether definite or indefinite, invariably
precedes the noun : *he hale, ka hale,* "a house, the
house," *une maison, la maison,* εἰς δομος, ὁ δομος.

In Polynesian the attributive adjective follows the
noun, the predicative precedes it : *he hale ula,* "a red
house ;" *ula ka hale,* "red (is) the house ;" *he waa loloa,*
"a long boat or vessel ;" *loloa ka waa,* "long (is) the
boat ;" *he makua alii,* "a noble parent;" *alii ka makua,*
"noble (is) the parent," &c. Professor Sayce, in his
valuable work so often referred to, calls attention to the
fact that the Aryan (Indo-Europ.) languages, with the
exception of the Romance branches of the Latin, placed
the adjective before the noun " unless it implied a sentence
of predication." [1]   But as it is admitted that there was
a period of Aryan speech when the inflections were not
yet formed and exercised their influence on the current
of thought and the position of words in a sentence ; when
the nude words which gave expression to the speaker's

---

[1] *Loc. cit.* vol. i. pp. 434-435.

thoughts must have stood side by side in the same order
that those thoughts arose in the speaker's mind,—at which
period, perhaps little later, the Polynesians separated
from the Aryan stock,—it is possible, nay, probable, that
the thoughts of the Aryan, *par excellence* the Indo-European of that time, followed the same order as that of his
disowned Polynesian brother, as that of his immediate
neighbours the Accadian—an agglutinative language—
and the Semitic—an inflectional language. Professor
Sayce [1] justly remarks that "in the primitive sentence
the object would have come first, then the attribute and
verb, and lastly the subject." To that natural and
" primitive " order of thought in the Aryan's mind and
manner of expressing it the Polynesian bears witness.
The *hale*, the *waa*, the *makua* (house, ship, parent), in
the examples quoted above, were the objects of the
speaker's thoughts; the *ula, loloa, alii* (red, long, noble),
were the attributes, the adjectives that described and
qualified the object. And the same order of thought
and expression held good in compound words.

I would not venture to contradict so eminent a philologist as Professor Sayce when he states, as a rule, that
the earlier Aryan, through all its branches, placed the
adjective, the qualifying word, the attribute, before the
noun. But the question may innocently be asked, how
early, or when, did the Aryan depart from that " primitive order of thought and expression in the primitive
sentence " to which I have just referred on Professor
Sayce's own authority? If such was the order of the
Aryan " primitive sentence "—and that it was such the
Polynesian attests, from my point of view—then the
placing the adjective before the noun, the object, must
have been a subsequent, a later change, in which the
Polynesians did not participate, as they did not in the
inflectional development. The "altered position of the
adjective in the Romance languages " would then be

[1] *Loc. cit.* vol. i. p. 436.

simply a return to the "primitive" order of a sentence, brought about under peculiar conditions—the loss or corruption, perhaps, of some of the inflections.

As regards compound words, Professor Sayce refers to the Latin *credo*, "I believe," which has the same origin as the Sanskrit *srad-dadhâmi*, "heart-placing-I." The Polynesian offers numerous instances of similar compounds: *ke-manao-lana-nei*[1] *a'u*, "I hope," literally, *ke*, article, indicating pres. ind.; *manao*, "mind;" *lana*, "floating, buoying up;" *a'u*, "I;" *lihi-launa*, "arriving at," lit. "edge-reaching;" *waha-hee*, "to lie, to falsify," lit. "mouth-slipping," &c.

Again, Professor Sayce remarks, that "at the time when an Aryan syntax was first forming itself, there was as yet no distinction between noun and verb"[2] As the Aryan was then, so has the Polynesian remained up till now. *Noho*, s. is "a seat;" *noho*, v. "to sit;" *nono*, s. "a red purple colour;" *nono*, v. "to be red in the face from exertion;" *kilo*, v. "to gaze earnestly;" *kilo*, s. "a star-gazer;" *opu*, v. "to expand;" *opu*, s. "a protuberance, belly;" *hewa*, s. "error;" *hewa*, v. "to be wrong;" and numerous others. The prefixed article alone distinguishes the one from the other, as it probably did with Aryan words at that early time when "the Aryan syntax was first forming itself."

In the forthcoming work I have endeavoured to heed Professor Sayce's warning, that "in comparing languages[3] we have first to compare their grammars, not their vocabularies. It is in the sentence, not in the isolated word, that languages agree or differ, and grammar deals with the relations that the several parts of the sentence bear to one another. Single words may accidentally resemble each other in both sound and sense, and yet belong to languages which have nothing in common." But in

---

[1] *Nei* is an article, expressing "here, now, at present."
[2] *Loc. cit.* vol. i. p. 431.   [3] *Loc. cit.* vol. i. p. 148.

order to institute a just comparison, the two things to be
compared must stand on an equal footing.   One does
not compare a full-grown man with a child, nor the
grammar of a highly inflectional language with a grammar
that is " first forming itself." I have endeavoured to
show that the Polynesians must have separated from
their Aryan congeners during some pre-Vedic period when
the syntax of the latter was still in its infancy. It is,
therefore, with Aryan speech as it was then, with the
order of words in a sentence that then obtained, that the
Polynesian must be compared.   It is to be regretted that
so little of that ancient Aryan speech and mode of expression has been preserved.   But Professor Sayce has
kindly furnished not a few illustrations, which I have
sought to utilise and combine. It is true that " single
words may accidentally resemble each other both in
sound and sense, and yet not belong to a common
language." But when, in addition to similarity of grammar, so far as such can be pointed out and identified, not
a few " isolated " words, but a host of words, including
articles and numerals, as well as words of primary
necessity to express thought, are found in two languages,
however far separate their geographical position,—their
resemblance in sound and sense must be something more
than " accidental," and I think we are justified in seeking
a common origin for both.   And as ethnologists now are
beginning to discern and acknowledge that the Polynesians
owe nothing to the Malays ethnically, it may not perhaps
be too great a heresy to seek the origin of their language
outside of the Malays.

But " language," we are told by Professor Sayce,[1] " is
no test of race, merely of social contact, and so, too, the
possession of a common stock of myths proves nothing
more than neighbourly intercourse." And in another
place he says : " Language belongs to the community,
not to the race ; it can therefore testify only to social

[1] *Loc. cit.* vol. ii. p. 267.

contact, never to racial kinsmanship. Tribes and races lose their own tongues and adopt those of others. . . . Language is an aid to the historian, not to the ethnologist. So far as ethnology is concerned, identity or relationship of language can do no more than raise a presumption in favour of a common racial origin. . . . If ethnology demonstrates kinship of race, kinship of speech may be used to support the argument; but we cannot reverse the process, and argue from language to race. To do so is to repeat the error of third-hand writers on language, who claim the black-skinned Hindu as a brother, on the ground of linguistic relationship, or identify the whole race with the speakers of Aryan tongues." [1]

There is undoubtedly much sound wisdom in the above utterances. The English or Spanish speaking Negro in North or South America has no ethnic kinship with the Goth or the Latin or their Aryan forefathers. There is in that case a palpable ethnic dissimilarity which no appropriation of a foreign language can hide or explain away. But when not only language—not merely a number of vocables, but the grammar and the foundation of grammar—but also the ethnic and physical characteristics point in the same direction, then they mutually support each other, and what at first may have appeared dark and dubious in one receives light and confirmation from the other. Professor Sayce admits that identity or relationship of language " raises a presumption in favour of a common racial origin," but no more. It was this identity or relationship that raised a presumption in Bopp's mind, and which presumption subsequent inquirers have strengthened by ethnological and historical data. It was probably this "presumption" which caused Professor Max Müller to write: " No authority could have been strong enough to persuade the Grecian army that their gods and their hero-ancestors were the same as those of King Porus, or to convince the English soldier that the

[1] *Loc. cit.* vol. ii. pp. 315-317.

same blood was running in his veins as in the veins of the dark Bengalee. And yet there is not an English jury now-a-days which, after examining the hoary documents of language, would reject the claim of a common descent and a legitimate relationship between Hindu, Greek, and Teuton. . . . Though the historian may shake his head, though the physiologist may doubt, and the poet scorn the idea, all must yield before the facts furnished by language."[1] Even so cautious and reliable a writer on this subject as Professor W. D. Whitney, after indicating the various objections to language as a racial or ethnic test, sums up by saying that "it still remains true that, upon the whole, language is a tolerably sure indication of race." And in another place he says that "language shows ethnic descent, not as men have chosen to preserve such evidence of their kindred with other communities and races, but as it cannot be effaced without special effort directed to that end."[2] It is not usual, I believe, to class Professor Max Müller or Professor Whitney among "third-hand writers on language," and yet the positivism on the one side is perhaps as instructive as the positivism of the other, and I and others may be excused for seeking a *via media* between the two.

Let us now more closely, and so far as it can be done, compare the grammars, the component parts of a sentence, of the Polynesians and Indo-Europeans, such as it presumably was when the former separated from the latter. I have shown by the testimony of the ablest Indo-European savants of the present day that there was a time when the Indo-European languages were in a transition state from being agglutinative to becoming inflectional, and that their grammar must have corresponded to the linguistic requirements and intellectual

[1] "The Languages of the Seat of War in the East," p. 29. See also "India : What can it Teach us?" by same author, p. 36.

[2] "Language and the Study of Language," p. 374 and p. 51.

status of that period. What causes, what motives, what pressure, induce a people whom an agglutinative form of speech has satisfied for unnumbered ages, to change that form—however gradual that change may come about— for an inflectional, is beyond my power to state. It is enough for my purpose that that fact is acknowledged. Nor yet is it relevant to my object whether that change be an improvement, a development for the better, indicating higher culture, a certain mental superiority, as some assert and others doubt. It is enough for my purpose that, whether for better or worse, such a change was in operation within the Aryan family of speech at or about the time that the Polynesian branch broke off from the parent stock. No "inscribed monuments," no surviving specimen among the Indo-European branches, exists to attest the condition and appearance of the Aryan tongue previous to or during that transition period. When first historically known to us, their transition period was passed, and we only know them as emerging from the profoundest obscurity with a most wonderful wealth and symmetric arrangement of inflections, from which they, each and all, have in subsequent ages been receding, and, as it were, returning to a less complicated mode of expressing men's thoughts. Professor Tegnér in the essay quoted on p. 6 says: "Flections have their real source, not in the thought of man, but in his tongue; they rise, not from thinking quicker, but from speaking quicker; not from thinking more correctly, but from speaking more incorrectly."[1] But whatever the origin of flections, whether from decay or from growth, they were not the primary mode of expression of the ancient Aryan race. Of that primary mode we can only "catch glimpses" by analyses which reveal to us that there was a time, as Professor Sayce has told us, when there was no distinction between an Aryan verb and an Aryan noun, when the casus-endings had not yet been developed, when even

[1] *Loc. cit.* p. 54.

genders were unknown, and, apart from the imperative, the Aryan verb had no moods nor tenses. We have here a tolerably good outline of the condition of the Polynesian of this day, with this addition, that a few flections had already crept into the latter before separation and isolation arrested their further development.

Bearing in mind what Professor Whitney says, that "the boundaries of every great family, again, are likely to be somewhat dubious, there can hardly fail to be branches which either parted so early from the general stock, or have, owing to peculiar circumstances in their history, varied so rapidly and fundamentally since they left it, that the tokens of their origin have become effaced almost or quite beyond recognition;"[1] bearing this in mind, let us now compare the different parts of speech which present themselves for comparison within the Polynesian and Indo-European branches.

ARTICLES.

It is said by Professor Whitney[2] that the articles in the Indo-European branches of the Aryan are of "a decidedly modern date; the definite article always growing out of a demonstrative pronoun, the indefinite out of the numeral one." Such order of genesis in the evolution of speech is probably correct; but if "modern" in relation to the growth of language, it is still old enough to have been shared in by the Polynesian branch of the Aryan stock before its separation.

Within the Polynesian area the indefinite article is expressed by: Samoa, Fakaafo, *se ;* Tonga, New Zealand, Hawaiian, *he ;* Tahiti, Rarotonga, Mangarewa, Marquesas, *e ;* ex. gr. *se mata,* "an eye;" *he ilio,* "a dog;" *e wahine,* "a woman." This refers to Sanskrit *sa,* "originally one" (Benfey), and probably reappears in the Greek ἑ-εις, the

---

[1] *Loc. cit.* p. 290.   *Loc. cit.* p. 276.

Epir. for εἰς, "one;" in the Greek ὁ, ἡ, οἱ, αἱ; in the Gothic *sa, se;* A. Sax. *se, seo;* Latin *hi-c, hæ-c, ho-c.*

The definite articles in Polynesian are : Hawaii, *ka* and *ke;* in South Polynesia generally *te: ka hale,* " the house;" *ke kumu,* " the reason;" *te tapa,* " the cloth." The Samoan definite article *le* must have been of very recent adoption, for it is not found or used in groups that were professedly, and known to be, peopled from the Samoas. To this article corresponds the Sanskrit *ta-d,* the Greek ὅς, ἡ, το (Liddell and Scott infer an original τος, τη, το, from the Homeric gen. τοιος), the Latin *-te, -ta, -tud,* in *iste, ista, istud;* Goth. *thata, thai;* Sax. *the, thæt.*

NOUNS.

The nouns in Polynesia are not distinguishable in appearance from the verbs. Numbers are marked by prefixes or duplications. Genders, as an inflection, are unknown, but marked by suffixing " male " or " female " terms. Casus-endings are also unknown. In short, the Polynesian noun is as nude as was the Aryan noun at the time referred to on pp. 11, 12.

PRONOUNS.

Among the Polynesian pronouns there are some that force themselves on our attention by their apparent, and, I venture to say, undoubted connection with Indo-European words of the same character. The principal pronouns in Polynesia are :—

1st pers. sing., Samoa, Hawaii, Marquesas, Tahiti, Hervey Group, Easter Island, *a'u,* emphatically, *o-a'u, owa'u, wa'u;* New Zealand, *ahau,* but in the possessive, *n'aku;* Javanese and Malay, *aku,* Mentawei Islands, *aku;* Tagal, *aco;* Celebes (Garontalo), *wau;* Malgasse, *aho, zaho.*

2nd pers. sing., Polynesia (*ubique*), *koe*, *'oe*; Java and Malay, *ang-kau*, *kau*, *kweh*, " thou."

3rd pers. sing., Polynesia (*ubique*), *ia*, " he, she, it ; " Malay, *dia* or *iya*; Sumatra (Singkel), *ieja*; Pulo Nias, *iaija*. The Polynesian *la* or *ra* and *na*, now only occurring in compounds forming demonstratives and possessives, were doubtless at some previous period independent pronouns of the 3rd pers. They now occur as *te-ra*, *ke-la*, *te-na*, *ke-na*, *lo-na*, *o-na*, *ko-na*, *ka-na*, *a-na*, " that, its, his, her."

No trace can be found in the Polynesian of a form of 1st pers. sing. in *ma*, yet *ma* is the base of the 1st pers. dual and plural, and as such retained pure in the Samoan and Tongan. In all other dialects coupled with *lua* in the dual and with *tolu* in the plural. 1st pers. dual, *ma'ua*, " we two ; " 1st pers. plur. *ma-to'u*, or in Tonga *ma-tolu*, " we three, we all ; " 2nd pers. dual, *ou-lua*, *ko-lua*, *o-lua*, " you two ; " 2nd pers. plur. *kou-to'u*, *ou-to'u*, *ou-ko'u*, " you three, you all ; " 3rd pers. dual, *la-'ua*, *ra-'ua*, *na* and *na-'ua* (Tong.), " they two ; " 3rd pers. plur. *la-ko'u*, *ra-to'u*, *nau* and *nau-tolu* (Tong.), " they three, they all."

Of the two forms, *aku* and *ma*, which the Polynesian retains, one in the 1st pers. sing. and the other in the 1st pers. dual and plural, the West Aryan dialects offer the following relatives : Gothic, *ik*, *mis*, *mik*; A. Saxon, *ic*, *me*; Greek, ἐγω, με, μου ἡ-μεις; Œol. αμ-μες; Latin, *ego*, *me*, *mihi*; Sanskrit, *as-ma*, *mâ*, *mat*, different cases of *aham*.

The New Zealand *ahau* stands alone among the Polynesian dialects, but its relation to the Malgasse *aho* cannot well be doubted. How far both refer to, and retain an older form of, the Sanskrit *aham*, I leave to those more conversant with Sanskrit than myself to determine, though I strongly believe in the relation until disproven.

As the Gothic 1st pers. plural and dual, *weis*, *wit*, with an apparent base of *wi*, have no kindred, so far as I know, within the Indo-European dialects, it may be possible that a similar permutation of *w* for *m*, as is not unknown in Polynesian as well as in the Indo-European branches,[1] may have taken place here, and thus *wi* represents an older *mi*, akin to the Polynesian *ma*, Sanskrit *mâ*, Greek *με*, &c.

Of the Polynesian 2nd pers. sing. and plur. I find no well-preserved relative or analogue within the Indo-European branches, unless the Sanskrit *yu*, *tu*, *tva*, pronominal bases of 2nd pers. and preserved in Latin *tu*, Greek *τυ*, *συ*, *ὑ-μεις*, Gothic *tu*, *yus*, A. Saxon *eow*, eventually refer themselves to what Mr. Gaussin ("Du Dialecte de Tahiti," 1853, p. 157) calls the second form of the 2nd pers. sing. of Polynesian personal pronouns, viz., *u*, and which now never appears except in the possessive pron. *ta-u*, *to-u*, *na-u*, *no-u*, "thine, your."

To the Polynesian 3rd pers. sing. I find related the Gothic *ija*, "she, they," *iains*, "yon, that," Germ. *iener*. If the Latin *is*, *ea*, *id*, is connected with the Polynesian *ia*, the primary base of both must have been *i*, which Benfey offers as a pronominal base of the Latin and Gothic, as well as the Sanskrit *i-d* and *i-dam*.

Indo-European relatives of the Polynesian 3rd pers., *la*, *ra*, *na*, "he, they," I find none, unless the Sanskrit *na* in *a-na*, *e-na*, "this," be one.

Among the interrogative Polynesian pronouns are found the forms of *wai*, *hai*, *ai*, "who," *aha*, *ha*, *a*, "what," *fe*, *fea*, *hea*, "how, which, where," the two latter frequently accompanied with a prefix, *pe*, whose original meaning is now lost. To these forms probably ally themselves the Greek *πού*, Ionic *κοῦ*, "where," *ποι* "whither," *πῆ*, Ionic *κῆ*, Doric *κα*, "how," Latin *quis*, *qua*, *quod*, *qualis*, &c. ; Gothic *hwas*, *hwo*, *hwa*, "who," *hwan*,

---

[1] In New Zealand, *kumara*, Greek *ἀ-μαξα*, "vehicle, cart;" "potatoes;" Hawaii, *uwala*, id. Sanskrit, *vaha*, *vahja*, id. Greek, Samoan, *male*, " to hawk and *μαλλος*; Latin *vellus*. Greek, *μαντις*; spit;" Hawaii, *wale*, "spittle." Latin *vates*.

"when," *hwaiwa*, "how," &c.; Sanskrit *ka*, *kas*, "who," *kva*, "where," &c.

COPULATIVES AND CONJUNCTIONS.

In this category may be noticed *akā*, *atā*, *'a* (Haw., Marqu., Samoa), "but, as, if." I would refer them to the Gothic *ath-than*, *ak*, *akei*, "but, however;" to the Latin *at*, "but," perhaps also *ac ;* to Sanskrit *atha*, "but, if."

ADVERBS.

Among the Polynesian negative adverbs we meet with the Tahitian *ai-ta*, *ai-ma*, *ai-na*, *ai-pa*, "not, no," used with the past only, and *ei-ma*, *ei-na*, *ei-ta*, used with the future; Marquesas, *ai-e*, "no, not;" Tonga, *i-kai* and *tai*, "no, not ;" Fakaafo, *ai* with suffix *ala*, e.g., *ai-ala*, *tai-ala*, "no, not;" Rotumah, *inke*, *indi*, "no ;" Malay, *ti*, *tia*, *tiada*, "no, not ;" Sunda, *ente*, id. ; Malgasse, *tsi*, id. I would consider all these different forms as merely dialectical variations of a common and original negative, whose form was probably *i*. By analysing the Tahitian forms I arrive at that conclusion. The last syllables, *-ta*, *-ma*, *-na*, are suffixes, making the negative more or less emphatic, but whose original meaning I am unable to state. The *-pa* in *-ai-pa*, however, is known to imply a qualification, and to "include an idea of doubt or contingency," and is probably a contraction of the general adverb *paha*, "perhaps." Remains therefore the *ai*, which we find alone in the Fakaafo dialect, and nearly so in the Marquesan *ai-e*, some of the other dialects having prefixed a *t* or *k*, as the Tonga. But the *a* in *ai* is as much euphonic as the *a* in *a-ole*, that other Polynesian negative current in the Hawaiian and other groups; and its euphonic prefixual character is moreover evidenced by its being changed into *e* when the negative is applied to the future, *ai-ta* becoming *ei-ta*, &c. There remains, then, only the original *i* as an expression of negation, which we find reproduced in the Tonga *i-kai* and the Rotumah *i-nke*, and which probably meets us with prefixed *t* or *ts* in the Malay *ti* and the Malgasse *tsi*, "no, not."

Among the Indo-European languages it is often difficult to ascertain which vowel-sound in a common root or stem was the primary or original one. Hence, though the Sanskrit and Greek have their *a* privativum, expressing an idea of negation, which in the former becomes *an* before vowels, yet the Latin and Gothic express the same idea with *in* and *un*, the Scandinavian with *o ;* the absolute negative particle in Greek is *ού*. In all these the simple vowel was the original sign and expression of negation; but was that vowel *a, i, u,* or *o ?* If I am sustained in considering the Polynesian as an older branch than either of the above, I should hold that the Polynesian *i* was the primary form, from which itself as well as the others have deviated ; for not only do traces remain of this original *i* in the Latin *in,* but also in the Scandinavian *ej, inte, icke,* adverbs of negation, and. *ingen,* " none."

Another Polynesian negative deserves consideration. It is *mai* (Haw.), *u-moi* (Marqu.), with a prohibitive sense used imperatively, " do not;" *mai hele oe,* " do not go you;" *mai hana*, "don't do it." It corresponds in sense and use as well as sound to the Greek *μή*, the Sanskrit *mâ,* the Latin *ne*, " do not, no."

Some of the Polynesian affirmatives also proclaim their affinity to the West Aryan branches. Thus in Tonga, Samoa, Fakaafo, *io,* " yes," Hawaii, *io,* " truly, verily ;" Fiji, *io* and *ia*, " yes ;" Malgasse, *ie,* Malay, *ija,* Sunda, *nja ;* all which show a remarkable family likeness to the Gothic *ja, jai,* " yes, yea," the Scandinavian *ia, jo, ju,* id. ; perhaps the Greek *εἶα,* Latin *eia, eia vero,* "very well." The other Polynesian affirmative, *e, o-e, io-e,* Pulo Nias, *eh,* " yes," probably refers itself to the Greek *ἦ,* " in truth, verily."

VERBS.

The Polynesian present participial ending, verb active, Hawaiian *-ana,* New Zealand *-ana, -enga,* is by some philologists classed as a verbal particle, but is none the less a pure inflection, whose original meaning when standing alone or merely agglutinated can no longer be explained. It corresponds to the Indo-European participial endings in : Latin *-ans, -ens,* Greek *-ων,* Gothic *-ands, -onds,* Sanskrit *-ana,* and others. And I find that the manner of converting a verbal participle into a noun substantive, by help of this flection or particle, is the same in the Polynesian and the Sanskrit and other Indo-European branches. Thus in Polynesian, *hanau,* "to bring forth ; " *hanau-ana,* " birth ; " *moe,* " to sleep ; " *mo'-ena, moe'-nga,* contracted from *moe-ana,* "a sleeping place, mat, or mattress ; " and numerous others. Compare Sanskrit *kânch-ana,* "gold," from *kanch,* "to shine ; " *krodhâna,* " anger," from *krudh,* " be wroth ; " *gam-ana,* " gait," from *gam,* " to go ; " *budh-âna,* "teacher," from *budh,* "to understand ; " *yudh-ana,* " enemy," from *yudh,* " to fight ; " and so throughout the Indo-European branches down to the English *hear-ing, see-ing, fight-ing, bleed-ing,* &c., used substantively.

The sign of the passive voice of the verb throughout Polynesia is *-ia.* It is frequently for euphony's sake preceded by a consonant, such as *t, h, l, m, s, ng, f,* and sometimes contracted to *a* alone. Whatever its meaning as an independent word might have been has been lost; but though generally suffixed to the verb and incorporated with it as a flection, either by the additional consonant or by the loss of its own first vowel, or pure and simple, its place is not yet so fixed but that it admits frequently a qualifying adverb between the verb and itself, and thus shows a transition period from an independent verbal particle, bearing a sense and form of its own, to a fixed meaningless flection. Ex. gr., *hana-ia na mea a pau,*

" done were all things ; " *ike-a na olelo a Ku,* " understood were the words of Ku ; " *auhuli-hia ke aupuni o Lono,* " overturned is the government of Lono ; " *kau-lia ka paku,* " hung up is the curtain ; " *kini-tia,* " pinched ; " *sii-tea,* " lifted up ; " *fau-sia,* " bound together ; " *tao-fia,* " held ; " *tanu-mia,* " buried ; " *hana-ole-ia,* " not done ; " *holo-mua-ia,* " gone before," &c.

This verbal particle, if such it be, this sign of the passive Polynesian verb, just hovering on the verge of becoming a pure inflection, seems to me to belong to that class of words from which the Indo-European branches in after-times developed some of their passive inflections and signs of different stages of their passive verbs. I find the participle of the future passive in Sanskrit formed of a verbal ending or inflection in *-ya*, in *chush-ya,* " to be sucked ; " *abhi-nand-ya,* " to be rejoiced ; " *a-pur-ya,* " not to be satisfied ; " *yaj-ya,* " to be offered," &c. I find the Greek pass. aor. ending in -εις and -θεις, the Gothic past part. pass. ending in *-iths* and *-aiths,* the Sanskrit ending in *-ita,* the Latin in *-tus.* Now all these verbal endings are merely agglutinated words, like the Polynesian *-ana, -enga, -ia, -hia, -tia,* &c., whose original meaning has been lost, and whose original form it would be difficult to say where best preserved. The similarity of form and the similarity of purpose indicated in these Indo-European and Polynesian agglutinated verbal endings, particles, or flections, active and passive, seem to me to proclaim a common origin, and that, at the time of the Polynesian separation, the Aryan language had reached that stage of development.

" Apart from the imperative," says Professor A. H. Sayce in his " Introduction to the Science of Language," vol. ii. p. 156, " whose second personal singular sometimes ended in *-dhi* (-θι), sometimes in *-si* (δος, Vedic *mâ-si*), sometimes had no termination at all, the verb of the undivided Aryan community possessed no other tenses or moods. It was left to the separate branches of the family each to work out its verbal system in its new home and in its own way, adding new forms, forgetting others, now amalgamating, now dissociating." With due respect for so great authority, yet, from the foregoing comparison, I think it passably evident that " the undivided Aryan community," at the time when the Polynesians separated from it, already had a part. pres. act. and a pret. pass. in common throughout its various branches, and had arrived so far together in the development of their verbs. If the termination indicating the imperative was developed and common property of the undivided Aryan, it has been lost in the Polynesian, as it has been lost in some members of the Gothic branch and in some of the Romance descendants of the Latin; or else it was developed subsequent to the pres. part. act. and pret. pass. terminations above referred to, and after the separation of the Polynesians.

Again, speaking of the formations of case-endings of nouns, the same author says :[1] " We can trace the history of the verb with far greater completeness and certainty than we can the history of the noun. The history of the noun is one of continuous decay. We may catch glimpses, indeed, of a time when the cases were not as yet sharply defined, when the stem could be furnished with a number of unmeaning suffixes, and when these suffixes could be used indifferently to express the various relations of the sentence. But long before the age of Aryan separation, the several relations in which a word might stand within a sentence had been clearly evolved, and certain terminations had been adapted and set apart to denote these relations. The creative epoch had passed, and the cases and numbers of the noun had entered on their period of decay. But with the verb it was quite otherwise. Here we can ascend to a time when as yet an Aryan verb did not exist, when, in fact, the primitive Aryan conception of the sentence was much the. same as

---

[1] *Loc. cit.* ii. pp. 145–150.

that of the modern Dyak. Most verbs presuppose a noun, that is to say, their stems are identical with those of nouns. The Greek μελαίνω for μελαν-γω presupposes the nominal μελαν, just as much as the Latin *amo* for *ama-yo* presupposes *ama*." If "glimpses" can be caught of a time when the cases were not as yet sharply defined, &c., that time must have been synchronous with or posterior to the separation of the Polynesians; for in their language no glimpses can be caught of either meaning or unmeaning suffixes wherewith to express the cases and numbers of nouns. Their relations of a sentence were invariably expressed by prefixes, a mode of expression not devoid of precedent within the Indo-European branches.

PREPOSITIONS.

Some of the Polynesian forms of prepositions are probably the older. The Polynesian *a* and *o*, "of," seem to me the primary, because the simpler, forms of the Latin *a, ab*, the Greek ἀπο, Sanskrit *apa*, Gothic *af*, English *of*.

The Polynesian *e*, "by, from, through means of," calls up the Latin *e, ex*, Greek ἐκ, ἐξ.

The Polynesian *i*, "in, at, to," calls up the Latin *in*, the Greek ἐν, the Gothic *in*, Celtic *en, yn*, Old Norse, Swedish, and Danish *i*, all with same or similar meanings, and governing the same cases of a noun. The fact that the Old Norse of the Eddas and Runes, which cannot well be called a deteriorated scion of the Gothic, has retained the form of this proposition in *i*, seems to favour the view that the final *n* in the other Indo-European branches was a dialectical variation of a primary form in *i*, of which the Polynesian and the Old Norse alone retained the vestiges.

INTERJECTIONS.

These, being mostly onomatopeian in all languages, may not afford the best means of comparison; yet I would offer one interjection not commonly current in other families of language. The Polynesian *ue* and *au-we*, I think, claims kindred with the Latin *vae*, the Saxon *wa*, the Gothic *wai*, the Greek *ὀυαι*. In the Malay it has been preserved under the forms of *wah* and *wayi*, "alas."

NUMERALS.

In the first volume of "The Polynesian Race," &c., pp. 144 *et seq.*, I have shown that the first four numerals of the Polynesian, 1, 2, 3, 4, are of undoubted Aryan origin, and that the undivided Aryan family had arrived so far in its numeral system when the Polynesian branch broke off and developed the rest of its numeral system under different, and, so to say, foreign associations. I there express the opinion that, when adopting the quinary system of computation, the Polynesians were already beyond the influence of the parent stock, inasmuch as their term for five (*lima*), though an Aryan word, was not the term which the other still united Aryan tribes gave to that number. I have there, also, intimated that the higher Polynesian numerals, from five to ten, were drawn from probable Dravidian, possibly Cushite or Accadian sources, or perhaps both.

I have thus in a measure endeavoured to justify my boldness in instituting a comparison between the Polynesian and Indo-European languages, in order to show their linguistic relationship. It was a link in the chain of reasoning which made me conclude that the Polynesians were originally a branch of the Aryan stock—whatever incidents might have befallen that branch in after-life through admixture with others, and through isolation—and that link had to be taken up to the best of my ability.

Since publishing the first volume of my work on "The Polynesian Race, its Origin and Migrations" (1878),

I have come into possession of three works which, had I known them sooner, would have been of great assistance to me in filling certain gaps in the mythological references made by me, and in giving me greater assurance in asserting the non-Malay origin of the Polynesian family.

I refer to "Myths and Songs of the South Pacific," by Rev. W. W. Gill (London, 1876), a work on which too much praise cannot be bestowed for its many merits as a most valuable contribution to the knowledge of ancient Polynesian thought and life.

I refer to "Les Polynésiens," by Dr. A. Lesson (Paris, 1880–82), which, however much I may differ from the conclusions arrived at, is a most unrivalled work of reference on nearly every one of the Indonesian and Polynesian groups.

And I refer to Mr. A. H. Keane's treatise "On the Relations of the Indo-Chinese and Inter-Oceanic Races and Languages," in the Journal of the Anthropological Institute of Great Britain and Ireland (February 1880), which is a clear, outspoken protest against the misleading habit of representing the Polynesians as descendants, or even kindred, of the Malays. Mr. Keane, moreover, seeks the origin of the Eastern Polynesians in a "white Caucasian" race, of which remnants are still to be found in the Khmêrs of Cambodja, from which direction he thinks they arrived in the Indian Archipelago anterior to the appearance there of the Mongoloid Malays. I go entirely with Mr. Keane in deriving the Polynesians from a "white, Caucasian, Indo-European" Aryan race, and their priority in the Indian Archipelago; but I differ somewhat as to the locality whence they entered the Archipelago.

The perfect physical resemblance of those Cambodjan Khmêrs to the Polynesians is admitted; that the speech of both is polysyllabic and *recto tono* is also admitted, but that the Khmêr language, as represented in E. Aymonier's "Dictionnaire Khmêr-Français" (Saigon,

1878)—the only exponent of said language in my possession—has any appreciable resemblance in its vocabulary
to any of the dialects of the Eastern Pacific Polynesians, I
think admits of considerable doubt. And the " peculiarly
distinctive feature," which Mr. Keane lays great stress
upon as marking the linguistic connection between " the
Khmêr and Malaysian tongues," viz., " the use of identical
infixes," is entirely unknown to the Eastern Polynesians,
whom Mr. Keane classifies as as pure Caucasians as the
original Khmêrs.[1]

If life is spared, I may review more fully Mr. Keane's
opinion as set forth in the said treatise. It is sufficient
for my present purpose that he emphatically supports
me in maintaining the independence and non-relation of
the Eastern Polynesians to the Malays, as well as asserting their descent from " a fair, a Caucasian, an Indo-
European," or Aryan race. As to the divergence of
opinions between Mr. Keane and me regarding the
Asiatic home of the Polynesians, I would be willing to
make the following compromise :—If, what I believe the
majority of European savants still uphold,[2] the valleys
abutting on the plateau of Pamir in Central Asia were
the " Berceau des Aryas," it is not improbable that two
streams of migration may have left for lower latitudes ;
one going to the south-west, crossing the Hindu-Kush,
and, following the affluents of the Indus, landing in

---

[1] Mr. Keane refers to the Mentawey Islanders, off the coast of
Sumatra, as the purest specimen of
Khmêr immigrants still remaining
in Malaysia, and he looks upon
them as the clearest link connecting
the Polynesians with the Khmêrs.
He refers to their dialect as being
decidedly Polynesian. So it is, to a
great extent ; but the question here,
it seems to me, is : are the Mentawey words which Mr. Keane
quotes also Khmêr words ? Of the
ten Mentawey words, taken from
H. von Rosenberg's "Der Malayische
Archipel-Land und Leute," I can
only recognise three as having any
claim to Polynesian kindred, although
out of the whole list of eighty-two
words put down by Herr von Rosenberg nearly one-fifth—16 to 82—are
good Polynesian, either simply or as
compounds. Are the other four-
fifths Khmêr or Mongol?

[2] I am aware that from the days
of Latham several honoured names,
like Geiger, Spiegel, Benfey, Poesche,
and latterly Penka and Schrader,
are committed in defending an European, in opposition to an Asiatic,
origin of the Indo-Europeans. But
I am no convert to their theory.

Deccan; the other going in a south-easterly direction, descending the river systems of the Irawaddy, Salwen, and Mekong, landing in Laos, Yunnan, and Cambodja, both streams of migration eventually meeting in the Indian Archipelago ages before the arrival there of the Mongol or Mongoloid Malays.

There is no more historic evidence for the Polynesians debouching in the Archipelago from trans-Gangetic India than from cis-Gangetic, and they may certainly have come from both directions. But until it is shown that the Khmêr and Polynesian languages are closely related, and that the creeds, legends, and customs—the peculiarly Polynesian folk-lore—which the Polynesians either picked up *en route* or developed in the Archipelago, and brought with them as a prehistoric heritage into the Pacific, are shared in by, or at least not unknown to, the Khmêrs, I think myself justified in believing that the immigrants coming from the north-west, from Deccan, were the preponderating majority, and absorbed into themselves those who came from the north and north-east, from Further India. *En attendant*, I am grateful to Mr. Keane for the destructive portion of his treatise, unsparingly destructive of the long-cherished "Malayo-Polynesian" error.

COMPARATIVE VOCABULARY

OF

POLYNESIAN AND INDO-EUROPEAN LANGUAGES.

———◆———

A'E, *v.* Haw., to pass over, morally or physically, from one condition or place to another; to assent, to permit; to embark, as on board a ship; to mount, as on a horse; to raise or lift up, as the head with joy; to vomit, as in sea-sickness. *A'e, adv.* yes. Tah., *a'e,* to ascend, to mount. Mangar., *ake,* up, upward, over. New Zeal., Rarot., *kake,* to ascend, to mount. Tong., *hake,* up, upward; *hahake,* eastward, windward (*i.e.,* up). Sam., *a'e,* to go up, ascend; *sasa'e,* the east. Fiji., *cake,* upward. Malgass., *ma-kate,* to get up, to mount. Mal., *atas,* up, upward.

Sanskr., *ak,* to wind or move tortuously; *akhu,* a rat, a mouse; *akheta,* hunting.

AI, *v.* Haw., to eat; *s.* food, vegetable food, in distinction from *ia,* meat; *ai-na,* for *ai-ana,* eating, means of eating, fruits of the land; hence land, field, country. New Zeal., *kai,* to eat; *kainga,* food, meal, home, residence, country. Tong., *kai,* to eat. Sam., *'ai,* to eat; *ainga,* family, kindred. Marqu., *kaika, kainga,* food, meal. Tagal., *cain,* to eat.

Zend., *gaya,* life; *gaetha,* the world; *gava,* land, country. Vedic, *gaya,* house, family (A. Pictet). Sanskr., *ghâsa,* food; *ghas,* devour.

Greek, *αἰα, γαια, γη,* different forms occurring in

Homer, land, country, cultivated land; γειος, indigenous; γειτων,, a neighbour; ἠια, provisions for a journey.

Goth., *gawi, gauja,* country, region.

Germ., *gau.*

Lat., *ganea,* eating-house; *ganeo,* glutton.

Lith., *goyas;* Ant. Slav. and Russ., *gai,* "past-rage," nemus.

Polish, *gay,* id.

Mr. A. Pictet, in his "Les Origines Indo-Europ.," vol. ii. p. 15, says that the Vedic and Zend *gaya* "n'ont surement aucun rapport avec le grec γαῖα." This assertion evokes a doubt, inasmuch as, as late as in Homer's time, two other dialectical variations of this word existed in the Greek, viz., αια and δα or δη, in δη-μητηρ, contracted from some ancient form in δαια, as γη and γα, from γαια. As neither of these can be supposed to be derived from, or be a phonetic corruption of, the other, it seems to me that they must have come down abreast from primeval times, thus indicating that the original root was differently pronounced by various sections of the still united Aryan stock; and I believe that this root, in its archaic forms, still survives in the Polynesian *ai* and *kai,* to eat. The Sanskrit *go,* land, the earth, from which Benfey derives a hypothetical *gavyâ* and a Greek γαϝια—by elimination γαια—is probably itself a contraction from the Vedic and Zend *gaya,* as the Greek γη and γα, as the ancient Saxon *gâ* and *gô,* pagus, regio, and the ancient Slav. *gai,* nemus, are contractions from derivations of that ancient root still found in Polynesia. The above derivatives in sound and sense certainly refer themselves better to some ancient *ai* or *kai,* food, the fruits of the forest or the roots of the field, than to the Sanskrit *go,* bull, cow, cattle; for the Aryan family undoubtedly had one or more names for eating and for food before its various divisions applied themselves to the herding of cattle. The Sanskrit *ghas, ghâsa,* the Latin *ganea, ganeo,* point strongly to the underlying original sense of eating and food.

According to Professor A. H. Sayce, in " Introduction to the Science of Language," vol. ii. p. 19, it is probable that the Latin *edere,* to eat, is a compound word = *e-dere,* like *ab-dere, con-dere, cre-dere,* and others, thus leaving *e* as the root.

How far that *e* may have been a dialectical variant or a phonetic decay of an older form more nearly allied to the Polynesian *ai, kai,* I leave to abler philologists to determine.

Ao, *s.* Haw., light, day, metaph. the world. Sam., *aso,* day. Tong., *aho,* id. Tah., *ao,* light, day. Rotuma, *aso, as,* day, sun ; *asoa,* white men. Marqu., *ao-mati,* the sun. Bugui, *oso,* day. Gilolo (Galela), *osa,* moon. Malg., *azo-horo,* the moon; *azo-hali,* Jupiter (planet); *azan,* clearness, brightness.

Sanskr., *aha, ahan,* a day. Ved., *ahâ,* id.; *aho-râtra,* lit. day and night, a day of twenty-four hours. In the Hindu-Kush dialects, Gilgit (Shina), *âcho,* to-day; *dazo,* mid-day.

'Au[1], *v.* Haw., to swim, to float, convey as on a raft, primarily to stretch out, reach after ; *au, v.* to long after, be wholly bent on ; *s.* current in the ocean, the action of the mind ; ex. gr., *ke au nei ko'u manao,* my mind is exercising. Sam., *a'au,* to swim ; *au,* a current at sea ; *v.* to reach to. Tong., *kau,* to swim; *kakau,* id. New Zeal., *kau-kau,* id. Deriv., Haw., *au-a,* to think so much of a thing as not' to part with it ; to be stingy, keep back, refuse, forbid. New Zeal., *kau-a ;* Sam., *au-a ;* Tong., *ou-a ;* Tah., *au-aa,* desist, forbear. Fiji., *katu,* to stretch, as the arms ; a fathom.

Sanskr., *ao,* to be pleased, desire, take care, excite affection, obtain, embrace.

Greek, *ἀω* (comp. Liddell and Scott), to satiate.

Lat., *aveo,* desire earnestly, to long for, to crave; *avidus,* desirous, eager, covetous.

It is possible, until a better etymon is found, that *avis*, bird, refers itself to a primary, material sense of *aveo*, as stretching out, reaching after, akin to the Polynesian *au*. If so, the compounds *au-gur*, *au-ger*, *au-ceps*, *au-cupium*, recall the ancient form of *avis*.

AU², *s.* Haw., handle of an axe, staff, or spear. Sam., 'au, handle, stalk of a plant; 'au-'au, the ridge-pole of a house.

Greek, *αὖς* (Lacon. and Cret.), an ear, a handle; *οὖς*, Att., id. ; Mod. Greek, *αυτιον*, id. ; Dor., *ὦς*, id.

Lat., *auris*, the ear; *audio*, to hear ; *aus-culto*, to listen, hear.

Goth., *auso*, ear; *hausjan*, to hear. Sax., *ear*. Germ., *ohr*, ear. Lith., *ausis*, ear.

The application of this word to designate ear occurs also in the Polynesian : Tah., *pepe-i-au*, the ear; Haw., *pepe-i-ao*, composed of *au*, *ao*, whose primary meaning seems to have been a protuberance of anything, a projection, and of *pepe*, broken, flattened down, bent, pliable. Hence, literally, the flattened protuberance or handle, scil. of the face or head. The same word occurs in another compound, *maki-ao* or *ma'i-ao*, nails of fingers or toes, hoofs of animals, claws of birds; from *maki*, to fasten, hold on to, and *ao* = the protuberance that fastens to or holds on to a thing.

AU³, *s.* Haw., time, period of time, lifetime, season ; *au-ae*, to spend time idly, be lazy ; *au-a-nei*, present time, now, soon; *au-makua,* ancestors; *au-moe*, midnight. Tah., *au-hd*, an aged person. Sam., *au-anga*, to continue to act, to live on; *au-fua*, to begin. Marqu., *au-hi*, later, by-and-bye.

Sanskr., *dyus*, life, lifetime ; *cata-dyus*, a centenarian, very old ; *avuka*, ancestor, parent (Pictet).

Lat. *ævum*, *ætas*, age, lifetime, life ; *avus*, grandparent ; *avia*, grandmother ; *avitus*, ancestral.

Greek, *ἀει*, *ἀιει,* ever, always ; *αιων,* lifetime, age, space of time.

Goth., *aiws*, time, a long time, age; *aiw*, continually, ever; *awo*, grandmother. Sax., *awa, aefre*, ever. Icel., *ae, ei*, ever; *afe*, grandfather. O. H. Germ., *ewa*, eternity, habit, custom, law; *ewig*, eternal. Dutch, *eeuwig*, id.

Welsh, *ewa*, uncle. Lith., *awynas*, uncle (maternal).

A. Pictet (Or. Ind.-Eur., ii. 349) derives the Sanskr. *avuka* and its West Aryàn congeners from the Sanskr. *av* "tueri, juvare," and the Vedic *êwa* (course of time, custom, usage) from the root *i*, to go (ibid., p. 429). Benfey (Sanskr.-Engl. Dict.) refers the Latin *œvum* and its Gothic relatives to the Sanskr. *âyus*, life. I would have accepted Pictet's derivation of *avuka* from *av*, had not the Hawaiian *au-makua* indicated an application of the Polynesian *au* to family relations, as well as to time generally. The Sanskr. *av* offers a plausible solution, but only to one-half of the derivatives referred to, whereas the Polynesian *au* satisfactorily accounts for its derivatives in both directions.

It might be interesting to ascertain, if possible, whether the *y, i*, and *e* in the Sanskr., Lat., Greek, and Goth., after the first *a*, was an original factor in the root from which those words sprang, and then was elided from *avu-ka, av-us, aw-o, aw-a, aw-ynas*, or whether they were comparatively later and dialectical additions, as in the Sanskr. *vâyus* (wind), Goth. *wajan* (blow), Slav. *veja* (breathe), which Liddell and Scott and Benfey refer to a root Ϝα, *va*, or, as Benfey indicates, "originally *av-â*." Benfey gives no root to *âyus*, and Liddell and Scott give αιϜ as the root of ἀεί, *âyus*, &c.; but αιϜ, whose original sense is not given, and is simply hypothetical, if it explains ἀίει, αἰών, *âyus*, and *aiws*, does not explain the form or the sense of *avuka, awo, avus*, &c., unless we assume its original form to have been *au*, as in the Polynesian, with a subsequent *y, i*, or *e* inserted.

AUI, *v.* Haw., to decline, as the sun in the afternoon, turn aside, vary; *auina* (scil. "ka la" = the sun), afternoon. Tah., *aui*, to the left. Sam., *m-aui*, to fall down, to subside, ebb as the tide ; New Zeal., *mawi.* Marqu., *moui.* Rarot., *kaui,* left, left hand. Fiji., *yawi, yakawi, kajawi,* evening ; *yawa,* far off, distant. Malag., *an-kawi,* to the left ; *avi-ha,* left hand.

Sanskr., *ava,* away, off, down, below ; *awara,* posterior, inferior, behind, occidental, western ; *avama,* low ; *avanati,* setting of the sun.

Pers., *iwar, aywar,* evening. Kurd., *evar,* id.

Irish, *iwar, iar,* west.

AHA, *s.* Haw., a company or assembly of people for any purpose ; *aha-aha, adv.* sitting squarely, uprightly. Malg., *mi-ahan,* to stop ; *foha,* be seated.

Sanskr., *ás,* to sit, stay ; *ásana,* seat.

Greek, ἧμαι, to be seated, be still.

This word, so common in the Hawaiian group, either single or in compounds, appears to have become lost or obsolete in the other Polynesian groups. In Fiji alone I find *yasa,* signifying a place, a part of a land, a district.

AHI, *s.* Haw., fire. Sam., Tong., *afi,* id. Rarot. and Mangar., *a'i,* id. Tah., *auahi,* id. New Zeal., *ahi,* id. Mal., *api,* id. Ceram. (Ahtiago), *yaf,* id. Matabello, *efi,* id. Sumatra (Singkel), *agie,* id. Banjak Islands, *ahé,* id. Teor, *ahi,* id. Goram, *ahi,* id. Malg., *af,* id. There is another series of words in the Polynesian family, expressing the sense of fire and its derivatives, which probably is allied to the former class, though uniformly distinct in the last vowel. This uniform distinction I am inclined to consider as arising from a very ancient dialectical variation of a common root, or else the two classes of words proceed from two nearly similar roots. That second class is : Tah., *ahu, v.* to be burnt or scalded ; *s.* heat, fever. Sam., *asu,* smoke. Tong., *ahu,* id. Haw., *m-ahu,* smoke, steam. Tidore, *afu,* fire. Tagal, *apuy,* id. Buru, *ahu,* id. Ceram. (Tetuti), *yafo,* id. Gilolo (Gani), *iaso,* smoke.

The former class I would refer to :—

Sanskr., *agni, agira, angate,* fire.   Bengal., *agin, aag,* id.
Shina (Gilgit), *agár,* id.   Kurd., *agher, aghri,* id.

Lat., *ignis,* fire.

Slav., *ogni,* fire; Lith., *ugnis,* id.

Cymr., *engyl,* fire.

The latter class I would refer to:—

Sanskr., *açira,* fire, heat.   Ved., *áshtrî,* hearth, cooking-place.   Belut., *ás,* fire.   Pers., *ásh,* cooked.

A.-Sax., *ast,* fireplace, oven.

Irish, *asaim,* to light a fire.

Lat., *asso,* to roast; *assus.*

A. Pictet (Orig. Ind.-Europ.) seeks a common root for the first family of words (West Aryan) in the Sanskr. *ag, angh,* to move tortuously, to move, to hasten, "de la mobilité de cet élément," and he thinks the second family derives from the Sanskr. *aç,* "edere, vorare;" fut. partcp. *ashtá* and *açitá.* Benfey (Sanskr.-Engl. Dict.) derives *agni* and its congeners "probably from *añj* in its original signification to shine;" and the same authority makes no reference to any derivations from *aç,* to eat, consume, as signifying fire.

In this uncertainty, and with such unsatisfactory solution, it evidently becomes necessary, if possible, to go higher than the Sanskrit in search of some form or forms around which all these dialectical variants of a once common speech may rally themselves as around a common ancestor. I believe the Polynesian *afi* and *asu* or *ahu* offer such ancestral forms. *Afi* rallying to itself the Aryan variants in *g, agni, ogni, ignis,* &c., and *asu, ahu,* those in *s* and *ç, ás, açira, asso, asaim.* It must be admitted, however, that *afi, ahi,* and *asu, ahu,* are themselves but variants of some still older, but now forgotten, form or forms. They stand abreast in Polynesian speech, and the one is not a derivation or corruption of the other.

There are some other words in the West Aryan tongues whose relationship to the foregoing family seems to me preferable to that which eminent philologists have hitherto assigned them. The Sanskr. *asta*, "home," the Greek ἄστυ, "town, city," have been referred, the former by A. Pictet (*loc. cit.*, ii. 243) to Sanskr. *as*, "esse, to be;" the latter by Liddell and Scott (Greek-Engl. Dict.) and by Benfey (Sanskr.-Engl. Dict.) to a root ϝας, Sanskr. *vas*, "to dwell." I may be permitted to ask under what circumstances the digamma in the supposed ϝαστυ has been lost without being replaced by an aspirate ʻ? That ἑστιά, like the Lat. *vesta*, refers itself to a root in ϝας or *vas*, is evident enough, but not so with ἄστυ. There is another Greek word, ἐσ-χάρα, with the sense of "the hearth, fireplace," which has no etymon assigned it by Liddell and Scott, but which I should consider a relative of ἄστυ; for both doubtless go back, like the A.-Sax. *ast* and the Belut. *ăs*, to the same root as the Polynesian *asu*, the Vedic *ăshtrî*, the Latin *asso*, *assus*. To this family may also be referred the Sax. *as-ca*, the Goth. *az-go*, "ashes, cinders." Benfey refers the Sanskr. *asta* to *as*, but does not indicate whether to *as*[1], "to be," as Pictet has it, or to *as*[3], "to shine." The first seems rather too forced an etymology; the latter, if such be the inference from Benfey, would bring it in harmony with ἐσ-χαρα, with *ast*, *ăs*, *asu*, and ἄστυ. There is little doubt in my mind that, in the early savage or nomadic life of the Aryan, wherever he stopped to dress his fire, by day or night, there was his home for the time being. Hence *asta*, "a home, dwelling," where the fire was lighted; hence ἄστυ, "a town," a congeries of dwellings or homes.

Aho, *s.* Haw., breath, met. spirit, courage; *i nui ke aho*, let the breath be long, *i.e.*, be patient. Tah. and Marqu., *aho*, breath. Rarot., *ao*, id.

Sanskr., *asu*, the five vital breaths of the body, life; *asura*, eternal.

Zend., *ahŭ*, *aŭhu*, spirit, life, God, the world.

Commenting on Dr. Spiegel's derivation of the Persian *Ahura*, as a name of the Deity, from the root *ah*, the Sanskrit *as*, " to be," Professor Max Müller, in his " Chips from a German Workshop," i. 156 (Scribner's ed.), says : " The root *as* no doubt means to be, but it has that meaning because it originally meant to breathe. From it, in its original sense of breathing, the Hindus formed *asu*, breath, and *Asura*, the name of God, whether it meant the breathing one or the giver of breath."

AHU, *v.* Haw., to collect, gather together, pile up, cover up, to clothe; *s.* assembly, collection of things, clothing; *ahua*, an elevated place, a raised pathway, sandbank formed at the mouth of a river. Tah., *ahu*, to pile up, throw things together; *ahu-api*, cloth doubled together, a quilt; *ahu-arii*, a raised pavement for the king; *ahu-mamau*, old garment; *ahu-ena*, property; *ahu-pare*, a fort. Sam., *afu*, a wrapper of cloth (Siapo); *afu-loto*, bed-clothes. Tong., *kafu*, id. New Zeal., *kahu*, *kakahu*, clothes. Marqu., *kahu*, id. Fiji., *qavu*, to clasp with the two arms; *s.* property, goods, what can be clasped in the arms.

Sanskr., *aj*, to drive, direct; *aji*, battle; *ajman*, id.; *ajra*, a field; *ajira*, a court.

Greek, ἀγω, to bring, bring together, to carry, conduct; ἀγων, a gathering, an assembly, struggle, combat; ἀγυια, a street, public place; ἀγυρις, ἀγορα, assembly, crowd, place of assembly, market; ἀγρα, a catching, hunting, booty, prey; ἀγρος, an estate, a field; ἀγος· a leader, chief; ἀγειρω, to gather, collect, bring together, assemble; ἀγελη, herd, flock, company; ὀγμος, a furrow, a row, a path, orbit.

Lat., *ago*, to drive, collect, carry away, to lead; *agmen*, multitude, crowd, motion; *ager*, land, field.

Irish, *agh*, battle; *aighe*, valiant.

Goth., *akrs*, a field; *akran*, fruit; *aigan*, to possess, own; *aigis*, property, possessions. O. Norse, *aka*, to drive. Swed., *öka*, increase, augment.

It may be noticed that the application of this word to clothing, so prevalent in the Polynesian branch, is wholly wanting in the West Aryan branches. It may have been supplanted by the latter with other synonyms, or it may have been adopted by the former after its separation from the common stock.

AKA[1], *s.* Haw., knuckle-joint, protuberance of the ankle, vertebræ of the back. Tah., *ata*, the tops, buds, or shoots of plants. Fiji., *gata*, sharp, as of a knife or a point, sharpness, peakedness; when of a country, hilly; *yaka*, to sharpen.

Sanskr., *aç* vel *ço*, to sharpen; *açri*, edge, corner; *aç-man*, a stone; *açani*, Indra's thunderbolt.

Greek, ἀκη, point, edge; ἀκανθα, thorn, vertebræ; ἀκαζω, to point, sharpen; ἀκονη, whetstone; ἀκις, point, barb of a 'hook; ἀκρος, topmost, highest.

, Latin, *acus*, a needle; *acuo*, to point, sharpen; *acumen*, *acies*.

Goth., *ahs*, an ear of corn; *ahsa* or *amsa*, shoulder. Germ., *achsel*, shoulder. Sax., *ecg*, point, edge.

Lith., *akmu*, stone.

Welsh, *awc*, point, edge. Irish, *aicde*, needle.

AKA[2], *adv.* Haw., now used only in compounds, "with care;" *aka-hele*, carefully; *aka-hai*, gentle, modest. New Zeal., *ata-whai*, kindly, with pity. Sam., *ata-mai*, *v.* to understand, be clever; *s.* the mind. Tah., *ata-ma*, wise, intelligent. Malg., *ata-he*, caresses; *ata-hets*, to pacify; *ata-rien*, generosity.

Greek, ἀκα, ἠκα, quietly, gently; ἀκαλος, peaceful, still; ἀκην, ἀκεων.

O. Norse., *akta*, to make account of. Swed., *akt*, care, heed; *akta*, to consider, take care of. North Engl., *ack* to heed, regard.

AKA[3], *v.* Haw., to laugh, deride. South Polynes., ubique, *ata*, *kata*, id. Mentawej Isl., *gah-gah*, to laugh.

Sanskr., *kakh*, *gaggh*, to laugh.

Greek, καχαζω, to laugh aloud.

Lat., *cachinno*, id.

O. H. Germ., *hôh*, sneer.

AKA[4], *conj.* Haw., but, if not; generally expressing strong opposition of idea. Marqu., *atia*, but. Tong., *ka*, but. Sam., *'a*, but.

Sanskr., *atha, atho, conj.* but.

Greek, ατap, but.

Lat., *at*, but.

Goth., *ak, akei,* but.

AKA[5], *s.* Haw., the shadow of a person; the figure or outline of a thing; likeness; dawn or light of the moon before rising; *v.* to light up, as the moon before rising; to go up and down, as on a hilly road; *akaka,* to be plain, clear, intelligible; *adj.* lucid, bright, as the moon; *kakahi-aka,* dawn of day, morning, lit. breaking up the shadows, scil. of night. Sam., *ata,* a shadow, reflected image, a spirit, the morning dawn; *ata-ata,* the red sky after sunset; *ata-e-ao,* when it is morning, to-morrow; *atangia,* to glisten, become evident; *ata-lii,* a son, *i.e.,* a little image. Tah., *ata,* cloud, shadow, twilight; *a'ahi-ata,* dawn of day; *ata liilii,* the great morning clouds. Marqu., *ho-ata;* Tonga, *tio-ata,* a mirror. Mangar., *ata-riki,* the eldest son. Fiji., *matata,* to clear up, be plain; *mataka,* morning; *yata-yata,* move about tremulously or as a thing near dying.

Sanskr., *at,* to go, move continuously; *atasa,* wind, spirit; *âtman,* breath, soul, intelligence, a person, one's self; *âtma-ja,* a son = one's own born.

Greek, ἀτμος, ἀτμη, ἀτμις, vapour, exhalation, steam, smoke; ἀταλος, tender, tremulous.

The Sanskrit *âtman* seems to have had a variety of etymons assigned it. Referring to it in "Orig. Indo-Europ.," ii. 541, Mr. Pictet says :—"Le sanksr. *âtman,* souffle, âme vitale, intelligence, puis la personne, le soi, est encore obscur, quant à son origine. Pott (Et. F., i. 196), présume une contraction de *â-vâtman,* rac. *vâ,* flare, et compare αὔτμην, souffle. Benfey (Gr. W. L., i. 265), part d'une racine hypothétique *av = vâ.* Bopp (Gl. Scr.) pense à la rac. *at,* ire, d'où dérive *atasa,* vent et âme; mais ailleurs (Veogl. Gr., i. § 140) il incline vers la racine *ah,* parler et reconnaître, et compare le goth. *ahma,* âme. Enfin, le Dict. de Pétersbourg recourt à la rac. *an,* spirare, mais sans s'expliquer sur la formation de *âtman*, dont le *t* resterait énigmatique.

" On voit que les hypothèses ne manquent pas, mais, d'après l'observation de Max Müller (Anc. Sanskr. Littér., p. 21), elles tombent toutes en présence du vêdique *tman*, Zend *thman*, qui remplace souvent *âtman*, et où l'élision de l'*â* ne saurait être expliquée. Toutefois Müller ne tente aucune conjecture nouvelle."

As Mr. Pictet adopts none of the foregoing hypotheses, it is but just to give his own explanation of this crucial word. He says, in continuation of the foregoing :—

" Je décomposerais le mot en question en *â-tman*, pour le rattacher à la rac. *tam*, étouffer, suffoquer, perdre le souffle, d'où *tamaka*, *tamana*, oppression, asthme. Ce sens, au premier abord, parait le contraire de celui que l'on exigerait, mais il passe aisément à la signification de respirer fortement, *anhelare*, ce que l'on fait quand on étouffe. Nous pouvons d'ailleurs nous appuyer d'un rapport tout semblable entre l'anc. slave *duchati*, spirare, *dusha*, anima, et le russe *dushiti*, suffoquer, *dushenie*, suffocation, *dushniku*, soupirail, &c. ; ainsi qu'entre le lith. *duzzia*, âme, *dausa*, air, souffle, et *dusti*, respirer avec effort, *dusas*, respiration difficile, *dusulys*, asthme, &c. La transition de sens est ici manifeste. Les autres acceptions de la racine *tam*, confici mœrore, languescere, desiderare, cupere (cf. *tamata*, désireux, avide), s'expliquent par le double sens d'être oppressé, et *d'aspirer* à quelque chose, et *tama*, *tamas*, désigne l'obscurité en tant qu'elle produit un sentiment d'anxiété, Ainsi *âtman* pour *â-taman*, de *â-tam*, et le vedique *tman* pour *taman*, par une contraction analogue à celle de *dhmâ*, flare, pour *dham* peut-être primitivement allié à *tam*, signifierait proprement une respiration forte et agitée, puis secondairement l'âme active et passionnée, de même que le grec θυμος vient de θυα = Sanskr. *dhû*, agitare.

" La rac. *tam* et ses dérivés, surtout ceux qui expriment l'obscurité, ont beaucoup de corrélatifs européens qu'il serait hors de propos d'enumérer ici. Je me borne à remarquer que le sanskr. *átman* trouve son équivalent presque complet dans l'anc. saxon *athom*, ang.-sax. *aedhm*, anc. all. *ádum*, *átum*, halitus et spiritus, all. mod. *odem*, *athem*, souffle, respiration, &c. Je ne sais si l'on peut y rattacher l'irlandais *adhm*, connaissance, science, *adhma*, peritus, que donnent Lhuyd et O'Reilly, et dont le sens serait plus abstrait. Quant au grec ἀϋτμὴν et ἀτμὸς, ἀτμὴ, souffle et vapeur, fumée qui suffoque, ils paraissent composés avec le préfixe *ava* au lieu de *á*."

Liddell and Scott (Gr.-Engl. Dict.) refer ἀτμος, -η, -ις, to ἀω, to blow, and that to a root, Ϝα = to Sanskrit *vá*.

In this conflict of opinions it may not, perhaps, be presumptuous in me, in view of the Polynesian *ata* and its various meanings, if I concur with Bopp in referring *átman* to the Sanskrit *at*, to go, to move continuously, which may possibly be related to *ak*, to wind, move tortuously, and its derivative *ákáça*, ether, sky, open air, and which latter has an unmistakable family likeness to the *atasa*, wind, spirit, referred to by Pictet. If I am right, this would bring *átman*, *atasa*, *ákáça*, *en rapport* with the Fiji. *yata-yata*, the Haw. *aka*, the Sam. and Tah. *ata*, the Greek ἀτμος and ἀταλος. The Polynesian vocables certainly offer a much less forced explanation than the process of deriving breath, life, soul, from choking, darkness, and death.

AKE[1], *s.* Haw., liver; name of several internal organs, according to the qualifying compound. South Polynes.; *ate*, id. Malg., *ate*, *aten*, *atine*, heart, liver, pith, marrow or middle of a thing. Jav., *ati*, heart, in the sense of affections. Fiji., *yate*, liver.

Greek, ἦτορ, the heart, as a part of the body, as a seat of feeling; ἦτρον, the part below the navel, abdomen.

Liddell and Scott give no etymon to ἦτορ. By separating the substantive termination, however, there remains as stem or root ἦτ or ατ, which strongly points to the same root as the previous, *ata*, *aka*[5]. With that remarkable intuition, which so seldom made default, though he could not always prove himself right, Bopp refers the

Polynesian *ate* to the same root from which the Sanskrit *átman* sprang; but he looked upon the former as a corrupted form of the latter.

AKE[2], *v.* Haw., to tattle, blab, slander, lie. Sam., *ati*, speech, oration. Marqu., *atia*, in truth, certainly.

Sanskr., *ah* ("*h* for *gh*," Benfey), say, speak, pronounce, specify.

Lat., *ajo* ("for *agjo*," Benfey), to say, affirm; *ad-ag-ium*, proverb; *ne'go*, deny.

Greek, ἠχη; Dor., ἀχα, sound, noise, roar; ἠχος, ἠχω, echo, sound.

A.-Sax., *aqu*, jay, magpie.

AKI, *v.* Haw., to bite, bite in two; meton. to revile, backbite. Tong., *achi*, to pierce. Sam., *ati*; Tah., *ati*, to bite, bite through. Rarot., *kati*, to bite. New Zeal., *kati*, sufficient, enough, *i.e.*, bitten through. Ceram. (Awaiya), *aati*, a chopper. Malg., *fatsi*, sting, goad, thorn.

Sanskr., *aç*, to pervade, penetrate, attain to; *aksh*, id.; *áçi*, fang of a serpent.

A. Pictet (Or. Ind.-Eur., i. 500) refers the Sanskrit *ahi*, a snake, serpent, to a Vedic root, *ah*, amplecti, pervadere, "d'où *ahi* celui qui enserre sa proie, comme fait le serpent, le constrictor. De là aussi, avec une nasale intercalée comme souvent, les dérivés *añhu*, étroit, serré, *añhas*, anxiété, malheur, péché, &c. La forme primitive de cette racine a dû être *agh*, *angh*, à en juger par *agha*, mauvais, dangereux, mal, douleur, péché, *angha*, *anghas*, péché = *añhas*." And he says further, " Ces deux formes, *agh* et *angh*, se retrouvent d'ailleurs avec une foule de dérivés, et des transitions du sens matériel au moral, dans toute la famille arienne. Elles se maintiennent souvent à côté l'une de l'autre, et suivent fidèlement les variations phoniques du nom du serpent." Benfey, also (Sanskr.-Engl. Dict.), refers *ahi*, snake, to *amhas*, and *amhas* to " a lost verb, *angh* = to the Greek.ἀγχω." And both these eminent philologists refer, among numerous other derivatives and correlatives, the Greek ἐχις, viper, snake, serpent, and ἐχινος, hedgehog and sea-urchin, to this Sanskrit *ahi* and its Zend equivalents *azi* and *aji;* while Pictet (*loc. cit.,* i. 454), in accounting for the derivation of ἐχῖνος from ἐχις, says: " On ne s'étonnera pas que le hérisson soit comparé à un reptile, car il rampe plutôt qu'il ne marche."

With due respect for so eminent authorities, I would remark that the snakes, and serpents, and vipers with whom the early Aryans came in contact in their primitive homes, in Bactria and beyond, were probably not of the " constrictor" kind; but that their knowledge of them, gained from sad experience, came from being bitten or stung by them. Granted that the dialectical forms of *ah, ac,* and its desid. *aksh,* signify to penetrate, pervade, attain to, occupy (vid. Benfey), in West Aryan tongues, yet the Polynesian dialects have retained what was probably the oldest meaning of the original word in the sense of biting, piercing, stinging. While the Hawaiian retains the form of *ac, ak,* in *aki,* to bite, and, going " from the material to the moral sense," to revile, to backbite, the Tahitian has retained the form of *ah* in *ahi-ahi,* to be wounded, a wound, the transition from which to a moral sense is found in the Hawaiian *ahi-ahi,* to complain falsely, to slander, defame, synon. with *ake.* In view, therefore, of the light which the Polynesian forms and meanings throw upon this subject, it would seem to me preferable to trace the Sanskrit *ahi,* the Zend *azi, aji,* the Greek ἐχις, to this primal form in *ah, ac,* or *ak,* with its primal sense of biting, piercing, stinging, and thus render *ahi* as the biter, the stinger, rather than the constrictor, the strangler. With such a rendering, the derivation and appropriateness of ἐχῖνος from ἐχις becomes plain and intelligible. Mr. Pictet's explanation of the derivation of ἐχῖνος seems to me wholly untenable, as neither *ah, ac,* or *ak,* nor *ah, agh,* or *angh,* have been shown to mean to crawl (*ramper*). Under these considerations it seems to me proper to separate the former family of words from the latter as represented by the Sanskrit *angh,* the Latin *ango,* the Greek ἄγχω, and their West Aryan relatives and derivatives. We shall find their kindred and equivalents under the Polynesian *ana,* quod vide. The remaining relatives of the former family I find in—

Icel., *eglir,* snake, adder. A.-Sax., *igil,* hedgehog. Act. Germ., *ecala, egala,* leech.

Welsh, *asg,* a splinter. Gæl., *asc,* a serpent.

ALA[1], *v.* Haw., to anoint; *adj.* perfumed, spicy; *a'ala,* fragrant odour. Tong., *kakala,* fragrant, a flower wreath. N. Zeal., Mangar., *kakara,* fragrant. Marqu., *kakaa,* id., odoriferous. In Tah. the word seems lost, unless retained in *ara-nua,* name of an odoriferous shrub = the fragrant "Nua." (In Sam. *nua-nua* is the name of a shrub.)

Sanskr., *al,* adorn.

Benfey (Sanskr.-Engl. Dict.) gives no derivatives from *al,* unless *sutra-âli,* a necklace; apparently composed of *sûtra,* the thread or string, and *âli,* probably representing the ornaments—flowers or other things—which are held together by the *sûtra,* and thus form the necklace. Another Sanskrit word for which no etymon is given may refer itself to this *al* or Polynesian *ala.* It is *ara-vinda,* a lotus. Perhaps *alaka,* a curl, may also refer itself to *al,* in the sense of an ornament.*

ALA[2], *adj.* Haw., dim-sighted, as old people, blind; fair-eyed, but staring, as if unable to distinguish. Tah., *ara-ara,* glaring, as the eyes of animals. Sam., *alafa,* shining, phosphorescent, a kind of fungus.

Greek, ἀλαος, blind; ἀλαιος, ἠλεος, crazy, distraught; referred by Liddell and Scott to ἀλη, ἀλαομαι, wandering, roving, straying. If so, probably akin to the next.

ALA[3], *s.* Haw., smooth round stones worn by water; a road, a path. Tah., *ara,* road, path; *ara-poa,* the throat, the gullet. Sam., *ala,* stone worn smooth by water, path, road, a division of a village. Marqu., *aa,* road. Tong., *hala,* a road. Fiji., *sala,* road, path.

Sanskr., *sri,* to flow, to blow, to go, extend; *sal,* to go =

---

[1] Possibly the Greek ἀρωμα, spice, sweet herb, on whose origin philologists are divided, may connect with the Polynesian *ala.* Pott refers it to Sanksrit *ghrâ,* to smell; Max Müller to ἀροω, to plough, the smell of a ploughed field. Vid. Liddell and Scott (Gr.-Engl. Dict.)

sṛi; saranî, path, road; *carani*, id.; *kshar* and *kshal*, to stream, pass away.

Greek, ἀλαω, ἀλημι, to wander, rove. Perhaps σωλην, a channel, gutter.

ALA-EA, *s.* Haw., also *ala-ula*, red earth, from which, according to the legends, mankind was made; *ala-alai*, argillaceous earth, clay; *alaa*, to cultivate, dig off the greensward. Tah., *ara-ea*, red earth; *maraea*, id.; *marari*, to clear off land, cultivated; *araia*, one's own place of birth, native soil. Marqu., *kaaea*, red ochre.

Sanskr., *ira, ila, ida*, earth; *âra*, oxide of iron.

Greek, ἐρα, earth.

Goth., *airtha*; H. Germ., *era*, earth. Icel., *eyri*, gravelly. A.-Sax., *ora, ore*, mineral.

Gæl., *ar-gyll*, quasi *ara-Gœl*, the land of Gæl. Irish, *iris*, bronze.

Pehlwi, *artâ*, land, field.

A. Pictet (Or. Ind.-Eur., ii. 75) derives the Greek, Sanskrit, and Gothic words from a Sanskrit root, *ṛ, ṛi, ir, ar*, with the general sense of lædere, and the words ἀρω, *aro, arjan*, &c., in Greek, Latin, and Gothic, to the same root, and explains the derivation of earth, "en tant que labourée, c'est-à-dire blessée, déchirée." The transition of sense from *ṛ, ar, ṛi*, and *îr*, lædere (sc. terram), to ἀρω, *arjan*, &c., and their derivatives, to dig, plough, cultivate, and from these again to land as a cultivation, plantation, Greek ἀγ-ουρα, Lat. *arvum*, Lith. *arim-mas*, Armor. *aor*, Erse *iom-air, im-ir*, is intelligible and natural; but that *ira, ἐρα, airtha, âra, ora, iris*, signifying earth, mineral, oxides, and even bronze, should derive from that Sanskrit *ṛ, ar, ṛi*, or *îr*, in any of its various senses, is not so clear, especially in view of the positive Polynesian *ala, ara*, earth, clay, soil, ochre, and possibly the Samoan *ele, ele-ele* (other Polynes. dial. *kele*), earth, soil, dirt. And it certainly must be supposed that the Aryans had some general archaic name for the earth, soil, and dust beneath their feet long before they attempted to utilise it by cultivation. The Sanskrit *ṛ, ar, ṛi*, and *îr*, in the sense of to rise, to meet, to move, to raise, to deliver, and restore, and even to hurt, lædere, have evident relatives in the Polynesian *ala*, *ara*, to wake, to rise up, and with the Caus. *hoo*, to lift up, to raise, to excite, stir up, to deliver, to repair. Even the Sanskrit *arus*, *îrma*, wound, *irina*, a notch, a furrow, have their kindred and analogies in the Polynesian *ali*, a scar; *alina*, scarred, badly burned, spotted; *s. alina-lina*, a mark, a sign, a low servant, a slave. But the direct application of this root *r*, *ar*, &c., to cultivation and planting, which the Sanskrit lacks or has lost, while it remains in all the European branches, is found also in Polynesian *eri*, *eli*, *keli*, to dig, *quod vide*, and thus supports A. Pictet's argument against those who hold " que l'agriculture ne s'est développée de part et d'autre que postérieurement à l'époque de l'unité primitive et de la vie pastorale."

ALALA, *s.* Haw., the cry of young animals, crying, squealing, weeping. Tah., *arara*, hoarse through much calling or speaking. Sam., *alanga*, to shout; *alalanga*, a shout. Marqu., *aaka*, to growl, complain.

Greek, ἀλαλή; Dor., ἀλαλα, a loud cry; ἀλαλάζω, to cry aloud, shout; ἀλαλαι, exclamation of joy.

Liddell and Scott refer this ἀλαλη to λαλεω, to talk, prop. to chatter, prattle, chirp, opp. to articulate speech, and they refer to Lat. *lallo*, Germ. *lallen*, as relatives. They are probably right, and we shall find another Polynesian relative under the sect. *Lelo*, tongue. The identical development, however, in both directions, of the Polynesian *alala* and the Greek ἀλαλα, or their retention by each from the hoariest antiquity, when either branch shouted to the other in intelligible speech, is, to say the least, remarkable.

ALANA, *s.* Haw., a sacrifice, offering, present. Tah., *ara*, to importune the gods with prayers or presents.

Greek, ἀρα, a prayer, a curse; ἀραομαι, to pray, vow, invoke. No reference given in Liddell and Scott.

ALANGA, *s.* Sam., shoulder or leg of an animal. Tong., *alanga*, a haunch, a limb. . Haw., *alaea*, the fore-part of the thigh. Sunda., *lengen*, the arm. Malg., *elan*, a wing.

Sanskr., *ara-tni*, the elbow.

Greek, ὠλενη, elbow, and arm from elbow down.

Lat., *ulna*, elbow.

Goth., *aleina*, a cubit. Sax., *elne-boga*, elbow.

Benfey intimates that *aratni* is composed of *ara* and a verb *tan*, to draw, spread out, extend. Doubtless correctly; but what was the original sense of *ara*? From the Polynesian suffixes *nga* and *na*, I should judge the root or stem was *ala*, *ara*, whose primary sense was probably a limb generally; for in Samoan we find the kind of limb designated by a compound; *a-langa-lima*, the shoulder, the fore-quarter of an animal; *ala-nga-vae*, the leg, the hind-quarter.

Benfey refers the first compound of *aratni* to that immensely prolific Sanskrit root *ri* or *ar*. I am not competent to decide. I think, however, that the Sanskrit *aratni* and the Polynesian *alanga* have come down through the ages abreast, from the time when *ara* signified a limb generally, a joint, without particular specification.

ALANI, *s.* Haw., a timber tree used in fitting up canoes. The Polynesians of the archaic, pre-Pacific period must have had some generic name for wood, trees, forest, like *ara* or *ala*. We thus find in Hawaiian, besides the foregoing, *ala-hee*, name of a tree, very hard, from which instruments for digging the soil (*oo*) were made; *ala-hii*, the bastard sandal-wood; *ala-ala-wai-nui*, a large tree whose fruit was used in dyeing; *ala-ala-puloa*, a shrub with yellow blossoms. In Sam., *alaa*, the name of a tree; in Tah., *ara*, branches, twigs; Malg., *ala*, wood, forest.

Sanskr., *arani*, wood used for kindling fire by attrition; *aranya*, a forest.

ALE[1], *s.* Haw., wave, billow, crest of the sea, undulation of water; met. the sea. Tah., *are*, wave, billow. Rarot., Mangar., *kare*, id. N. Zeal., *kare*, reflection of light from running water, flashing, glancing. Sam., *ua-ale*, shower of rain. Malg., *mare*, a torrent. Ceram. (Gah.), *arr-lehu*, a river; *arr*, water.

Sanskr., *ârdra*, wet, moist, fresh.

Greek, ἀρδω, to moisten, to water, to irrigate; ὀρος, watery part in milk, blood, &c.

Armen., *alik*, a wave.

Liddell and Scott submit ῥαινω, to sprinkle, as related to ἀρδω and *ârdra*, and propose *ard* as a root. Benfey gives no root to *ârdra*. I leave the question to be settled by abler hands than mine; but Sanskrit scholars may yet find that *ârdra* is a compound word, of which *âr* is the subject and *dra* the attribute, whether the latter may connect with *drâ*, to run, or with *dhara*, bearing, holding. The *ar* thus left falls easily in line with the Polynesian *ale*, the arm, *alik*, and the Greek ὀρος.

ALE[2], *v.* Haw., to swallow, to drink, to gulp down, absorb; also to well up, as tears in the eyes. Sunda., *ngale*, to drink; probably allied to the foregoing.

Lith., *alus*, a kind of native beer.

Anc. Slav., *olovina*, Sicera.

A.-Sax., *eala*, *alodh*, ale.

Irish, *ol*, a drink; *olaim*, to drink.

Sanskr., *ali*, some kind of spirituous liquor, referred to by Pictet (*loc. cit.*, ii. 320), who adds: "la racine primitive est incertaine."

ALI, *s.* Haw., a scar on the face; *ali-ali*, to be scarred; *aali*, a small, low place between two larger or higher ones; *pu-ali*, a place compressed, a neck of land, an isthmus; *pu-ale*, a ravine. N. Zeal., *pu-are*, a hollow, open place. Tah., *ari*, a great deep or hollow; *adj.* empty, as the stomach; *v.* to scoop out, to hollow; *ari-ari*, thin, worn-out.

Sanskr., *arus*, a wound; *irma*, id.; *irina*, notch, furrow.

Swed., *ärr*, scar.

ALII, *s.* Haw., *a* euph., a king, a chief. Rarot., Paum., *ariki*, id. Fakaafo, *aliki*, id. Mangar., *akariki*, id. Tong., *eiki*, id. Marqu., *aiki*, *hakaiki*, id. N. Zeal., *ariki*, chief and high-priest. Tah., *arii*, chief. Sam., *alii*, chief.

Sanskr., *rij* (for primitive Vedic *râj*, to govern, Benfey), to stand or be firm, be strong; *râj*, *râjan*, king.

Goth., *reiki*, dominion; *reiks*, king, chief.   Sax., *rik*, noble; *rici*, dominion, state.   Icel., *rikr*, in compounds as *ul-rikr*, *e-rikr*.   Swed., *rik*, rich; *rike*, kingdom.

Irish, *righ*, king; *airigh*, chief.   Welsh, *-rix*, a frequent suffix in the names of nobles.

Zend, *ragi*, kingdom (A. Pictet).

Lat., *rex*, king; *rego*, *rectus*.

ALO, *v.*   Haw., to pass from one place to another, to dodge, skip; *alo-alo*, turn this way and that.   Tong., *alo*, to hunt; *kalo*, to dodge, parry, elude; *alo-alo*, to fan.   Sam., *alo*, to fan, to paddle; rdpl. to avoid, dodge.   Tah., *aro*, wage war, to fight.   Mal., *alih*, to shift, change.   Malg., *mi-valik*, turn about.

Sanskr., *ara*, rapid (Pictet, *loc. cit.*, i. 456, *r*, *ar*, to go, to move); *arna*, agitated, impetuous.   Ved., *arnava*, ocean.

Greek, ἐλαω, ἐλαυνω, to drive, urge, beat.

Lat., *ala*, wing; *ala-cer*, swift.

Goth., *ara*, eagle.   A.-Sax., *earn*, id.   Act. Germ., *aro*, id.; *ilan*, to hasten.

Lith., *eris*, eagle.   Illyr., *ora*, id.

Irish, *allaim*, *ailim*, to go, move; *allach*, activity.

Doubtless related to *alo*, as a phonetic variation, is the Haw. *alu-alu*, to pursue, chase, persecute; the Sam. *alu*, to go backward and forward; *alu-alu*, to drive, chase; Tah., *aru-aru*, to hunt, pursue.   Perhaps the Greek ἀλης, ἀλις, throng, crowd, connect with the same root as the Polynesian *alu*.

AMA, *s.*   Haw., the outrigger of a canoe; *amana*, two branches crossing each other, the crotch of a tree; *adj.* crossing.   Tah., *ama*, outrigger; *amaa*, branches of trees, division of a subject; *ama-ha*, a split, a crack.   Sam., *ama*, outrigger.   Rotum., *sama*.   Tong., *hama*.   Fiji., *cama*, id.; *amo*, *v.* ubique, to carry on the shoulder.   Sam., *amonga*, a burden, also name of Orion's belt in that constellation.

Sanskr., *aṁs*, to divide, to break asunder; *aṁça*, a part, share; *aṁsa*, the shoulder.

Lat., *ansa*, handle, haft, ear of vessels; *ames*, a pole or fork for spreading nets with; *humerus*, shoulder.

Greek, *ἀσιλλα*, a yoke for the shoulders to carry with; *ὦμος*, the shoulder; *ὦμια*, corner, side.

AMI-AMI, *v.* Tah., to be in dread or fear; to wink the eyes as if apprehensive of a blow; to move the lips quickly, as if panting for breath.

Sanskr. (Ved.), *am*, to be ill; *am-îva*, pain; *am-aya*, sickness.

ANA[1], *v.* Haw., to measure, in any manner or direction, to set aside, set back, restrain, be satiated, have enough; *s.* a measure; *ana-aina*, lit. a circle for eating purposes, a congregation of people for any purpose, provided a space be left in the centre, a congregation; *ana-aina*, land-surveying; *ana-hua*, *kana-hua*, bending over, stoop-shouldered; *ana-na*, a fathom, to measure. Tah., *aa*, to measure; *aa-mau*, twenty fathoms in length. Mangar., *anga*, a fathom measure. Sam., *anga*, a span. Fiji., *canga*, a span, a stretch of the fingers. The Sam. *anga*, to move or turn oneself in this or that direction, to turn towards or turn from, probably refers to this family.

Sanskr., *aṅg*, to go, to mark; *anga*, a limb, a part, a division; *angula*, a finger's-breadth, as a linear measure; *aṅgulî*, finger; *aṅgulîya*, a finger-ring; *aṅga-da*, bracelet; *aṅka*, a hook, mark, the flank, the arm; *aṅkuça*, a hook; *aṅch*, to bend, curve. Perhaps *anas*, a cart.

Zend., *angust*, a finger-ring.

Welsh, *angu*, embrace, contain; *ang*, large, capacious.

Greek, *ἀγκαλη*, the bent arm; *ἀγκη*, id.; *ἀγκας*, in the arms; *ἀγκων*, the bend or hollow of the arm, the elbow, any nook or bend; *ἀγκος*, bend, hollow, glen, valley; *ὀγκος*, a hook, barb.

Lat., *uncus*, bent, curved, a hook; *anulus*, a ring, a link.

Benfey refers *aṅgula* to a lost base, *aṅgu*, whose meaning is not given, however. A. Pictet (*loc. cit.*, i. 501) refers

the Welsh *angu* to the Sanskrit *agh, angh,* "amplecti, pervadere." I see no reason why the one or the other should
not refer itself in a nearer degree to this Polynesian *ana,
anga.* Pictet's derivation, by contraries, of the Welsh
angu and *ang,* "to embrace, contain, large, capacious,"
from the Sanskrit *anhu,* "étroit, serré," seems to me more
ingenious than satisfactory in view of the Polynesian word
with its primitive meaning, "to measure in any direction,"
straight or circular. The original differentiation of meaning in the kindreds and derivatives of the Sanskrit *agh* or
angh I thing best displayed in the Polynesian forms *aki*
and *ana.*

Though the West Aryan branches generally have lost
of this word the sense of to measure, or supplanted it
with other synonyms, it is probable that the Persian word
ἄγγαρος,—a messenger, a courier kept ready at regular
stages throughout Persia to carry royal despatches,—and
adopted by the Greeks, may recall the original sense of
" measuring a distance."

ANA[2], *v.* Haw., to suffer, be grieved, troubled; *s.* grief,
sadness, sorrow; *ana-ana,* to practise witchcraft, procure
the death of one by sorcery, also to be in a tremor, agitated;
s. contraction of the muscles; *ana-anai,* to be angry. Tah.,
anae, anxiety; *anau,* sorrow, grief, regret. N. Zeal., *kanga,*
to swear, curse. Sam., *ana-ana,* to go into danger; *ana-
gofie,* easily perished, perishable.

Sanskr., *agha* (fr. a *v. angh,* Benfey), sin, impurity;
agas, crime, fault; *amhas,* pain, sin. Ved., *anhu* (Pictet),
narrow, light; *anhas,* anxiety, misfortune.

Lat., *ango,* press together, choke; *angustus,* narrow,
close; *angor, angina,* sore throat, anguish, vexation,
trouble; *anguis,* a snake, serpent; *anxietas.*

Greek, ἄγχω, press tight, strangle, choke; ἄγχι, near,
close by; ἄχος, grief, pain, distress; ἐγγύς, near, nigh.

Goth., *aggvus,* narrow, straight; *agis,* fright; *agan,* to
fear. Sax., *ange,* vexed, troubled; *enge,* narrow strait;
angst.

Irish, *agh*, fear; *ang, ing,* peril, danger. Welsh, *ing,* narrow strait.

Lith., *anksztis,* narrow; *angis,* serpent.

I have followed Benfey and Pictet in these comparisons and derivations. It may appear as if the Hawaiian *ana-ana,* contraction of the muscles, to be in a tremor, agitated, did not fully correspond to the idea of nearness, closeness, which seems to be the primary and prominent sense of the West Aryan vocables. The original material sense of *ana* is no longer to be found in any of the Polynesian dialects, so far as I can ascertain, but some of them have preserved two vocables nearly akin to *ana,* which express that idea of nearness, closeness, and compression. The one is *ane, v.* Haw., to be near, to be almost; *adv.* nearly, scarcely, with difficulty; *ane-ane, adv.* nearly, almost; *s.* a vacancy, compression of the stomach for want of food or from sickness; *adj.* be exhausted, faint, feeble; *v.* to be near doing a thing, be almost at a place. The other is *ene,* Haw., *v.* to creep along, draw near an object; Tah., *ene,* to approach; *ene-ene,* to press upon, insist upon. With these words supplementing the material sense lost in the Polynesian *ana, anga,* its relation to the Sanskrit Vedic *aṅhu,* the Greek ἀγχι, the Saxon *enge,* the Welsh *ing,* cannot well be called in question.

ANA[3], *s.* Haw., cave, hollow, cleft in the rocks, the hollow part of the mouth. Sam., *ana,* cave, a room, a cabin. Tah., *ana,* cave; *ana-ana,* indented; *ana-pape,* the bed of a river. *Quære, tanga,* Sam., a shark's stomach, a bag; *tanga-ai,* the crop of birds.

Sanskr., *aṅjali,* the cavity formed by putting the hands together and hollowing the palms, this cavity as a measure, two handfuls (Benfey); *ânana,* i.e. *an-ana* (Benfey), the mouth, face; *ânaka,* a drum.

Benfey refers *ânana* to *an,* to blow, breathe, but gives no reference for *aṅjali* and *ânaka.* It is possible, but, in view of *aṅjali* and *ânaka,* hardly probable. There doubtless was a primary *ana,* with the sense of cavity, hollow, to which *ânana* and *ânaka* refer themselves as well as *añjali.* There is a composite of *ánaka* in Sanskrit which seems to me inexplicable unless on the assumption that the primary sense of *ánaka* embodied the idea of hollowness, cavity. That word is *cata-ánaka,* lit. a hundred drums, but conventionally a cemetery. With the primary sense of cavity resting in *ánaka,* one can understand that a hundred graves, caves, or holes, might conventionally be called a cemetery, but not otherwise.

The Lat. *inguen,* the groin, the abdomen, possibly goes back to this primitive *ana* for its root.

The Greek ἀντρον, Lat. *antrum,* of which Liddell and Scott give no etymon, may also be referred to the same root. Perhaps also Sanskr. *antar,* within; Lat. *inter.*

ANI, *v.* Haw., to pass over a surface as with the hand, to draw, to wave, beckon, blow softly; *s.* a gentle breeze; *ani-ani,* to cool, refresh, blow gently; *ma-kani,* wind, breeze, air in motion; *ane-ane,* blow gently. Rarot., Mangar., *angi,* gentle breeze. Sam., Tong., N. Zeal., *matangi,* wind; *angi,* to blow. Tah., *matai,* wind. Marqu., *metani.* Fiji., *cangi,* air. Nias, *angi,* id. Teor., *anin,* id. Malg., *anghin,* air, wind; *angats,* spirit, phantom.

Sanskr., *an,* to breathe, blow as wind, to live; *anila,* wind; *anas,* a living being; *apána,* the anus; *prána,* breath, wind.

Greek, ἀνεμος, wind, breath; ἠνεμοεις, Dor. ἀνεμοεις, windy, airy.

Lat., *anima,* air, breath, soul; *animus, animal, inanis,* and *anus.*

Goth., *anam,* to breathe; *uz-ana,* expire. O. H. Germ., *un-st,* storm. Swed., *ande,* breath, spirit; *andas,* breathe.

Gael., *anam,* breath, soul; *anail,* respiration, puff. Welsh, *en,* soul, spirit; *en-vil,* a being. Armor., *ane-val,* animal.

Pers., *an,* intelligence.

The Greek ἐνηης, soft, gentle, kind; προς-ηνης, Dor. προς-αυης, and ποτανης, with the same meaning, ἀπηνης, harsh, rough, unkind, of whose root lexicographers are in doubt, probably refer to this family of words, and seem to coincide with the Polynesian sense of a soft, gentle breeze.

ANO, s. Sam., the innermost substance of a thing, the kernel. Tong., *kano*, id., seeds; *kano-o-he-mata*, eyeball. Haw., *ano-ano*, seeds of fruits, the semen, descendants, children; *onohi*, the eye, the pupil of the eye, centre of things. N. Zeal., *kanohi*, the eye. Marqu., *kakano;* Mangar., *kanokano*, seeds, kernels. Tah., *ano-ano*, id.

Sanskr., *kana*, grain, broken rice, a drop, a spark, a little bit; *kanika*, seed; *kanîgams*, very small.

This reference is strengthened by several pre-Malay terms for "small, little," viz., Amboyna (Battumerah), *ana;* Ceram. (Teluti), *anan;* Ceram. (Ahtiago), *anaanin;* Salibabo, *anion;* Matabello, *enena.*

APO, v. Haw., to catch at, to span, encircle, receive, contain, apprehend intellectually; s. a hoop, a band, a ring; *apo-apo*, to snatch, seize. Sam., *sapo*. Tong., *habo*, to catch, materially or mentally; *'apo*, take care of, attend to, to cling to. Tah., *apo*, to catch; *apu*, the shell of nuts, seeds; and *apu-rima*, the hollow of the hand. Fiji., *kabo-ta*, take hold of with something in the hand that it may not burn or dirty; take up food with a leaf; akin to Haw., *apu*, a cup; Rarot., *kapu*, id.; Mangar., *kapu*, to enclose, contain, a cup; Marqu., *kapu-kapu*, take up water with a cup; Sam., *'apu*, a cup or dish made of a leaf; Mal., *tang-kap*, to catch; Sund., *tjap*, a ring.

Sanskr., *âp*, to attain, obtain; *adj.* fit, trusted, near; *apas*, work, diligent, active. Ved., *apnas-vant*, efficacious.

Lat., *apto*, to fit, from obs. *apo*, *aptus*, joined, fastened to, fit; *apiscor*, reach, get; *opus*, *copia*.

Greek, ἅπτω, fasten to, cling to, touch; πρεπω for προ-επω, be becoming, to suit; ἀφη, touch, laying hold, grasping.

Welsh, *hap*, *hab*, luck, chance, what comes suddenly; *hafiaw*, snatch; *hapiaw*, happen.

The Latin *capio*, *capto*, *capax*, &c., doubtless refer themselves to this family of *apo*, as well as *capulus* and *capsa*, though Benfey refers them to the Caus. of Sanskr. *chi* = *chapayámi*, to arrange, to heap, collect; and the Sax. *hæftan*, to seize, *hæft*, a handle, haft, claim, also kindred to the same.

Awa[1], *s.* Haw., harbour, cove, creek, channel; *awaá*, to dig as a pit, a ditch; *awawa*, a valley, space between two prominences, space between the fingers or toes. Tah., *ava*, a harbour, channel. Sam., *ava*, a boat-passage, opening in the reef, anchorage; *v.* be open, as a doorway. Marqu., *ava*, interval, passage.

The Malgasse *ava*, a rainbow, may refer to this family, in the sense of an arch, a bay, a hollow, curved space on the firmament.

Sanskr., *avaṭa*, a pit; *avata*, a well; *avatas*, below, in the lower regions; *ava-káca*, space, interval; *avama*, low, opp. to high, probably all referring themselves to *ava*, prep. with the primary sense of " down, below, away, off," as its derivatives plainly indicate.

Awa[2], *s.* Haw., fine rain, mist. Tong., Sam., *afa*, storm, hurricane; *afu*, a waterfall. N. Zeal., *awa*, a river. Fiji., *cava*, a storm. Mal., *awap*, mist, dew. Sangvir Island, *sawan*, a river. Rotti, Ofa, id. Tagal., *abo-abo*, rain. Malg., *zav*, mist, fog.

Sanskr., *ap*, *apas*, water.

Lat., *aqua ;* Romain, *ava*, water, rain-water.

Goth., *ahwa ;* O. H. Germ., *ouwa,* water. Germ., *aue*, *au*, brook. Swed., *å,* id.

Irish, *abh*, water; *abhan*, river. Welsh, *aw*, fluid.

Pers., *âw*, *âb*, water.

A. Pictet (*loc. cit.*, i. 137) refers the Celtic and Persian forms to a Sánskrit root *av*, " ire," whence *avana*, rapidity, *avani*, river; and he refers the Latin and Gothic forms to a Sanskrit root *ac* or *ak*, " permeare, occupare," from which spring a number of derivatives expressive of " le mouvement rapide, la force pénétrante " (ii. p. 552). In view of the Polynesian forms, Haw., Sam., Tagal., and their meanings, I prefer to follow Benfey and Bopp in referring the West Aryan as well as the Polynesian forms to the

Sanskrit *ap*, whether that be the original form itself or a contracted modification of it.

It seems to me to have been in the very nature of language that men in the olden times should have commenced by giving distinct and instantaneous names to objects around them, and to natural phenomena, before they invested those objects with names derived by after-thought and reflection from this or that quality characteristic of those objects. Many, if not most, of such original names were doubtless lost in the course of ages, and supplanted by synonyms derived from and expressive of some quality or other in the objects named; but many still survive to baffle the analysis of philologists, and to assert their claims to priority over synonyms that must necessarily have been of later formation.

AWA³, *s.* Haw., Sam., Tah., name of a plant of a bitter taste, but highly relished throughout Polynesia—"Piper Methysticum"—from which an intoxicating drink is made; the name of the liquor itself. Tong., N. Zeal., Rarot., Marqu., *kawa,* id. Haw., *awa-awa,* bitter. Sam., *a'awa,* id. Tong., N. Zeal., *kakawa,* sweet.

Sanskr., *av,* to please, satisfy, desire (Benfey); *ava,* nourishment (Pictet).

Pers., *âwâ,* nourishment; *abâ,* bread.

Lat., *aveo,* crave after, long for; *avena,* oats. See AU¹.

E, *adv.* and *ppr.* Haw., from, away, off, by, through, means of; also, adverbially, something other, something strange, new; *adj.* contrary, opposed, adverse, other, foreign. Sam., *e, ppr.* by, of; *ese,* other, different, strange. Tah., *e, ppr.* by, through, from; *adv.* away, off; *adj.* different, strange, distant; *ee,* strange. N. Zeal., *ke,* strange, different. Malg., *eze,* of, by.

Greek, *ἐκ, ἐξ,* from out of, from, by, of; *ἐκει,* in that place, opp. to *ἐνθαδε,* in some other place than that of the speaker, thither; *ἐκας,* afar, afar off.

Lat., *e, ex,* out of, from.

Liddell and Scott (Gr.-Engl. Dict., s. v.) say: "The

root of ἔτ-ερος is said to be the same as Sanskr. *ant-aras*, Goth. *auth-ar*, Germ. *and-er*, Lat. *alt-er, aut*, French *aut-rui*, our *eith-er, oth-er, itara = alius*, also in Sanskrit." Whatever the root of *ant-aras, auth-àr, alter*, it seems to me that ἕκας shows nearer kindred to the Polynesian *e, ke, ee, ese, eze*, than to forms so developed as *ant-ar, ant-ara*, &c.

EHA, *v.* Haw., be hurt, sore, painful; *s.* pain, suffering, affliction. Tah., *eha-eha*, to be spoiled, as of food kept too long. Probably the Haw. *ehe-ehe*, to cough, to hack, and Tah. *ma-ehe*, withered, scorched by the sun, are connected with this word.

Sanskr., *ej*, to stir, tremble, quake.

Greek, ἐπ-ειγω, press upon, urge, drive; αἰγις, a rushing wind, a storm; ἀΐσσω, dart, shoot, force; αἰγειρος, the poplar tree.

Lat., *æger*, sick, suffering, troubled.

In the Polynesian form of *eha*, nothing remains of the probably primitive sense of rapid motion, pressure, trembling, as retained in the Sanskrit *ej*, the Greek ἐπ-ειγω, αἰγις, and αἰγειρος, though the forms in *ehe-ehe* and *ehe* may in a measure recall it. But the Polynesian *eke*, with its variants, which doubtless also goes back to a Sanskrit or older *ej*, has well preserved that original sense, as well as the later derivative one of pain or distress. We thus have: Haw., *e-eke*, to start away as in fear, to shrink from, the motion of the hand when one has burnt his finger, to twinge or writhe with pain; *eke-eke*, to brush off, as a fly or insect; *s.* a piercing, stinging pain; *ekeke*, the wing of a bird (from its fluttering rapid motion). Tah., *ete*, to flinch, shrink back; *ete-ete*, shocked, ashamed.

ELE, *v.* Haw., be dark, black; *adj.* dark-coloured, black, blue, dark-red, brown; *ele-ele*, id. Tah., *ere-ere*, dark, black, blue. Rarot., *kerekere*, id. Marqu., *kekee*, id.; *kee-voo*, darkness, gloom.

The application of this word to colour is doubtless derivative from the Polynes. Haw. *kele*, mud, mire (*quod vide*), Tong. *kèle-kere*, earth soil, dirt, Sam. *'ele* and *'ele-ele*, red

earth, dirt, rust; *elea*, Tong., *kelea*, rusty, dirty; probably
all akin to *ala*, *ara*, in *ala-ea*, earth, clay (vid. pp. 51, 52).

Jav., *iran*, black. N. Celebes (Kema), *hirun*, id.

In the following Greek words the first constituent proclaims their affinity to the Polynesian *ere*, *ele*:—

ἔρεβος, darkness of the grave, the dark passage from
earth to Hades; ἐρεβεννος, dark, gloomy; ἐρεμνος, sync.
fr. previous word, black, swarthy; ἐρεφω, to cover; ὀρφνη,
darkness of night; ὀρφνος, dark, dusty; ὀροφη, roof of
a house.

Sanskr., *aruṇa*, tawny, dark, red; *s.* the dawn, the sun;
aruṇita, made red.

. Benfey refers the Sanskrit word to *arus*, a wound.
Liddell and Scott refer the Greek words to ἐρεφω, to
cover. They are plausible; but are they the true roots
or stems, in view of the Polynesian *ele*, *ere?* Dr. J.
Pickering, in his Greek Lexicon, derives ἔρεβος "from
ἔρα (the earth) or ἐρεφω (to cover)." The former seems
to me the better reference.

ELE², *prefix.* Haw., an intensitive added to many words,
imparting a meaning of "very much, greatly;" *ele-u*,
alert, quick; *ele-ma-kule*, old, aged, helpless; *ele-mio*, tapering to a point; *ele-ku*, easily broken, very brittle; *ele-hei*,
too short. Tah., *ere-huru*, encumbered, too much of a
thing.

A. Pictet (*loc. cit.*, ii. 757) says, apropos of the derivation
of the word *Erin:* "L'irlandais *er* comme adjectif magnus,
nobilis, paraît être identique à l'*er* intensitif de l'irlandais et du cymrique, considéré comme une particule
inséparable, et qui serait ainsi proprement un adjectif.
Il est à remarquer en confirmation, que le zend *airya* =
sanskr. *arya* avec l'acception de bon, juste, est également
devenu *ér* dans les composés du Pârsi, comme *ér-maneshu*
bon esprit, *er-tan*, bon corps (Spiegel, Avesta, i. 6). De
là à un sens intensitif, transition était facile." Why not
widen the philological horizon by admitting the Polynesian *ere*, *ele*, to consideration as well as the Irish,
Welsh, or Parsi? And why may not the O. Norse *ar*,

early, first; *aerir*, messengers; the Sax. *er*, before, in time, go up to the same root as those others?

ELI, *v.* Haw., to loosen or break up earth, to dig in the ground. Tah., *eri, eru*, id. Tong., N. Zeal., Fiji., *keri, keli*, id. Sunda, *kali, ngali*, to dig.

Sanskr., *ar*, to plough; Lat., *aro;* Greek, ἀροω; Irish, *arain;* Goth., *arjan*, and their numerous derivatives.

EMU, *v.* Haw., to cast away, throw away; *emi*, to decrease; subside, retire, despond, to ebb as the tide. Mangar., *kemi*, to depart, disappear. The Haw. *emo*, to put off, delay, is probably but a phonetic variation.

Greek, ἐμεω, to vomit, throw up.

Sax., *aemti, aemtian*, to evacuate, be vacant, idle; *aemta*, ease, leisure. Engl., *empty.*

Benfey and Liddell and Scott refer the Greek ἐμεω to the Sanskr. *vam*, to vomit, spit out; Lat., *vomo*, id. It may be so; but why is not the Sanskr. *v* represented by the digamma or the aspirate in Greek? Benfey further refers the Greek ἐμεω to the Goth., *wamm*, a spot, *ga-wamms*, spotted, tainted; but W. W. Skeat, in Mœso-Goth. Glossary, derives *wamm* from *wimman*, to blemish. In this uncertainty I think the Polynesian etymon the preferable.

I[1], *prep.* Haw., to, towards, in, at, unto; *iho*, a verbal direction implying motion downward, succession; *v.* to descend from a higher to a lower level; *io, v.* to flee, hasten away; *s.* a forerunner, a herald. In the S. Polynes. dialects, *i* and *ki, prep.* to, towards, at, in, on. Sam., *ifo;* Tah., *iho;* Tong., *hifo;* Mangar., Rarot., *io*, down, downward, to descend. Sam., *ifu*, to run away. Tah., *ihu*, be lost, go astray. Fiji., *civo*, downwards. Buru., *iko* and *wiko*, to go. Ceram. (Teluti), *itai*, id. Amboyna, *oi*, id.

Sanskr., *i*, to go, to go to; *ay*, id.; *it*, id.; *yâ*, id.

Greek, ἐω, ειω, ιημι, ειμι, and their numerous forms retaining the original *i*, denoting motion, to go, to pass; ιτος passable; ιθμα, a step, motion.

Lat., *eo, ire*, to go; *iter*, journey, road; *itio*, &c.

Goth., *iddja*, I went.

I², *v.* Haw. and Tah., to speak, to say. Sam., *i*, to cry. Mangar., *ki*, id. N. Zeal., Rarot., *ki*, to say, to answer. Tong., *ki*, to whistle. Fiji., *gi*, to squeak, shrill voice. Haw., *ii*, rejoice with audible voice. Sam., *ii*, a prolonged scream.

Sanskr., *id*, to implore, to praise; *ida*, speech; *iti*, calamity.

Greek, *ia*, a voice, cry; *ἰωή*, shout, clamour; *ἰαζω*, cry aloud.

IA¹, *pron.* Polynes., ubique, he, she, it. Malay., *iya*, id. Malg., *isi*, id.

Lat., *is, ea*, id.

Goth., *is, si* (acc. f. *ija*), *ita*. (See Introduction.)

IA², *s.* Haw., Tah., Sam., fish. Tong., N. Zeal., Marqu., *ika*, id. Mal., *ikan;* Pulo Nias, *iah*, id. Gilolo (Galela), *ian*, id. Saparua, *ian*, id. Teor., *ikan*, id.

Greek, *ἰχθύς*, fish.

In the earlier pre-historic residence of the Greeks on the coasts and islands of the Mediterranean, there must have been in the language which then obtained such a word for fish as *ika* or *icha*. One of the ancient names of Sardinia was *'Ιχνουσα*, evidently a composite word, from *νουσα*—a word which, whatever its original derivation, prevailed extensively at one time with the signification of "island," from the Pillars of Hercules to the Straits of Gilolo, and from thence was borne into the Pacific—and *ἰχ*, for which Greek lexicographers offer no explanation or etymon. Pausanias, Pliny, and Silius Italicus refer the name of *'Ιχνουσα* to the Greek *ἰχνος*, vestigium, a track of the human foot, from its apparent shape ; but C. Ritter ("Die Vorhalle Europ. Völker-Geschichten") has, in a measure, upset that theory, though his own is hardly more probable, and neither the one nor the other will account for the termination of *-νουσα* in the names of numerous other islands ; and thus, in the case of *'Ιχνουσα*, the first syllable still remains unexplained. There is another Greek word in which I recognise the existence of this

ancient ἰχα or ἰχ : it is ταριχος, "salted or pickled fish,"
"smoked or dried fish or meat," "a mummy." No etymon
is given by Liddell and Scott. The first component of
this word possibly refers to ταρασσω, or the stem upon
which ταρασσω was formed, with the sense of "to stir up,
to mix, to agitate, to trouble," with a probably conventional or understood sense of "to prepare pickle (by stir-
ring, mixing), to pickle, to cure." The second component
I claim as that ancient ἰχ or ἰχα which gave its name to
Sardinia. The etymology of the name of 'Ικαρος, an
island off Samos in the Ægean Sea, has, I believe, not yet
been satisfactorily settled. According to Anthon (Class.
Dict.), Bochart inclines towards a Phœnician derivation,
and assigns as the etymology of the name *i-caure*, *i.e.*,
"insula piscium," the island of fish. In support of this
explanation he refers to Athenæus, Stephanus Byzantinus,
and others, according to whom one of the early Greek
names of the island was 'Ιχθυοεσσα, *i.e.*, "abounding in
fish." The reference to "fish" as the foundation of the
name rather confirms my opinion that ἰκα, ἰχα, was an
ancient name of that class of animals, but had become
obsolete before the adoption of the comparatively later
and composite ἰχθυς; and, under previous considerations,
it is fairly probable that the city of 'Ιχνη, mentioned by
Herodotus (vii. 123) as "near the sea," in the neighbour-
hood of the river Axius, which divided the territories of
Mygdonia and Bottiæis, is another memento of the original
long-forgotten name of fish, ἰχα, ἰκα, ία.

A. Pictet (Or. Ind.-Eur., i. 509), after rejecting Benfey's
etymon of the Latin *piscis*, and the connection of ἰχθυς
thereto, says : "Quant à 'Ιχθυς, qui est tout-à-fait isolé,
la question est beaucoup plus obscure. C'est là, peut-être,
un composé purement grec, où θυς me paraît se lier à
θυω = sanskr. *dhu*, agitare, commovere, et ἰχα, un ancien
nom de l'eau dont la trace est restée dans ἰκμας, humidité.
Cf. *aqua*, Goth. *ahva*, Anc. All. *aha*, Cymr. *ach*, Irlande
oiche, eau, &c., et les rac. sanskr. *ak*, volvi, *aç*, permeare,
&c. Cet *ik* hypothétic, identique à sa racine comme

beaucoup d'autres noms, se serait changé en $i\chi$ devant le θ de $\theta v\omega$, et $i\chi\theta v\varsigma$, signifierait ainsi *qui agite l'eau,* épithète bien adaptée au poisson." There can be little doubt of the latter syllable deriving from $\theta v\omega$ or $\theta v v\omega$, but whether the hypothetic $i\kappa$ of Mr. Pictet ever existed in the Greek language with the sense of water—*aqua*— may admit of a doubt, even though the Greek $i\kappa\mu a\varsigma$, moisture, would seem to favour the conjecture. Its association in $I\chi\text{-}vov\sigma a$ $\tau a\rho\text{-}i\chi o\varsigma$, $i\chi\text{-}v\eta$, perhaps $\Delta ov\lambda\text{-}i\chi iov$ of Homer (ii. 625), cannot thus be explained, but becomes readily intelligible if we admit the Polynesian *ika* to membership in the Aryan family.

IA³, *s.* Haw., name of the galaxy or milky way ; *iao, s.* name of the planet Jupiter when morning-star.

If in former ages this word and its associations with the Polynesians were invested with any divine- character, it has so long been lost or superseded that no trace thereof can now be found. *Ia* and *iao* now represent only a particular star or a cluster of stars. The stellar worship has been obliterated, but the to them now unmeaning name still remains to attest their former intimate relation to those peoples who, starting with common names for individual stars or cluster of stars, retained the names to designate the Author and Maker of " the hosts of heaven." The Chaldean, Syro-Phœnician *Iah,* the Greek $I a\omega$, of whom the Clarian oracle said, as reported by Macrobius, " $\Phi\rho a\zeta\epsilon\omega$ $\tau\omega v$ $\pi a v\tau\omega v$ $\dot{v}\pi a\tau ov$ $\theta\epsilon\dot{o}v$ $\ddot{\epsilon}\mu\mu\epsilon v$ $I a\omega$," attest the existence of the name in that part of the world. The Polynesians, in their development from stellar worship to the conception of individual deity, employed other words to express that conception, and to them *ia* and *iao* conveyed only the primary material sense of a star or cluster of stars. The Chaldeans and Greeks (and the latter probably borrowed from the former) in their development retained the name but forgot its original sense, and sought for etymons that seem to me more profound than conclusive.

IA⁴, *v.* Tah., to pitch, to daub ; *ia-loa, v.* Haw., to embalm by perfuming or otherwise; *s.* a dead body embalmed and preserved.

This word probably refers itself to the Greek *ιαινω*, to heat, melt, warm, cheer; *ιαομαι*, to heal, cure; *ιατηρ*, a surgeon, a healer; *ιαμα*, remedy, medicine.

IELE, *s.* Haw., a chief, a king. Tah., *ieieere*, consternation, amazement, awe.

Greek, *ιερος*, holy, hallowed, magnificent, vast, awful; *ιερευς*, a priest; *ιερεια*, sacrifice, festival; *ιεραξ*, a hawk, sacred to Apollo.

Liddell and Scott after Curtius, and A. Pictet after Kuhn, refer *ιερος* to the Sanskr. *ishira*, strong, lively, vigorous, robust, mighty, and hence divine, sacred; and Pictet suggests that the suppression of the *sh* is compensated by the initial spiritus asper. It may be so; but then, in view of the parallel Polynesian *iele*, the phonetic decay of *ishira* must be of an enormously ancient date.

Professor Max Müller, in " Chips from a German Workshop," i. 133 (Scribner's edition), says : " It is easy again to see that *ιερος* in Greek means something like the English sacred. But how, if it did so, the same adjective could likewise be applied to a fish or to a chariot, is a question which, if it is to be answered at all, can only be answered by an etymological analysis of the word. To say that *sacred* may mean *marvellous*, and therefore *big*, is saying nothing, particularly as Homer does not speak of catching big fish, but of catching fish in general." ` If Homer spoke of "fish in general" (Iliad, xvi. 407), why use the epithet *ιερος*? Whatever may be the etymology of *ιερος*, whether it refers itself to the Sanskrit *ishira*, or to the Polynesian *iele*, or both, it seems to me, under correction, that the sense of the word in Homer's time invariably conveyed the idea of something select, something remarkable, beyond ordinary things and persons, for its superior excellence, grandeur, solemnity, power, beauty, or elegance, thus reconciling its varying application, from a chariot, *ιερος διφρος* (Il. xvii. 464), up to the darkness, κνεφας ἱερον (Il. xi. 194), and to the day, ἱερον ἡμαρ (Il. viii. 66). And hence I infer that the ἱερος ἰχθυς, to which Homer refers, was not "fish in general," but some particular kind of fish known in his time by that epithet. Liddell and Scott quote Aristotle in explanation that the ἱερος ἰχθυς meant the fish otherwise known as the ἀνθιας.

The Tahitian *ieieere*, though somewhat corrupted in form, has probably retained the earlier sense of the word, and corresponds closely to the Greek senses of ἱερος, viz., wondrous, marvellous, extraordinary.

Io, *adj.* Haw., true, real; *adv.* truly, verily. Sam., *io*, *ioe*, yes. Tong., Fakaafo, *io*, yes. Fiji., *ia* and *io*, yes. Malg., *ie*, yes.

Goth., *ia, iai*, yes, verily. Swed., *ia, io*, yes, an affirmative.

Iu, *adj.* Haw., prohibited, sacred; *iuiu*, to be afar off, high up, to live in some sacred place; *s.* a place supposed to be afar off or high above the earth, or beneath the ocean, sacred to the dwelling-place of God. *Ke akua noho i ka iuiu*, the God dwells afar off; *i ka welau o ka makani*, at the farther end of the wind (Andrew's Dict.); *po-iu*, afar off, at a great distance, very high up, grand, solemn, glorious; *koiuiu*, far off, at a great height; *ko-iu-la*, to ascend as smoke, to float in the air as a cloud. Tah., *ioio*, handsome, brilliant. Haw., *io-lani*, the high, upper heaven.

Sanskr., *dyu, dio*, heaven, day; *deva*, god, deity, perhaps properly "the heavenly;" *dyâvâ-prithivi*, heaven and earth; *dyâus*, heaven personified; *diu-pate*, lord of heaven.

Greek, διος, divine; ἐνδιος, in the open air; Ζευς, Æol. Δευς, gen. Διος, chief of the Olympian deities; Διωνη, mother of Aphrodite; ἐν-δια, fair weather.

Lat., *divum, dium*, the sky; "*sub diu, sub divo*," in the open air; *Ju-piter* = Sanskr. *Dyu-pitar*, gen. *Jo-vis*, in Oscan *Dio-vei;* in the Iguvine tables *Juve-pater* = "in heaven the father" (Pictet); *Ju-no*, the wife and sister of Jupiter; *deus*, God; *dies*, day.

Goth., *tius*, gen. *tivis*; A.-Sax., *tiu*; O. Nors., *tyr*, gen. *tys*; A. Germ., *ziu* or *zio*, the most ancient of the Teutonic gods, and a personification of heaven (Pictet, *loc. cit.*, ii. 664).

It will be seen from the above comparison that the Polynesian *iu* and its composites have retained what was probably the very earliest sense of this word, as well as of its subsequent developments of sense. The idea of "high up," "far away," is not retained in the West Aryan tongues, except impliedly, as *diu* or *dio*, the heaven, in *dium*, the sky, in ἐν-διος, in the open air.

I have purposely omitted reference to the Greek θεος. Philologists seem to differ. Professor Sayce, in "Introduction to the Science of Language," ii. 136, says: "In spite of every effort that has been made to connect the Greek θεος with the common Aryan term that we meet with in the Latin *deus*, it still stands obstinately alone, and favours the view of Herodotus and Rödiger, that the Greek looked upon the gods as the 'placers' or 'creators' of that divinely arranged universe to which he afterwards gave the name of κοσμος, or order." Liddell and Scott (Greek-English Dictionary, *s. v.*) say: "We cannot admit the Greek derivation given by Herodotus[1] (2, 52), ὅτι κοσμωθέντες τὰ τάντα πρήγματα καὶ πάσας νομὰς εἶχον, or that of Plato (Crat., 397, C.), from θέειν, to run, because the first gods were the sun, moon, &c." In his notes to Herodotus, touching the passage above quoted, George Rawlinson justly remarks: "Both these derivations are purely fanciful, having reference to the Greek language only, whereas διος is a form of a very ancient word common to a number of the Indo-European tongues, and not to be explained from any one of them singly." In this dilemma the Polynesian *iu* offers a solvent for the forms in *dyu*, *iu*, &c., which we recommend to the above philologues. As to the θεος, vide Polynesian KEO, *post*.

IHA, *v.* Haw., be intent upon, desire strongly, persevere; *iha-iha*, strained, firmly drawn as a rope. Tah., *iha*, displeasure, grief, trouble; *iha-iha*, to palpitate from heat or

---

[1] Referred to by Professor Sayce, *vide supra*.

exertion. Sam., *isa*, exclamation of anger, contempt, indignation. Fiji., *isa*, interj. expressing disapprobation.

Sanskr., *ish²* (Benfey), to wish, cherish, approve ; *ishti*, wish; *îh*, to aim at, desire; *n.* exertion; *îhâ*, exertion, desire.

Greek, *ἵμερος*, desire, longing, and *ἰότης*, will, desire, interest in, are both referred to Sanskrit *ish* by Benfey and Liddell and Scott. They are probably correct, and the Greek shows no other correlatives ; but in the following branches the Sanskrit and Polynesian connection is certainly more apparent.

Zend., *ishud*, prayer.

Anc. Slav., *iskate* (pres. *ishta*), to seek, to ask.

Goth., *aîhtron*, to desire, to beg. A.-Sax., *aescian*, to seek, ask, inquire.

IHE, *s.* Haw., a spear, lance. Tah., *ihe*, id.

Sanskr., *ish¹* (Benfey), to throw, direct, send; *ishu*, an arrow; *ishîkâ*, a reed.

Greek, *ἰος* (contr. fr. *ἰσος*), arrow, shaft; *ἰς*, nerve, strength, force, and its composites.

Liddell and Scott refer *ἰς* to the Latin *vis*.

IHI, *adj.* Haw., dignified, majestic, sacred; a title applied to high chiefs. Tah., *ihi*, skill, wisdom, dexterity.

Sanskr., *îç*, to possess, be master, be able; *îça*, proprietor, master, ruler; *Içâna*, a name of Çiva; *îçin*, a governor.

Greek, *ἴφι*, splendidly, mightily, with might; *ἴφιος*, excellent; *ἴφια μελα*, fat sheep.

Liddell and Scott refer *ἴφι* to the Greek *ἰς*, power, strength, &c. But in view of the Polnes. *ihi*, the Sanskr. *îç*, the primary sense of both of which doubtless was that of excellence, superiority, I think the particularised Greek sense of *ἴφι*, " with might," is rather secondary and conventional than primary. The *ἴφια μελα* of Homer indicate excellence as the underlying sense, and not strength. Benfey refers the Goth. *aigan*, *aihan*, to own, possess, A.-Sax. *agan*, O. H. Germ. *eigan*, to the Sanskr. *îç*.

Ike[1], *v.* Haw., to see, perceive, know. Tah., *ite,* id. Mangar., Tong., N. Zeal., *kite,* id.

Sanskr., *íksh,* to look, behold, perceive, mind. Benfey calls this a desideratum of a lost verb analogous to *aksha.* That verb must then have been *ik,* which brings us near to the Polynesian form.

Ike[2], *v.* N. Zeal., to beat, to bruise the bark in making tapa. Marqu., Mangar., *ike,* name of the club or wooden mallet with which the bark is beaten out. Haw., Tah., Sam., *i'e,* id.

· Lat., *ico,* strike, beat, hit ; *ictus,* a blow, a stroke.

Ila, *s.* Haw., a dark spot on the skin. Sam., *ila,* a mother's mark, a mark in the skin, a defect ; *ila-ila,* marked, spotted. Tah., *ira,* a mole or mark on the skin. N. Zeal., *ira,* id. Tong., *ila,* id.

Greek, ἰλύς, mud, slime, dirt. Liddell and Scott think that ἰλύς comes " probably from εἰλύω, ἰλλω," to roll, fold up, to cover. If so, the connection in sense is so very distant, that it will perhaps be safer to connect ἰλύς with *ila,* as "mud" will make "spots" on the skin, whereas it is not evident that "rolling" or "folding" necessarily produces mud.

Ili[1], *s.* Haw., *ili-ili,* smooth, water-worn stones or pebbles. Tah., *iri-iri,* id. N. Zeal., *kiri-kiri,* id. Sam., *'ili-'ili,* gravel, pebbles, small stones. Flores (Ende), *keli,* mountain. Mal., *karang,* rock.

Sanskr., *çila,* a stone, rock ; *çilîndhra,* hail ; *çaila,* stony, rocky.

Armen., *kil,* slung-stone.

Lat., *silex,* flint.

It may be noted as an idiomatic correspondence, that as the Sanskrit *açman* and *açani,* rock, stone, are also applied as names for the thunderbolt ; and as the Greek κεραυνος, which Pictet derives from καρυς, καρυον, the nut or stone in fruit, has also become thunder and thunderbolt ; so by a similar process the Polynesian Haw. *he-kili,* thunder ; Tah., *pa-tiri,* id. ; N. Zeal., *wha-tetiri,* id.; Tong., *te-kili*, lightning; Sam., *fatu-tetili*, thunder, have received their applications.

The Sanskr. *giri*, a mountain, may possibly refer itself to this Polynesian *iri, ili, kiri.* Benfey says, *s. v.*, that *giri* stands "for original *gara ;* cf. Slav. *gora,* ὂρος, from *gur* for *gar.*" But see p. 85, *s. v.* OLO.

ILI², *s.* Haw., skin, bark, surface. Tah., *iri,* id. Tong. Fakaaf., *kili,* id. N. Zeal., Rarot., *kiri,* id. Sam., *ili-ui,* dark-skinned; *ili-ola,* the outer skin; *ili-ti-tai,* the bed of the sea (Haw., *ili-kai,* the surface of the sea); *ili,* a fan. Malg., *ulitz,* skin, bark. Sula Isl., *koli,* id. Amboyna, *uliti,* id. Teor., *holit,* id. Matalullo, *aliti,* id.

Sanskr., *chîra,* bark, a vesture of bark, a rag, a cloth. Benfey considers this word " a syncope perhaps of *chîvara,*" which he derives from *chï,* to arrange, collect, to cover. Pictet (*loc. cit.,* i. 203) refers this word to a primitive root *kr, kr̄,* "dans le sens de secare, lædere." In this dilemma I think it safer to refer it to its kindred Polynesian *ili, kiri,* and to look upon it as one of those ancestral words which have been retained by different sections of a common stock, but whose analysis it is impossible to determine because of our ignorance of the primitive form under which this word passed current. And certainly the early Aryans must have possessed some name for the bark of the trees and the skin of the animals before they adopted new words from the processes of obtaining them; *kritti,* hide, from *krit,* to cut off, divide, &c. The following possibly also belonged to the same family —:

O. Norse., *gera,* skin.

Lat., *ilia,* flanks of the body, loins.

The Haw. *hili,* general name for barks used in colouring and dyeing; *hili-koa,* koa bark; *hili-kolea,* &c., is probably but a dialectical transition from *kili* to *ili.*

ILIO, *s.* Haw., dog.

Greek, λις, lion, (Ep.) gen. λιος, acc. λιν, λεων, dat. pl. λειουσι, lion.

Lat., *leo,* lion.

Anc. Slav., *lisu, lisitsa,* fox.

Pictet (*loc. cit.*, i. 223) refers the Greek λεων to an ancient form, λεφων, and that to the Sanskr. *lû*, to cut off, destroy, whence *lavya*, secandus; and claims a purely Semitic origin for λις in the Hebr. *lais*, Arab. *lays*, and Chald. *laith*. To me the Semitic origin of λις seems more phonetic than real. So far as known, λις is as old a name for lion in the Greek language as λεων; they both occur in Homer's Iliad. The casus-endings of λις indicate that λι was its root, as well as the root of the Haw. *i-li-o*, where, as I consider, the initial *i* is euphonic.

It is somewhat singular, perhaps, that the Hawaiian word for dog has not, so far as I can learn, been retained in any of the other Polynesian dialects, in all of which the word *kuri* or *kuli* designates dog, except in the Marquesan, where *niche* stands alone as another remnant of former synonyms. The application of the word to a lion in one direction, and to fox and dog in other directions, but strengthens the presumption that it was one of the early generic names for that class of animals.

In regard to the root of this word, λεων, *lisu*, or *i-lis*, I think we must ascend higher than the Sanskrit *lavya*, a derivative or an inflection of *lû;* for it is almost certain that the Aryans were acquainted with and had named that class of animals long before the inflections of their language had developed themselves. Let us look to that earlier stage of the ·Aryan speech which the Polynesian has preserved, and we will find in the Haw. *li*, v. to be afraid, shrink back with dread; *li-o*, to fear, start suddenly; *adj*. fearful, affrighted; *li-o*, or *lei-o*, v. to open the eyes wide as a wild or affrighted animal, to act wildly or ferociously as an untamed animal, to bristle up as a wild hog. Hence *lio*, s. the name given to the horse when first introduced in the Haw. group. In the Sam. we find *lia-lia*, be afraid of; *lei-leia*, be frightened. In Tah., *riai*, be afraid.

On the fact that the West Aryan names for lion, and, I may add, the Polynesian (Haw.) name for dog, have no corresponding term in Sanskrit, Mr. Pictet very justly observes: " L'absence de ce nom de lion en sanscrit et en persan, ne

prouve pas qu'il n'ait jamais existé en Orient. Les ani-
maux qui frappent vivement l'imagination de l'homme,
reçoivent incessament de nouvelles denominations carac-
téristiques. Les Aryas de l'Inde, en contact journalier
avec le lion, lui ont donné de cinquante à soixante noms
descriptifs, et au milieu de cette profusion, quelques-uns
des plus anciens ont pu facilement se perdre."

IMO, *v.* Haw., to wink, as the eye, twinkle as a star;
imo-imo, v. to wink fast; *adv.* very high up, very far off,
i.e., it makes the eyes wink to look. This word is probably
akin, and but another, perhaps the earlier, form of *amo*, with
exactly the same meanings, singly or doubled. Tong.,
kame, to wink; *kema, id.* ; *kemo*, the eyelash; *kimoa*, a
rat, mouse. Sam., *emo*, to wink the eye, to flash as
lightning; *imoa*, a rat. Tah., *amo*, to wink, twinkle, flash.
N. Zeal., *kakamo*, to wink. Tikopia, *kakamo*, flash of
lightning. Marqu., *amo*, to twinkle; *kamo*, to steal.
Malg., *ambou, ambon*, on high, in the air, superior; *tan-
ambon*, a mountain.

Sanskr., *jihma*, oblique, squinting; *jihma-ga*, a snake;
jimûta, a cloud, a name of the sun. Benfey, it is true,
refers *jimûta* to *jihma*, and this to "*hvri*, probably for
primitive *jihvri, i.e.* redupl. *hvri-a.*" With due deference,
it seems to me that the Polynesian forms offer an easier
solution.

Greek, σιμος, snub-nosed, bent upward like the curved
slope of a hillside; τα σιμα, epithet applied to mountains,
"ardua acclivia." Liddell and Scott give no etymon for
σιμος.

Whether the Icelandic Old Norse *himin* and the
German *Himmel*, both signifying heaven, and of which the
latter was anciently a name applied to mountains, are not
allied to the Polynesian *imo*, I am not prepared to say,
but think it probable, in the absence of other or better
etymology. The German *Sims, Ge-sims*, a cornice, mantel,
or shelf, would also seem to ally itself to the Greek
αισιμαι, the ends of a lyre, parts of the cornice.

INU, *v.* Haw., to drink. Tah., and all other Polynesian

dialects, id., except Rotuma, *imu*, to drink. N. Guinea (Motu or Port Moresby), *inua*, to drink. Tagal. and Sunda, *inum*, *nginum*, *minum*, to drink. Malg., *minim*, *minon*, id.

Sanskr., *ino*, *inu*, to please, satisfy ("in the Vedas especially"—Benfey).

Greek, *αἰνυμαι*, to take hold of, to enjoy, feed on.

Probably the earliest craving of human nature was thirst, and the earliest satisfaction experienced was that of drinking when thirsty. Hence the name given to the act of drinking became also the name for the sentiment experienced from the act. The transition from the material to the moral sense of the word seems perfectly intelligible. The Polynesian branch has preserved the former, the Sanskrit and Greek the latter.

INO, *v.* Haw., to hurt, injure, be worthless; *adj.* bad, vile, wicked. Sam., *ino-ino*, bad, hateful. Tah., *ino*, bad, sinful. N. Zeal., Rarot., Mangar., Marqu., *kino*, bad, evil.

Zend., *eno*, sin.

Greek, *αἰνος*, dread, grim, horrible. Liddell and Scott refer this to *ai*, interj. of affright. It may be, but the Zend and Polynesian would indicate otherwise.

IWI, *s.* Haw., bone, midrib of a leaf, cocoa-nut shell, rind of sugar-cane, boundary-stones, broken materials, remnants; fig. descendants, near kindred; *v.* to turn aside, be curved, crooked. Tah., *ivi*, bone; *wahine-iwi*, a widow. Sam., *iwi*, bone. N. Zeal., Mangar., *iwi*, bone, also a family, a clan. Rarot., *iwi* and *iwa*, bone. In compds., Haw. *poo-hiwi*, N. Zeal. *poko-hiwi*, the shoulder; Haw. *kua-hiwi*, Sam. *tua-siwi*, Tah. *a-iwi*, backbone, ridge of a mountain; Fiji., *siwa*, a fish-hook.

Closely allied to this, if not a mere dialectical variation, is the Haw. *kiwi*, *v.* to bend, to crook; *adv.* side-ways; *s.* anything crooked, a sickle, a horn. Fiji., *tiwi-tiwi*, side-ways; *s.* a hatchet; *tibica*, to bend sharply.

Sanskr., *ibha*, elephant. Ved., *ibha*, family, household; *ibhya*, wealthy.

Greek, *ὑβος*, crooked.

Lat., *tibia*, shin-bone; *gibbus, gibba*, a hunch on the back.

Irish, *ibh*, country, tribe.

Anc. Germ., *eiba*. Lombard, *aib*, used in compounds of names of places, as *Wetar-eiba, Wingart-eiba*, indicating a district or territory. Perhaps the Goth. *ib-dali*, descent, refers also to the Ved. *ibha*, the Irish *ibh*, and the Polynes. *iwi*.

The Sax. *iw* or *eow*, the yew tree, from which archers' bows were made, the Icel. *ivr, yr*, a bow to shoot with, and the Germ. *eibe*, the yew tree, as well as the Welsh *yw, ywen*, the yew tree, doubtless ally themselves to the primary forms and sense of *iwi* and *kiwi*.

Benfey and Pictet refer the Greek ἴφι, ἴφιος, to the Sanskr. *ibhya*. (On p. 73 I have given my opinion.) The Sanskr. *ibha*, elephant, was no doubt so called from its prominent tusks, and thus indicates a close and primary relation to the Polynesian *iwi*, as doubtless does also the Latin *ebur*, ivory.

A. Pictet (*loc. cit.*, i. 230), following Kuhn, refers the Saxon and Celtic names for the yew tree to the Sanskr. Ved. *êwa*, "cours (de temps), cours habituel, coutume," analogous to the Anc. Germ. *êwa*, eternity, *ewin, ewig*, eternal, &c., on account of its remarkable longevity. I think the hypothesis untenable in view of the Polynesian *iwi* and its various developments, which seem to offer a better solution of the origin of these terms, either in regard to the use made of the yew tree for making bows, or in regard to its strength and durability, the former connecting it with *iwi* through its sense of curvature, the latter through its sense of hardness and strength; and in the absence of other etymons, I would also refer the Saxon *ifig*, the ivy, to some near, but to me unknown, relation of *iwi*.

OAKA, *v.* Haw., *owaka, hoaka*, to open suddenly, as the eyes or mouth, to open as a flower, to shine, to glisten; reflection of the sun on a luminous body, glimpse, glance, brightness, glory, the crescent or hollow of the new moon, the lintel or arch over a door. This word is probably allied to or derived from *aka*, to light up as the moon before rising, dawn of light (vid. p. 46); but in the ancient dialect of Kauai (Hawaiian group), *aka* means eye, and *aka-lapa-lapa*, large brilliant eyes. In Tah., *oata* is the hole or meshes in a net, the hole in a calabash, a central hole, the monkey's eyes on a cocoanut; *vata*, an opening, a rent. Fiji., *waqa*, to burn; *waqa-waqa*, hot, fiery, of anger, or of the eyes flashing.

The existence in a Hawaiian dialect, now obsolete, of the word *aka*, with an undoubted specific meaning of eye, with the derivative forms and their significations quoted above, will doubtless throw some light upon the descent of the Sanskr. *aksha, akshi*, the Greek ὄκκος, ὄσσε, the Lat. *oculus*, the Lith. *akis*, the Russ. *oko*, all designating eye, and each one coeval with, if not a development from, the Polynesian *aka*.

Among the tribes of the Hindu-Kush, the Gilgit dialect of the Shina has *achi*, eye; the Chiliss has *ache*, id.; Torwalak, *ashi*, id.; Bushgali, *achen*, id.

A. Pictet (*loc. cit.*, i. 553) rejects in a rather scornful manner the proposition of those philologists who claim relationship for the Goth. *augo*, the Sax. *ægh, eag*, &c., eye, with the Sanskr. *akshā*, and he proposes for them a Sanskr. root *ûh*, animadvertere, intelligere, and says that *ûh* "semblerait avoir eu dans l'origine la signification de voir, puis de faire attention, considérer, &c." Benfey, however, refers the Goth. *augo* to the Sanskr. *akshi*, and, I think, with greater probability of being correct.

Or[1], *v.* Haw., to project over, be more in any way, exceed, be better; *s.* excess, superiority, the sharp edge or point of a weapon; *adj.* first, greater, more excellent, sharp pointed; *oi-e*, an ancient name or epithet of the god Kane. Tah., *oi*, sharp, as the edge of a tool; *oioi*, rapid, swift.

Sanskr., *oj*, be strong, to live; *ojas*, strength, light, splendour.

Lat., *augeo*, make great, increase, strengthen; *augustus.*

Greek, αὐγη, bright, light, radiance, any light or gleam; αὐγαι, the two eyes.

Icel., *auka*, to increase. Sax., *eacan*, id. Swed., *öka*, id.

s. v. αὐγη, Liddell and Scott hesitate whether to refer it to "the same root as Lat. *oc-ulus*, Germ. *aug-e, i.e.*, Sanskr. *ic*, videre, or from the same root as ἀως, αὐως, *aurora.*"

s. v. ὀψ, the eye, they refer that as well as the Lat. *oculus*, the Goth. *augo*, the Sanskr. *aksham* (eye), *iksh* (to look), and several others to a root οπ, from which all those referred to are but "dialectical forms."

It ill becomes me to criticise my masters; but in such uncertainty it may be well to acknowledge the Polynesian as an elder dialect of Aryan speech, and take the aid it offers.

OI², *v.* Haw., to approach, draw near to. Tah., *oi, adv.* nearly, almost, Tong., *ofi*, near, to approach. Sam., *ofi*, to enter, to fit in, to cover, of the male animal. N. Zeal., *awi*, to approach, draw near.

Sanskr., *abhi*, towards, to, on, over; *abhi-tas*, on both sides, from every side, round about, near, towards; *abhi-gama*, approaching, visit, sexual intercourse.

Greek, ἀμφι, on both sides, on, about, over, at, by, near. Lat., *amb-*, as in *amb-ire.*

O. H. Germ., *umpi.* Goth., *bi*, at, by, near.

OHANA, *s.* Haw., a family, brood of birds, a litter, offspring, tribe. Tong., *ohana*, husband or wife, a spouse; *iiena*, a person. Sam., *ofanga*, a nest; *fanganga*, a herd. N. Zeal., *kohanga*, a nest. Tah., *ofaa*, id.; *v.* to nestle close, to brood. All these are derivatives of a once common word, whose primary meaning was "to bear, bring forth young, to breed," and the simple form of which no longer exists, but appears in compounds like the following: Haw., *hana-u*, to bear, to bring forth, breed; *hanau-na*, relations, generation; *hana-i*, to feed, to nurse. Sam., *fana-u*, bring forth young, be born; *s.* offspring, children; *fafanga*, to feed; *fanga-moa*, a hencoop. Tong., *fanga*, a brood, flock, family; *fafanga*, to feed, nourish. Tah., *fana-u*, be born;

fanau-a, an infant. Buru (Cajeli), *anai*, child. S. Celebes (Bouton), *oanana*, child. Malay and Jav., *anak*, child. Malg., *zana*, *zanak*, *zanaka*, children, offspring.

Sanskr., *jan*, to bring forth, produce, be born, to grow, to be caused, become; *jana*, creature, mankind, a person; *jani*, a woman; *jan-aka*, a father, producer; *jana-ta*, mankind, household servants, subjects; *jâte, i.e., janti*, birth, life, tribe, kind.

Zend, *zan*, to beget; *zantu*, tribe.

Greek, γενω, am born, made, become; γενεα, birth, origin, race, family; γυνη, a woman; γονη, produce, offspring; γενναω.

Lat., *geno, gigno*, bear, bring forth; *genus*, birth, descent, race, family; *gens nascor, i.e., gnascor*, be born, begotten; *natus, nata*, son, daughter, pl. children.

Irish, *genim, geanaim*, bring forth; *ginel, cine*, family, race. Welsh, *geni*, be born; *gan, genid*, birth.

Goth., *keinan*, to germinate, spring up, grow; *kuni*, kin, race, generation, tribe; *kwens, kweins*, a woman, a wife; *kwino*, woman.

Anc. Slave, *jena*, woman.

See further articles "Kanaka," "Kino."

OKA, *s.* Marqu. (Nuk.), the rafter of a roof. Haw., *o'a*, rafters of a house, timbers of a boat or ship; *oka-na*, a district or division of country. Tah., *oa*, the ribs or timbers of a vessel. Sam., *o'a-o'a*, a stake or pile stuck in the ground.

Sanskr., *oka, okas*, house, dwelling-place.

Lith., *ukis*, a rustic dwelling; *ukininkas*, landed proprietor, paterfamilias.

Benfey (Sanskr.-Engl. Dict.) and Pictet (*loc. cit.*, ii. 243) derive the Sanskr. *oka* from *uch*, to like, be accustomed to, suitable. It is at best an hypothesis.

OKI, *v.* Haw., to cut, sever, end, finish, cease from doing. Tong., *oki*, to end, complete; *koki*, to cut off, as hair. N. Zeal., *oti-oti*, to rest. Fiji., *koti*, clip, shear; *otia*, to finish; *oti-oti*, end, conclusion. Sunda, *ukir*, to cut, engrave.

Lat., *occo*, to harrow; *otium*, leisure, rest, exemption from business.

Greek, ὀξύς, sharp, keen, piercing; ὠκύς, swift, quick, sharp.

This word is doubtless a phonetic variation of *aki*, q. v. p. 49.

OKO, *adj.* Marqu. (Nuk.), strong, vigorous. Haw., *o'o*, ripe, mature, full-grown. Sam., *o'o*, id. Mangar., *oko*, hard, firm.

Sanskr., *okh*, be able.

OLA, *v.* Haw., be saved from danger, recover from sickness, to live; *s.* means of life, life itself, living, period of life. Sam., *ola*, to live, recover from sickness; *s.* life, prosperity; *ola-ola*, to flourish, to thrive. Other S. Polynes. dialects: *ora*, id. Fiji., *bula*, life, to live, recover from sickness, sound, either of body or mind, healthy, flourishing. Malg., *velon*, life, to live, healthy, sound.

Greek, οὖλος (the older Epir. and Ion. form, used by Homer and Hesiod), ὅλος, whole, entire, sound, safe; οὖλω, be whole or sound; οὖλε, a salutation like the Lat. *salve*. To the later Greek ὅλος refer themselves probably the Lat. *salus, salvus, solus* (?); the Goth. *hails*, hale, sound; Sax., *hal*, id.; *hæl*, health.

OLE[1], *v.* Haw., to speak through the throat, guttural, or through a trumpet; *s.* name of a large sea-shell; *ole-ole*, talk thickly or indistinctly, as one angry or scolding, to grin like the idols; *olo*, be loud, as a sound, as a voice of wailing; *olo-olo*, intens. to roar, rush, as the sound of waters. Sam., *ole*, to ask, beg; *olo*, to coo as a dove; *faa-olo*, to whistle for the wind. Tah., *oro-io*, to grieve to death; *ta-oro-oro*, make a noise, rumble at the bowels. Tong., *kole*, to beg. Fiji., *kodrau*, to squeal; *qolou*, to shout. Mal., *lulong*, to shout, howl.

Lat., *os, oris*, mouth; *oro*, speak, utter, pray; *ululo*, howl, yell; *ulula*, an owl.

O. Norse, *ôs*, mouth or opening of a river or lake. O. Engl., *ouse*, id. A.-Sax. and O. H. Germ., *ûla*, an owl.

Greek, ὀλολύζω, to cry aloud to the gods; ὀλολύγη, any

loud cry; ὀλολυγων, the croaking of frogs; ὑλαω, to bark, bay, howl.

OLE[2], *s.* Haw., the eye-tooth, name of a fish; *ole-ole, v.* to make notches in anything, to dovetail two pieces together. Tah., *ore-ore,* the teeth of sharks or of the ono fish.

Greek, ὄρυξ, a pickaxe, or any sharp tool for digging; ὀρυσσω, to dig. Ὄρυξ was also the name of a species of antelope or gazelle, so called from its "pointed horns" (Liddell and Scott); also the name of "a great fish, probably the narwhal; Lat. *orca*" (ibid.) Liddell and Scott, *loc. cit.,* refer ὀρυσσω to ἀρασσω, to strike hard, or to ῥησσω, to break. I believe neither etymon is the correct one— ὀρυσσω is evidently a denominative of ὄρυξ, but ὄρυξ has three distinct meanings, all converging to one common origin, of which the two latter, as given by Liddell and Scott, probably suggested the first one. The Polynesian *ole, ore,* eye-tooth, shark's teeth, gives the key to the Greek ὄρυξ, narwhal and sharp-horned antelope, and the Latin *orca,* grampus.

OLI, *v.* Haw., *oli-oli,* id.; to sing, be glad, exult; *s.* joy, exultation, gladness, a song. Sam., *oli, oli-oli,* joy, joyful; *faa-oli-oli,* to rejoice, to quiet a child by walking about with it. Tah., *ori,* to dance, to shake, to ramble about; *ori-ori,* to gad about; *faa-ori,* get up a dance. Rarot., *taoriori,* to stir up, excite. Sunda, *ulin,* to play, romp.

Greek, ὄρω, ὄρνυμι, raise, stir up, of bodily movements, urge, incite; ὀρυνω, id., agitare; ὀρουω, rush violently; ὄρνις, a bird.

Lat., *orior,* rise, get up, appear; *origo.*

Liddell and Scott refer the Greek ὄρω, &c., and Benfey refers the Latin *orior* to the Sanskr. *ri, ri-nómi,* to go, to rise, &c., &c. For my part, I should consider that the Polynes. *ole*[1], *olo,* and *oli* refer themselves for their primary meaning, as well as the Greek and Latin words quoted above, to the Polynes. *olo, oro* (Haw., Sam., Tah.), to rub, grate, saw, vibrate, swing; and I would endorse Judge Andrews' remark in his Haw.-Engl. Dict., *s. v.:* "It is not easy to see the connection between *olo-oloolo,* to sound, as the voice of wailing, and *olo-oloolo,* to swing, vibrate, &c., unless the latter be the radical meaning, and the voice of wailing be so expressed on account of the vibratory motion of the voice in mourning and wailing."

OLo, *s.* Haw,. the simple form is obsolete. In compound words it serves mostly as a synonym for mountain. We thus have *Olo-kui,* name of a mountain on Molokai; *Olo-mana* and *Olo-ku,* mountain peaks on the island of Oahu, Haw. group; *Oro-hina* and *Oro-tou,* mountains on Tahiti; *Oro-singa,* one of the Samoan islands. In Sam., *olo* means a place of refuge, a fortress; in Rarot., *koro* means a wall, enclosure; in Haw., *olo-alu* means a safe place where the property of the chief was stored; in Tah., *oro-matua* means lit. the skull of a parent, secondarily the spirits of dead relations, analogous to the Haw. *au-makua.* In the Motu dialect of New Guinea (Port Moresby), *ororo* means mountain. A dialectical form in *ulu* is common in Polynesia. Sam., *ulu,* head of man and animal, head of a club, the knob of a stick; *ulu-lá,* the top edge of a Samoan mat-sail; *ulu-poo,* the skull; *ulu-tula,* bald-headed. Tab., *uru,* skull. Marqu., *u'u,* club. Fiji., *ulu,* head; *ulu-mate,* wig. Throughout Polynesia *ulu* is also the name of the bread-fruit, doubtless from its shape and resemblance to a human head. Among the Malay Islands both forms prevail. Tagal, *olo,* head. Buguis, Batta, Banjak Island, Engano, Amboyna, Saparua, Ceram, *ulu, uru,* id. Sunda, *huru,* id. Buru, *olum, olun,* id.

Greek, ὄρος, mountain, hill, height; Ion. οὖρος, id.; ὀρογκοι, mountain tops.

Liddell and Scott, without giving their own opinion, state that "Curtius connects this word with Sanskr. *giris,* Zend. *gairis,* Slav. *gora,* all of the same signification." Unfortunately I do not possess the works of Mr. Curtius, and do not know to what root he refers *giris* and *gora.* But Mr. A. Pictet (*loc. cit.,* i. 122) refers them to a Sanskrit root, " *gr (gar),* effundere, conspergere, à cause des eaux qui descendent des hauts lieux et des montagnes

neigeuses." Mr. Pictet, however, refers the Greek ὄρος
to the Sanskrit *varâha*, mountain, ὄρος for ϝορος, and allied
to *vâra*, a heap, a pile, a multitude, and quotes the Irish
fair, faire, hill, eminence, as analogous. Because *vâra*
and *varâha, fair* and *faire*, indicate the presence of a
digamma, and *giri* and *gora* the presence of an initial
guttural, I do not see that it necessarily follows that ὄρος
must have lost either a primary digamma or a primary
guttural. Its two forms, ὄρος and οὖρος, have their exact
counterparts in the Polynesian *oro, ulu*, with the same
primary meaning of hill, height, tallness, mountain, &c. I
have no desire and still less ability to contend with so
eminent philologists as Curtius, Pictet, &c., but I simply
wish to present the claims of the Polynesian to recognition by European savants as a primitive member, however
much "weather-worn and travel-stained," of the great
Aryan stock; and call their attention to the fact that in
this language may be found the solution of many an etymological riddle in the Aryan family of speech. I hold,
therefore, that not only are *olo* and ὄρος related, but are
also far older names for mountain than their synonyms
varâha or *giri*, inasmuch as the idea of altitude, pro-
minence, in relation to mountains, must necessarily have
struck the beholder before the more complex ideas of
covering and protection, or the effusion of rain from lofty
mountains. The Polynesian *olo* and *ulu* were no doubt
only dialectical variations of a primary word conveying
the idea of tall, high, lofty, prominent, applied to head and
mountain, like the Celtic *pen*.

OPE, *s.* Haw., bundle; *v.* to bundle up; *opi-opi*, to tie up
tightly, to fold up as a cloth. Tah., *ope*, to collect, to
bring together; *ope-ope*, property, things of all descriptions,
which in the rage of war had been thrown into the rivers,
then carried to the sea, and afterwards thrown on shore
again; *opi, oopi*, to shut together, to close as the leaves of a
book. Marqu., *kopi*, to close, shut up, as the hand. Fiji.,
ovi-ca, to gather the young under her wings, as a hen;
oviovi, a nest. I consider these as dialectical variants of

another Polynesian form : Haw., *api*, to gather together, as people to one place, to bring into a small compass, as baggage. Sam., *api*, to lodge ; *s.* residence, lodging. Tong., *abi*, home, habitation. Rarot., *pu-api-nga*, property, possessions. Tah., *api*, folds of cloth ; *v.* to join together, to confederate, be filled, as a place ; *api-a*, closed, as oyster-shells ; *api-piti*, altogether ; *api-api*, crowded, as a road.

Lat., *ops, opis*, means, riches, wealth ; *Ops*, the goddess of earth, as the source of fruitfulness and riches; *opimus*, fruitful.

Greek, ἄφενος, wealth, abundance.

Lith., *apstas*, riches, abundance.

Benfey and Pictet refer the Latin *ops, opes*, to the Sanskrit *áp*, to attain to, obtain, to fit, whence the Latin *apto*, to fit; *opus*, work, &c. Liddell and Scott, following Curtius, refer ἄφενος to Sanskrit *apnas*, income, property, and allied to Latin *ops, opulentus, copia*. With due deference, I think that *ops*, ἄφενος, *apsta*, show a greater affinity to the Polynesian *opi, api*, than to the Sanskrit *áp*, which, on the other hand, certainly connects better with the Polynesian *apo*, q. v., p. 61.

Whence came the suffix *-ops, -opes*, which so many different peoples, or rather tribes of the same race, inhabiting the coasts of the Mediterranean in ancient times, shared in common, whatever their patronymic distinction ? We read of *Pel-opes, Mer-opes, Dry-opes, Dol-opes, Cere-opes, Aithi-opes, Opisci* (contracted *Osci*), and others. It has been generally referred to the Greek ὄψ, the voice or manner of speech, or to the Greek ὄψ, the eye, look, and appearance, and in course of time to have become a collective word for people, nation, tribe. It seems to me that neither ὄψ, the eye, nor ὄψ, the voice, fully satisfies the etymological demands of this word. If the former may apply to the Pel-opes or Aithi-opes, it certainly cannot apply to the Mer-opes or Dol-opes, nor can the latter apply with any greater appropriateness to the Pelopes and Aithiopes. A swarthy or sunburnt voice would be as unintelligible an expression as a wooden or articulated eye; and hence the

Greek ὄψ failing to be equally applicable to all the words in which it occurs as meaning a nation, people, or tribe, we must look outside the Greek among kindred tongues for an etymon that will render an intelligible meaning to all the cases where occurring, and will justify its application in expressing the idea of a people or a tribe. Such a word I find in the Polynesian *ope, api*. It may have existed in the Greek in far pre-Homeric times, indicating a collection, a gathering of men or things, and thus been applied to a people or tribe, as the Scandinavian *thiod* in Svithiod or Gauthiod indicated the Svea or Gota people; but no trace of its primary meaning remained in Homer's time, except perhaps in ἀφενος, whose derivative meaning has been retained also in the Latin *opes,* the Lithuanian *apsta,* as well as in the Polynesian *ope-ope* and *pu-àpingà*.

U, *v*. Haw., to protrude, rise up, draw out, to ooze or drip, as water, to drizzle, to weep, to be tinctured, impregnated, soaked; *s*. the breast of a female, pap, udder. Tah., *u*, to run against a thing, to touch, to be damp, wet; *s*. the breast of anything that gives milk. Sam., *u*, direct towards, turn to. Marqu., *u*, swell up, as boiling water, proceed out, breast of woman, milk; *uu*, proceed. Fiji., *ua*, to flow, of the tide, a wave; deriv. Haw., *uha*, the thigh, the ham of a hog, the lap of a woman, the rectum. Sam., *ufa*, the rectum, posteriors. Tah., *ufa*, females of beasts, the thigh. N. Zeal., *uwa*, id. Marqu., *pufa*, the thigh. N. Zeal., Tah., Marqu., *uma*, breast. Tong., *uma*, the shoulder. Haw., *umauma*, breast. Paum., *kouma*, heart. Sam., *uma*, a wide chest.

As this word is evidently either a primary form or a dialectical variation of the Polynesian *hu, su*, with almost identical meanings, I refer the reader to that for further remarks. But there are a few West Aryan words which seem to me to ally themselves nearer to the form *u* than to that of *hu, su,* and I here submit them.

Sanskr., *û-dhar*, udder.

Greek, οὐθαρ, udder.

Lat., *uterus,* womb; *uber,* teat, breast, udder; *uvidus,* wet; *udus.*

A.-Sax., *uder,* udder. Engl., *ooze?* Swed., *udde,* point, projection, cape; *udda,* odd, not even.

Benfey (Sanskr.-Engl. Dict.) refers the Sanskrit *údhar* to an original (so supposed) *vad-dhant;* but as no such word as *vad* answering to that purpose is found in the Sanskrit, I may be permitted to refer the first component to its Polynesian kindred *u,* and the second to the Sanskrit verb *dhâ,* to grant, confer. And when that agglutination of *u* and *dha* took place among the West Aryan branches, *u* must still have been a living, independent word, with the secondary meaning of milk, moisture, that it still retains in the Tahitian.

U^2, *v.* Sam., to emit a hollow sound, to roar, as the waves on the reef; *faia-u,* to cry with a loud moaning voice. Haw., *uō,* cry out, to bellow, roar. Tong., *uō,* to crow, as a cock. Tah., *uā,* to scream.

Sanskr., *u,* to sound.

UA, *s.* Haw., rain; *v.* to rain. Sam., Tah., N. Zeal., Marqu., id. Tong., *uha,* rain. Rotoma, *usa,* id. Sunda, *hua,* to rain. Sulu Isl., *huya,* rain. Ceram. (Camar), *ulani,* id. Gilolo (Gani), *ulau,* id.; (Galela), *hura,* id. Mentawej Isl., *urat,* id. Teor, *uran,* id. Tagal, *olon,* id. Malg., *oran,* id. Ceram. (Gah), *u'an,* id. Timor (Brissi), *oû,* water. Savn., *u iloko,* id. Rotti., *oe'e,* id. Fiji., *uca,* rain.

Sanskr., *udan,* water; *und,* to wet, moisten; *uksh* (Ved.), to wet, sprinkle.

Lat., *unda,* wave.

Icel., *und,* a spring of water, wave. O. Norse, *yda,* to flow together; *ûr-van,* a cloud, from *ûr,* pluvia (Grimm's Teuton. Myth., i. 332).

Whatever the meaning of the qualifying suffixes *-dan,* *-nd, -ksh, -r,* to the above West Aryan words, it is evident that the common base of those words was an original *u,* as it is in the Polynesian *u-a, u-ha, u-sa, u-ran, u-lan,* of which we find an almost literal reproduction in that old and half-forgotten member of the Iranian branch, the Ossetic, where *ua-ran* signifies "to rain."

I think it very probable that the Sanskrit *abhra*, a rain-cloud, Latin *imber*, rain, shower, *umbra*, shade, Greek ὄμβρος, thunderstorm, heavy rain, which lexicographers point out as closely related, without, however, giving an etymon, will, when properly analysed, be found to dissolve themselves into this primary Old Aryan *u*, meaning "water, moisture," and some common Aryan form of the Sanskrit *bhri*, to bear, to hold. Probably also the Latin *u-ber* refers itself to the same formation.

I have said nothing of the Greek ὕδωρ or the Latin *sudor*. Authorities differ. The initial aspirate and sibilant indicate their connection with the Polynesian *hu*, *su*, q. v., and which was probably a later form, though with similar meaning, than that in *u*.

In regard to the Gothic *wato*, water, whose base, *watan*, Benfey says, "represents the organic form of the verb *und*," I fear it will be found to have no relation to *u*, *ud*, *und*, whatever. My reasons will be shown s. v. WAI.

UILA, *s.* Haw., also *uwila*, *u* prefix or euphon., lightning. Sam., *u-ila*, and in most of the Southern dialects, *u-ira*, lightning. In Tong., *u-hila*, lightning, we approach the original form of the word, which we find in the Sam. *sila*, *s.* an extremity of the rainbow, *v.* to be ashamed. Haw., *hila-hila*, blushing of the face, quick suffusion of blood, shame. Tah., *hira*, bashfulness. Fiji., *cila*, to shine, of the heavenly bodies. Malg., *helet*, lightning. Sunda, *gelap*, lightning; *gilap*, to shine, glitter; *sirab*, streak of lightning; *ira*, shame. Malay, *kilat*, lightning. Celebes (Goront), *ilata*, id.

Sanskr., *hîra*, Indra's thunderbolt, a diamond; *hirana*, gold; *hriniya*, be angry, ashamed, bashful.

Greek, σέλας, flash of lightning, light, brightness; σελήνη, moon; ἕλη, the heat or light of the sun; ἑλανη, a torch; ἠέλιος, ἥλιος, sun, daylight. Liddell and Scott refer the Greek σείριος, scorching, and the Sanskrit *sûra*, *sûrya*, sun, *sol*, to the same family. It may be so, but it may be "faute de mieux."

Germ., *helle*, clearness, brightness, brilliancy.

UKA, *s.* Haw., the country inland from the sea, up towards the mountains. S. Polynes., *uta*, id. Motu (N. Guinea), *uta*, forest. Mal., *utan*, wilderness, forest, jungle; *utara*, north. Bisayan (Phil. Isl.), *yuta*, earth, land.

Sanskr., *ud*, up, upward, out; *udañch*, upper, northern; *uchcha*, high; *uttara*, superior, northern, *i.e.*, upper region.

Welch, *uc*, high, elevated.

Goth., Sax., *ut*, *uta*, out of, from.

In Polynesian the *uta* corresponds exactly to the Sanskrit *ut-tara*, the inland, higher country, in contradistinction from the lower, coast land. The Malay *utara*, north, is probably an importation in after-ages of the Sanskrit *uttara*, which itself, doubtless, only became indicative of a northern region after the Aryans had descended from the Hindu-Kush, and when to go northward was equivalent to going upward. In no part of Polynesia proper does the sense of north connect with the word *uta*. It means simply up from the lowlands, or inland from the seaboard, whatever point of the compass one starts from. When the Polynesians left the Aryan stock, the Vedic Aryans had apparently not yet descended from the mountains which afterwards formed their northern barrier.

ULA, *adj.* Haw., red as a blaze, purple, scarlet, name of a lobster. Tah., *ura*, flame, to blaze, be red; *ura-ura*, red. Sam., *ula*, red; *ula*, lobster. Mangar., *ura*, blaze, flame. Tong., *ula*, id.; *kula-kula*, red. N. Zeal., *kura*, red. Marqu., *kua*, id. Fiji, *kula-kula*, red. Sunda, *urung*, flame. Ceram. (Awauja), *ausa*, fire. Pulo Nias, *auso*, yellow. Matabello, *ululi*, red. Tidore, *kur-achi*, yellow. Gilolo (Galela), *kur-achi*, gold.

Sanskr., *ush*, to burn, and its numerous derivatives; *ulkâ*, a firebrand, meteor, fireball; *ulmuka*, id.

Lat., *uro*, burn, *ustus*, *ustio;* *aurum*, gold; *aurora*, the redness of the dawn, dawn.

Greek, *αὔω*, kindle, light a fire; *ἠώς*, *ἀώς*, *αἰώς*, for *ἀϝώς*, the morning red, dawn; *αὔριον*, to-morrow; *αὖρον*, gold; *εὔω*, to singe.

Irish, *ur*, fire. Welsh, *ysu*, burn; *aur*, gold. Corn., *eur*, id.

Lith., *auksas*, gold; *auszra*, the dawn. Anc. Pruss., *ausis*, gold.

Zend, *ushâ*, *ushô*, *usâ*, morning, dawn.

O. Norse, *usli*, fire. A.-Sax., *ysli*, a live coal. Anc. Germ., *usil*, yellow.

Benfey refers the Sanskrit *ulkâ* to " probably " *jval*, to blaze, burn. Again it is possible; but is it so in face of the Latin, Greek, and Polynesian congeners ?

In the Dravidian, Canarese, and Tulu occurs the word *ur-i*, signifying to burn.

The same tendencies to commute *r* and *s* are as apparent in the Polynesian family as in the Indo-European.

ULI, *s.* Haw., the blue sky; *adj.* blue, cerulean, green; *uli-uli*, verdure; *adj.* green, dark-coloured, black. Sam., Tong., Fak., *uli;* Tah., *uri*, blue-black, any dark colour.

I find no application of this word in the West Aryan dialects, unless it forms the component part of the Latin *cær-ula*, *cær-uleus*, the blue colour of the sky, dark-blue, dark-coloured; *cær* or *coer* being a contraction of *cælus* or *coelum*, *r* and *l* commuted.

ULE, *v.* Haw., to hang, to swing, to project; *s.* the genitals of male animals, the tenon for a mortise ; *ule-ule*, pendulous, projecting; *uli*, *v.* to steer a canoe; *hoe-uli*, a rudder, a steering oar or paddle; *ulili*, a ladder, a bamboo whistle. Fiji., *uli*, the steering oar of a canoe. Tah., *uri*, the pilot-fish, the dog.

Greek, *οὐρά*, the tail of an animal, the rear; *ὄρος*, *ὄῤῥος*, tail, rump, bottom; *ὄρυα*, a sausage; probably *οὖρον*, urine; *οὐρέω*.

Lat., *urina*, urine; *urinor*, dive under water; *urinator*, a diver; possibly so named from the action, if the process was diving head foremost; probably akin to *οὐρία*, a water-bird.

Sanskr., *úru*, the thigh; *uras*, the breast; *ura-ga*, a snake; *urmi*, a wave. Benfey refers the three first to *vri*, to guard, screen, cover, conceal, and the last to *hvri* ("orig. *dhvri*"), to bend, be crooked. Under correction, I believe that the Polynesian *ule, uli*, pendulous, swinging, would be a safer and more satisfactory etymon, as to original sense and subsequent derivatives, than either *vri* or *dhvri*.

ULU, *v.* Haw., to grow up as a plant, to increase, be strong; *ulu-ulu*, grow up thick, collect, assemble. Sam., *ulu*, a grove of trees; *ulu-ulu*, foliage, bushy, umbrageous; *ulu-ia*, be increased, as property. Tah., *uru*, a thicket of wood, also of coral; *uru-hi, uru-pa*, id., growing rapidly.

Sanskr., *uru*, large; *urvi*, the earth.

Zend, *uru, urva*, grand, large; *urvara*, a tree.

Greek, εὐρύς, wide, broad, spacious, far-spreading.

Lat., *oleo*, to grow; *ad-oleo, sub-oles.*

In Dravidian, *uru* signifies "to be strong;" *uru-di*, strength. Vid. Drav. Gram., Caldwell.

UMA, *v.* Haw., to screw, press, grasp; *ume*, to pull, draw out; *umi*, to press upon, choke, to crowd; *mea-ume*, something drawing, attractive, the mistress of a lover. N. Zeal., Mangar., *kumi*, to squeeze, press; *kume*, to pull, draw out. Tah., *uma*, to pinch; *ume*, to pull, draw. Tong., *uma*, a kiss, salutation by pressing noses; *omi*, to draw out; *kumi*, to search, explore. Sam., *umi*, to lengthen out.

Sanskr., *chumb*, to kiss; *chumb-aka*, a loadstone.

UNU[1], *v.* Haw., to prop up, help, hold up; *s.* small stones for propping up and sustaining larger ones, prop, wedge; *unu-unu*, to pile up; *unu*, also a place of worship, temple, Heiau. Tah., *unu*, an ornament in the Marae, the crest on a cock's head. Mal. and Sunda, *gunung*, mountain; *guna*, profitable, useful.

Greek, ὀνυνημι, aor. 2, ὠνημην, to profit, help, aid, support. Liddell and Scott give a root *ον*, but without stating what its primary material meaning may have been. Ὄνειαρ, what helps or strengthens.

UNU[2], *v.* Tah., to pass away as a season or an age;

unuhi, to draw out as a sword, to withdraw, depart, as the soul at death, to swoon, to substract. N. Zeal., *unu*, to take off, draw out. Marqu., *unuhi*, to take away, reduce. Sam., *unusi*, to pick out, select.

Sanskr., *úna*, lessened, inferior, wanting.

Greek, εὖνυς, bereft of, bereaved.

Goth., *wans*, waning, lacking, wanting. O. H. Germ., *wenag*, few.

Lat., *vanus*, empty, void ; *vanesco*, to vanish, disappear ; *unde* (?), whence, from what quarter.

Benfey (*loc. cit.*, s. v.) refers *úna* to "*va-na* from *van* = Goth. *van, vans*," &c. It may be so, but I do not find in the Sanskrit *van*, either 1st or 2nd, as given by Benfey in his Sanskr.-Engl. Dict., any sense or meaning that could possibly connect it with the sense of loss or privation, which apparently underlies, and probably was the original sense of the Sanskr. *úna*, the Goth. *wans*, the Polynes. *unu*. Liddell and Scott give no etymon to the Greek εὖνυς.

UPENA, *s.* Haw., et ubique, a net, a snare. Tong., *kobenga ;* N. Zeal., *kupenga ;* Sam., *upenga*, id. Tah., *upea*, id. ; *ufene*, to be filled, crammed, to compress, squeeze ; *ufeu*, abundant. In Sam. *upeti* is the braided frame used for printing native cloth.

The Polynesian words are evidently derivatives of some ancient form in *upe* which no longer exists in the language, unless the Fiji. *ube*, " again, repeatedly," with an underlying sense of going to a place and returning, "to go and hurry back," leads us to the sense of net-making, knitting, weaving, in one direction, and to cramming, filling, compressing, in another.

Sanskr., *ubh, umbh*, to fill (Ved.), to compress (properly "to incurvate," vid. Benfey, Sanskr.-Engl. Dict., s. v. *Kuvinda*, a weaver).

Greek, ὑφη, ὑφος, a web ; ὑφαω, ὑφαινω, to weave.

Zend, *ubdaêna*, what is woven, a web.

Liddell and Scott refer ὑφη to Sanskr. *ve*, to weave, caus. *vâpaya*. Benfey says it may be allied to *ve*, but refers it to *ubh*. A. Pictet, following Aufrecht (Or. Ind.-

Eur., i. 521, and ii. 168), refers ὑφη to a lost Sanskr. root, *vabh = ubh*, to which the A.-Sax. *wefan*, to weave, and its congeners ally themselves. It is possible that the Greek ὑφ-η, the Zend *ub-da*, the Sax. *wef-an*, &c., are all reminiscences of a causative form of an original root in *ve* or *va*, but of which form no traces now exist in the Sanskrit, for the *vápaya* referred to is purely hypothetical, according to Benfey's own admission. It may be permitted, therefore, to suggest that ὑφ-, *ub-*, and *wef-*, refer themselves to a root of which the form and the primary sense have been retained in the Sanskr. *ubh = vabh*, and the Polynes. *upe*, *ufe*, *ube*.

UPU, *v.* Haw., also *upo*, "to desire strongly, covet, to swear, make a vow; *kupua*, sorcerer, wizard. Marqu., *kupu*, to curse. Tah., *upu*, invocation to the gods, prayer. N. Zeal., *kupu*, word, language. Sam., *upu*, word, speech, language; *upuia*, to be reproved, found fault with; *uputoina*, to be cursed; *upu-tu'u*, tradition.

Sanskr., *kup* (1), become excited, angry; *kup* (2), to speak, shine (Benfey).

Lat., *cupio*, to desire, long for.

UWALA, *s.* Haw., sweet potato (Convolvulus batatus). N. Zeal., *kumara;* Tah., *umara;* Sam., *umala;* Sunda, *kumeli*, id.

Sanskr., *kumará*, name of several plants; *kuvala*, the water-lily.

Lat., *cu-cumis, cu-cumeris*, a cucumber. The genitive seems to indicate an earlier form in *cumer*.

HA[1], *s.* Haw., a trough for water, a water-pipe, a ditch. Tah., *fa-a*, valley, in compounds. Tong., *ma-ha*, a crack, rent, fissure. Sam., *ma-fa*, pudendum muliebre. Fiji., *ma-ga*, id. Haw., *ma-ha*, to rend, make a hole, tear in two; *na-ha*, to split, crack open; *no-ha*, id.; *ha-iki*, a narrow passage, pinched, scant; *ha-wale*, lying, deceitful, lit. "mouth only." Marqu., *fa-fa*, an opening generally, mouth; *ha-ake*, to separate, divide. N. Zeal., *wha-iti*, a narrow passage. Rarot., *o-iti*, id. Sam., *fa-nga*, a bay, a fish-trap.

Intimately connected with the above, and probably originally only a dialectical variation, is the general Polynesian word *wa*, "the space between two objects in space or in time," the different derivations of which interlace and confound themselves, in sound and sense, with those of *ha*. Vid. *s. v.* WA.

Sanskr. *hâ¹* (Ved.), to give way; *hanû*, the jaw.

Greek, χαος, primary meaning, doubtless, space, expanse, applied also to time, the nether abyss, any vast gulf or chasm, also applied to the gaping jaws of the crocodile; χαζομαι, χαινω, χασκω, to give way, recede, relinquish; χατεω, to open the mouth; χασμα, a yawning hollow, the open mouth, any gulf or wide expanse; χηρα (Liddell and Scott), widow, relict; χωρις, separately, asunder. Liddell and Scott admit the radical connection of these words with the Sanskr. *hâ*. Γενυς, the under-jaw; γενειον, the upper-jaw, also the chin; γναθος, the jaw, mouth; referred by Liddell and Scott and by Benfey to the Sanskr. *hanû*, jaw.

Lat., *gena*, cheek, perhaps *cedo*, go away, leave (Liddell and Scott). *Hio*, to open, gape, yawn, is also referred by lexicographers to the Sanskr. *hâ*. *Fauces*, a narrow passage, the gullet.

Goth., *kinnus*, the cheek. Sax., *cinne*, chin; *ceoca*, cheek.

HA², *v.* Haw., to breathe strongly, a forced breath, breathe out, breathe upon, puff, blow, expire; *ha-u*, to swallow, gulp down, inhale, snuff up, snort. Tong., *fa*, breathe strongly, strong expiration of the breath. Mangar., *a*, id. Sam., *fa, fafa*, hoarse, hoarseness. Tah., *fa-o*, speak through the nose, a snuffler.

From these roots and stems we have the following derivatives :—Haw., *ha-nou* and *ha-nō*, the asthma, a wheezing breath; *ha-nu, ha-no*, to breathe, the natural breath; "na mea hanu," the breathing things, *i.e.*, the people; *hanu-hanu*, to scent, to smell, as a dog following a track. Tong., *fa-fango*, to whisper; *fango-fango*, to blow the nose, play on the nose-flute. Sam. *fangu-fangu*, a flute;

fano, to die, perish. Tah., *faa-fano,* to go out, as the spirit of one possessed, as the spirit or breath of one dying. N. Zeal., *whango,* to groan.

Sanskr., *van, van, ban,* to sound; *vâna,* a pipe, a flute; *vânî,* speech, voice (?). Perhaps *bhash,* to bark; *bhasha,* dog; *bhastrâ,* a bellows, as well as *bhâsh,* to speak, refer themselves to the same root as the Sanskrit *van, van,* the Polynesian *hano, fano.*

As I have found no adequate etymon for the Latin *halo,* to breathe forth, exhale, I refer to it here, *n* and *l* commuted, a not uncommon occurrence in several of the Aryan branches.

In regard to the Sanskrit *van,* Pictet (Or. Ind.-Eur., ii. 474) says: "Au sanskr. *vâna,* flûte, pipeau, de *van, van,* sonare (Dhatup), répond peut-être directement, par le changement de *n* en *l,* comme dans ἀλλος, alius = sanskr. *anya,* le grec αὐλος, flute (cf. Z. S. X., 246 note). Il faudrait alors le séparer de αὐω, ἀω = sanskr. *vâ,* flare, bien que les rac. *vâ, van, van,* puissent être primitivement alliées. Cf. aussi *vên, ven,* organum musicum canendi causa sumere, fidibus canere, *vêna,* musicien, *vênu,* flûte et roseau, et peut-être *vînâ,* le luth indien. La rac. *van,* sonare, se retrouve dans l'irlandais *fonnaim,* chanter, *fonn,* chant, *fonnmhar,* melodieux, et, sous la forme *vin,* dans l'anc. all. *weinôn,* ejulare, flere, ululare, scand. *veina,* lamentare, angl. *whine;* cf. anc. all. *winisôn,* murmurare, &c."

HAOA, *adj.* Haw., hot, burning, as the sun or fire, pungent, bitter, heart-burn; *s.* the fierce heat of summer. Tah., *fa,* to appear, come in sight. Celebes (Buton), *wha,* fire. Buru, *bá-na,* id. Saparua, *hao,* id. Ceram. (Camar.), *hao,* id.; (Wahai), *aow,* id.

Sanskr., *bhâ,* to shine, be bright, to appear; *bha,* a star; *bhâ,* light, the sun; *bhâ-tu, bhâ-lu,* the sun; *bhâs,* &c.

Greek, φαω, to light, shine; φαος, light; φαινω, &c.

Lat., *fax,* a torch; *focus,* hearth, fireplace; *foveo,* to warm, keep warm; *febris,* fever.

Connected with *hao-a* is doubtless the Hawaiian word

hao-le, which, so far as I know, does not occur in any other Polynesian dialect. Its meaning is "white," and was generally applied to hogs with white bristles. It was also applied to foreigners—"white people"—and occurs as such in the celebrated chant of *Kualii*, which was composed and recited long before Captain Cook visited the Hawaiian group.

HAKA[1], *v.* Haw., to stare, look earnestly at, to contend, quarrel; *haka-ka*, id., to fight. Marqu., *hakata*, a mirror.

Greek, ἀγη, wonder, awe, envy, malice; ἀγαμαι, to wonder, be astonished, feel envy, be angry; ἀγαιομαι, be indignant.

HAKA[2], *s.* Haw., a ladder, *i.e.*, a pole with cross sticks, the hole or opening between the sticks, a hole generally, also an artificial henroost; *adj.* full of holes or crevices; *haka-haka*, be hollow, empty. Sam., Tong., Tah., Marqu., *fata*, shelf, a litter, scaffold, loft, altar. N. Zeal., *whata*, id. Tah., *fata-fata*, open, not enclosed, empty. Niua, *fata*, the chest, breast. Tong., Sam., *fata-fata*, id. Marqu., *fata*, to spread out, raise up; *fata-a*, staging, shelf, bed, altar. Fiji., *vata*, loft, shelf, a bedstead. Malg., *fata*, fireplace, hearth; *fatan*, crowfoot, pan, warming-pan.

Sanskr., *pach* (2), *panch*, make evident, state fully, to spread—vid. Benfey; the latter meaning probably the primary one; *vakshas*, breast, bosom.

Lat., *pectus*, breast; *pecten*, comb; *pecto*, to comb, hackle, card.

Greek, πεκω, to comb, card.

It will be seen that the primary underlying sense of these references is "to expand, to spread out," and that the sense of hollowness, chest, breast, must be a secondary, but still extremely ancient, application of the word, occurring as it does in Sanskrit, Latin, and Polynesian.

For further Polynesian connections to Sanskrit *pach* (2), see *s. v.* PAKA, *post.*

HAKA[3], *s.* Marqu., in compounds, *haka-iki* (for Haka-ariki), chief, lord. Sam., '*ata*, a hero, a strong man; *sata-'alaua*, a name of respect given to the Tongans. Fiji., *saka*, equivalent to " Sir " in addressing a person, probably allied to *haku*, q. v.

Sanskr., *çak*, to endure, be able, powerful; *çakti*, strength, power; *Çakra*, name of Indra, a king; *çakune*, a bird, the Indian kite; *çâka*, power.

O. Norse, *haukr*, a hawk, falcon; *hagr*, the right hand, dexter.

HAKI, *v.* Haw., also *ha'i* and *ha'e*, primary meaning to break open, separate, as the lips about to speak, to break, as a bone or other brittle thing, to break off, to stop, tear, rend, to speak, tell, bark as a dog; *hahai*, to break away, follow, pursue, chase; *hai*, a broken place, a joint; *hakina*, a portion, part; *ha'ina*, a saying; *hae*, something torn, as a piece of kapa or cloth, a flag, ensign. Sam., *fati*, to break, break off; *fa'i*, to break off, pluck off, as a leaf, wrench off; *fai*, to say, speak, abuse, deride; *sae*, to tear off, rend; *ma-sae*, torn. Tah., *fati*, to break, break up, broken; *fai*, confess, reveal, deceive; *faifai*, to gather or pick fruit; *haea*, torn, rent; *s.* deceit, duplicity; *hae-hae*, tear anything, break an agreement; *hahae*, id. Tong., *fati*, break, rend. Marqu., *fati*, *fe-fati*, to break, tear, rend; *fai*, to tell, confess; *fefai*, to dispute. The same double meaning of " to break " and " to say " is found in the New Zealand and other Polynesian dialects. Malg., *hai*, *haïk*, voice, address, call.

Lat., *seco*, cut off, cleave, divide; *securis*, hatchet; *segmentum*, cutting, division, fragment; *seculum* (sc. temporis), *sector*, follow eagerly, chase, pursue; *sequor*, follow; *sica*, a dagger; *sicilis*, id., a knife; *saga*, *sagus*, a fortune-teller.

Greek, ἀγνυμι, break, snap, shiver, from root Ϝαγ (Liddell and Scott); ἀγη, breakage, fragment; ἑκας, *adv.* far off, far away.[1]

---

[1] Liddell and Scott consider ἑκας akin to ἑκαστος, each, every, " in the sense of apart, by itself," and they refer to the analysis of Curtius of " ἑ- = εἱς, ἑν, and -καστος, &c., comparing Sanskrit *kas*, *kâ*, *kat* (quis, qua, quid), who of two, of many, &c." Doubtless ἑκας and ἑκαστος are akin " in the sense of apart, by itself," but that sense arises from the previous sense of separating, cutting off, breaking off, and thus

Sanskr., *sach,* to follow.   Zend, *hach,* id.   (Vid. Haug, " Essay on Parsis.")

I am well aware that most, perhaps all, prominent philologists of the present time—" whose shoe-strings I am not worthy to unlace "—refer the Latin *sequor, secus,* even *sacer,* and the Greek ἕπω, ἕπομαι, to this Sanskrit *sach.* Benfey even refers the Greek ἕκας to this *sach,* as explanatory of its origin and meaning.   But, under correction, and even without the Polynesian congeners, I should hold that *sach,* " to follow," in order to be a relative of *sacer,* doubtless originally meaning " set apart," then " devoted, holy," and of ἕκας, " far off," doubtless originally meaning something " separated," " cut off from, apart from," must also originally have had a meaning of " to be separated from, apart from," and then derivatively " to come after, to follow."   The sense of " to follow " implies the sense of " to be apart from, to come after," something preceding.   The links of this connection in sense are lost in the Sanskrit, but still survive in the Polynesian *haki, fati,* and its contracted form *hai, fai, hahai,* as shown above.   I am therefore inclined to rank the Latin *sequor* as a derivative of *seco,* " to cut off, take off."

Welsh, *haciaw,* to hack; *hag,* a gash, cut; *segur,* apart, separate; *segru,* to put apart; *hoc,* a bill-hook; *hicel,* id.

A.-Sax., *saga,* a saw; *seax,* knife; *haccan,* to cut, hack; *sægan,* to saw; *saga,* speech, story; *secan,* to seek.   Anc. Germ., *seh, sech,* a ploughshare.   Perhaps the Goth. *hakul,* A.-Sax. *hacele,* a cloak, ultimately refer themselves to the Polynes. *hae,* a piece of cloth, a flag.

Anc. Slav., *sieshti (siekā),* to cut; *siekyra,* hatchet.

Judge Andrews in his Hawaiian-English Dictionary observes the connection in Hawaiian ideas between "speaking, declaring," and " breaking."   The primary idea, which probably underlies both, is found in the Hawaiian " to open, to separate, as the lips in speaking or about to

more naturally connects itself with the Latin *sec-o, sac-er,* and that family of words and ideas, than with such a forced compound as εἰς and κας.

speak;" and it will be observed that the same development in two directions shows itself in all the Polynesian dialects, as well as in several of the West Aryan dialects also.

HAKU[1], *s.* Haw., lord, master. Tah., *fatu;* Rarot., *atu,* id. I am not aware that this word, in this, probably the full form, occurs in the other Polynesian dialects with that meaning. We find it, however, in Pulo Nias, off Sumatra, where *batu* is an epithet and name of deity. The Sumatra, Bali, and Tagal *batara, bathala,* as a name for God, may possibly refer to the Sanskrit *bhaṭṭâra,* venerable, derived from *bhartri* and *bhṛi,* but I think it doubtful. In all the Polynesian dialects, however, occurs a contracted form of *haku, fatu, k* or *t* elided, viz., Sam., *sau;* Tong., *hau;* Tah., *fau,* king, chief. Principal, Haw., *hau,* a title of chief, a noble, a descendant of kings; Rarot., Mangar., *au,* kingdom, government. The verbs follow the same forms: Haw., *haku,* to dispose, arrange, rule, compose, as a song; *hahau, haua,* to whip, chastise. Sam., *fatu,* to make a girdle, to plait, to compose a song; *fatufatu,* to fold up, to lay up words, commit to memory; *fatu-pese, fatu-siva,* a poet; *fau,* to tie together, to build; *fau-mau,* to hold firmly, be obstinate; *sausau,* to build up, repair; *saua,* cruel, despotic. Tah., *fatu,* to braid, plait; *fatu-pehe,* a composer of songs, poet; *faufaua,* to make straight, arrange; *fafau,* to tie together. N. Zeal., *whatu,* to weave by hand, to braid, as a mat; *whaka-hau,* to command. Tong., Marqu., *fatu,* to fold, roll up.

This word is doubtless related to, or another form of, the Marqu. *haka*—vid. p. 198.

Greek, ἔχω, ἔξω, to have in hand, to hold, to rule, keep, check, keep on, with a sense of present duration; ἔκτωρ, holding fast, epithet of Zeus; also applied to anchors, a prop, a stay, a proper name; ἔχυρος, strong, secure; ὀχυρος, id.; ἔχμα.

A.-Sax., *secg.* Scand., *seggr,* vir fortis, miles, strenuus, illustris; *seigr,* firmus; *sigi, sege,* victory. Goth., *sigis,* id.

Irish, *seighion,* warrior, hero.

The Greek forms are referred by both Benfey and Liddell and Scott to the Sanskrit *sah*, to bear, endure, be able, and the Teutonic forms by Benfey and Pictet to the same Sanskrit˙ root, and the latter quotes the Vedic *sahuri*, victorious (Or. Ind.-Eur., ii. 197). It seems to me quite probable that the Sanskrit *sah*, *sagh*, and *çak*, with precisely similar meanings, are but dialectical forms of a once common word, whose primitive sense has been best retained in the Polynesian and in the Greek.

To the same primitive sense of holding fast, being strong, I think may also, with good reason, be referred:

HAKU², *s.* Haw., a hard lump of anything, a hard bunch in the flesh, the ball of the eye. With *po* intens. *po-haku*, general name of stones, rocks, pebbles, &c. Sam., *fatu*, seed, the heart of a thing, stone; *adj.* hard; *fatufatu*, stony; *fatu-ngao*, the kidneys. Tah., *fatu*, the core of an abscess; *fatu-rei*, the stones at the bottom of a fish-net. Marqu., *fatu*, stone, teat. Nina, Fakaafo, *fatu*, stone. N. Zeal., *watu*, hail; *ko·watu*, stone. Mang., *atu*, seed; *po-atu*, stone. Fiji., *vatu*, stone, rock; *vatu-ni-balawa*, a whale's tooth; *vatu-ni-taba*, the shoulder-blade. Sunda, *batu*, stone. Pulo Nias, *bàtu*, id. Engano, *paku*, id. Aru. Isl. (Wammer), *fatu*, id. Amboyna (Liang), *hatu-aka*, the belly. Malg., *vatu*, stone. Timor. Laut., *vatu*, id.

Lat., *saxum*, rock, crag. Probably *satum*, which has been sown, the seed, the grain; *satus*, *sator*, also refer to a form equally akin to *saxum* and the Polynesian *haku*.

Greek, σηκος, a weight in the balance; certainly a very distant, if any, relation to σηκος, a pen, a fold. Liddell and Scott give no etymon to either. Σηκος, weight, no doubt represented originally a stone or some hard ˙substance conventionally used as a weight; perhaps σιτος, grain, corn, wheat. The correspondence of the Greek σιτος and Sunda *siki*, seed, kernel, may be accidental; and yet I think it a fair inference that σιτος refers itself to σηκος within the Hellenic group, as *siki* does to *haku* within the

Polynesian group, and that both σηκος and *haku* had a common Aryan origin.

In the valleys of the Hindu-Kush the old form is still retained. We find in Gilgit (Shina), *but*, stone; Chiliss, *bât*, id.; Torwalak, *bâd*, id.; Gowro., *bât*, id.; Narisati, *wutt*, id.; Kowar, *bôt*, id.

Professor Sayce, in "Introduction to Science of Language," vol. ii. p. 132, speaking of the early Teutonic family in Europe, says : "Gold, silver, and bronze were the three metals known, though implements of stone still continued in use; and even after their arrival in Europe we find the Teutonic Aryans naming the 'dagger' *seahs*, from the stone (Lat. *saxum*) of which it was made."

HALA, *v.* Haw., to proceed, pass on or over, to miss the object aimed at; *s. hala*, transgression, trespass, offence; *adj.* sinful, wicked. Sam., *sala, adj.* wrong, incorrect; *s.* punishment, fine; *v.* to lop, cut off; *sasala*, be diffused as a perfume, to spread about; *ma-sala*, great, in any way; *tu-sala*, stand in the wrong place. Tah., *hara*, sin, transgression, guilt; *adj.* unequal, not hitting the mark; *v.* to deviate, be wrong (the word is also pronounced *hapa* in Tahitian); *hahara*, to divide unequally. Marqu., *haa*, offence, aversion, anger. Sunda, *sala*, fault. Malg., *hala*, hate, to hate; *halak*, pain, confusion; *hala*, withdraw, retire; *mi-hala*, to leave, to let; *halet*, punishment.

Sanskr., *char*, to move, to go through, over, or along, to behave; with *ati-*, to overstep, trespass, offend; *chal*, to tremble, to move, go away, swerve, be troubled; *chhala*, fraud, deceit; *skhal*, to stumble, fall, err, fail; *ċal*, to shake, tremble. Benfey refers *chal* to *char*, and *char* to a hypothetical *cchar*, and *chhala* to *skhal*. I am inclined, in view of the Sanskrit *ċal* and the Greek σαλος, σαλα, not to mention the Polynesian affinities, to consider the simplest form of the word as the oldest. The guttural additions may have grown up as dialectical variations on an earlier, more simple, and more diffused root or stem.

Greek, σαλος, any unsteady tossing motion, the swell

of the sea, restlessness, distemper, perplexity ; σαλα, distress, anguish ; σαλευω, to shake, to rock ; ζαλη, the surging of the᾽ sea ; pl. storms, distresses ; ἀλλομαι, ἀλεσθαι, inf. to spring, leap,᾽ bound ; ἁλμα, ἁλσις, &c. Liddell and Scott, *s. v.*, indicate that an old form was Ϝαλλομαι. That would only show that within the West Aryan branches the permutation, in ancient times, of *s, h,* and *f* was as common an occurrence as within the Polynesian group.

Lat., *salio,* to leap, jump ; *saltus, salto, salum,* the open sea, tossing ·at sea ; *scelus,* a wicked action, crime, sin, disaster. Benfey refers *culpa,* guilt, fault, blame, to the Sanskr. *skhal ;* Pictet refers it to *klṛp, kalp.*

Goth., *skulan,* ᾽to owe ; *skula,* debtor ; *sair,* sorrow. A.-Sax., *sar,* pain, grievous ; *scyld,* debt, offence.

Lith., *skilti, skelēti,* to owe ; *skóla,* debt.

HALAU, *v.* Haw., to extend, stretch out, be long ; *s.* a shed for keeping canoes in. The word occurs in the old Hawaiian legends with the meaning of a large canoe or vessel, but that sense is now obsolete. Tah., *farau,* a long shed generally, canoe-shed. Tong., *felau, folau,* canoe, fleet, voyage, navigating. Sam., *folau,* large vessel, ship ; *v.* go on a voyage. Fiji., *bola,* war-canoe from another land. N. Celebes, *bolata,* boat. Ceram.᾽ (Wahai), *polutu,* id. Mal., *praau,* id. Malg., *paraho,* " embarcation, barque ; " *alou,* a shed. ᾽ Sunda, *parahu,* boat.

Sanskr., *pṛi,* to bring over (Ved.) ; *para,* distant, opposite, beyond, exceeding ; *pâra,* the opposite bank of a river ; *pâra-ga,* crossing, passing over ; *para-tua,* length, of distance and of time.

Zend, *pere,* to bring over. Pers., *parîdan,* to fly, to traverse the air ; *parandah,* boat, vessel, bird.

Greek, περαν, on the other᾽ side, across = trans. περα, beyond, over, farther = ultra ; περαω, to pass over, to cross over ; παρων, a light skiff or boat ; πορος, a ford, a ferry.

A.-Sax., *faer.* Scand., *far,* a ship, a vessel. Goth., *faran, farjan,* " ire, vehi (nave, curru) ; " *fiord.*

Lith., *paramas,* a raft.

Anc. Slav., *pariti*, to fly.

Logan, in his "Ethnology of the Indo-Pacific Islands," part ii., pp. 146–147, derives the Polynesian *falau* from the Dravidian (Telugu) *pada-va*, boat. But whatever the Polynesians may owe to their contact with the Dravidian, it is evident from the varying applications of the word *falau* that it is not a borrowed or imported word, but a legitimate development of the verb "to extend, stretch out, be long," as much so as the Pers. *parandah*, the Greek παρων, the A.-Sax. *faer*, the Lith. *paramas*.

I am inclined to consider this word as a derivative of the previous *hala*, "to proceed, pass on or over," and should thus be written *hala-u*. It certainly is not a contraction of the Dravidian *pada-va*. Had it been a borrowed word, it would have been adopted entire, according to the phonetic laws which govern Polynesian speech.

HALE, *s.* Haw., house, habitation, dwelling-place. Sam., Tong., *fale*, id. Tah., *fare*, id. Marqu., *fae*, id. N. Zeal., *whare*. Fiji., *vale*, id. Salebabo, *barch*. Sanguir, *bali*, id. Tidore, *fola*, id. N. Celebes, *bore*, id. Aru (Wammer), *balei*, id.

Sanskr., *vṛi* or *vṛî*, to conceal, to screen, to cover, surround; *varana*, enclosure, raised on a mound of earth, what screens or covers; *varanda*, a portico; *vâra*, a gate; *vala*, enclosure.

Zend, *ware*, enclosure. Pehloi, *ware* or *ouar*, fortified enclosure. Pers., *wârah*, house, dwelling. Kurd., *war*, house for winter.

A.-Sax., *war*, fence, enclosure. O. Norse, *ver*, a homestead.

Irish, *forus*, dwelling-place. Erse, *bhaile* or *vaile*, a town.

I am not aware of the application of this word, or rather its root or stem, in Greek or Latin to designate a dwelling, habitation, house, unless the Greek ἤριον, a mound, barrow, tomb, refers to it. This has by some been referred to ἐρα, the earth; but Liddell and Scott say that it was "a raised mound," and that "it has the digamma in Homer."

The Latin *foris*, gate, like the Sanskrit *vára*, gate, may perhaps derive from the same primitive word and conception.

HALI[1], *v.* Haw., to bring to and fro, carry, bear, convey.

Sanskr., *hri*, to bring, carry to or away, convey, fetch, take, seize; *hára*, taking, seizing; *harana*, the hand, the arm; *hary*, to take (Ved.); *hara*, a co-heir; *hartri*, a robber.

Greek, χειρ, hand, arm; αιρεω, to take by the hand, grasp, catch.

Latin, *heres*, heir, possessor; *hir*, hand.

HALI[2], *s.* Haw., obj. *pu-hali*, stinginess, covetousness, name of a delicate little sea-shell. Sam., *sali*, to scrape, scoop out, pluck out, take away, rake out, as embers of a fire. Fiji., *salia*, to dig a channel for water; *n.* the entrance or channel through a reef; *sedre*, a bowl, large or small. Malg., *sary*, a case, a sheath; *hadi*, hole, cave; *hadiu*, to dig a hole.

Greek, σαιρω, draw back the lips and show the teeth, grin like a dog; hence to gape like an open wound, to sweep off, to clean up; σηραγξ, a hole, hollow, cleft; σηλια, a flat tray or board with a raised edge; a sieve, the hoop of a sieve; σηλιον, a small vessel used by bakers.

The original word is lost or obsolete in the Hawaiian, but its derivative, *pu-hali*, stingy, covetous, corresponds well, in its conception, to the Greek conception of σαιρω, a dog grinning over a bone; while the Samoan *sali*, to scrape, scoop out, probably represents the primitive sense, as retained in the Greek σηραγξ and σηλιον.

HAMO, *v.* Haw., to stroke with the hand, to rub, besmear with blood or lime, anoint with oil; to bend or crook the arm as in doing the foregoing, bend round, be circular; *hamole*, *adj.* round, smooth, as the edge of a board; *hamo-hamo*, to rub the hand over a surface, to touch. Sam., *sama*, to rub and colour the body with turmeric; *amo*, to rub the fibres of a cocoa-nut husk so as to separate them; *amo-amo*, to repaint black native cloth. Fiji., *sama-ka*, to rub with the hands, to anoint, rub oil on the body; *yamo-ca*, to feel for a thing with the hand, to run the hand over.

Greek, ἀμη, ἀμῆ, a shovel, mattock, harrow, sickle, bill-hook; ἀμαω, to reap, gather, cut off; ἀμαλλα, a bundle of ears of corn, a sheaf.

Lat,, *hamus*, hook; *hamulus*, id. and angle; *hamatus*, crooked, bent like a hook.

HAMU, *v.* Haw., to eat fragments of food; *s.* the refuse of food. Sam., *samu*, to chew, crunch; *samu-samu*, to eat the remains of food. Tah., *amu*, to eat; *amu-amu*, eat a little at a time; *hamu*, gluttonous. N. Zeal., Mang., *amu*, eat fragments. Malg., *homau*, to eat. Mal., *djamu-an*, a feast, a meal.

Sanskr., *jam*, to eat, to chew.

O. H. Germ., *gauma*, a meal. Germ., *gaum*, palate. A.-Sax., *goma*, the gum.

Lat., *gumia*, a glutton.

Greek, γαμφαι, the jaws; γομφιος, a grinder-tooth, a molar.

HANA[1], *v.* Haw., to do, to work, labour, produce; *s.* work, labour, calling, trade; *hana-hana; v.* to be severe, to be hard, to afflict, as a famine, to be fatal or deadly, as a sickness; *adj.* disagreeable, offensive, stinking. N. Zeal., *anga*, to work, &c. Sam., *sanga*, *adv.* continually, without intermission; *s.* the dowry or property given by a woman's family at her marriage; *v.* to face, be opposite; *anga*, to do, to act; *s.* conduct. Tong., *anga*, custom, habit. Marqu., *hana*, to work. Tah., *haa*, to work, operate in any way. Fiji., *onga*, engaged, employed; *yanga*, to do, act, use, useful. Malg., *angan*, to do, to make; *fanau, fanganon*, custom, usage, habitude.

Sanskr., *han*, to strike, to peck (" probably from original *dhan*," Benfey); *dhan*[1], to put in motion, to bear or produce grains, &c.; *hanana*, multiplication (sc. increase); *hatnu*, i.e., *han+tnu*, sickness; *hataka*, miserable; compare Tah., *hana*, fatigued, mournful; *ghana* (" i.e., *han+a*," Benfey), firm, hard, solid; *ghat* (" akin partly to *han*, partly to *ghatt*," Benfey), to endeavour, to work; *dhana*, property of any description, abundance; *dhanus, dhanvan* ("i.e., probably *han + vant,*" Benfey), a bow, a desert.

Goth., *ginnan, du-ginnan,* perf. *gann,* to begin, undertake. Sax., *ginnan,* id.

Greek, I will not refer to θανατος, θνῄσκω, θεινω, which Benfey refers to Sanskr. *han,* but to which Liddell and Scott give different roots. But the Greek εὐ-θενεω, εὐ-θηνια, to flourish, prosper, abundance, may probably maintain their relation to the Sanskr. *dhana.*

HANA[2], *v.* Haw., mostly used in frequ. and compounds; *hahana,* to be warm; *hanahana,* warm, heated; *koe-hana, ma-hana,* id.; *mehana,* heat, generally of the sun or the weather, sometimes warmth arising from exercise. Sam., Tong., *ma-fana,* hot, warm; *faa-fana,* warm up food. Tah., *ma-hana,* the sun, day; *ma-hana-hana,* hot, warm; *hana-hana,* bright, glorious. Marqu., *fana,* warm, ardent, materially and mentally. Paum., *hana,* the sun. Jav., *panas,* warm. Sunda, *hanet,* id. Tagal., *banas,* id. Buru (Waiapo), *hangat,* sun. Ceram. (Gah), *mo-fanes,* hot. Malg., *fan, ma-fan,* hot, be warm.

Sanskr., *bhâ,* to shine, appear, the sun, light, splendour; *bhânu, bhâma.* Vid. p. 97, *s. v.* HAOA.

Greek, βαννος, furnace, forge; βαναυσος, working by the fire, mechanical, a mechanic, an artisan. Liddell and Scott refer these to αὐω, to light, to kindle a fire; but whence the β and the βαν?

HAWA, *v.* Haw., to be daubed, defiled; *hawa-hawa,* filthy, dirty; *hawawa,* rude, ignorant, awkward; *hau-kai,* filthiness; *haumia,* to defile, pollute; *hau-na,* strong, offensive smell; *haunaele,* be in confusion, as a mob, riotous. Sam., *sava,* filth, ordure; *v.* to be daubed with filth; *faua,* spittle; *v.* to drivel. Tah., *haua,* scent of any kind; *fau-fau,* vile, filthy, base; *hava,* dirty, filthy; *auaua,* slovenly done. N. Zeal., *haunga,* bad smell.

Sanskr., *cav,* to alter, change, destroy; *cava,* a dead body, carcass; *câva,* dead, deadly; *câvara,* low, vile, fault, sin, wickedness; *cavala,* spotted.

Greek, σαυκος, σαυχμος, σαυσαρος, easily rubbed to

pieces, brittle, dry ; σαυλos, σαυνοs, mincing in gait, conceited, affected. Liddell and Scott refer the first three to αὶω, to kindle, burn. I think the Polynesian *hau, sau, fau,* offers a better etymon.

Lat., *sœvus,* excited, raving, cruel ; *saucius,* wounded, weak, hurt, debilitated.

I am inclined to consider the Polynesian sense of *hawa, sava,* " bedaubed, defiled," as the primary sense of the Sanskrit *cav,* which reappears nearly in *câvara,* but more plainly in *cavala,* " spotted, variegated in colour, brown, yellow, brindled," as would be the effect of being daubed with mud, filth, ordure. From *cav,* to " change, destroy," the transition is easy and intelligible to the Greek σαυκos, &c., and the Latin *saucius.*

Benfey considers the Sanskrit *carvarî,* night, " as akin to κερβερos, and derives it from *çrî,* to hurt, wound." Prof. Max Müller, in " Chips from a German Workshop," ii. 180, considers *çavara* " as a modified form of *çarvara,* in the sense of dark, pale, or nocturnal," and as akin to the Greek κερβερos. It is not for me to gainsay so high authorities, but neither of them was probably aware of the existence of the Polynesian *sava* and its kindred to the Sanskrit *çav.*

Following the researches of the most eminent philologists whose works have come under my notice, and comparing the same with the genius and idiom of the Polynesian language, it becomes apparent to me that the early Aryan in pre-Vedic times designated the left, left hand, left side, with words whose primary sense implied defect of some kind, inferiority, shortcoming, or opposition. Proceeding on that assumption, I would include the Sanskrit *sav-ya,* rendered by Benfey as " left, left hand,[1] southern, south, backward, reverse, contrary," among the derivatives of *çav,* although Benfey gives it no etymon,

---

[1] Benfey gives *savya* as " south, southern," as well as " left, left hand." A. Pictet in " Orig. Ind.-Europ.," ii. 495, plainly states that *savya* signified the north, and refers it to the Slave *Sieveru, Boreas,* Illyr. *Siever,* id. Having no other works of reference at hand, I am unable to reconcile the two, and am forced to conclude that the " south " of Benfey is a misprint.

and refers it to the Greek σκαιος, the Latin *scævus*, and "probably also sinister." Pictet, *loc. cit.*, ii. 493, refers σκαιος and *scævus* to Sanskr. *sku*, *tegere*, to cover. Liddell and Scott refer σκαιος to *savya* and *scævus*, and the Engl. *skew*. With this difference of opinion between such eminent authorities I am not concerned ; *scævus* and σκαιος may refer to Sanskr. *sku*, *tegere*, or to *sku*, "to go by leaps," irregular motion, and I am inclined to favour the latter ; but *savya* hardly refers to *sku* for its origin, nor yet to *su*, "to beset, bring forth, to express as juice," and with *abhi*, "to sprinkle," as Pictet assumes, ibid., p. 490. I have no reason to doubt the fact which Pictet refers to in the place just cited ; but so far from explaining the meaning of *savya* with "*manus purificanda abluendo*," I think the natural and primary meaning was simply "*manus immunda*," the unclean, filthy hand. Certes it was the sense of deficiency, weakness, impurity which gave the designation to the left hand, not *vice versa*, nor the necessity of cleaning it after the operation it had performed.

Within the Polynesian area proper, I am not aware of any designation of "the left" that can be fairly traced to this *sava*, *hawa*, or *çav*, the Tahitian *aui*, "left," and its Malgasse correlative *aviha*, *havia*, "left, to the left," probably referring themselves to the Polynes. (Haw., Sam.) *aui*, *aui-a*, to decline as the sun, be slender. Some other Polynes. designations for the "left," the N. Zeal. *maui*, the Marqu. *moui*, and others of that class, refer themselves to the Polynes. (Sam.) *maui*, to diminish, subside, to fall ; while still others, like Haw., Tong., Hema., Mang., Ema., Fiji., *sema*, "left," refer themselves to the Tah., *hema*, be deceived, imposed upon ; Haw., *hema-hema*, awkward, destitute, wanting ; Sam., *sema*, to beg.

HE, *s.* Haw., a grave, sepulchre ; *heana*, corpse, carcass. Tah., *hea*, name of various diseases ; *mahea*, be pale, from fear ; to cease, of rain. Marqu., *heaka*, a human victim. Sam., *senga-senga*, to be yellowish from disease ; *senga-vale*, shine dimly, as the sun through a mist, be pale from fear ; *sengi-sengi*, twilight ; *se-se*, nearly blind.

Sanskr., *sâya*, end, evening. Benfey refers this word to *so*, to destroy, to finish. Pictet is in doubt whether to refer it to *so* or *sâ*, as Benfey has done, or to *si*, to bind, whence *sîmun*, limit, boundary. Both Benfey and Pictet, however, refer the Lat. *serus*, late, and *serum*, evening, to the Sanskr. *sâya*.

In the Dravidian (Tamil) *sâ* and (Tulu) *sei* signify " to die."

HELE[1], *v.* Haw., *hele-hele*, to cut up, divide asunder, as with a knife; *mahele*, *v.* divide, cut in pieces, separate. Sam., *sele*, to cut, a bamboo-knife; *sele-sele*, to cut in pieces, to shear. Tong., *hele*, to cut, a knife; *mahele*, to cut, gash. Tah., *pa-here*, to pare the rind of fruit. Fiji., *sele*, bamboo-knife; *sele-ta*, sword. Malg., *fer*, a cut, a sore.

Sanskr., *çrî*, to hurt, wound, be broken, split to pieces; *çara*, *çaru*, an arrow, any weapon; *çari*, hurtful; *çiri*, a sword, a murderer.

Greek, κλαω, to break, break off, break in pieces; κλημα, a cutting, a slip; κλαδος, id.; κληρος, lot; κρινω, to pick out, assort, choose, decide.

Lat., *cerno* (orig. to separate), to distinguish, know apart, to decide; *certo*, to contest, strive together; *certamen*, fight; *cribrum*, a sieve; *crimen* (orig. sentence).

Goth., *hairus*, sword. A.-Sax., *hyrt*, hurt, wounded, struck.

The analogy of the Latin *cerno*, to separate, and the Greek κρινω, to pick out, which lexicographers refer to Sanskrit *krî*, to cast, to scatter, seems to indicate that *krî* and *çrî* were but different forms of an older word, whose primitive meaning, as retained in the Polynesian, the Latin, and the Greek, was " to sunder, to separate," and that the conception of " to hurt, to wound," and the derivatives based upon that conception, were subsequent and secondary to the former meaning, and incident to the act of " sundering, separating."

To this family of words, rather than to the next, belong the Haw. *helei*, to open, spread open, as the legs, to straddle;

helelei, to throw away, to scatter, to fall, as seed sown. Sam., *selei,* to cut, slash.

HELE[2], *v.* Haw., to move in any way, to walk, to go; *haele,* id. Tah., *haere,* to go, to come. N. Zeal., *haere,* id. Sam., *saele,* to swing the arms in walking.

Sanskr., *sel* or *cel,* to go or move.

This word seems to have no derivation in the West Aryan branches. In Dr. Caldwell's Dravidian Grammar, I see that in Tamil *sél* is "to go, proceed." Is the word Ayran in itself, or did the Hindus as well as the Polynesians receive it from their intercourse with the Dravidians after entering India?

HELE[3], *v.* Haw., a noose, a snare for catching birds; *pa-hele,* id.; also deceit, treachery. Tong., *hele,* snare, noose; *nau-hele,* to snare. N. Zeal., *here,* to tie, bind; *where-where,* to hang, suspend. Rarot., *ere,* id. Sam., *sele,* a snare, to snare. Tah., *here,* a snare, cord; *v.* to entangle.

Greek, εἴρω, fasten together, string, plait; ἕρματα, ear-rings; ὅρμος, cord, chain, necklace; εἴρερος, bondage, slavery; εἱρμός, a series, a train; σειρα, cord, string, rope, noose.

Lat., *sero, serui,* to bind, tie, connect, entwine; *series,* a row, series; *serta,* wreath, garland; *servus,* a slave.

A.-Sax., *serian,* to set in order.

Anc. Slav., *u-seregu, u-serezi;* Russ., *seriga,* ear-ring; *sherenga,* series, row.

Armen., *sarich,* a cord.

HELU, *v.* Haw., to scratch the ground as a hen, to dig or scratch the ground with the fingers, to paw, to count, compute, to tell, relate. Tong., *helu,* to comb. Sam., *selu,* a comb, to comb; *seselu,* comb the hair with the fingers, to praise. N. Zeal., *heru,* comb. Tah., *heru,* scratch as a hen; *pa-heru,* id., search thoroughly; *tu-feru,* id. Marqu., *feu,* to rub, scrub. Fiji., *seru,* a comb. Mal. and Sunda, *sisir,* comb.

Lat., *sero, sevi,* scatter as seed, sow. Benfey refers this word to the Sanskrit *sri,* to flow, blow, go, in caus. to extend. But the Latin *sero* evidently does not derive from the Sanskrit causative form, and is possibly as old a word in its own dialect as the Sanskrit word, with the retention of the earlier sense "to scatter," apparently lost in the Sanskrit *sṛi*, if ever it had it. Pictet, following Bopp, refers *sero* to a Sanskrit *sâ, san,* " donner, répandre," in order to find a place for the Gothic *saian,* A.-Sax. *sâwan,* to sow, and the Greek σαω, σηθω, "cribler, c'est-á-dire répandre." The Latin *satum,* the Greek σηθω, the Gothic *seths,* &c., may probably refer to a root in *so, sâ,* or *san;* but the Latin *sero,* in my opinion, has no more etymological connection with *satum* than *fero* has with *latum.* The sense of "scattering," though not retained in the Polynesian in connection with planting or sowing, is yet manifest in two other directions, viz., numbering, counting, and combing, unravelling the hair. I am therefore inclined to refer the Polynesian *hele*[1], *helu,* the Latin *sero,* and the Sanskrit *çrî,* to a common root, whose primary meaning was "to scratch," and, in so doing, in one direction "to wound," *çrî,* in another "to scatter," *sero.*

HEMA, *adj.* Haw., left, the left hand, south, southern; *hema-hema,* left-handed, awkward, destitute, needy. Tong., *hema,* left. Mang., *ema,* id. Tah., *hema,* to be deceived; *faa-hema,* a deceiver. Sam., *sema,* to beg for various things. Fiji., *sema,* the left hand. Malg., *simis,* be in need, to fail.

Greek, ζημια, loss, damage, penalty; ἥμερος, tamed, quiet, gentle; ἡνια, bridle, reins; ἐφ ἡνιαν, wheeling "to the left," the bridle-hand being the left hand. Benfey refers these three words to Sanskrit *yam,* to restrain, to tame. Liddell and Scott refer ζημια to Sanskrit *dam, damyâmï,* to tame; they refer ἥμερος to ἥμαι, to sit down, and ἥμαι to Sanskrit *'âs, âsmê,* " *sedeo,*" and they give no etymon of ἡνια.

In this uncertainty I may be permitted to doubt if ἡνια belongs to the same family as ἥμερος and ζημια. The underlying sense of the former is that of strength, power, restraining, governing; the underlying sense of the two latter is that of loss, deficiency, weakness, want. Hence the former may be allied to the Sanskrit *yam,* as Benfey suggests, but hardly the two latter. Of these, however, ἥμερος may doubtless refer through ἥμαι to Sanskrit âs, although the primary sense of âs is not one of weakness, deficiency, but rather of strength and freedom of action : " I sit, I stay, I abide, I perform." Ζημια, again, as Liddell and Scott intimate, may refer, through the Cretan δαμια, to Sanskrit dam, to tame, " coercere," and dam-a, chastisement, fine; but in this case I think it possible that the analogy of sound may have produced an analogy of sense, ζημια, δαμια, when the result in both was " loss, damage." There is this difference, however, between the two, as I think, that in ζημια the sense of loss, &c., seems to be inherent in the thing or person referred to, whereas in dam-a, δαμια, damnum, the sense of loss seems to arise from an imposition ab extra, the sense of inherent loss, weakness, defect, cropping out in expressions like φανερα ζημια, lit. evident loss, good-for-nothing, worthless, &c. I would therefore seek the connection of ζημια, ἥμερος, and the Polynesian sema, hema, in the Sanskrit çam, whose " original signification," Benfey says, is " to get tired," then to cease, to be quiet, meek, humble.

I remarked, p. 110, that the designation of the left could generally be traced to a sense of weakness, inferiority, defect; and to name the left hand " the quiet, the still," &c., sc. hand, in contradistinction from the right hand, is a correct analogy to sav-ya, whether that be interpreted " manus immunda " or " manus purificanda abluendo."

The Hawaiian is the only Polynesian dialect which has retained hema to designate south as well as left, and the origin of that designation arises from the fact that the Polynesians looked to the west when designating the cardinal points.

To the Sanskrit çam Benfey refers the Greek καμνω, to work oneself weary, be tired, ill, to suffer; καματος, toil, trouble, distress.

Liddell and Scott refer to the German sanft in connection with ἥμερος, as related to ἥμαι. I know not the etymology of sanft, but if it is related to ἥμερος, I think it better to refer it to the Sanskrit *cam* and its derivative *cantva* = *cam-tva*, conciliating, mild.

HENE, *v.* Haw., *hene-hene*, to laugh at, to mock, deride, despise. (Not found in other Polynesian dialects.)

Goth., *hauns*, humble, base, contemptible; *haunjan*, to humiliate. A.-Sax., *hynan*, to humble. Germ., *hohn*, scorn, derision, scoff; *höhnen*, to deride, to scoff at. Swed., *hån*, derision, mockery, scorn.

Lat., *hinnio*, to neigh. Comp. latter part of *cachinnus*.

HI, *v.* Haw., to flow away, as evacuations, to blow out with force from the mouth, as liquids, droop, be weak; *s.* purging, dysentery, a hissing sound, as the rapid flow of a liquid. Tong., *sisi*, to hiss; *ifi*, to blow with the mouth. Sam., *si*, semen emittere; *sisi*, to make a hissing sound, as green wood burning, to trickle down. Tah., *hi*, to gush out, as water, to flux. Deriv., *hio*, Haw., eructatio ventris; *hio-hio*, to draw in the breath, as if eating something hot; *hihio*, to blow, rush violently. N. Zeal., *whio*, to whistle. Mang., *vivio*, id. Paum., *hiohio*, id. Tah., *hio*, to puff, as out of breath, to whistle.

Sanskr., *hi*, to go, send, discharge, as an arrow, dispatch, jacere, projicere; *sich*, to sprinkle, discharge, effundere; *çik* or *sik*, to sprinkle; *çikara*, drop of water, thin rain, spray.

Greek, σιζω, to hiss, the sound of frying in a pan; σικχος, squeamish, sickening; σικχασια, nausea; σιγμος, a hissing; σιξις, id.; ζεω, to boil, seethe; ζεστος, boiling hot; ζυμη, leaven; ζυθος, beer. Liddell and Scott refer the four last to Sanskrit *yas*, to make strenuous exertions, to endeavour, and they refer σιγη, silence, to σιζω.

A.-Sax., *hysian*, *hiscan*, to hiss, to whiz, whence Engl. *hist*, a word of attention, commanding silence; *sythan*, *seathan*, to seethe, boil; *seoc*, sick; *sife*, *syfe*, a sieve. O. H. Germ., *sîhan*, to strain, sift; *seihjan*, mingere. Goth., *siukan*, be sick, be still.

Lat., *sibilo*, hiss, whistle.

Lith., *setas*, a sieve; *sijoti*, to sift.

HIA, *v.* Haw., der. of an obsol. *hi*, to entangle, to catch, as in a net; *hihi*, duplicate form of the original root, to branch, spread out, as vines or limbs of trees, grow thick together; *adj.* spreading, creeping, entwining; *hihia*, be perplexed, entangled; *s.* difficulty, trouble, a thicket of forest, a snarl. Tong., *fihi, fihifihi*, to entangle, entwine. N. Zeal., *wiwi*, rushes, also entangled; *ta-wiwi*, to ensnare. Mangar., *i'i*, ensnaring. Marqu., *fifi*, to envelop. Tah., *fifi*, entangled, intricate, a chain; *hi*, to fish with hook and line, angle; *hihi*, rays of the sun, whiskers of a cat or mouse. Fiji., *vivi-a*, to roll up, to coil. Malg., *a-fehai*, to knot; *a-fiezi*, to tie, to make fast; *fiheho*, bound.

Sanskr., *si*, to bind; *sita*, bound; *sîmâ, sîman*, boundary, limit, nape of the neck.

Greek, *ἱμας*, a thong, strap, rope, girdle, latch-string.

O. Sax., *simo*, bond.

HIO, *v.* Haw., to lean over, to slant, to swing to and fro, to lean upon, trust in, to wander about; *hihio*, to sleep, fall asleep, to dream; *hiohiona*, the gait and personal appearance of a person. Sam., *sioa*, wearied, exhausted. Marqu., *fio*, to rove about.

Sanskr., *çî*, to lie, as on the ground, lie down, repose, sleep; *çaya*, asleep, sleep, a snake, a tiger; *çayyâ*, a bed.

Greek, *κειω, κεω, κειμαι*, to lie, be laid, lie asleep, repose; *κοιμαω*, to lull or hush to sleep, fall asleep, lie down, have sexual intercourse, keep watch at night; *κωμα*, deep sleep; *κωμη*, an unwalled village; *κοιτη*, bed, couch; *κοιτος*.

Lat., *quies*, rest, cessation of labour, repose; *cio, cieo*, to put in motion, to move, stir, shake; *civis*, a citizen, member of a village or tribe. Liddell and Scott refer the Greek *κυπτω*, to bend forward, stoop down, as akin to the Latin *cubo*, to lie, recline; and they refer *cubo* to Sanskrit *çî*. For my reasons for differing from such analysis, vid. *s. v.* KUPA.

Anc. Slav., *po-citi*, quiescere; *po-koi*, quiet.

Lith., *kiemas*, village; *kaimynas*, neighbour.

Goth., *haims*, a village; *haithi*, a field, heath; *hethjo*, a sleeping-place.

HIKI, *v.* Haw., to come to, arrive at, to happen, be able;

hikina, i.e., *hiki-ana* (sc. *a ka la*), the rising of the sun, the east. Tah., *hiti*, id.; *hitia*, sunrise, east. Nuh., Fak., Sam., *fiti*, id. N. Zeal., *witi;* Rarot., *iti*, to rise, as the sun, appear, to come.

Greek, *ἵκω*, *ἱκανω*, *ἱκνεομαι*, to come, come to, reach to, approach, befall, befit; *ἱκανος*, befitting, sufficient, able, strong. Liddell and Scott give no Indo-European relatives of this word. Benfey refers *ἵκω*, &c., to the Sanskrit *viç*, to enter, enter in, begin; with *pra*, to appear; and also intimates the relation of the Gothic *waihts*, a whit, a thing, a slight appearance.

HILI, *v.* Haw., to braid, plait, twist, turn over, spin; *wili*, id.; *wili, s.* a ribbon, a roll; *wili-wili*, to stir round, to mix; another dialectical variation is *hilo*, to twist, turn, spin. Sam., *fili*, to plait, as sinnet; *filo*, to mix, *s.* twine, thread; *vili*, a gimlet, a whirlpool. Marqu., *fau-fii*, twist, braid. N. Zeal., *wiri*, id. Rarot., *iro*, id. Tah., *firi*, id.; *hiro*, id. Fiji., *siri*, askew, not nicely in a row, wrong, in error. Tagal and Bisaya, *hilig*, a woof.

Greek, *εἴλω*, to roll up, to press together, pass to and fro, to wind, turn round; *ἑλισσω*, turn round or about, roll, whirl; *ἑλιξ, adj.* twisted, curled; *s.* anything of a spiral shape, twist, curl, coil; *ἰλλω*, to roll, of the eyes, to squint, look askance; *ἰλλος*, squinting; *ἰλλας*, a rope, band; *ἰλιγξ*, a whirlpool.

Sanskr., *vel, vehl*, to shake, tremble; *vellita*, crooked; *anu-vellita*, a bandage. To this Sanskrit *vel* Benfey refers the Greek *εἴλω*, the Latin *volvo*, and the Gothic *walo-jan*. Liddell and Scott also incline to connect *εἴλω* and *volvo* with the same root. To me it would seem as if the Sanskrit *vrij*, whose "original signification," Benfey says, is "to bend," and the Sanskrit *vrit*, whose "original signification," Benfey says, is "to turn," were nearer akin to the primary form from which the Greek *εἴλω*, *ἰλλω*, and the Polynesian *hili, wiri*, descend: that primary form being *vri*, now lost to the Sanskrit, with a primary sense of to bend, twist, turn over, braid, and of which *vel, vell,* or *vehl*, is possibly another secondary and attenuated form. With

such a Sanskrit *vri*, surviving in *vrij* and *vrit*, the derivation of the Latin *filum*, thread, as twisted, spun ; of the
Latin *varus*, bent asunder, parting from each other, *varix*,
crookedness ; of the Saxon *wile*, deceit ; of the Swedish
willa, confusion, error, *wilse*, astray, becomes easy and
intelligible.

HILU, *adj.* Haw., still, quiet, reserved, dignified, glorious.

Sanskr., *cil*, to meditate, adore, worship.

Greek, ἰλαω, ἰλασκομαι, to appease, propitiate ; ἰλαος,
gracious.

Lat., *sileo*, be still, silent.

HINA[1], *v.* Haw., to lean from an upright position, to
fall, fall down, tumble over, to fall morally as well as
materially, to offend. Tong., N. Zeal., *hinga*, id. Paumotu, *hinga*, dead, *i.e.*, fallen. Tah., *hia*, to fall. Sam.,
s.sina, to drop down. Marqu., *hika*, to fall, slide, lean, to
die ; *hina*, id. Malg., *tsinga*, to lean to, incline. Malay.,
tiggelam, to sink.

Lat., *sino*, let down, lay down, suffer, permit ; *pono* =
po-sino, put down ; *sinus*, a bending, a curving ; *sinuo*,
sinister.

Goth., *sigghwan*, to sink, to set, of the sun. A.-Sax.,
sigan, fall ; *sincan*, sink.

HINA[2], *adj.* Haw., grey, hoary, as hair or beard ; *hina-
hina*, id., withered as fruit ; *poo-hina*, grey-haired, aged ;
po-hina, white, whitish, silvery, grey ; *ma-hina*, moon.
Sam., *sina*, white or grey, of the hair ; *faa-sinasina*, to
whiten, whitewash ; *ma-sina*, the moon. Tong., *hina*,
grey, white ; *ma-hina*, moon. Mang., *ina*, white, grey ;
ma-ina, moon. Tah., *hina-hina*, grey hairs. Marqu., *hina*,
white ; *ma-hina*, moon. N. Zeal., *hina*, grey, white, of
hair. Fiji., *sika*, grey-headed ; *singa*, the sun, day ; *singa-
singau*, white. Sunda and Mal., *sinar*, a ray of light, sunbeam. Sulu Isl., *fa-sina*, the moon. Tagal, *quinas*, to
shine ; *quinan*, a glance. Malg., *fassin*, grey ; *hina*, *hign*,
an oyster ; *hinign*, the flash of a gun.

Lat., *senex*, old, aged, hoary-headed ; *seneo*, *senesco*.

Goth., *sins*, old.

I have not found any Sanskrit root that may refer to the Polynesian *sina* or *hina* in its application as white, bright, shining, or its further application as a name for the moon. Yet I find *siṁhala*, tin, brass, cassia-bark; *siṁhana*, rust of iron, the mucus of the nose; *ciṅghâṅa*, froth, foam, the mucus of the nose, rust of iron, a glass vessel, all which certainly indicate their connection with a root conveying the sense of whiteness, brightness, &c.

HINAI, *s.* Haw., a braided container, a basket. Sam., *sina*, gourd, calabash. Tong., *hina*, gourd, bottle. Tah., *hinai*, a sort of basket. Fiji., *sinai*, full; *sinai-ta*, do up the mouth of a basket. Malg., *sini*, vase, pot.

Lat., *sinum*, a large, round drinking vessel.

Anthon, Lat. Dict., *s. v.*, refers *sinum* to *sinus*, a bend, a curve. If so, it derives from *sino*, as the Haw. and Tah. *hinai* may derive from *hina*[1].

HINI, *adj.* Haw., *hini-hini*, *u-hini*, small, thin, feeble, speaking in a small, thin voice, whispering. Tah., *uine*, to chirp as chickens. Malg., *hinti*, to tinkle.

Sanskr., *cinj*, to tinkle; *cinja*, tinkling, a bowstring.

HINU, *s.* Haw., ointment; *v.* to anoint, besmear with oil or grease, be smooth, shining. Tah., N. Zeal., *hinu*, oil, grease. Rarot., *inu*, id. Marqu., *hinu*, ointment, ink, tincture from the tutui nut. Tikop., *sinu*, cocoa-nut oil. Fiji., *sinusinu*, id. Ceram. (Camariau), *wai-li-sini*, oil Saparua, *wa-ri-sini*, id.

Sanskr., *cyâna*, *cina*, thick, viscous, adhesive; *prate-cina*, melted, fluid.

HIWA, *adj.* Haw., dear, valued, beloved, precious; applied mostly to that which was used in sacrifice to the gods, in which the black colour was preferred, as a black hog, a black kapa, a black cocoa-nut, &c.; hence black, clear black. Sam., Fak., *siwa;* Tong., *hiwa*, song, dance, festivity. Tah., *hiwa*, family, company; *hiwa-hiwa*, abundance, plenty.

Sanskr., *civa*, prosperous, happy, complacent, well-being;

name of one of the Sanskrit Triad, distinguished by his black or blue-black neck.

I note, but leave to abler hands to explain, the coincidence, if such it be, of the Tah. *hiwa,* family, company, clan, and the A.-Sax. *hiwa,* family; O. Germ., *hiwa,* a wife, &c., which latter Benfey refers to the Sanskrit *çî,* to lie down, while he refers *çiva* to a root *çvi,* to swell, increase. Benfey also refers the Sanskrit *çeva,* happiness, to *çî.* Why not *çiva* also, or the Polynesian *hiwa ?*

Ho, *v.* Haw., to cry in a clamorous manner, to shout, cry out for fear or distress, breathe hard; *hoho,* id., to snore; *s.* asthma, lowing of cattle. Tah., *ho,* a war-shout of triumph or rejoicing.

Sanskr., *hve,* Ved., *hû,* to call, to name, invoke, challenge; *hvânâ,* a cry; *gu,* to sound; *guy,* to buzz; *ghu, ghur, ghush,* id., to proclaim.

Greek, βοη, loud shout, cry; βοαω, to roar, howl, call aloud; γοος, wailing, lamentation; γοαω, to wail, groan, weep.

Lat., *re-boo,* resound; *voveo,* to vow, promise; *hoi, interj.* oh, alas!

Goth., *gaunon,* mourn, lament. A.-Sax., *hveop,* to cry, call out; *wepan,* to weep.

HOA, *v.* Haw., to tie, bind, wind round; *s.* companion, friend, assistant; *hoai,* mix, unite two things; *s.* union, suture, as of bones; *hoai-manawa,* coronal suture, &c. Sam., *soa,* companion, friend. Tikop., *soa,* id. Tong., *nga-hoa,* a pair. N. Zeal., *hoa,* to help. Tah., *hoa,* friend; *faa-hoa,* make friends. Fiji., *so,* to assemble; *soso,* an assembly; *sota,* to meet, meet accidentally. Malg., *zokhe,* friend, comrade, brother.

I am induced to believe that the form *hoa* is a contraction of an orignal *hoka,* which occurs in a duplicated form; Haw., *hokahokai,* to mix, as two ingredients. The Fiji. *so* probably represents the primary root, now obsolete in Polynesia, but with the primary sense retained in the Hawaiian *hoa, v.,* which probably underlies the formation of the

Lat., *socius*, a companion, partner; *sodalis*, friend, comrade, assistant.

Ho'o, Ha'a. Haw., a causative prefix to verbs. Tah., *ha'a, fa'a*, id. Marqu., *haa, faa*, and *haka ;* Sam., *faa* and *faka ;* N. Zeal., *whaka*, id., to cause to be or do a thing. Paum., *faka ;* Rarot., *aka*, id.

Lat., *facio*, imp. *fac*, pret. *factum*, do, make, cause to be; *facies*, figure, face, shape. Benfey refers *facio* to Sanskrit *bhû*, to become, to be; but I am not aware of any West Aryan forms to explain the transitions.

So far as I know, none of the West Aryan branches make use of a causative prefix to verbs, the Zend and Vedic alone expressing the causative by suffixes, which have already lost their primary sense and become mere unmeaning flexions. It would be interesting, therefore, to know if any trace of a causative prefix can be found within the Indo-European lines. Was the prefix, as found in the Polynesian, an older form of expressing the causative, which afterwards, for reasons now unknown, became obsolete and was replaced by suffixes, or was it a form of speech acquired and adopted by the Polynesians from long and intimate intercourse with the Cushite-Chaldeans? But if the Polynesian causative prefix has no analogy in Sanskrit or Iranian, it has an undoubted Aryan relative in the Latin *facio*, and that *facio* was certainly used at times as a causative, and, though it was not agglutinated to the verb which it governed, but stood apart, yet it preceded it, and did not follow it, like the Sanskrit or Zend causative suffixes. The Greek, Latin, and Gothic did not use causative suffixes, but expressed that sense, as their descendants do to-day, by what I may call auxiliary verbs, independent in form and sense, placed *before* and not *after* the verb which they affected, and in so far the construction of their sentences, their idioms, corresponds to the Polynesian. I think, therefore, that I may be permitted to infer, from the absence of causative suffixes in such prominent branches of the Aryan stock as the Greek, Latin, Gothic, and Polynesian, that such suffixes were of later development and adoption in some of the other branches.

HOKA, *v.* Haw., to squeeze, press, take hold of, to search, examine into, to strike, attack, be destitute, fail, be disappointed. Sam., *so'a-so'a, soso'a,* to spear a thing, to husk cocoa-nuts. Tah., *hota,* to cough. N. Zeal., Mangar., *hoka,* a sharp-pointed instrument. Tong., *hoka,* to stab, thrust. Fiji., *voca,* to strike against. Malg., *hota,* fault, vice, defect; *hota-lela,* to stutter. Sunda, *suker,* in trouble, difficulty.

Sanskr., *sûch,* to point out, indicate, betray, espy; *sûchî,* piercing, a needle, indication by signs; *sûcha,* piercing, gesticulation; *sûchana,* information, piercing, gesticulation, wickedness.

Goth., *sokjan,* to seek, desire, question with, dispute; *sakan,* pt. *sok,* to rebuke, strive, dispute; *sakjis,* a brawler, a striker. Engl., *sake* in *forsake;* Swed., *för-saka;* Germ., *such* in *versuchen;* Swed., *för-söka.*

HOLA, *v.* Haw., to open, spread out; *hola-hola,* id., to smooth; *hohola,* id., unfold; *mohola,* to open, expand, unfold, as leaves of plants or flowers, blooming; *po-hola,* id. Sam., Tong., *fola, fofola;* N. Zeal., Tah., *hora, hohora,* to spread out, unfold; *ma-hora,* developed, clear, explicit. Related to these as dialectical variations are doubtless the Hawaiian *mo-halu,* clearness, fulness, as the full moon; *holi,* to commence, the first appearance of a thing. Tah., *po-hori,* new shoots, buds. Tong., *foli,* to spread, expand, as vegetation. Marqu., *po-hoe,* living things; and the ubiquitous *hala, hara, fala, fara,* the Polynesian name for the pandanus. Fiji., *volā,* to make a mark, to mark; *volā-bongi,* evening or midnight star; *volā-singa,* morning star. Malg., *fala* or *fola-tangh,* the open hand, the palm; *fola-tombuk,* plante de pied; *felan,* blossom.

Sanskr., *phal,* to burst, to produce, to bear fruit; *phulla,* blown, expanded, as a flower, opened, as the eyes with pleasure; *phalin,* bearing fruit; *phalya,* a flower; *phull,* to blossom. Benfey considers *phal* as derived from an older form in *spar, sphar,* and *sphur,* to tremble, palpitate, flash. In view of the Polynesian and of the Latin, Greek, and Gothic, quoted below, the *s* is more likely to be a subsequent prosthetic than an original constitutent of the word.

Lat., *folium*, leaf; *flos*, flower.

Greek, φυλλον, leaf, foliage, flower.

Goth., *bloma*; A.-Sax., *blosm*, bloom, blossom.

Liddell and Scott refer φυλλον and *folium* and *flos*, &c., to a root represented by the Greek φλεω, φλυω, βλυω, to gush, swell up, overflow. Benfey, however, refers *flos* and *bloma* to the Sanskrit *phal*. Pictet (Or. Ind.-Eur,. i. 205 *sq*.) refers both φυλλον and φλεω, with all their derivatives and correlatives, as well as *folium*, *flos*, and *bloma*, to the Sanskrit *phal* and *phull*, which brings us back to the Polynesian forms in *fola, hola, fala*, and *hala*, &c.

It may be interesting to observe with Pictet that the various European names for apple refer themselves back to either of those two forms in *phul* or *phal*; Welsh, *afal*; Irish, *abhal, ubhal*; A.-Sax., *appel*; Anc. Germ., *aphul*; Lith., *obolys*; Anc. Slav., *jabulko*.

The name of a festival in Deccan, of very ancient date, to celebrate the vernal equinox and the return of spring, and called *holi*, does singularly enough associate itself to the Hawaiian *holi*, the first appearance of a thing, to commence, and to the Tongan *foli*, to spread, expand, as vegetation.

HOLO[1], *v.* Haw., to move swiftly, to run, to flee; *hooholo*, to stretch out, reach forth, as the hand, to slip, slide; *holoi*, to wash, to scrape, brush, wipe, blot out, to clean; *holoholoi*, to rub with pressure and quick motion, rub off dirt, rub down, smooth; *holo-ke*, to run or rub against some opposing object. Sam., *solo*, to slide, fall down, pass along, to wipe, as after bathing; *s.* a towel; *adj.* swift; *soloi*, to wipe, to break gradually, as a wave fit to glide on; *solo-solo*, to slip away, as a landslip; *sola*, to run away, to flee. Tong., *hola*, id.; *holoi*, to chafe, to wipe; *hoholo*, to grind, sharpen. N. Zeal., Tah., *horo*, to run; *s.* a landslip; *horohoro*, swiftly, quickly; *horoi*, to wash, cleanse.

Fiji., *solo-ta*, to rub or grind, to wipe or dry oneself after washing. Malg., *sora*, *tsora*, a file, a hedgehog.

Sanskr., *kshar*, to stream, pass away, to let escape, to yield; *kshal*, to purify, make clean, remove; *kshâlana*, washing.

Greek, σαρος, broom; σαροω, σαιρω, to sweep, clean. Lat., *sarrio*, to rake, hoe.

Russ., *soru*, sweepings, offal. Pol., *szor*, *szur*, detritus, alluvium; *szorowach*, nettoyer, frotter. Lith., *szlota*, broom.

Pers., *sharîdan*, to flow, run, pour out; *shâr*, flood, flux; *shârûf*, broom.

Goth., *skiuran*, to scour; *skura*, a shower.

To the Sanskrit *kshar* Benfey refers the Latin *scortum*, a whore, and the Gothic *hors*, a whoremonger.

HOLO[2], *s.* Haw., a bundle. Fiji., *sole*, *sole-sole*, a bundle, package.

Greek, σωρος, a heap, a pile; σωρακος, a basket, box; σορος, a vessel for holding anything, a container.

HONUA, *s.* Haw., flat land, in distinction from the mountains, the bottom of a deep place. Marqu., Tah., *fenua*, land, country. N. Zeal., *whenua*, id. Tong., *fonua*. Sam., *fanua*, id. Paum., *henua*, id. Fiji., *vanua*, id. Malay., *benua*, id.

Goth., *fani*, clay, mud. Sax. and O. Engl., *fen*, lowland, moor, boggy.

HOPE, *s.* Haw., the end or beginning of a thing, termination, result, consequence; *adv.* behind, after, last. Tah., *hope*, the tail of a bird, the hair of a man tied behind; *v.* to be finished, ended; *hopea*, the end or extremity of a thing. Sam., *sope*, lock of hair left as an ornament. Rarot., Mang., *ope*, end, extremity. Marqu., *hope-hope*, the buttocks, rump. Fiji., *sobe-ta*, to cleave to, to ascend or descend, as by a rope.

Greek, ὀπις, the consequence of things, good or bad, retribution, vengeance, favour; ὀπισθεν, behind, at the back, after, in place or time; ὀπισω, behind, hereafter. Liddell and Scott are in doubt whether to refer ὀπις to ὀψομαι or to ἐπω, ἐπομαι. But ἐπω has been referred by them and Benfey to Sanskrit *sach*, Latin *sequor*. Why not refer ὅπις and *hope* to Sanskrit *sap*, *sev*, connect, follow?

Hopo, *v.* Haw., to shrink back through fear, be afraid, agitated, troubled. Sam., *sopo*, step over, pass over; *soposopo*, id., transgress. Tong., *hopo*, to jump, to caper. Marqu., *hopo*, to fear, tremble.

Greek, σοβεω, to scare or drive away, to shake, beat, to walk pompously, strut; σοβας, a kind of dance; σοβη, horse's tail; σοβησις, agitation, excitement. Liddell and Scott consider σοβεω akin to σευω, to hunt, chase. I think the connection doubtful. They refer, moreover, to the Old German *sweif* (*schweif*), a tail, a train, which seems a more probable connection.

Sax., *hoppan*, to leap, jump. Icel., *skopa*, to leap, spring. Engl., *skip, hop, hobble.*

Hu, *v.* Haw., to rise or swell up, effervesce, to rise up, as a thought, to overflow, run over, to shed or pour out, to ooze quietly, to appear, *i.e.*, to heave up in sight, as a ship at a distance, to whistle, as the wind (Germ. *brausen, sausen*); *hu*, *s.* a rising, swelling, a top; *hu-kani*, a humming-top; *huhu*, be angry, scolding, storming; *hua*, *v.* to swell, foam, to sprout, bud, bear fruit, grow, increase; *s.* fruit, offspring, production, froth, an egg, a kidney, seed, as of grain, human testicles; *huai*, to open, as a native oven, as a windbag, as a grave; *hua-huai*, to boil up, as water in a spring. Tong., *hu*, to boil a stew; *hua*, general name for liquids; *huai*, to pour out; *huhu*, the nipple of the breast; *fua*, fruit. Sam., *su, susu*, wet; *susu*, the breast, teats of animals; *sua*, liquids; *fua*, to begin, to start, *s.* fruit. N. Zeal., *hua*, to sprout, grow, *s.* fruit; *kohua*, to boil; *huka*, foam. Tah., *hu*, wind on the stomach; *hua*, grain, particles; *hu'a*, testicles; *huaa*, ancestors; *huai*, to open an oven; *huhua*, top of a mountain. Marqu., *hu*, break wind; *huaa*, people, family; *huhua*, to swell up. Rarot., *ua*, fruit. Mang., *uai*, to begin. Fiji., *su*, the water in which food has been boiled, soup; *sua-sua*, wet, moist; *susu*, be born, bring forth young, to suck, suckle; *vu*, to cough; *vua*, fruit, produce, *v.* to bear fruit, to overflow; *vua*, family, tribe; *vusa*, tribe genealogy; *vuso*, froth, foam. Timor Laut., *susu*, the breast. Sunda and Malay., *buah*, fruit. Jav., *wowoan*, id. Buru, *fuan*, id. Amboyna, *hua*, id. Ceram. (Gah.), *voya*, id. Malg., *vua*, *voa*, id.; *sosoa*, potage, bouillon. Motu. (N. Guinea), *huahua*, fruit.

Sanskr., *su* and *sû*, to beget, bear, bring forth; *sûna*, born, produced, blown, as a flower; *sûnu*, a son; *sû*, s. birth, bringing forth, yielding; *sûma*, milk, water; *sûti*, birth, offspring, source; *sutin*, father; *suma*, a flower; *sûsh*, *cûsh*, to bring forth, bear; *hu*, to sacrifice; *homa* (for *huma*), oblation; *home*, fire, clarified butter, water. Pictet (Or. Ind.-Eur., ii. 702) thinks the Sanskrit *hu* is wrongly compared with the Greek θνω, and that its primitive sense might have been "projicere, effundere, et libare." He is probably correct, and the sacrifice contemplated consisted in the "pouring out" of the clarified butter or the soma juice as a libation. If so, it brings the Sanskrit still more *en rapport* with the Polynesian form and primary sense. The Sanskr. *sûnu*, son, which is retained in the Goth. *sunus*, Lith. *sunus*, Anc. Slav. *synu*, with almost identical form, has its exact counterpart in the Polynes. Haw. *hunona*, child-in-law; Tah., *hunoa*; N. Zeal., *hunaonga*; Rarot., *unonga*, id. Fiji., *vungona*, son or daughter in law, or father or mother in law; N. Zeal., Marqu., *hungoni*, a parent-in-law.

Greek, ὑω, to wet, to water, to rain; ὑετος, rain; υἱος, a son; ὑσμα, rain; ὑστερα, womb; ὑδνης, watery, moist, nourishing. Benfey refers ὑω to Sanskrit *su*, but Liddell and Scott refer it to ὑδωρ, while they admit that Curtius will not connect ὑδωρ with ὑω. At the same time they refer υἱος to Sanskrit *su*, generare. The primary sense of "to rise, swell up, to bear or bring forth," had evidently become obsolete in Greek when ὑω was reduced to writing, though indications of such a form remained in υἱος, son, ὑς or συς, swine, probably in ὑλη, a wood, forest, ὑσγη, a shrub.

Lat., *humor*, moisture, liquid; *humidus, humectus, sucus*

juice; *sugo,* to suck; *sumen, sugmen,* udder, teat; *fundo, fudi,* pour out, shed, spread, bring forth, produce; *fuse,* copiously.

Goth., *giutan,* to pour out; *Guth,* God; according to Pictet (Or. Ind.-Eur., ii. 660), he to whom libations are poured out = Ved. *huta.*

Zend, *zu,* to sacrifice.

Afghan, *sui,* son.

Irish, *soth,* progenitor.

Alban., *sua,* race, family.

Pictet (*loc. cit.,* i. 194) inclines to refer the Greek ὕλη and the Latin *sylva* to Sanskrit *sâla,* tree, through some obsolete or hypothetical form, *sâlava;* but the Sanskrit *sâla* or *çâla* is fully and correctly represented in the Polynesian *hala, fala,* the Pandanus odorif., and ὕλη and ὕσγη doubtless connect themselves with ὕω in some of its primary but forgotten meanings, as much as ὕιος and ὕς.

I have purposely not referred to the Greek χύω, χεύω, χέω, to pour out, scatter, &c., and its numerous derivatives. Benfey and Pictet refer it to Sanskrit *hu,* but Liddell and Scott to ἕω, ἵημι. The connection of the Polynesian *hu* with the other Aryan branches is sufficiently established without it.

Hu², *s.* Tong., a royal appellation.

Welsh, *Hu,* name of a solar deity, also called *Huon* and *Huan.*

Zend, *Hu,* the sun.

Sanskr., *suvana, sûta, sûnu,* sun, from root *su,* to beget, bring forth—vid. *supra.*

Greek, ὕης, ὕευς, title of Bacchus, as the god of fertilising moisture—vid. ὕω, Liddell and Scott.

Goth., *sunno* and *sunna,* sun.

Huali, *adj.* Haw., bright, clean, pure, white, glittering, shining. A synonym of this word, but of the same formation, is the Hawaiian *huaka,* clear, as pure water, bright, white, shining. *Huali* is composed of *hu* or *hua,* froth, foam, bubble (obsolete as liquids), and *ali* or *aliali,* white, as snow, or paper, or salt; Tah., *ari-ari,* transparent.

Huaka is composed of *hu* and *aka,* to be light, as moonrise or morning ; *akaka,* clear, transparent, as glass or a liquid.

Greek, ὑαλος or ὑελος, any clear, transparent stone ; in later times glass, said by Jablonski to be an Egyptian word, but by others to be derived from ὑω (vid. Liddell and Scott, *s. v.*), ὑακινθος, a precious stone, perhaps the amethyst, also a flower of that name. The Hawaiian correlatives will afford a satisfactory analysis of both ὑαλος and ὑακινθος, without going to Egypt. Another kindred word, the Latin *vaccinium,* a kind of plant, the whortleberry, confirms the Aryan home-growth of this branch of derivatives. The Latin *succinum* or *sucinum,* amber, and the Greek σουχιον, id., like *vaccinium,* ὑαλος, and ὑακινθος, probably also go back to the same formation as the Polynesian *hu-ali, hu-aka.*

Hui[1], *v.* Haw., to unite together, to mix, to add one to another, to assemble, meet ; *s.* cluster, collection of things ; *huihui,* a bunch, cluster ; *huiuna* (for *huiana*), a seam in a garment ; *la-hui,* collection of people, a nation. Sam., *sui,* to dilute, to add ingredients to a thing ; *sui,* to sew, to thread beads ; *susui,* to mend, repair ; *susuia,* to fasten the ridge-pole of a house. Tong., *hui,* mingle, mix, join ; *fufui,* a flock of birds. N. Zeal., *hui, huhui,* to gather, mix, unite ; *ra-hui,* a company ; *ka-hui,* a herd, a flock. Tah., *hui,* a collection of persons, a company ; *huihui-manu,* flock of birds ; *hui-tara-wa,* Orion's belt. Marqu., *huhui,* a bundle of taro.

Sanskr., *yu,* to bind, join, mix ; *yuj,* to join ; *yuga,* a yoke, a pair, a couple ; *yûti,* mixing ; *yûtha,* flock of birds or beasts.

Greek, ζευγνυμι, to join, put to, yoke up, bind, fasten ; ζευγος, a yoke of beasts, pair, couple ; ζυγον, the yoke ; ζωνη, belt, girdle.

Lat., *jugum,* a yoke ; *jugo,* bind up, tie together ; *jungo,* bind, join, unite.

Goth., *juk,* a yoke. A.-Sax., *geok,* id. Scand., *ok,* id.

Armen., *zugel,* attach together, yoke up ; *zoygkh,* a couple, a pair. Pers., *yûgh,* a yoke.

Irish, *ughaim*, harness. Welsh, *jow*, yoke.

Lett., *jûgs*, yoke. Anc. Slav., *jgo*, yoke. Bohem., *gho*, id. Lith., *jungas*, id.

A singular coincidence of application, if it has no nearer connection, by the Polynesian and the Latin of this word to similar purposes, occurs in the *huhui* and *hui-tarawa* of the former and *jugulæ* of the latter. In Hawaiian *huhui* designates a constellation generally, but especially that of the Pleiades; in Tahitian *hui-tarawa*, lit. the transverse or horizontal cluster, designates the stars generally called Orion's belt, and in Latin *jugulæ* represents the very same stars in the constellation Orion.

HUI[2], *v.* Haw., to ache, be in pain; *s.* bodily pain; *niho-hui*, the toothache; *hui, huihui*, cold, chilly, as morning air or cold water; *hukeki, hukiki*, cold, shivering on account of wet. N. Zeal., *huka*, cold. Tah., *hui, hui-hui*, to throb as an artery, twitchings in the flesh.

Sanskr., *çuch*[1], to be afflicted, grieve; *çuch*[2], to be wet, fetid; *çuch, s.* sorrow, grief; quære *suçîma*, cold? To this Sanksr. *çuch* Benfey refers the Goth. *hiufau*, to mourn, lament, and the O. H. Germ. *huvo*, an owl.

HUKA, *s.* Haw., a term used in calling hogs.

I am not aware that this word is used for that purpose in any of the other Polynesian groups, nor that any of those groups have a name for hogs or swine that will ally itself to this Hawaiian *huka*, unless we find it in the Fijian *vonga*, a sow, which has the appearance of a foreign word in Fijian speech, and as a remnant from the time when the Polynesians sojourned in Fiji. But this Hawaiian *huka* has doubtless a lingual affinity to the following Indo-European terms used in calling hogs :—

Lett., *chûka*, a hog; *chuck-chuck*, a term for calling hogs.

Russ., *chushka*, pig; *chu-chu*, a call to hogs.

Sax., *chuck*, a term used in calling hogs, probably in more ancient times a name for swine, as we find it still retained in the word " *wood-chuck.*" The Welsh *hwch*, a pig, from which we have the English *hog*, according to

Pictet, makes the relation still plainer, whether *chuck,* *hwch,* or *huka* refer themselves to the Sanskrit *su* or Polynesian *hu,* or, as Pictet prefers, are onomatopoetic.

HULI, *v.* Haw., to turn generally in any way, to turn over, roll over, search, change. Sam., *fuli,* turn over, roll along. Tah., *huri,* turn over, roll as a cask; *huri-ea,* to deliberate, turn a subject over in one's mind. N. Zeal., *huri,* turn. Related to this is the Haw. *hula,* the **Tah.** *hura,* to bend over, fall over, move from place to place, shake, tremble, dance, dancing, dancing and singing, a Polynesian chorus, an expression of joy. Fiji., *voli,* to go round about. Sunda, *buled,* to be round. Malg., *mi-holak,* to turn round; *hulik, holak,* a turn; *vola, bola, buri,* round. Malay., *guling,* to roll, turn.

Sanskr., *ghûrn,* to reel, move to and fro, roll, as the eye; *ghûrṇa,* vacillating, shaking, staggering; *ghurṇ,* to whirl; *guda, gola,* a ball; *gulpha,* the ankle.

Pers., *gûli, gôli,* a pill; *garuhah,* a ball.

Greek, γυρος, round, crooked, a ring, a circle; γυροω, to round, to bend. No etymon *s. v.* by Liddell and Scott. Χορος, the movement of dancers in a ring, a dance, dancing with singing; χορωνος, a crown.

Lat., *curvus,* crooked, bent.

HULU, *s.* Haw., feathers of birds, hair of other animals. Tah., *huru-huru,* hair, wool, feathers. Tong., Sam., *fulu,* hair, feathers. Marqu., *huu,* id. In all other Polynesian groups, *fulu, huru, uru,* hair, fur, feathers. Fiji., *vulua,* hair about the privates, a tabu word; *vulu-vulu-ka-ni-mata,* eyelashes. Mal., *bulu,* feather; *bulu-kambing,* wool; *burong,* a bird. Malg., *vulu,* hair. Amboyna, *huru,* feather. Buru, *fulun, folun,* feather; *folo,* hair. Ceram. (Tobo), *ulon,* hair; *fulin,* feather. Amblaw, *ol-nati,* hair; *boloi,* feathers.

The West Aryan connections of this word, as designating hair, feathers, are not many nor very apparent. The application to express a quantity, at first indefinite and conventionally adopted as ten, within the Polynesian area, might lead us to refer it to the Sanskrit (Ved.) *pûru—*

which Benfey derives from *prî*—"much, many, exceeding."
But its limited use as a quantitative expression alongside
of its synonyms, as well as the total absence of the
application of this word to other matters conveying a
sense of quantity, leads me to infer that the quantitative
sense of *fulu*, as used singly or in compounds to express
the numeral ten, is secondary and derivative of the
original sense of hair, feathers, and has no connection with
the Sanskrit *pûru* or *prî*, unless it can be shown that these
latter are themselves derivative, in sense at least, if not
in form, from some older word with a primary meaning of
hair or feathers. I find, however, I think, a relative of
hulu, fulu, &c. in the

Greek *ιουλος*, down, the first growth of beard, the
down on some plants. Liddell and Scott refer *ιουλος* to
ουλος, iv. (vid. Greek-Engl. Dict., *s. v.*) It may be so ;
both words occur in Homer. But I notice that Homer
always uses *ουλος* as an adjective, an attribute of *θριξ*,
κομη, καρηνον, &c., whereas he uses *ιουλος* as a substantive
having its own well-defined meaning. *Ουλος*, conveying
the sense of "stout, thick, strong, crisp," may appropri-
ately apply to hair, beard, wool, and the like, but its
application to *ιουλος* would be destructive of the sense,
and I therefore consider that there is no connection in
root or derivation between them.

HUNA, *v.* Haw., to hide, conceal, protect, defend. N.
Zeal., Tah., *huna*, id. Rarot., Mang., *una*, id. Sam., *funa*,
conceal; *funai*, id. Fiji., *vuni*, hid, concealed. Derivs.
Haw., *huna, s.* the private parts, pudenda; *huna-huna*,
caves in mountains or underground where people took
refuge in time of war. Fiji., *vuni-langi*, the horizon.
Malg., *a-vuni*, to conceal, secrete. The root of this word is
doubtless found in the Tong. *fu-fu*, with same meaning,
"to conceal," and in the Sam. *fu*, with a derivative
meaning, "vagina, pudendum;" perhaps also in the Tah.
huhu, to close the mouth of a bag, to brail up a sail.

Sanskr., *guh*, to conceal, hide; *guhya*, hidden, a secret,
pudendum; *guhâ*, a cave, the heart; *gudh*, to cover,

referred by Benfey to *kuh*, surprise, deceive; *kuh-aka*, a juggler; *kuh-ara*, a cavern, cave.

Greek, κευθω, cover up, hide.

Sax., *hydan*, to hide. O. H. Germ., *hutta*, a hut; vid. Liddell and Scott, *s. v.* κευθω. Quær. Swed. *gynna*, to favour, befriend, protect; *gunst*, favour?

HUNE, *adj.* Haw., anciently it signified a collection of people, a class, tribe, or nation, as shown from the compound *Mene-hune*, the people of Mene. When that signification became obsolete, its meaning became equivalent to " a poor man, destitute, poor," with two derivatives, *ma-hune*, *ili-hune*, both meaning poor, destitute. Sam., *songa*, a chief's upper servant, exempt from the precautions of the tapu. N. Zeal., *hunga*, the common people, those who were not " Ariki " or " Rangatira." Rarot., *unga*, the tenants of the chiefs, labourers. Tah., *mana-hune*, the common people. In Haw. occurs also the simple form *hu*, designating a class of the common people, nearly synonymous with " Makaainana," the farmers.

The probable primary meaning of the Haw., Tah., *hune* and *hu*, N. Zeal., *hunga*, as a collection of men, a people or class of people, connects this word with the Polynes. *hui* in its etymon, *q. v.* p. 128.

HUPE. *s.* Haw., mucus from the nose, snot, slime. Tah., *hupe*, mucus, night-dew; *hupe-hupe*, dirty, despicable, mean. Sam., *sofe-sofe*, native dish of yam cooked in juice of cocoa-nut. Fiji., *sove, ka-sove*, soft, muddy, of earth. Akin to

Sanskr., *sûpa*, broth, soup, sauce.

Goth., *supon, sukwon*, to season, as with salt. Sax. *sipan, supan;* O. H. Germ., *supan, saufjan*, to sup up, drink greedily, as beasts. All referable to the Sanskr.-Polynes. *su, hu*, and its family of derivatives.

Greek, ὀπος, juice, vegetable juice.

Possibly Lat. *sapa*, thickened must, new wine boiled down, connects itself with the foregoing.

HUPO, *adj.* Haw., savage, ignorant, barbarous.

Sanskr., *yup*, to confuse, to trouble.

KA, *v.* Haw., to strike, dash, radiate, overthrow, finish, to curse, be angry, to doom. Tah., *ta,* to strike, to tattoo, repeat, relate. Sam., Marqu., *ta,* id., to reprove. Fiji., *ta,* to chop, cut lightly; *ca,* evil, bad, destroyed, spoiled. This word is the root of numerous derivatives, which will be referred to as they occur. I am not aware that this root has been preserved in any of·the West Aryan tongues, though its duplicated and derivative forms are abundant.

In Hawaiian *ka* is also an interjection of surprise and strong disapprobation. The Fijian *caca,* plural form of *ca,* is probably the nearest Polynesian correlative of

Greek, κακος, bad, evil. No etymon assigned by Liddell and Scott. In "Or. Ind.-Eur.," ii. 110, A. Pictet suggests that κακος is derived from Sanskrit *kak,* be unstable, vacillate, and that its primary meaning was "lâche, tremblant." But Sanskrit *kak* is probably itself a derivative or duplicated form of the original, and in the Polynesian preserved *ka,* in the sense of radiating, striking; whereas the Hawaiian *ka,* in the sense of to curse, be angry, and the Fijian *ca, caca,* bad; *ca-ta,* to hate, intr. *caca,* id., certainly correspond better with the Greek κακος.

KA'A,[1] *v.* Haw., to radiate, as rays of light from the sun, as cinders from a red-hot iron, to turn round, roll over, as a wheel, to pass off, away, from, to remove. Tong., *taka,* to go round, turn, roll. Sam., *ta'a,* to go at large, as animals and fish. Tah., *ta'a,* to fall, to remove; *tata,* to strike, to beat. Marqu., *tata,* to grind, triturate. Mang., *po-taka,* go round and round. Tong., Fak., N. Zeal., Tah., *takai, ta'au,* to bind round, to tie up; *s.* a ball. Sam., *ta'ai,* to wind round, to circle round, as smoke. Haw., *ka'ai,* to bind round, to girdle. In Tah., *ta'a* is also the chin of the face, a circular piece of wood under the rafters of a native house, separated, *i.e.,* struck off, cut off. In Haw., *ka'a* is a branch of a vine, a strand of a cord. Fiji., *qata,* surround, enclose.

Sanskr., *kak,* be unsteady; *kaksha,* a spreading creeper, the side or flank; *kakshâ,* armpit, end of the lower garment tucked into the waistband, a girdle, enclosure; *kakshya,* a girdle, an enclosed court, the cup of a balance; *chakra*, a wheel, a circle, a discus.

Pers., *chak*, a cart.

Greek, κυκλος, a ring, circle, wheel, a circular motion, a sphere, globe; κιρκος, a falcon or hawk that flies in circles or wheels, a circle; κιρκοω, to hoop round, secure with rings. Vid. Liddell and Scott, *s. v.*

Lat., *circus*, circle; *circino*, to round.

KA'A², *s.* Haw., also *ka'ao*, a tradition, a legend. Tah., *ta*, to repeat, relate; *ta'a-raa*, explication, separation; *ta'o*, *s.* a word, speech; *v.* to speak, address, bid, command. Tong., *ta'anga*, song, poetry. Sam., *ta*, to strike with a stick, beat as a drum, play on an instrument with the hands, to reprove, to tattoo; *ta'a-nio*, a roundabout way of speaking. Marqu., Mang., *takao*, to speak, tell, a word, information. Fiji., *tata*, speak indistinctly; *s.* an order, command. Malg., *tata*, acknowledgment, profession; *takho*, echo; *takon*, secret, mystery.

Sanskr., *kath*, to tell, announce, declare, converse, command; *kathá*, a tale, a speech, discourse; *katth*, to boast, praise, blame.

KA'I¹, *v.* Haw., to lift up the hand and carry, to lift up the foot and walk, to lead, guide, direct, bring, take in hand; *ka'i-ka'i*, to lift up, as the hands or the eyes, to take up, carry off, carry tenderly, as a child; *kaka'i*, to go in company, travel together, follow; *s.* a family, including servants, dependants, &c. Marqu., *taki*, to take, seize, remove. Fak., Tong., Mang., *taki*, to convey, bring along, lead, direct. Sam., *ta'i*, *ta'i-tai;* Tah., *ta'ita'i*, id. Rarot., *ta'i-ta'i*, a leader, conductor. Malg., *tak*, a gift, portion, settlement; *taten*, to bring along, apporter. Fiji., *taki-va*, carry water or food on a tray.

Sanskr., *tak*, to start (Ved.); *taksh*, to slice off, cut off, prepare, form (Ved.); *takshan*, a carpenter; *dagh*, to attain (Ved.)

Greek, τασσω, to arrange, put in order, to form; ταχυς comp. θασσων, sup. ταχιστος, quick, swift, fleet; τικτω, to bring into the world, to beget; τεχνη, art, skill, craft;

τοσσαις, Dor. aor. part. of an unknown pres., to happen, to be; τεκτων, a carpenter, craftsman; δεχομαι, to take, accept, receive.

Lat., *tango, tactum*, to touch, take, reach, arrive at; *tignum*, building materials; *texo*, to put together, make, frame, weave.

Goth., *tecan*, pt. t. *taitok*, to touch. Sax., *tœcan*, to take. Swed., *taga*, id. O. Norse, *tegia*, touch lightly, to tap. Sax. *teogan*, to pull, draw. Goth., *tiuhan*, pt. t. *tauh*, to tow, pull, draw, hence to lead, to guide; *mith-ga-tiuhan*, carry away; *bi-tiuhan*, to lead about. Swed., *tåg;* Germ., *zug*, expedition, procession, march, passage.

For other relatives vid. *s. v.* KAHA.

KAI², *s.* Haw., sea, salt water, brine, pickle, in opp. to *wai*, or fresh water. Tah., *ta'i*, id. Sam., *tai*, the sea, the tide. Tong., *tahi*, the sea, sea-water. Marqu., *tai*, id. Fiji., *taci*, the sea. Malg., *taikh*, the sea. In the pre-Malay dialects of the Indian Archipelago this word is applied to both sea and salt, as in Ceram. (Ahtiago), *tasi*, the sea; *tai-sin*, id.; *teisim*, salt. Matabello, *tahi*, the sea. Amboyna, *tasi*, salt. Saparua, *tasi*, id. Sunda, *tjai, tjahi*, water.

Sanskr., *kâç*, be visible, to shine; *kâçita*, resplendent; *kâçin*, shining; *kâsâra*, a pond.

The formation of a word to express sea and salt from a root conveying the sense of " shining, resplendent," has strong analogies throughout the Aryan family, and is as legitimate a process, and perhaps older in conception, as the Sanskr. *mîra*, Lat. *mare*, from *mri*, to die; as the Lat. *vastum*, desert; Sanskr., *vasra*, death; *vasu*, dry, sterile; *vasuku* and *vaçira*, sea-salt, from Sanskr. *vas* or *vast*, interficere, occidere, according to Pictet (*loc. cit.*, i. § 16). The sense of " shining, brightness," as applied to the Polynesian *taci, tahi*, or *ta'i*, is nearly obsolete, but lingers still in some of the composites, as in the Tah. *tai-ao*, dawn (brightness of the day or sky); as in the Marqu. *tai-tai*, proper, neat, bright; perhaps also in the Haw. *ai-ai*, bright, as moonlight, fair, white. The Sanskr.

kâsâra, pond, from *kaç*, to shine, is doubtless due to a similar conception, and confirms the Polynesian relation of *tai* or *kai*. In the Sunda dialect, alongside of *tjahi*, water, occurs *tjahaya*, to shine, to blink: there also the Sanskrit form and analogy of application are manifest.

KAO-KAO, *v.* Haw., be red. Root and primary meaning obsolete in Haw. Sam., *tao*, to bake. Marqu., *tao*, bake, roast, sacrifice. Tah., *tao*, baked, boiled, cooked.

Greek, καιω, Old Att. καω, to light, kindle, burn, scorch. According to Liddell and Scott, Pott refers καιω to Sanskrit *çush*, be dry, but Curtius rejects this.

In Dravid. (Tamil), *kay*, to be hot, burn.

KAU, *v.* Haw., to hang up, suspend, to tie or gird on, to put or place a thing, to fall upon, to put on, as a burden, to set or fix, as boundaries of a land, or a decree, to promulgate, as a law; in a neuter sense, to light down, as a bird, as a spiritual influence; *adj.* a setting of the sun, a resting, a roost for fowls; *kau-a*, to hesitate, be in doubt, suspense, to beg off; *kau-o*, to draw, as a load; morally, to endure, to incline to, to pray for some special blessing; *kau-oha*, a dying charge, bequest, covenant, commission, command; *kau-kai*, to wait for an event, to expect; *kau-kau*, to take counsel, to resolve, to chide, to reprove, to explain, make clear; *kau-la*, a rope, cord, tendon, a prophet, a seer; *kau-la-i*, to hang up, put up in the sun; *kau-lana*, fame, report, renown; *ma-kau*, be ready, prepared; *akau*, the right hand (dexter), to the right, to the north, north. In the Southern dialects we find: Tong., *tau*, to hang, overhang, impend, extend to, fit, be suitable; *ma-tau*, the right hand; *ta-tau*, equal, like (balanced); *tau-la*, a cable; *tau-ranga*, an anchoring place. Sam., *tau*, to rest on, light on, fall on; *faa-ta-tau*, to compare; *tau*, what is proper and right; *tau-au*, to tend towards, either decline or increase; *tau-me*, stretch up the hand and not reach, to desire and not obtain; *tau-i*, reward, payment, revenge; *tau-la*, an anchor, to anchor, the priest of a god; *tau-la-i*, to hang up to; *tau-langa*, a sacred offering, an anchorage; *tau-lalo*, let the hands drop in fighting, be conquered; *tau-tau*, to hang, hang up; *ma-tau*, right-hand side, an axe; *faa-tau*, equally, alike; *v.* to buy, barter, sell; *faa-tau-oa*, a merchant. Marqu., *tau*, to carry on the back; *tau-tau*, suspended, hung up; *ta-tau*, to count, reckon; *tau-a*, a rope, a priest; *a-tau*, *ka-tau*, an anchor. N. Zeal., *tau*, besides previous meanings, to meet; *ma-tau*, expert, dexterous, shrewd, Tah., *tau*, to hang upon, an anchor; *tau-ai*, to hang up, spread out, as clothes to dry; *tau-i*, price, cost, to exchange, buy; *tau-ra*, cord, a troop, crowd, be inspired, a prophet; *tau-e*, a swing, see-saw; *tau-piri*, tail for a kite; *tau-mata*, a visor, a mask; *tau-mi*, a breastplate, plastron; *a-tau*, right hand, to the right. Fiji., *tau*, to fall, as of rain, to fall upon; *tau-ca*, to place or put down a thing; *tau-nga*, a swinging shelf. Malg., *mang-hatau, mana-tao*, to place, put.

Sanskr., *kavi*, a wise man, a poet; *kâv-ya*, coming from old sages, a bard, a poem; *kavi-tâ*, poetry, wisdom. Benfey refers this word to *kû*, to cry, sound. Pictet, on the other hand (*loc. cit.*, ii. 480) remarks: " D'après le Dict. de Pétersbourg, l'origine de *kavi* est probablement la même que celle de *âkûta* ou *âkûti*, intention, motif, ce qui conduirait à une racine *kû* ou *ku*, perdue en sanskrit, mais conservée dans plusieurs langues européennes avec le sens de voir, prévoir, connaître, &c. Ici, sans doute, le grec κοεω, κοαω, pour κοϝεω, connaître, ainsi que ἀκούω, entendre—ἀκοη, audition, &c. Ensuite de latin *caveo*, prendre garde, être prudent, d'où *cautus, cautio*, &c.; l'anc. slave *ҫute*, cognoscere, *cutüe*, cognitio, *po-cuvati*, custodire, &c.; et, enfin, avec *s* prosthétique, l'ang.-sax. *scawian;* anc. all. *scawôn*, mod. *schauen*, conspicere, considerare, intueri, speculari, &c. La vraie signification de *kavi*, sage, prudent, et proprement voyant, explique comment ce nom, ainsi que *kavâ*, est devenu en zend celui du roi, dont l'office est de prévoir, de surveiller, de diriger avec sagesse et prudence. De là *kâvya*, royal, et le persan *kay*, grand roi, héros, et noble, &c. C'est ce qui empêche de rattacher, avec Benfey (Samav. Gl.), *kavi* à la rac. *ku*, sonare canere, qui expliquerait bien le sens de poête, mais non pas celui de sage et de roi."

May not that *ku* or *kû*, "perdue en sanskrit," be only a contracted and dialectical form of the still living Polynesian *kau, tau*, in its moral and secondary sense, "to be in doubt, to deliberate, to endure, to wait, take counsel, explain, a prophet, a seer, a priest?"

While thus the root, as well as the derivatives of this word, in its moral sense, have been retained and diffused throughout the Aryan family east and west, the analogies to the material and primary sense, so widely adopted in the Polynesian branch, seem to be totally wanting, or at least very deficient, in the West Aryan branches. I find, however, the following words, which may perhaps be classed in that category, and whose etymons are as yet doubtful or unsatisfactory:—

Sanskr., *kavaka*, a mushroom; *kavacha*, mail-armour; *kavara*, a braid of hair; *kavan-dha, kaban-dha*, a cloud, vapour; *kaulika*, a weaver. Of the last Benfey says, "*i.e.*, probably *kula-ika;*" but *kula*, a herd, flock, multitude, family, conveys no idea from which the name or occupation of a weaver can be derived. The other words stand in Benfey's Dictionary without any reference whatever.

Lat., *cautes*, a crag, peaked rock, as overhanging?

Greek, καυκαλις, an umbelliferous herb; καναξ, κηυξ, a gull, a seamew; καυκαλιας, a kind of bird—probably both so called from the floating, suspended character of their flight.

KAHA[1], *v.* Haw., to cut, hew, as timber, cut open; *kahe*, cut longitudinally, to slit; *kahi*, to cut, shave, slit, comb, rub gently. These three forms doubtless proceed from the same root. Sam., *tafa*, to cut, gash, scarify; *tafi*, to brush, sweep, shave. Tah., *taha*, a side; *taha-hu*, to skim, bale, ladle; *taha-taha*, declining, as the sun, wandering, as the eye; *tahi-tahi*, to brush with the hand, weed, wipe off, separate. Marqu., *kahi-kahi*, thin, slender, mince. Fiji., *tasi*, a razor; *tasi-a*, to shave; *tava*, to cut generally;

tavi-a, to brush the head with the hand, to slap a thing. Malg., *katsa*, incisions; *tatatch*, scarification. Timor, *taha*, a cleaver. Ceram. (Ahtiago), *tafim*, a chopper.

Sanskr., *taksh*, to slice wood, cut to pieces, to wound, to prepare, form; *takshan*, a carpenter; *tvaksh*, to produce, to work, to pare.

Zend, *tash*, to cut, fashion, to make, smoothe.

For other relatives see *s. v.* KA'I, TAKI, p. 135. I therefore only refer to—

Greek, τυκος, a hammer or pick; τυκανη, instrument for thrashing.

A.-Sax., *thixl, thisl;* O. H. Germ., *dishila, desha*, axe, adze.

Lith., *taszyti*, to cut with an axe; *taisyti,* arrange, prepare. Anc. Slav., *tesati*, to cut. Pol., *tasak*, cutlass.

It is very probable that the Polynesian N. Zeal. *toki to i, koi* (Sam. and Haw.), adze, hatchet, refers itself to this same family and its kindred forms expressive of the instrument of cutting.

It may be interesting to note in the development of language that the original root of this was probably subject to a twofold pronunciation, a guttural and a sibilant, of which some dialects have retained one, others the other, and some both. For instance:—Ved., *tak;* Zend, *tash;* Sanskr., *taksh;* Greek, τασσω, τεταχα; Lat., *tago, tactum;* Slav., *tesati;* Goth., *tekan;* Polynes., *taki, toki, tasi*, with sub-dialects *tafi, tahi.*

KAHA[2], *s.* Haw., the crack, as of a whip; the report, as of a pistol. Tah., *tafa,* sonorous, loud-sounding.

Sanskr., *kac,* to sound; *kaca, kashâ,* a whip.

KAHE, *v.* Haw., to run, as water, to flow, as a stream, to spill, pour out, drop, trickle. Sam., Tong., *tafe;* Tah., *tahe,* id. Malg., *tazun*, run out, leak, flow.

Sanskr., *cac (cas)*, jump, to move irregularly by leaping.

Irish, *casaim*, move about crookedly and rapidly; *cais*, a stream; *cas*, rapid, agile.

Armor., *kas*, quickness, speed.

To the Sanskrit *cac, cas*, or, as Pictet suggests, a still

older *kas,* refers the Sanskrit *çaça,* a horse, a rabbit; the O. H. Germ. *haso,* Mod. Germ. *hase,* Eng. *hare,* and Germ., Scand., Eng., *hast, haste, hasten.*

KAHU, *v.* Haw., to kindle or make fire, to burn, as lime in a pit, to cook, bake. Tah., *tahu,* id., to conjure, act as a sorcerer. Marqu., *tahu,* light fire, to cook. Sam., Tong., *tafu,* make up the fire; *tafu-la'i,* a large fire; *tafu-tafu,* an oven of lime. Rarot., *tau,* make fire. N. Zeal., *tahuna,* id. Fiji., *taou-na,* to broil, roast, set on fire; *tavu,* *s.* charred sticks; *tavu-cawa,* a steam-bath; *tavu-tavu,* to burn down, to clear the ground for planting; *tavu-teke,* a frying-pan. Perhaps the Malg. *tsembuk,* smoke, vapour, incense, refers itself to this family.

Sanskr., *tap,* to warm, to heat, to burn up, consume, mortify oneself; *tapa,* heat, hot season; *tapas,* fire, penance, mortification; *tapana,* warming, tormenting, the sun.

Zend, *tap,* to become warm; *tafnu,* burning. Pers., *taftan,* to burn.

Greek, θαπτω, perform funeral rites. Those rites in early times were performed by burning the body and burying the ashes; hence, doubtless, the original sense of the word was to burn. Ταφος, funeral, place of burial; τεφρη, ashes. Liddell and Scott remark that θαπτω is a "strengthened form of a root, ταφ, which appears in the fut. and aor. 2 pass., and in ταφος." They are probably correct, and that brings the Greek more in accord with the Zend *trafnu,* the Polynes. *tafu,* and the A.-Sax. *thefian.*

Lat., *tepeo,* be warm; *tepidus.*

A. Sax., *thefian,* æstuare.

Irish, *teboth,* heat.

Anc. Slav., *teplu, toply,* warm.

Scyth., *Tabiti,* the fire-goddess. Vid. Rawlinson's "Herodotus," iii. 160.

To this Polynesian *kahu, tafu,* refer themselves two words in a derivative sense, as a reminiscence of the times when the making and procuring fire was the greatest art discovered. One is Haw. *kahu,* *s.* an upper servant, guardian, nurse, feeder, keeper. Marqu., *tahu*, a cook. N. Zeal., *tahu*, a husband. The other is Haw. *kahuna*, a general name of an artificer exercising some trade or profession, and in a special sense applied to the priesthood. Tah., *tahua*, an artificer, a workman ; *tahu-tahu*, a class of priests, a sorcerer. Sam., *tufunga*, a carpenter, a tattoo-marker. N. Zeal., *tohunga*, a workman, artificer. Marqu., *tuhuka*, skilful, a priest. Probably also the Malg. *ampi-tahe*, a doctor, medicus.

KALA[1], *v.* Haw., only used in dupl. and comp. forms ; *kalakala*, rough, sharp, scraggy, knotty, harsh ; *kakala*, be rough, sharp ; *s.* the breaking of the surf, the point of a needle, the spur of a cock ; *hookala*, to sharpen, to whet ; fig. to sharpen the tongue, to speak injuriously of one. Tong., *tala*, thorn ; *tala-tala*, thorny, rough, prickly. N. Zeal., *tara-tara*, id.; *tara*, the upright poles in a fence. Tah., *tara*, thorn, sharp point, cock's spur ; *to-tara*, the sea-urchin, echinus. Sam., *tala*, a thorn, the barb of a spear ; *tala-tala*, prickly, rough. In all the foregoing, *tara*, *tala*, and *kala* also mean the gable end of a house. Fiji., *karo*, prickly. Matabello and Teor, *gala-gala*, a spear. Biaju, *ti-kala*, a post. Malg.; *tolan*, adze, angle, fish-bone, bone.

Sanskr., *kara*, the tip of the hand or of a ray ; *karkata*, a crab ; *karkara*, hard, firm, harsh, cruel ; *karj*, to pain ; *kâranâ*, torture ; *kârâ*, jail, prison ; *khara*, solid, sharp, hoarse, *s.* an ass ; *kharj*, to creak ; *châraka*, prison.

Pers., *charas*, prison, pain, torture.

Greek, καραβος, a beetle ; καρκινος, a crab, a pair of tongs ; καρκαρον, prison ; καρδος, a thistle ; καρις, lobster ; καρχαρος, sharp-pointed, jagged ; χαραξ, a pointed stake ; καρχαριας, a shark ; χαραδρά, a mountain torrent.

Lat., *calx*, heel ; *calcar*, spur ; *carcer*, prison ; *cancer*, crab ; *horreo*, stand on end, as hair, bristle, be rough, shiver.

A.-Sax., *hearm*, damage, injury ; *harrow*, *v.* and *s.* *hallus*, rock, stone. Goth., *kara*, care, anxiety. Swed., *kärf*, rough, rude, harsh.

Anc. Slav., *karati*, to quarrel. Russ., *kara*, punishment. Lith., *kora*, id.; *kaline*, prison.

KĀLA², *v.* Haw., to loosen, untie, separate from, put off, absolve, spare; *kala-i*, to hew, cut, pare, divide out, apportion. Sam., *tala*, to loosen, untie; *tatala*, id., release from contract or obligation; *tala-to*, to undo, to let go a thing; *tala-i*, to adze, chip off; *tala-ia*, be relieved, freed. N. Zeal., *tara*. Tah., *tara, tatara*, untie, set free; *tara-i*, to chop or adze, as a piece of timber; *tara-e-hara*, expiation, forgiveness of sin. Marqu., *taa-i*, to cut off, chop, chip; *taai-taai*, to carve. Fiji., *tala*, to send off, a messenger; *tala-voka*, a landslip. Sunda, *tulun*, to loosen, unbind. Tagal., *tolon*, to help. Malg., *hala*, take off, remove from; *mang-hala*, to steal, pillage, divest; *mang-hala-mifant*, release from an oath (= Sam., *tatala*), *mi-hala*, to leave, quit.

Sanskr., *kart*, to loosen; *kartrikâ*, a hunter's knife; *krit*, to cut down, cut off, extract; *karhtarî*, scissors.

Greek, χαλαω, to slack, loosen, rend, let go, be indulgent, to pardon; χαλ-ειμας, loose-robed, ungirt, of the Bachantes; κλαω, break off, break in pieces; κλασις, fracture. Perhaps κειρω, cut short, as hair, to shave, shear, cut or hew out, to ravage, pillage. This latter word Liddell and Scott refer to Sanskrit *crî*, to hurt, wound, be broken, while they give no etymon for χαλαω, nor for κλαω. Benfey, however, refers κλαω to *cri*. I think more probable that κλαω is but a contraction of χαλαω. To *kart* and *krit* Benfey refers the Lat. *culter*, Sanskr. *karttrikâ*, but Liddell and Scott refer *culter* to Sanskr. *crî*, Greek κειρω. The Polynesian offers an easier, and, I venture to say, an older etymon to all these varying forms, even to *crî*, if wanted.

Lat., *clades*, breaking, breakage, damage, loss; *classis*, a division, a class; *talea,* a cutting, branch, stake, any small piece cut off; *colo*, with perhaps a primary sense of "to break," to till, to cultivate; *culter* a ploughshare, a knife generally; *cortex*, back, rind.

Irish, *tallan*, cut off. Welsh, *toli*, separate.

Icel., *talga*, hew, chip off, smoothe. Swed., *tälja*, to cut, chip, carve. A.-Sax., *scearan*, to share, divide. In Norse and N. Engl. *scar*, a cut off, precipitous rock, retained in names of places, as "*Scar*-borough," &c. Swed., *skär*, broken, scattered rocks off a coast.

To this Polynesian *kala, tala*, in the sense of separating, dividing, apportion, I think may justly be referred the Sanskrit *kalâ*, a small part, a portion, a division of time, as well as *kâla*, time period. Benfey refers *kalâ* to *kri ;* but the compounds *nish-kala*, undivided, and *sa-kala*, whole, as well as *kalâ-pa* (vb. 2. *pâ*), a bundle, totality, imply a root indicating previous separation, division, &c., rather than "making, doing, performing," the primary sense of *kri*. In the Polynesian (Haw.) *kala* is also applied to time, but always accompanied with a negative, as "*aole e kala*," not lately, some time ago, long ago ; and from its conventional use it is evident that time was not its primary sense, any more than it is of the Sanskrit *kalâ* or *kâla*. Probably in the same way that the English *tale*, *tally*, and *score*, derived from the same root, were applied to numbers, so *kala* was applied conventionally to time, and the Haw. "*aole e kala*," lit. "not to be scored," while preserving the primary sense, came to signify time past and long gone. Outside of the Polynesian and Sanskrit I am not aware that this word in its application to time has any analogues in the other Aryan branches.

Another derivative, probably, is the Hawaiian *kalana*, to strain, filter, as through a cloth or the fibres of the cocoa-nut husk, to separate ; *s.* a strainer, filter. Its correlative, I think, is the Latin *colum*, a strainer, *colo-are*, to strain, purify. Pictet (Or. Ind.-Eur., ii. 286) refers *colum* to the Sanskrit *chal*, to move, tremble, shake, and *châlanî*, a sieve. Though the result may be the same, yet it seems to me that there is a great difference in the underlying sense of a "sieve," that must be shaken, and a "strainer" or "filter," that must be squeezed or perform their function while at rest, in order to separate the good from the worthless. The Latins—so far as my reading goes—did not use the words *colum* and *cribrum* interchangeably. One represented one method of separation, the other another. I prefer, therefore, to ally the Latin *colum* to the Polynesian *kala* and *kalana.*

KALA[3], *v.* Haw., to proclaim, cry, publish, call out, invite, send for; *ku-kala,* id. ; *s.* a public crier. Tong., *tala,* to speak, tell, bid. Sam., *tala,* to tell, relate, a narrative, news; *tala-i,* to proclaim; *tala-a-lelo,* to lie ; *tala-u,* to make a noise, as a number of people talking together; *tala-tala,* converse, relate ; *tala-tala-o,* to cackle as a hen, to scold. Mang., *tala-u,* to call. N. Zeal., *karanga,* to call. Malg., *talakh, talak,* public, regard, evidence.

Greek, καλεω, to call, invite, invoke, to name ; κλεος, rumour, report, fame; καλανδρα, a lark.

Lat., *calo,* to call, call out, convoke ; *calator, calendæ, clamo.*

Icel., *tel,* to call, to name. Scand., *tala,* to speak, say, tell. Swed., *kalla,* to call, to name; *tolka,* to interpret, explain.

Sanskr., *kal,* to sound, to count ; *kala-kala,* confused noise ; *kala,* dumb (Ved.), indistinct, confused, low-voiced; *kalaha,* a quarrel.

KALI, *v.* Haw., to wait, to tarry, to stay, expect, hesitate ; *s.* slowness, hesitancy of speech, the edge of a board, leaf, &c. ; *kakali,* to wait, be detained ; *kali-kali,* to fall behind, be not quite even with something else. Sam., *tali,* to wait for, to answer, to receive, *adv.* nearly ; *tatali,* to wait for. Tah., *tatari,* to wait, expect, delay. N. Zeal., *tatari,* id.

Lat., *tardus,* slow, tardy.

Germ., *harren,* to stay, wait for, delay, tarry. Swed., *dröja,* stay, tarry, stop.

I know not what Zend or Sanskrit word may be akin to Latin *tardus,* but, until a better one is found, I think myself justified in referring it to the Polynesian *kali, tari.* It may be noted that, according to Dr. Caldwell's Comp. Gram. Dravid. Lang., in the Tamil *tari* signifies " to remain." Have the Dravidians borrowed it from pre-

Vedic Aryans, or have the Polynesians borrowed from the Dravidians?

KALO, *s.* Haw., one of the class of gods called "*Akua noho*," the fixed or stable gods; *kalo-kalo*, to pray to the gods. Tah., *taro-faro*, id. Sam., *talo-sanga, talo-talonga,* a prayer, praying. Fiji., *kalo-kalo*, a star; *kalo-u*, a god, also a falling star, which the natives take for a god. Malg., *terak-afu*, feux-follets, météores; *terak-anru*, dawn, day-break; *terak-hal*, twilight. This word, with the meaning of "a star," perhaps also of "sun," still survives in several of the pre-Malay dialects of Asonesia. S. Celebes (Bouton), *kati-popo*, a star. Buru (Massaratty), *tolo-ti*, id. Ceram. (Tobo), *tol*, id. Gilolo (Gani), *be-tol*, id. Matabello, *tolu*, id. Biajau, *kuli-ginta*, id. Salibabo, *alo*, the sun. Celebes (Salayer), *mata-alo*, id.

Sanskr., *târa*, a star, the pupil of the eye; *târâ*, a meteor, a shooting star, the name of deities.

Greek, τειρεα, the heavenly constellations, signs; τερας, a sign, wonder, omen, signs in the heaven, star, meteor.

Benfey refers *târa*, a star, to an "original *stâra*, cf. 3 *stri*," and refers this 3 *stri* to "probably 2 *as*+*tri*," a shooter, from 2 *as*, to throw. Max Müller and others refer *târa* to original *stâra*, from 1 *stri*, to spread, expand, to strew. Liddell and Scott, after Curtius, refer Sanskr. *staras, târâ,* Zend *açtar, çtar*, Greek τειρος, τερας, Lat. *astrum, stella,* &c., to a root ἀστρ; but *s. v.* τειρος they seem to doubt its connection with ἀστηρ, *staras, târâ*. Without presuming to decide between such authorities, it seems to me that the existence of the cognate Polynesian terms in *kalo, kali, terak, tolo, kuli,* as names for stars and meteors, would indicate an older and a common formation of *târâ*, τερας, τειρος, and the Polynesian terms from some root other than the comparatively later *stri* or a supposed compound like *as*+*tri*. Whether the Polynesian, Sanskrit, and Greek forms connect themselves in preference to Sanskrit *tri* (*taritum*, inf.), to pass over, to hasten, or to *tur* (Ved.), to hasten, or to *tvar*, make haste, be swift, I leave abler men to decide, though probably all go back to some primary form from which they diverged with different shades of meaning. The employment of the Sanskrit *târâ* as "a name of deities," and of the compound *Turâ-sâh* as a name or epithet of Indra and Vishnu, brings it *en rapport* with the Polynesian *kalo, kalo-u,* a class of gods, a god.

The Fijian, where so much Polynesian archaic lore was deposited, seems to be, in this case, the connecting link between the Asonesian (pre-Malay) and Sanskrit primary conception of the word as a star, a meteor, now lost in Polynesia proper, and the secondary conception of it as a deity and a religious performance.

KAMA[1], *s.* Haw., first husband of a wife; *kama-i,* to play the whoremonger for hire; *kama-kama,* to practise prostitution; *hoo-kama-kama, s.* a prostitute; probably akin to Marqu., *kami-kami,* to desire; Fiji., *kami kami-ca,* sweet, agreeable, pleasant.

Sanskr., *kam,* to love, to desire; *kâm-ya,* agreeable; *kâma,* wish, desire, love, the god of love; *kâma-tva,* love of pleasure; *kâma-rasika,* libidinous; *kâmâtman,* voluptuous, sensual; *kâmin,* desiring, having sexual intercourse, a lover; *kânti* = *kam* + *ti,* beauty.

Lat., *carus* = *kam-ra,* beautiful, charming; *amo,* to love; *amœnus,* agreeable (Benfey).

KAMA[2], *v.* Haw., to bind, tie, make fast, tie up, as a bundle, to lead, direct; *kama-kama,* to bind, tie on. With Caus. *hov-,* to adopt as a child; "*keiki-hookama,*" an adopted child. Fiji., *tama-ta,* tame, domesticated.

Connected with this probably primary sense of "to tie, fasten, connect, direct," is the Polynesian word *kama, tama,* as expressing a family relation, mostly that of children, sometimes of the father, as in the Sam. and Fiji. *tamā,* and Tong. *tamai;* Malg., *tamaha,* tamed, a domestic; *taman,* habitude, custom, tamed, a heifer.

Sanskr., *dam,* to tame; *dam-ana,* subduing; *dam-pati,* master of a house. Ved., *dam, dama,* house, dwelling. Zend, *demâna,* house.

Greek, δαμαζω, δαμαω, to tame, break in, bring under

the yoke; δμως, a slave; δμητηρ, a tamer; δαμαλης, a subduer; δαμαλις, a heifer, a girl; δομος, a house; δομη, a building; δεμω, to build.

Lat., *domo*, to tame, subdue; *domitus, dominus, domus, domicilium.*

Irish, *damh, daimh*, house, family; *damh*, cattle; *domhan*, a young bull.

Pers., *dam*, any tame beast.

Armen., *dohm*, house, family.

A.-Sax., *tam*, tame; *tamjan*, to tame; *team*, family, race. Goth., *ga-tamjan*, to tame; *ga-timan*, to suit, agree with. O. H. Germ., *zamon*, to tame. Germ., *zaum*, bridle. Mod. Eng., *team*, two or more animals harnessed together. Swed., *töm*, reins to a bridle; *tam*, tame; *tomt*, a house, lot.

I cannot better explain the relation of the words signifying "house, family," to those signifying "to tame, to subdue," than by quoting from A. Pictet (Orig. Ind-Eur., ii. 237):—"La racine en sanskrit est *dam*, domitum, mitem esse et domare, et le Dict. de P. voit dans *dama*, non pas la maison matérielle, mais le lieu où règne et domine le chef de la famille, ce qui résulterait d'ailleurs de l'emploi de ce mot dans les Vêdas. Il y est ajouté que, d'après cela, il faudrait séparer le grec δομος de δεμω, construire, ce qui semble cependant fort difficile. Le grec pourrait bien ici, comme le pense Lassen (Anthol. Sans. Gloss.), avoir conservé, mieux que le sanskrit, le sens primitif de la racine *dam*, qui doit avoir été celui de lier. Cf. δεω, qui serait à δεμω, comme le sans. *dâ*, ligare, à *dam*, et comme *gâ*, ire, à *gam*. On conçoit, en effet, que, de la notion de lier, soient provenues secondairement, d'une part celle de dompter, de même que l'allemand *bändigen*, vient de *band* et de *binden*, et de l'autre celle de construire. La première est restée attachée au sanskrit *dam*, en accord avec plusieurs autres langues ariennes, grec δαμαω (auquel on ne saurait rapporter δομος), lat. *domo*, cymr. *dofi*, armor. *doñva*, goth. *tamjan*, &c.; la seconde ne s'est maintenue que dans le grec δεμω, car le goth. *timrjan*, ædificare, que l'on a comparé, est probablement tout différent (Cf. I. i. p. 209). Si *dama* et δομος dérivent en réalité de *dam* dans son acception la plus ancienne, ces noms auraient désigné la maison en tant que construction dont les parties sont *liées* entr'elles, ce qui peut s'entendre à la lettre du mode tout primitif de construire avec des bois et des branches entrelacées. Dans l'état de la question, une décision finale n'est guère possible." But the preservation of the primitive sense "to bind, tie on," in the Polynesian *kama*, *tama*, may greatly aid in arriving at that "decision;" and the family relation expressed in the Polynesian *kama*, *tama*, child, children, lit. qui connexe sunt, as well as the Caus. *hoo-kama*, to adopt as a child, lit. to cause to be connected, scil. with another, clearly indicate a very ancient mode of transition of sense, which I think may be recognised also in the A.-Sax. *team*, family, progeny, a word springing, doubtless, directly from some ancient form in *tam*, with the same sense of binding, connecting, as the Polynesian *kama*, *tama*.

Apropos of this A.-Sax. *team*, it is interesting to note how, in the evolution of language, words frequently, after centuries of service in secondary and derivative senses, return gradually and imperceptibly to the primitive sense, the root idea. The English *team* no longer signifies "family, progeny, race," but two or more animals harnessed together, because of their being bound or fastened together; and the Swed. *töm*, *tömmar*, the Germ. *zaum*, reins, bridle, no longer represent their immediate ancestors, the O. H. Germ. *zâmon* and the Goth. *tamjan*, to tame, subdue, but the far older and long-disused sense of to tie, to fasten, bind, connect.

The Fijian *tama-ta*, tame, domesticated, is especially valuable as showing the transition from the primitive sense of "to tie, to bind," to the West Aryan sense of "taming, subduing," in δαμαω, *tamjan*, *domo*, &c.

KAMA[3], *adj.* Fiji., burnt, fired; *kama-ca*, to burn, set on fire. Tah., *tama-u*, tinder on which to catch sparks of fire; *tamau-o*, keep burning, as a firebrand for the night.

Sam., *tamata,* to burn dimly, as the fire of an oven. Probably the Haw. *amau, amaumau,* fern, brake, used as tinder to catch the fire from the fire-sticks.

Greek, καμινος, oven, furnace, kiln; never an open fire.

Sanskr., *tâmra,* coppery-red colour, copper; *tâmarasa,* a lotus.

Liddell and Scott suggest that καμινος is derived "perhaps from καιω, καω," to light, to kindle, to burn, and indicate that καιω, καω, are altered forms of καϝω. Benfey refers *tâmra* to Sanskrit *tam,* Ved. to choke, *tamas,* darkness, gloom, night, and gives no etymon to *tâmarasa.* I think both those references are not well chosen. Liddell and Scott themselves seem to doubt the correctness of their reference. If καϝω is an older form of καιω, καω, would not that indicate a connection with ταφος, θαπτω, Sanskr. *tap,* Zend *tafnu,* Polynes. *tafu, kahu, q. v.?* In regard to the reference of *tâmra* by Benfey from *tam* and *tamas,* it is difficult to trace the connection and transition of sense from "to choke, to be dark, be night," to the "red colour of copper" and "the lotus." I hold, therefore, that there must have been, in more ancient times, a form in *kam* or *tam* corresponding in sense to the Polynesian "to burn" or "to be of a reddish colour," like fire, with which the Sanskrit *tâmra* and *tâmarasa* are connected, lost in Sanskrit but preserved in Polynesian.

KAMAA, *s.* Haw., shoes, sandals, any covering for the feet, made of kapa-cloth, rushes, or other materials, when travelling over scoria or other rough ground. Tah., *tamaa,* id. Rarot., *tamaka,* id.

Illyr., *zamaa,* boots. According to Pictet (*loc. cit.,* ii. 302), derived from the Persian *sham, shamam, shamal,* id. But what is the ancient form and the ancient meaning of the Persian; and why should the Illyrians have borrowed from the Persians? May not the Siapôsh *kamis,* cloth, stuff, Old Irish *caimmse,* covering, garment, Welsh *camse,* chemise, suggest an older form and an older sense, and thus lead back to the Polynesian *kama,* to tie up, bind on (*vide supra*), in the same way that the Sanskrit *upâ-nah* leads back to a similar meaning—"what is tied under," scil. the foot?

A. Pictet (*loc. cit.*, p. 300), speaking of the Siapôsh *kamis*, says: "Ce terme intéressant offre une preuve nouvelle de l'origine orientale de l'anc. irl. *caimmse*, vestis, cymr. *camse*, chemise, corn. *kams*, surplis, armor. *kamps*, aube, d'où Zeuss fait provenir le bas-latin *camisia*, &c. (Gr. Celt. 749). Cf. ags. *cemes*, du celtique ou du latin, et, pour les langues néo-latines, Diez, Roman. Spr. V. cit. L'arabe *gamic*, vêtement de dessous, qui n'a pas d'etymologie sémitique, paraît à Diez importé d'Europe, mais il pourrait l'être de la perse, si le mot Siapôsh venait à se retrouver dans les langues iraniennes. On a comparé, non sans raison peut-être, quant à la racine, le goth. *hamôn*, vetir, ags. *hama*, *homa*, peau, chemise, scand. *hamr*, *hams*, peau, anc. all. *hemithe*, *hemidi*, chemise, &c., mais les corrélatifs orientaux manquent jusqu'à présent." The Polynesian offers those "correlatives."

KAMALA, *s.* Haw., a booth, temporary house or shed; *v.* to thatch with uhi-leaves for a temporary house; *adj.* temporary, as such thatching or covering. Perhaps Malg., *tamanga*, tomb.

Sanskr., *kmar*, to be crooked. Perhaps also *kamatha*, a tortoise, whose relation to *kam* (to love), under which it is placed in Benfey's Sansk.-Eng. Dict., is certainly not very apparent, but which might be related to *kmar* on account of its "crooked" and vaulted back.

Zend, *kamere*, vault. Persian, *kamar*, id. Armen., *gamar*, id.

Greek, καμαρα, anything with an arched cover, a vaulted chamber, a covered carriage or boat; καμαρωσις, vaulting, arching over; καμαρος or καμμαρος, a kind of crab or lobster.

Lat., *camera*, a vault, an arched roof or ceiling.

KANA, *s.* Haw., only used in compounds. A prefix to numerals indicating a multiplier by ten, as *kana-kolu*, *kana-ha*, *kana-lima*, &c., ten times 3, 4, 5, *i.e.*, 30, 40, 50,

&c. Its original meaning was doubtless equivalent to a score, a tally, a total, a given conventional amount. In view of the Fijian *canga*, a span, the stretch of the fingers, I have no doubt that it is but a dialectical variation of *kano*, the bones of the fore-arm, a cubit measure, *q. v.* If so, a remarkable instance of early idiomatic affinity between the West Aryan and the Polynesian presents itself in the Haw. *kana-lua*, doubt, uncertainty, hesitation, lit. "two measures, two scores, two hands;" for the Lat. *dubius*, *dubito*, the Sax. *tweon*, *tweogan*, Goth. *tweifls*, the Germ. *zweifeln*, the Swed. *twifla*, bespeak the same origin in mode of thought and expression.

Liddell and Scott, *s. v.* ἑκατον, one hundred, "often loosely for very many," refer it to Sanskrit *çatas*, which they say "is a link between ἑκατον and *centum*." But *çata*, like *daça*, must originally have been but a conventional word to express a more or less definite number, having a previous meaning of its own, now perhaps lost, or at least doubtful. The presence of the *n* in the Latin *centum* and the Gothic *hund* are as likely to indicate the earlier form of this word as its absence in ἑκατον and *çata*. Granted that both are dialectical variants of an older form, are there any traces still to be found in the West Aryan branches that might lead us to the primary meaning of that older form before it settled down into the conventional signification of one hundred? Such meaning almost certainly was connected with the conception of a "hand-full," "an arm-full," a "capacity to hold or contain a certain quantity," or with the conception of "plenty, abundance," suggested by some natural object. Let it be borne in mind that the Sanskrit does not always convey the oldest form of a given word. The other West Aryan branches contain more or less vocables of older date and form than their relatives met with in the Sanskrit. Hence it is often difficult to decide whether such or such a word has retained its original, or at least most ancient, form, or been strengthened by subsequent addition or weakened by elision; as in this word now under consideration. Was *n* in *centum* a subsequent strengthening of an original or more ancient form, or was its absence in *catau* a weakening of the older form? In the Gothic and its congeners we find *hund*, hundred; *hinthan*, pft. *hanth*, pp. *hunthans*, to catch with the hand; *handus*, the hand; *hunths*, captivity; *hansa*, a company, a multitude, perhaps originally "a hand-full." Sax., *hund*, hundred; *hond, hand*, hand; *hentan*, to seize, take. Perhaps the German *ganz*, entire, all, total, full; Welsh, *cant*, a hundred, a complete circle, a hoop, a wheel. In Greek, κοντα in τριακοντα, τεσσαρακοντα, thirty, forty, &c., seems to be a multiplier by ten like the Polynesian *kana*, and was doubtless as old as *cata, centum*, or *hund*. In "Orig. Ind.-Eur.," ii. 570, this subject is fairly treated, though I must differ from Mr. Pictet as to the derivation of the different forms—*cat, can,* κατο, κοντα, *cem, cent,* &c. —to which he refers. He traces them to Sanskrit "*cam*, de *kam*, d'où dérive un nom de la main *cama*, pour *kama*. Au transitif au causatif *camay*, cette racine signifie sedare, quietare, et *cama* désigne la main qui apaise en caressant. . . . Le sens primitif semble avoir été celui de passer doucement la main sur quelque chose." I do not think it correct to derive the name of the agent from the act, in every instance at least, and especially in this. The ancient Aryans undoubtedly had some primary word or words wherewith to designate hand, foot, &c., without reference to what particular and varying uses these earliest objects of man's knowledge and consciousness may be put. I hold, therefore, that some primary word, common to the entire Aryan family in its earlier days, and with a general well-defined sense of "the hand," underlies the formation of such numerals as the Sanskr. *da-can*, the Goth. *tai-hun, te-hund, ti-gus, ti-guns*, the Lat. *-ginti, -ginta*, in *vi-ginti, tri-ginta*, &c., the Greek *-κοντα* in τρια-κοντα, &c., the Javan. (Basa Krima) *gan-sal* (5), the Sunda *gan-ap* (6), the Sulu Isl. *gane* (6), the Polynes. Haw. *kana* (10). That primary word with its primary sense nearly intact I find in the Malg. *tang, tangh*, hand, arm, claw, paw wing; Iawau. and Malay., *tangan*, hand; *tangkap*, to grasp, to catch with the hand; Mysol., *kanin*, hand; *kanin-pap*, foot; Fiji., *canga*, the stretch of the fingers, a span; Sam., *tenga*, upper part of the arm, also the thigh; *tango*, to touch, take hold, to feel; Haw., *kano*, the two bones of the lower arm, a cubit in measure, the handle of an axe, shovel, &c.; Marqu., *tano*, to catch, grasp; N. Zeal., *tango*, take in the hand; Timor Laut., *tanu-var*, fore-arm; Deriv. Greek, χανδανω, to take in, hold, contain; Lat., *hendo* in *pre-hendo*, to catch, grasp.

KANA², *s.* Haw., the outside of the neck; *kani-ai*, the throat, the windpipe, the Adam's apple. Sam., *tanga'ai*, the crop of a bird, the stomach. Fiji., *tanga*, a bag, pocket; *tanganga*, the neck, the head of a mast.

Sanskr., *kânana*, the throat; *kandhara*, the neck.

KANA³, *v.* Haw., to see, appear, get sight of. Sam., *tanga'i*, to look-out for; *tanga-tangai*, to look about, to look-out for. Probably related to this is the Polynesian *Kane, Tane*, the name of one of the oldest of their gods, the *deus deorum* among those tribes who retained his worship. From numerous prayers, legends, chants, and astronomical applications of the name, it is evident that it primarily represented a lingering reminiscence of planet-worship, and was a synonym for sunlight, the opposite to darkness and its associate ideas.

Sanskr., *kan*, to shine; *kanaka*, gold; *chand*, to shine; *chandana*, sandalwood, saffron, the moon; *chandra*, the moon.

Lat., *canus*, bright, clear, white, grey; *candeo*, be shining white; *caneo*, be white or grey; *candela*, a wax-taper, candle; *accendo*, set on fire, light up; *scintilla*, a spark.

Greek, ξανθος, golden yellow, bright yellow. Liddell and Scott say it is akin to ξουθος, tawny, yellowish, and derive this from ξεω, ξυω, to plane, smoothe, polish, scrape. Scraping, polishing, may produce a "shining" surface, but why that sheen should necessarily be of a yellow or golden colour, more than of green, blue, or black, I fail to see.

Benfey refers both ξανθος and ξουθος to *chand*, to shine; σπινθηρ, a spark.

Welsh, *can* or *cain*, bright, fair, white. Irish, *cann*, full moon.

To the same family of words and their etymon doubtless refer themselves the Greek *Zαν*, the Latin *Janus*. *Zαν* was the older, the Doric appellation of *Ζευς*, and Italy knew no older god than *Janus*. On Cretan coins *Zαν* was written *Ταν* (Liddell and Scott, *s. v.*)

KANAKA, *s.* Haw., man, human, mankind, a common man in distinction from chiefs. Sam., N. Zeal., Tong., *tangata*, id. Tah., *taata*, id. Marqu., *enata, enana*, id. Malg., *zanak, zanaka*, children, offspring. Javan., Sunda, Malay., S. Celebes, Sanguir, *anak*, child. Matabello, *enena*, id. Sula Isl., *ninana*, id. Bouton (Celebes), *oanana*, id.

Sanskr., *janatâ*, mankind; *janaka*, a father, a producer; *janana*, id.; *jana*, creature, mankind collectively, and individually a person; *jantu*, a creature, a man, from *v. jan*, to bring forth, produce, be born, to grow.

Zend, *zan*, nasci, oriri; *zantu*, a tribe.

Lat., *genus, gens, gigno*, old form *geno*, &c.

Greek, γενος, race, stock, family, offspring; γιγνομαι, γενεσις, γονη, &c.

A.-Sax., *cyn*, race, stock. Goth., *kuni*, sex. Swed., *kön*, id. O. H. Germ. *kind*, child; *kuning*, king.

To the Sanskrit *janaka* Benfey refers the Greek ἀναξ, in Homer ϝαναξ, lord, master. Liddell and Scott give no etymon to ἀναξ.

KANA-LOA. Haw., one of the ancient gods from the time of chaos; in most of the Southern Polynesian groups considered and worshipped as the creator of the world, and superior to other gods; in Hawaiian mythology sometimes, though rarely, considered the equal of *Kane, Ku,* and *Lono*, but in the older legends referred to as god of the infernal regions, sometimes distinct from, sometimes the same as, Milu. Sam., N. Zeal., *Tangaloa;* Tong. *Tanaloa;* Marqu., *Tanaoa;* Tah., *Taaroa*. It is a compound word—*Tana* and *loa*, "the great, large Tana." In, a Marquesan legend of the creation it is said that before light (*Atea*) and sound (*Ono*) were evolved or stepped forth from the primeval night, chaos (*Po*), *Tanaoa*, and *Mutuhei* —which are explained to mean "darkness" and "silence" —ruled supreme. So far as I know, but one Polynesian word is now current signifying "darkness" or its correlatives, that may be considered akin to *tana*, and that is the Marquesan *tano, tanzo, tako*, "shade, shadowy, obscure." It was a tabu word, and, as such in many other instances, fell out of use and became obsolete for common uses in the vernacular. In the West Aryan branches this word is not frequent. I find, however, Latin *tenebræ*, darkness, gloom, a composite word like *fune-bris, lugu-bris*, &c. Benfey refers *tenebræ* to the Sanskrit *tamas*, darkness, gloom, and also the Anglo-Saxon *dun, thystre*. I think the Saxon *dunn*, a dark, black-brown colour, the English *tan, tawney*, the Swedish *dunkel*, gloomy, dark, *dåna*, to faint, swoon, *dån-ögd*, dim-eyed, ally themselves to the Latin and Polynesian group.

KANE, *s.* Haw., a man, a male, a husband; S. Polyn. ubique, *tane*, id. Refers doubtless to the same root as *kanaka*, viz., the Sanskrit *jan* or the Zend *zan*, vid. p. 154. It was held by some of the Hawaiian priesthood that man was called *kane*, after his maker, the god *Kane;* but that is apparently a priestly gloss in comparatively later heathen times.

KANI, *v.* Haw., to make a noise, to hum, sound, cry, to strike, as a clock, to rumble, as thunder, to squeak, as shoes, to crow, as a cock ; *s.* a singing, ringing sound, with numerous compounds. Tah., *ta'i*, to cry, to lament, to sound as an instrument. N. Zeal., Tong., Sam., *tangi*, to cry, to weep, to chirp, to roar, to sing. Marqu., *tangi, taki*, make noise, hum, sound, howl. Fiji., *tangi*, cry, weep, lament, to sing as birds.

Sanskr., *tan 2* (Ved.), to sound ; *tåna*, a musical tone; *tåntra*, instrumental music ; *stan*, to sound, sigh, thunder; *stanana*, groaning, Benfey refers Sanskrit *tan* to *stan*, as being "akin," and refers the Latin *tono* and the A.-Sax *thunor* to both. Liddell and Scott, following Curtius, refer *tono* and A.-Sax. *thunjan* to the Greek τείνω and Sanskrit *tan* 1, to draw, to spread. In view of the Polynesian affinities, I prefer to follow Benfey, and, considering *s* in *stan* as a prosthetic merely, I would refer *tono*, *tonitru*, and *thunjan*, *thunor*, to *tan* 2, and to the Polynesian *tangi*, *kani*. Also,

Icel., *stynja*, to sigh, groan; Germ., *stöhnen*, id., *donner*, thunder.

Greek, στένω, to groan, lament.

Lat., *cano*, to sing, cry, sound; *tono*, to thunder, and their derivatives.

Welsh, *can*, a song; *canu*, to sing; Armor., *cana*, *canein*, id.

KANU, *v.* Haw., to cover up in the earth, to plant, to bury, as a corpse. Sam., N. Zeal., Tah., S. Polyn. ubique, *tanu*, id. Javan. and Malay., *tanam*, to bury; *tanaman*, to plant.

Sanskr., *khan*, to dig, pierce, inter.; *khani*, a mine; *khanaka*, a digger; *khanitra*, a spade.

Pers. *kandan*, to dig; *kân*, excavation. Armor., *kân*, canal, tube, valley.

Lat., *canalis*, groove, gutter.

KAPA[1], *adj.* Haw., rustling, rattling; *s.* cloth made of bark, cloth of any kind. Sam., *tapa*, to beckon with the hand, to demand; *s.* the white border of a siapo; *tapa-au*, mat made of cocoa-nut leaf. Tong., *tapa*, id.; *kapa-kapa*, to flap with a noise as wings of birds. Marqu., *tapa*, bark cloth. Tah., *tapa-ie*, envelop in leaves; *apa*, the lining of a garment; *apa-a*, thick cloth made by men, not by the women; *'apa'apa*, to flap as a sail or the wings of a bird. Fiji., *kava*, a roll of sinnet; *kaba*, to climb. Motu (N. Guinea), *kava*, bark girdle for men. Biaju, *tepoh*, a mat. Salayer (Celebes), *tupur*, id. Malag., *komba*, a monkey. Kawi, *kapala*, a horse.

Sanskr., *kamp*, to move to and fro, to tremble; *chapala* ("*i.e.*, kamp-ala," Benfey), trembling, unsteady, giddy; *châpala*, quickness; *kapi* ("*i.e.*, kamp-i," Benfey), a monkey. Perhaps *kambala*, a woollen blanket.

Greek, καμπη, bending, winding, as a river, turn, trick, sudden change.

A. Pictet (Orig. Ind.-Eur., i. 347–348) derives the Greek καβαλλης, a nag, and other kindred West Aryan forms for horse and its varieties, as well as καπρος, a wild boar, and *caper*, a buck, from the Kawi or obsolete Sanskrit application of the original sense, " to tremble, rustle, flap," found in the Sanskrit *kap*, *kamp*, and the Polynesian *kapa*, *tapa*.

KAPA², *s.* Haw., a bank, shore, side, as of a river, lake, wood, or the like. Rarot., *tapa*, id. Tah., *apa'apa*, one side of a thing when divided, the side of a house. Sam., *tafa*, the side of a hill; *v.* to turn on one side; *tafa-fa*, four-sided; *tafatafa*, the side; *tafa-tasi*, one-sided; *tafa-to*, perpendicular, steep as seen from above; *tafa-tu*, id., as seen from below. Marqu., *tapa-hai*, coral; *kapa-i*, on the side of the sea. Fiji., *taba*, wing, shoulder, branch, one side. Malg., *taf*, *tafo*, the roof of a house; *tambon*, above.

Welsh, *tab*, *tav*, an extended surface, a spread; *tob*, *top*, top, crest; *cop*, summit. Irish, *capat*, head. Armor., *kab*, id.

Lat., *tabula*, board, plank, table; *caput*, head.

Sanskr., *kapala*, skull, head, either half of an egg; *kapola*, cheek, the temples of the head. Pers., *kabah*, elevation, eminence; *tabrak*, *tabûk*, table, flat.

Greek, κεφαλη, head, top, upper end.

Goth., *haubith*, head. Sax., *heafod*, id.; *hafala*, *hafula*, head, casque. Anc. Germ., *haupit*, head; *hufela*, the temples. Germ., *kopf*, head.

A. Pictet (*loc. cit.*, ii. 273) refers the Persian *tabrak* and the Latin *tabula* to Sanskrit *sthâ*, or perhaps *stabh*, *tabula*, for *stabula*, and (i. 308) he says, speaking of the Sanskrit *kapala* and its West Aryan relations:—" J'y trouve un composé de *pâla*, protecteur, avec l'interrogatif *ka*, dans le sens laudatif. Quel (bon) protecteur! on ne saurait mieux caractériser le rôle naturel du crâne. Or *kapât* et *kapâ* ou *kapa* auraient la même signification; car *pât*, *pâ*, *pa*, à la fin des composés, sont synonymes de *pâla*, et dérivent également de la racine *pâ*, tueri."

Under correction, the "quel bon protecteur" of Mr. Pictet appears to me a singular and fatal misnomer of the most prominent and most exposed part of the body. The original meaning of the Polynesian word was probably something raised, spread out, obtruding, projecting, beyond or above the common level of things. Hence such compound words in the Polynesian as *kapa-au*, Haw., the raised place in the Heiau (temple), where the image of the god stood and offerings were laid; *'apa-'au*, Sam., a wing; *'apa-'apa*, the fin of a fish; *apa-ta*, to clap the wings. The West Aryan forms: Lat., *cap-ut*, *cap-pilus* (*capillus*); the Irish *cap-at*, alongside of *ceap* and *cap*; the double forms in the Goth. and Sax., *haub-ith*, *heaf-od*, and *hafa-la*, *hofu-la*, seem to indicate a different composition and root for themselves, as well as the Sanskrit and Greek, than what Mr. Pictet offers. And the probable primary sense of " elevation, eminence," in the root-word has survived in the Persian *kabah*, the Armorican *kab*, the Welsh *tob* or *top*.

KAPU, *v.* Haw., to set apart, restrict, prohibit, interdict, make sacred. S. Polynes., ubique, *tapu*, id. Fiji., *tabu*, *tambu*, id. Sumatra (Pessumah), *dempu*, sacred. Tagal, *cabunian, cambunian*, general name for god, divinity, sacred, holy.

I am not aware of any West Aryan word that can be positively classified as akin to the Polynesian *kapu* or *tabu*. In the Cingalese, however, where so many old and obsolete Sanskrit words have been preserved, I find the word *kapu* as the name of a scarlet string tied round the arm or wrist, to indicate that the wearer is engaged in a sacred cause and will not be interrupted. I note the coincidence, but I leave to abler philologists to trace out the relation, if any. In so doing, it may be well to bear in mind that one of Siva's names is *Çambhu*, which Benfey derives from *çam* and *bhû* (a happy being), but which derivation may admit of question in view of the Tagal, Sumatra, and Fijian forms of the word, where doubtless the primary sense of the word is " to restrict, prohibit, interdict," as it is in the

Polynesian. In Tahitian the rainbow is called *tapu-tea ;* in Samoan the evening-star is called *tapu-i-tea.*

KEA, *adj.* Haw., also *keo, keo-keo,* white, lucid, clear; *a-kea,* openly, public; *au-akea,* at noon, midday. Sam., *tea-tea-vale,* be pale; *ao-atea,* forenoon; *atea-tea,* wide, spacious. Tah., *tea,* white; *teo-teo,* pride, haughtiness; *atea,* clear, distinct, far off. Marqu., *tea, atea,* white, broad daylight, also name of the principal god; light generally, as opposed to darkness. Fiji., *cea-cea,* pale, deathlike; *cecea,* daybreak, light of morning. Malg., *tziok,* brilliant, snowwhite. Ceram. (Mahai), *teen,* a star.

Greek, θεος, m. θεα, f. god, goddess, divinity generally. In Greek, θεος signified no god in particular, but was applied to almost all the gods, though perhaps more often to the sun. As the first gods were the sun, moon, &c., their brilliancy and whiteness were the underlying sense of the names given them. That primary sense was apparently lost in the Greek and the other West Aryan branches, though in the Polynesian both the primary and derivative sense has been preserved, as in the Marqu. *atea,* both god and light, in the Tah. *tapu-tea,* the rainbow, and the Sam. *tapu-i-tea,* the evening star, mentioned in previous article.

Liddell and Scott give no root nor reference to θεος.

KE'E, *v.* Haw., to bend, crook, oppose; *keke'e* and *ke'eke'e,* id., also to strive, contend, obstruct; *hau-keke,* shivering with cold. Sam., *tete,* to shake, quake, as with fear or cold; *tete-e,* to refuse, reject, oppose; *faa-tetetete,* to quaver, as the voice; *tete-mu,* to tremble; *nga-tete,* tremble, be troubled. Haw., *na-keke,* move back and forth, to rattle, shake to and fro. Fiji., *keke,* be pained in the back, go stooping. Malg., *tetez,* a bridge.

In Sanskrit two forms present themselves, either or both of which I refer to the Polynesian. Benfey gives them in his Dictionary, but without root or reference: (1.) *cheta,* slave, servant; *chit,* to send off; (2.) *çik-ya,* the string suspended from either end of a pole to receive burdens, the strings of a balance.

Lat., *catena*, chain, fetter.

Germ., *kette*, chain.

KELA, *v.* Haw., to exceed, go beyond, project, be more; *kele*, *v.* to slip, slide, glide, sail out to sea; *kele-kele*, to sail about, to ride the surf in a canoe. Tah., *tere*, spread out, extend, advance, sail, slide. Sam., *tele*, large, great; *tele-a'i*, run quickly; *tele-tele*, to step out, be quick; *fa'a-tele*, to enlarge, increase. Marqu., *tee*, to be off, depart. Rarot., *tele*, a fleet of canoes. Fiji., *cere*, *cecere*, high, hight; *vaka-cere-a*, to lift up, make high. From the Haw. *kela* comes the intensitive *kela-kela*, to boast, brag, enlarge one's desires. From the Sam. *tele*, the intensitive *fa'a-teletele-ai*, be oppressive, overbearing. Malg., *tera*, proud, haughty = Sam., *tela-tela*, bad-tempered.

Lat., *cello*, obsolete root of *ex-cello*, to surpass, exceed; *celsus*, high, lofty; *culmen*, summit; *celer*, swift; *celox*, a light swift vessel; *pro-cello*, throw down, cast away; *pro-cul*, afar off, away from. Probably *pro-cerus*, long, high, tall;[1] *pro-ceres*, nobles, leading men, chiefs.

Greek, κελλω, to drive on, to urge on, to run a ship ashore; κελομαι, to urge on, exhort; κελης, a courser, a light vessel.

Sanskr., Liddell and Scott and Benfey refer the Latin *cello*, *celer*, *celox*, and the Greek κελλω, κελης, to a root *kal*, to impel, to drive ("akin to kṛi," Benfey), to pour out, to cast; *kali*, a die.

O. H. Germ., *halôn*, *holên*, to haul, to drag with force (Benfey).

Though the Polynesian forms in *tere*, *tera*, *kele*, *kela*, may be akin to the Sanskrit *kal*, yet I think them closer allied to the Sanskrit *tri*, to pass over, beyond, to hasten, accomplish, conquer, with its numerous and varied kindred in the West Aryan dialects.

Dr. Caldwell (Dravid. Gram., p. 480) suggests that the Greek κελλω, κελης, are related to the Sanskrit *sel*, *çel*, to

---

[1] Benfey refers *pro-cerus* to Sanskrit kṛî, to pour out, to cast, to cover. I fail to see the connection in sense; at least the Polynesian offers a better.

go, to move, and its affinity to the Drav. (Tamil) *sel*, to go, to proceed. I note the suggestion, but, in view of the formation of the West Aryan comparatives, prefer to connect *kela, kele, tere*, with the Sanskrit *tri*.

KELE, *s.* Haw., mud, mire, fat of animals, grease. Tong., *kele*, earth, mould, mud. Fiji., *qele*, earth, soil. (Vid. 'ELE, p. 64.) Sunda and Malay., *gala-gala*, tar, pitch.

Greek, κηρος, beeswax, mixture, impurity; κεραω, to mix; κεραμος, potter's earth, clay; κηρ, corruption, decay, death, goddess of death or doom; κηρα μελαιναν, II. v. 22; τελμα, standing water, pool, pond, the mud of a swamp, mud for building, mortar; τελμις, mud, slime; Liddell and Scott give no etymon; κηλις, stain, spot, defilement; κελαινος, black, swarthy.

Sanskr., *kâla*, dark blue, black; *kalanka*, rust, iron rust, a spot; *kalusha*, turbid, impure, dirt; *kalmasha*, dirt, sediment, a spot.

Lat., *caligo*, vapour, mist, fog, obscurity; *cera*, wax; *squalor*, dirtiness, filth (Liddell and Scott after Curtius).

Sax., *keld*, a spring, fountain, stagnant oily water in still places of lakes or rivers; *tare, tyr, tar*. O. Norse, *kelda*, wet, marshy place. Swed., *kan*, id.; *tjara*, tar.

KENA, *s.* Obsolete in Polynesia except in the Paumotu group, where we find *tena*, signifying land, district. The two divisions of the island Mature-wa-wao are called *tena-raro* and *tena-runga* = the leeward and windward district. It is possibly akin to the Tongan *tonga*, plantation, property, and Samoan *tonga*, a grove, a plantation. N. Zeal., *taonga*. Tah., *taoa*, property, possessions. Malg., *tan*, land, country, district; *tane*, id.; *tana-a*, a village; *tong-tonh*, place, residence. Sunda, *taneh*, land. Mal., *tanah*, id.

Greek, χθων, the earth, the ground, especially the level surface of it, gen. χθονος; θις, θιν, θην, a heap, beach, seashore, deposit of sea or rivers. Liddell and Scott refer χθων to χαμαι, with θ inserted, analogy χθαμαλος, on the ground, low, and they refer θιν, θην to the same root as the Germ. *dünen*, Engl. *downs*.

Irish, *tan*, region, country, territory ; *tanaiste,* a chief possessor of land.

Icel., *tuna,* a town, village; *tana,* a cave, hollow place, valley. Sax., *tun,* garden, enclosure, village ; *dun,* a sandy, barren tract.

KI, *v.* Haw., to squirt water, as with a syringe, to blow from the mouth, to sift, strain, make fine by separating the coarse. Tong., *ki,* to throw, toss, cast off. Deriv. Haw., *ki-i,* to go after a thing, to bring, to fetch. Tah., *ti-i,* id. N. Zeal., Rarot., Mang., *tiki,* to fetch, to go for, to seek. Haw., *ki-ai,* to watch over, to guard. N. Zeal., Rarot., Marqu., *tiaki,* id. Tah., *ti-ai,* wait, keep watch; *ti-ahi,* expel, drive away. Tong., *ti-aki.* Sam., *ti-ai,* throw away, reject, separate. Haw., *ki-ee, ki-ei,* look into, scrutinise, peep at, to watch. Tah., *ti-ei,* to reach over and look, to turn the head to look ; *ti-o-mata,* to stare, gaze at ; *ti-ao,* to search, seek out. Tong., *ki-o,* to stare, look, peep ; *ki-ata,* looking-glass, mirror. Sam., *ti-o,* sharp-looking, of the eyes ; *ti-o-ata,* a glass. Haw., *ki-u,* to spy. Sunda, *ti-angan,* to seek.

The Polynesian root *ki* or *ti* alone retains the primary, material sense of " sifting, straining, separating," which apparently has been lost in the

Sanskr. (Ved.), *ki,* to know ; *chi* 2 (Benfey), to search; *chit,* to perceive, and their West Aryan kindred, τιω, τινω, τιμη, *timeo,* &c.

KIA, *s.* Haw., pillar or inner post of a house supporting the roof, any kind of pillar or post, a mast of a vessel ; *kia-aina,* a supporter of the land, a governor of a province. Marqu., *tia,* id. Sam., *ti'a,* the stick used in *tanga-tia,* a man's head (abusively) ; *tia-pula,* taro-tops cut off for planting. Sunda, *tihang.* Mal., *tiang,* a pillar.

Greek, κιων, a pillar, support of the roof, the identical sense of the Polynesian usage of the word. Liddell and Scott give no etymology or connections of κιων.

KIHEI, *s.* Haw., a loose garment, mantle thrown over the shoulders, wrapper, coverlet. Marqu., *tifa, tiha,* to close together, a covering. Tah., *tifa,* to join together, dovetail; *tifa-i,* a patch, to patch, mend; *tihi,* a sort of petticoat, a large quantity of cloth wrapped round the waist; *tihi-ura,* a native shawl with stained borders. Sam., *tifi,* to 'adorn.

Sanskr., *chîv, chîb,* or *chîy,* to cover; *chî-vara,* the tattered dress of a mendicant.

KIKO, *v.* Haw., to reach after, pluck, peck, break the shell as chickens in hatching; to mark; *s.* a dot or point, marks made in tattooing; *adj.* spotted, speckled, striped; *kiko-kiko,* to nibble as fish. Tah., *tito,* to peck as a fowl, to fight as cocks, go softly on tip-toe as a thief. Marqu., *tito* and *tito-tito,* to dart, fall headlong, peck, nibble. Sam., *tito,* id. Sanskr., *tij,* be sharp (Ved.); caus. to sharpen, stir up; *tîkshna,* sharp, hot, energetic.

Greek, κιχημι, κιχανω, to reach, hit, or light upon; κικω, ἐκιξα, cause to go away, shake or blow off; κικυς, strength, vigour; κικκος, a cock; στιζω (s. prosth.), to mark with a pointed instrument, to prick; στικτος, pricked, punctured; στιγμη, &c.

Lat., *-stinguo, -stinctus, -sti(g)mulus, stilus, in-stigo,* et al.; perhaps *cica-trix,* scar, mark of a wound.

Goth., *stiggan, stikan,* to sting, stick, prick; *stiks,* a point, a moment (of time). Probably Engl. *tick,* to beat, as a watch, to beat, pat, *tickle.*

Welsh, *ys-tigaw,* to stick, prick, mark.

KILA, *adj.* Haw., strong, stout, able; *lana-kila,* id., victorious; *kila-kila,* id., an expression of admiration, equivalent to "long may it flourish," "long live the king." Tah., *tira,* the mast of a vessel, a pole stuck up in the Marae; *tira-tira,* to put up a high house, to invest a person with authority; *raa-tira,* an inferior chief, a freeholder. Sam., *tila,* sprit of a sail, mast of a vessel; *matila,* a fishing-rod. N. Zeal., *ranga-tira,* a chief. Fiji., *kila,* wild, as animals.

Sanskr., *kîla,* a stake, a pillar; *Kila-kila,* a name of Siwa, a cry expressing joy. Benfey, Sansk.-Engl. Dict., refers *çiras,* head, top of mountain or tree, a chief, to an original *çaras;* cf. Zend. *çara* and *çîrsha.* It seems to me that because *çara* and *çîrsha* are synonyms in the Zend, it does not necessarily follow that *çîrsha* in Zend or *çiras* in Sanskrit are weakened forms of *çara* or *çaras*.

KIMU, *v.* Obsolete in Haw.; in Sam. *timu*, rain; *v.* to rain; *timunga,* great continued rain. Tah., *timutimu,* also *timatima,* be lost in obscurity, obscured by distance. Marqu., *kimi,* to pour out, spill, shed.

Sanskr., *tim, tîm, stim,* be wet; *timita, stimita,* wet, benumbed; *s.* moisture; *timira,* dark, darkness. Benfey considers the latter as akin to *tamas,* perhaps for original *tam + ira.* I think not, in view of the Polynesian, which has so well preserved the connection between rain and obscurity, the latter so frequently being a result of the former.

KINA[1], *s.* Haw., blemish, sin, error, any untoward or troublesome event. Sam., Fak., *tinga,* *s.* pain, trouble, distress; *v.* to be in pain or distress.

Sanskr., *kînâca,* a poor labourer, a poor man.

In the Greek I find a number of composite words whose first constituent would seem to indicate a relation, from early times, with the Polynesian; *e.g.,* κινα-βευμα, a knavish trick; κινα-βρα, the rank smell of a he-goat; κινα-δος, a Sicilian word for a fox, generally a beast, a monster; κινα-βρευματα, stinking refuse; κιναιδος, a lewd fellow; κινδυνος, risk, hazard, danger. Benfey intimates a relationship of κινδυνος to Sanskr. *khid, khinad, khinna,* be afflicted, despair, tired. Liddell and Scott merely note the origin of κινδυνος as "uncertain."

KINA[2], *v.* Haw., to drive on, to urge, oppress. Sam., *tina,* to split; *s.* a wedge; *titina,* to strangle, choke. Tah., *ti'aia,* strike the foot against something, to stumble; *faa-ti'aia,* to touch with hand or foot, to push against.

Greek, θεινω, to strike, beat, dash upon or against.

Lat., *fendo* in *offendo,* to strike against, &c. (Liddell and Scott, *s. v.* θεινω).

KINANA, *s.* Haw., a hen that has hatched chickens. Sam., *tina,* a mother. Tong., *tina-manu,* a sow that had a litter. Tah., *ti'a,* the lower part of the stomach, below the navel. Fiji., *tina,* mother; *tina-tina,* mother of inferior animals. N. Zeal., *tinana,* the buttocks, trunk, body.

This word, with somewhat varying but not far separate meanings, I am inclined to consider as related to the

Goth., *kwens, kwino,* a woman; *kwina-kunds* and *kwineins,* female; and possibly *kwithus,* the womb, the stomach, if that is a syncope of an original *kwinthus.*

Greek, γυνη, woman; according to Professor A. H. Sayce, who, in " Introduction to the Science of Language," vol. i. p. 298, says that "the primitive Aryan speech must have possessed a row of labialised or ' velar gutturals,' *kw, gw, ghw,* of which the Latin *qu* and our own *cw, qu,* are descendants. . . . So far back as we can go in the history of Indo-European speech, the two classes of gutturals exist side by side, and the groups of words containing them remain unallied and unmixed. *Γυνη* and *queen* (*quean*) must be separated from γενος, *genetrix, kinder,* and other derivations of the root which we have in the Sanskrit *janâmi,* the Greek γιγνομαι, &c." Professor Sayce may probably be correct as regards the relationship of West Aryan dialects *inter se,* but whether the " primitive Aryan speech," in its primitive condition, was loaded with those velar gutturals I think may admit of a question. From the simple to the complex I think was the rule of development in language as well as in other things. " There is nothing to show," says Professor Sayce, " that these velar gutturals were ever developed out of the simple gutturals." But how can that be shown when the history of Indo-European speech only goes back some three thousand years, and then already presents itself in its full-fledged inflectional condition ? Where is the history of its childhood ? I think it right, but on other grounds, to say that the Gothic *kwino* and the Latin *quies* are not related to the Sanskrit *jan* or the Greek κειμαι. But to say that they could not possibly be related on account of the velar gutturals in the one set and simple gutturals in the other, seems to me to be assuming too much.

I know not how philologists derive or affiliate the

Scandinavian *kona*, *kone*, female. If, as I am inclined to believe, it is related to the Gothic *kwens*, *kwino*, it either shows the return of a velar guttural to a simple guttural, or that both are but dialectical variations of a still older word, whose oldest known form may be found in the Polynesian *kina*.

KINA, *s.* Haw., an indefinitely great number; specifically equal to 40,000, or 10 *manu;* a train of followers; *kini-kini*, *s.* a multitude; *na kini akua*, innumerable spirits. N. Zeal., *tini*, many, a crowd, 10,000. Tah., *tini*, innumerable. Sam., *tino*, ten in counting men; *tino-lua*, twenty. Marqu., *tini*, much, many times, multiplied. Fiji., *tini*, ten. Ceram. (Camarian), *tinein*, ten.

In view of the permutation of *l* and *n*, not uncommon in the Greek as well as in other Aryan branches, it is possible that this Polynesian word refers itself to χιλι-ας, a thousand, generally an indefinite but large number; χιλι-οι, a thousand, of which lexicographers give no etymon, and which seems to stand alone without kindred in the West Aryan dialects.

KEPA, *v.* Haw., turn aside from a direct path, turn in and lodge, turn off, as water in watering a field. Sam.,' *tipa*, to glide, move on one side, rebound. Malg., *kiban*, a bed.

A.-Sax., *scyftan*, to diverge, decline, distribute, shift. Goth., *skiuban*, push, shove. Germ., *schieben*, id., to slide, move out of place. Engl., *skip*, leap, bound. Dan., *kipper*, id. Swed., *kippa*, slip, slide, bound, rebound; *skifta*, change, distribute; *skipa*, distribute, dispense, administer.

KO'E-KO'E, *adj.* Haw., wet and cold, cold from being wet; *s.* dampness, chilliness. N. Zeal., *ma-toke*, cold, chilly; *hau-toke*, winter. Rarot., *toke-toke*, cold, chilling. Tah., *to'e-to'e*, id.

Sanskr., *tue*, to sprinkle (Ved.); *tushára*, cold, mist, thin rain, dew, frost, snow; *tuhina*, mist, dew, snow.

Goth., *twahan*, pt.t. *thwoh*, to wash. A.-Sax., *thwean*, id.; *deau*, dew.

KOI, *v.* Haw., to flow, rush, like water over a dam;

koi-ei-ei, a rapid current; *koi-ele,* to overflow. N. Zeal., *toi,* to dip in water, to duck. Iaw., *toya,* water.

Sanskr., *toya,* water. Apparently there is no etymon for this word in Sanskrit or Vedic, for Benfey suggests that it derives "perhaps from *tu.*" But the primary, at least the Vedic, meaning of *tu* is "to be all-powerful." Taking the New Zealand term as the best-preserved among the Polynesian dialects, it certainly offers a better etymon to the Sanskrit *toya* than the Vedic *tu.*

KOLE, *v.* Haw., be red, raw, skinned, shaved, as the head; *adj.* red, like raw meat raw, inflamed, sore; *kole-kole, s.* red earth, reddish; *o-kole,* rump, anus. Tah., *tore,* checkered, striped; *v.* to grow, as proud flesh in a sore. Sam., *tole, s.* clitoris. Marqu., *to'e,* id., rump, buttocks.

Sanskr., *kravya,* raw flesh; *krûra,* sore (Ved.), cruel, harsh; *krudh,* be wrathful, wrath. Perhaps *kruç,* to cry out, to revile.

Greek, κρεας, raw flesh, flesh, meat, a cadaver; κραυρα, a scrofulous disease.

Zend, *khrui,* cruel.

Lith., *kraujas,* bloody. Illyr., *karv,* id.

Irish, *cear,* blood; *cru,* bloody; *cruadh,* harsh, severe; *cruas,* cruelty.

Goth., *hraiw,* a carcass.

Lat., *cruor,* blood from a wound, blood generally; *caro,* flesh; *cruentus,* blood-stained, blood-red, red; *crudus,* raw, unripe; *crudelis,* unmerciful, cruel.

Liddell and Scott (Gr.-Engl. Dict.), by referring the Latin *cruor* to both κρεας and κρυος (icy-cold, frost), seem to indicate that they all spring from the same root. The same authorities refer *caro* to κρεας and *kravya.* A. Pictet denies the relation, but does not explain why so. The Illyrian *karv,* however, seems to confirm the relation of *caro* to this family of words, of which the Polynesian term is but one of many varieties.

KOLI, *v.* Haw., to pare, shave off, cut, trim, whittle; *s.* something moving through the air, a meteor; *kolii,* to diminish, taper off, grow less. Sam., Tong., *toli,* to gather fruit from high trees; *toli-u,* to burst inwardly, as an abscess. Fiji., *toro-ya,* to shave; *toro-i,* a razor; *coronga,* a grater; *kure,* shake the fruit of a tree. Mal., *chukur,* a razor; *kukur,* a rasp; *kurang,* to diminish; *churie,* to sever, separate.

Sanskr., *khur,* to cut, to break; *kshur,* to cut, scratch, make furrows; *kshura,* a razor.

Greek, κολος, docked, stunted; κολουω, cut short, curtail, clip; κολαζω, curtail, dock, prune. Perhaps σκυλλω, to skin, flay, strip off; σκυλον, σκυλα, what has been stripped off, as skins of animals, arms of enemies, spoils of war. Benfey refers ξυρος, razor, to Sanskrit *kshur.* Liddell and Scott refer ξυρος and ξυω, to scrape, plane, to ξεω with similar meaning, and quote Aufrecht as comparing it with "the (Vedic) Sanskrit to whet." They cannot both be right. In the absence of the Polynesian it might be an open question. Liddell and Scott give κολος as "akin to κυλλος, crooked, crippled," and derive κυλλος from ("prob") κυεω, to have in the womb, and refer that to κυω, to hold, contain, and both to Sanskrit ςvi, to swell, increase. I may be charged with fanciful comparisons, but, under correction, I fail to see the connection between ςvi, κυω, to swell, increase, and κολος, docked, stunted.

Lat., *calvus,* bald, hairless; *curtus* (perhaps), though Liddell and Scott refer it to κειρω.

Armen., *sur,* knife, sword.

Russ., *gol,* bald, naked; *goleyu,* stripped. In Drav. (Tamil.), *kuru* is short, brief; *kuru-gu,* to diminish.

KOLO[1], *v.* Haw., to creep, crawl, shoot sideways, as plants, to penetrate downwards, as roots. Sam., *tolo,* to push forwards, as a fish-net with the feet, to keep back, to stir round the hot stones in an oven; *totolo,* to crawl, creep. Marqu., *toto'o,* humpbacked, crawling, feeling around in the dark, commit adultery. Tah., *toro,* to creep, stretch out, as roots. N. Zeal., *kolo-pupuu,* to boil, to simmer. Malg., *kora-kora,* a snail, insect, a screw. Fiji., *dolo,* to creep, move as snakes.

Sanskr., *char,* to move, to graze, go through, over, along; *chal,* to tremble, go away, swerve.

Greek, κορος, a shoot, sprout, scion of a tree, a boy, lad; -κολος in βου-κολος, a herdsman, cowherd, derived from κολεω, "a word which only occurs in compounds; cf. Lat. *colo*" (Liddell and Scott).

Lat., *colo,* to till, tend, cultivate.

A further connection may be found in the Latin *torqueo,* to turn, distort, twist; Sanskrit *tarku,* a spindle; Greek ἀ-τρακτος, a spindle; ἀ-τρεκης, true, just, strict, *i.e.,* not crooked or warped. Liddell and Scott, after Curtius, refer *torqueo* and ἀτρακτος to Greek τρεπω, to turn, turn round. Benfey refers them to Sanskrit *tark,* to suppose, find out, reflect. Neither of these "suppositions" seem to me plausible with the Polynesian *kolo, tolo,* before us.

KOLO², *v.* Obsolete in all the Polynesian dialects except in Sam., *tolo,* to singe, to kindle a fire by rubbing sticks together; *tolo-i,* smoky to the taste. Fiji., *coro-ya,* to singe, scorch. Malg., *horu,* a burn, a scald. Mal., *chulor,* a scald. Celebes (Gerontalo), *tulu,* fire.

Saskr., *kûl,* to singe; *chûr,* to burn.

KONI, *v.* Haw., to throb, beat, as the pulse, to try, taste; *koni-koni,* to nibble, as fish; *ki-koni,* to smooth off and finish, as a canoe after it is dug out; *hi-koni,* a slave marked on the forehead. Tong., Sam., *tongi,* engrave, carve, to peck, as a fowl, to throw or cast, as a stone; *totongi,* to peck, nibble, as a fish, to drive of, as a hen her chickens.

Greek, κεντεω, to prick, goad, urge on; κοντος, a pole, shaft of a pike; τενδω, τενθω, to gnaw, nibble, eat daintily; τενθευομαι, eat greedily; τενθης, a gourmand, a dainty eater. No references given to either of these words by Liddell and Scott.

KU, *v.* Haw., to rise up, stand, let go, let fall, hit, strike against, resist; *ku-e,* to oppose, resist; *ku-i,* to pound, beat, knock; *ku'-u,* let go, loosen, put down; *ku-ku,* to strike, beat, stand up, be high, excel; *ku-a,* to strike horizontally, to cut down, as trees, to fell, throw away. N. Zeal., *tu,* stand; *tuki,* beat, knock; *tuku,* allow, permit.

Sam., *tu*, stand up, arise, to take place, come to pass; *s.* a custom, habit; *tu-i*, to thump, beat, pound; *s.* a blow with the fist, a curse; *tu'ia*, to strike, as the foot against a stone; *tu'i-fao*, a blacksmith (mod.), lit. a pounder of nails; *tu'u*, to place, appoint, permit, let go, set free, cut down, desist. Tah., *tu*, stand erect, to fit, agree; *tu-a*, to cut, to rest or wait; *tu-e*, to impel, strike with the foot, hit against; *tu'e-tu'e*, to oppose; *tu-i*, to butt, strike, smite; *tutu*, to strike, beat; *tu'u*, let go, dismiss, yield. Fiji., *tu*, to stand; *tuki*, beat, knock; *tuku*, let go, slack up. Sunda, *tutut*, loose, slack.

The same dialectical variations in form and sense obtain through all the Polynesian groups. Two original conceptions seem to have attached themselves to the Polynesian root-word *ku*, *tu*, viz., (1.) "To rise, stand, be prominent;" (2.) "To strike, put down, let go." The West Aryan relatives of this Polynesian *ku*, *tu*, appear to have confined themselves to the second conception of the word, "to strike, put down, let go," although the probably oldest of these forms, the Vedic *tu*, bears the general sense "to be powerful." To mention but a few of those Aryan correlatives, we find—

Sanskr., *tu* (Ved.), be powerful, to increase, to hurt; *tuy* and *tuñj*, to strike, push, abide, give or take; *tud*, to strike, sting; *tund*, be active; *tup, tump, tumbh*, to hurt, kill; *khud* (Ved.), *kshud*, to push, to pound.

Lat., *cudo*, strike, beat, sting; *incus*, an anvil; *tundo* (*tutudi*), to beat, strike, pound; *tussis*, a cough; *tueor*, guard, watch, keep; *tutus*, safe; *tuber, tumor, tumulus; stupeo*, be stunned, benumbed.

Greek, τυπος, a blow; τυπτω, ετυπον, to beat, strike; τυλη, τυλος, a knot or callus, a lump, hump, knob, a cushion; τυλιγμα, a wheal, swelling. Liddell and Scott refer this latter to Sanskrit *tu*.

Goth., *stautan*, to strike, smite. Germ., *stossen*. Dutch, *stooten*.

Benfey (Sansk.-Engl. Dict.) s. v. *Tud*, considers that the Gothic has retained an original *s*, which the Sanskrit and the other dialects have lost. With all due deference to so great authority, yet, if Professor Max Müller is correct, that the oldest forms of Aryan speech consisted of open syllables of one consonant and one vowel, or of one vowel, and judging from the analogy of the Polynesian, I should look upon all prefixes and suffixes to a simple root or stem as of later growth, and hence that the *s* in question, like the *s* in *stupeo*, indicates a later period than that when *tu* or *tup* were used to express the sense of striking, beating, stunning.

Anc. Slav., *kuti* or *kowati*, a smith. Lith., *kujis*, a hammer; *kauti*, to fight.

To this Vedic and Polynesian root *tu*, "to be powerful, increase, rise up," refers itself, doubtless, a word expressing family relation throughout Polynesia, but which in its simple form has become almost obsolete, except in Fiji. In the Polynesian groups proper it always occurs in composites, sometimes with the other family designation, *kai*, prefixed, sometimes with the intensive prefix *ma*, sometimes without either. That word is—

KUA, s. Haw., obsol. Fiji., *tuka*, a grandfather; *tua*, word used by children to their grandparents; *tuaka*, an elder brother or an elder sister. Sam., *tua'a*. N. Zeal., *tuaka-na*. Tah., *tu-a'ana*. Haw., *kai-kua'ana*. Marqu., *tuakana*, id. Sam., *tuangane*, a woman's brother. Haw., *kai-kunane*, id. Tah., *tuaane*, id. Marqu., *tuanane*, id. Sam., Tong., *tuafafine*. Haw., *kai-ku-wahine*. N. Zeal., Tah., *tuahine*; Marqu., *tuehine*, the sister of a man. Sam., Tong., N. Zeal., Haw., *ma-tua*, *ma-kua*, a parent. Rarot., Tah., *me-tua*, id. Mangar., *mo-tua*, id. It also signifies full-grown, old, elderly. In Tah., *oro-ma-tua* means ancestor. In Sam., *ulu-ma-tua* means the first-born, while *tua* simply means the child next to the oldest. In the Indian Archipelago this word meets us under analogous circumstances. Sula Islands, *tua*, husband. Malay., *tuan*, *tuhan*, master, lord. Pulo-Nias, *ira-matua*, husband. Kei Islands, *eb-tuan*, old. Malg., *tump*, *tumpu*, master, the top of a thing; *tupun*, id., chief of an expedition; *tu-vuan*, seed, increase; *tuku-tan*, a hill, rising ground.

Sanskr., *toka*, offspring, child.   Ved., *tuch*, offspring.

Greek, τοκας, she who has just brought forth, a mother; τοκος, birth, offspring, child.

Liddell and Scott refer these words to τικτω, to beget, bring forth, and τικτω, after Curtius, to one of three roots, τεκ, τυκ, τιχ, each one equivalent to the Sanskrit *taksh*, to prepare, form.   Under correction again, it does appear to me that if the Greek τικτω and its derivatives and variants refer themselves to the Sanskrit *taksh*, certainly the Vedic *tuch* does not descend to the same origin, but, on the contrary, allies itself with a better reason to the Zend *tuchm*, germ, seed, the Sanskrit *toka*, the Greek τοκας, the Polynesian *tuka*, whose common root would be the Vedic and Polynesian *tu*, prevalere, crescere, erigere. I am well aware of the frequent and often inexplicable permutation of vowels, not seldom leading to false analogy, in words descending from the same root, but, at the risk of making false analogy myself, I believe that, in the majority of cases, the Sanskrit nouns in *o* have their roots in *u*, and hence the Sanskrit *toka* may, with perfect propriety and almost absolute certainty, be referred direct and primarily to *tu*.

In Tahitian alone among the Polynesian dialects, so far as I know, this word, derived from *tu*, has retained a sense which brings it into close relation with some of the West Aryan tongues.   In Tahitian, *tua, s.* means also "a company of people, à flock, a herd."   Its Indo-European correlatives will be found in—

Irish, *tuath, tuad*, people.

Welsh, *tut*, people, nation.

Umbr., *tota, oscau, touto*, precinct of a town, primarily people or tribe (A. Pictet).

Lett., *tauta*, people, country.

Goth., *thiuda;* A.-Sax., *theod*, people.   For my remarks on the relation of the Polynesian word *atua*, god, spirit, supernatural being, to *ku* vel *tu* and *tua*, see my work, " Polynesian Race," &c., vol. ii. p. 365.

KULA, *s.*   Haw., the open country back of the sea-shore,

a field, uncultivated land. Sam., *tula*, bald, destitute of trees, a habitat, locality. Tong., *tula*, id.

Sanskr., *kûla*, a slope (Ved.), a bank.

Greek, χωρα, χωρος, place, space, region, country, tract of land. Liddell and Scott refer these words and χωρις to χαω, χανδανω, καζομαι. A more natural relationship, it seems to me, is to be found in the Sanskr. and Polynes. *kûla, kula*, which may, but possibly do not, refer themselves to any root in χα or *hâ*.

Irish, *cûl*, the back, tergum, dorsum.

KULE, *adj*. Haw., this word, in the simple form, does not appear in any of the Polynesian dialects that I am aware of, but in compounds we have in Haw. *ele-ma-kule, adj*. old, aged, decaying, in which *ele* and *ma* are two intensitives, according to L. Andrews (Hawaiian Dictionary), and correctly so. In Sam. we find *tule-fena, tule-moe*, to be wearied, to be sleepy, drowsy; *tule-i*, to be sick, to vomit; *tule-sisila*, with the eyes fixed, as in dying; *tule-soli*, to vex, torment, as a conquered party; in all which *kule, tule*, convey a primary sense of old age, decrepitude. We also find the duplicate form of Haw., *kukule*, dumpish, loth to move; Sam., *tutule*, the end, conclusion of a night-dance. In Malg. we find *kuru*, old, when speaking of things, not of persons.

Sanskr., *jûr;* Ved., *jur*, be old. According to A. Pictet, *jûr* signifies also an old woman. *Jujurva*, a grandparent. Benfey also gives *ghûr*, to become old.

Zend, *zaurva*, old age.

KULI[1], *s*. Haw., the knee; *kukuli*, to kneel. Sam., *tuli*, an outside corner, the knee; *tuli-lima*, the elbow; *too-tuti*, to kneel. Tah., *turi*, knee. N. Zeal., *turi*, id. Fiji., *duru*, the knee. Sunda., *tuur*, knee. Timor. Laut., *turad*, knee. Ke. Isl., *ead-tur*, id.

Sanskr., *kora*, a flexible joint, as of fingers; *kûr-para*, the elbow.

Anc. Slav., *koliena*, knee.

KULI[2], *v*. Haw., be stunned with noise, be deaf, be silent; *adj*. and *s*. deaf, deafness. N. Zeal., *turi*, deaf.

Marqu., *tui*, id. Tah., *turi*. Sam., *tuli*, id. Fiji., *tule*, ear-wax ; *adj.* deaf; *kuru*, to thunder. Malg., *tuli*, deaf. Sunda, *torrik*, id. Malg., *duru-duru*, taciturn; *mi-dola*, noise.

Sanskr., *kur*, to sound ;. *ghur*, to sound, be frightful.

Welsh, *tol, tolo*, loud noise, din. To this word and its primitive meaning of making great noise probably refers itself the Polynesian.

KURI, *s.* N. Zeal., Rarot., Mang., dog. Sam., *uli*, id. Tah., *uri*, id. Gilolo (Gani), *iyor*, dog.

Sanskr., *kurkura, kukura*, dog, perhaps also *kola*, a hog; *kolá-hala*, a great and confused noise, screaming.

Irish, *gyr*, dog ; *erse cuilean*, a young dog.

Greek, σκυλαξ, a young dog. Mod. Gr., κουλουκι, a little dog. Comp. A. Pictet, (Orig. Ind.-Eur., i. 378).

Pers., *gholin*, small dog.

A. Pictet, *loc. cit.*, inclines to refer the Irish, Greek, and Persian names to the Sanskrit *kula*, family. Liddell and Scott refer σκυλαξ to σκυλλω, to rend, to tear, But, in view of the Sanskrit and Polynesian analogies, σ may be prosthetic.

Goth., *gaurs*, mourning, grief; probably akin to Sanskr. *ghur, ghora* (Benfey).

KULO, *v.* Haw., to continue doing a thing, persevere, wait long. Probably akin to *kulu-iki*, to endure, be constant, persevere, and Sam., *tulu'i*, to endure, lasting.

Sanskr., *kul*, to proceed continuously, to accumulate.

KULU[1], *s.* Haw., a drop of any liquid, a globule ; *v.* to drop, as water, to leak, to flow, fall down, tumble over. Sam., *tului*, to drop into, as lotion in the eye; *tulu-vao*, drops from trees after rain ; *tulu-tulu*, the eaves of a house ; *tutulu*, to leak, as a house, to weep. Tah., *tuturu*, to drop,. as rain from a house. N. Zeal., *maturu-turu*, to drop, as rain. Fiji., *turu*, drop, as water ; *s.* eaves of a house, a drop of water. Malg., *kuala*, canal, watercourse.

Sanskr., *kulyâ*, a rivulet, a canal ; *kûlinî*, a river. Perhaps *guḍa, gola*, a ball.

In Dravidian (Tamil), *tûru*, means to drizzle, scatter, spread about.

KULU[2], *v.* Haw., sleep little, doze, dream, be in a trance; *kulukulu*, id. Jav., *turu*, sleep. Sunda, *kulem*, id. Malg., *ma-turu*, id. Tagal., *tolog*, id.

Icel., *dura*, sleep little, doze; *durnin*, sleepy. Sax., *dol*, wandering in intellect, stupid; *dwolian*, to wander, rave. Engl., *dolt*. Goth., *dwals*, foolish. Swed., *dwala*, trance.

KULU[3], *v.* Haw., obsol; *kukulu*, *v.* to set up, erect, to build. Tah., *turu*, prop, side-post of a house; *tuturu*, *tauturu*, to support, help, assist. Marqu., *tutu'u*, id. Paum., *turu*, a prop, post to support the roof. Mang., *turu*, id. Malg., *zuru*, column, support. Fiji., *duru*, the shorter posts of a house, on which the wall-plate rests.

Sanskr., *tul*, to lift, to weigh, ponder, attain; *tul-ana*, lifting; *tulâ*, balance; *dul*, to raise, to swing; *dolâ*, a swing.

Lat., *tollo*, *tuli*, to lift, raise, elevate; *tolero*, to bear, endure.

Greek, τλαω (ταλαω), to take upon oneself, to bear, suffer; τολμαω, to undertake, hold out, endure; ταλαντον, a balance; ταλαρος, a basket; τελαμων, a strap, belt; Ἀτλας, a mountain in Africa, supposed to support the heavens; ὀτλος, suffering, distress.

Goth,. *thulan*, to tolerate, suffer; *ga-thlahan*, take in the arms, caress.

KUMU, *s.* Haw., bottom, foundation of a thing, cause, beginning, root, stump, end, stalk. Marqu., *tumu*, id. Sam., *tumu*, be full; *tumu-tumu*, top, summit; *tumua'i*, crown of the head. Tah., *tumu*, root, origin, cause, foundation. N. Zeal., *tumu-ake*, crown of the head, upper part of a tree. Fiji., *kumu*, to collect, gather together. Ceram. (Wahai), *tamun*, root. Sunda, *tumbuk*, stump, foundation. Malg., *tumutch*, heel; *v.* squat down; *tombuk*, foot.

Lat., *humus*, earth, soil; *humi*, on the ground.

Greek, χαμαι, on the earth. Liddell and Scott, without giving an etymon for χαμαι, merely remark that the root is χαμ-, and that it is akin to *humus*, *humi*, &c. Lith., *zeme*, earth. Slav., *zembja*, id. But if *humus* and χαμαι are akin, which has preserved the primary vocalisation of the word ? The first man, or set of men, who expressed the underlying conception did not certainly pronounce that word in two ways. That difference must have arisen after the first name-givers had parted company and had no further opportunity to correct their pronunciation by reference to what was once the common mother-language. In such cases of dialectical divergence a *tertius medius* would be a welcome solvent of the difficulty. Such solvent the Polynesian offers ; and although the vowel sound within the Malaysian area of the dialects of this branch also differs from *u* to *a*, yet it is evident from the uniformity of the dialects of the Pacific area that *u* was the older sound, which brings the Latin and Polynesian nearer in accord.

KUNI, *v.* Haw., to kindle, to light, burn, blaze; *kukuni*, id. N. Zeal., *tungi*, id. Rarot., *tutuni*, id. Tah., *tutui*, id. Fiji., *tungi*, id. Jav., *guni*, fire. Celebes (Menado), *pu-tung*, id. Sangvir Island, *pu-tun*, id.

Welsh, *cynnen*, to kindle ; *sindw*, ashes, scoria of a forge.

Lat., *cinis*, ashes, cinders.

Greek, κονις, κονια, dust, ashes, sand.

Goth., *tundnan*, *tíndnan*, to burn ; *tandjan*, to kindle, to light. Sax., *tendan*, *tynan*, to kindle. Germ., *zünden*. Swed., *tända*.

KUNU, *v.* Haw., blow softly, to cough; *kunu-kunu*, to groan, complain. Marqu., *tono*, sorrow, dislike, pain. Mal., *kuntut*, break wind.

Sanskr., *dhû*, *dhûnu*, &c., to shake, shake out, off, &c., blow, as the wind, remove ; *dhûma*, smoke.

Greek, θυω, to rush on or along, of any violent motion, to storm, rage ; θυελλα, storm, hurricane ; θυιας, frantic ; θυμος, soul, life, breath (physically), strength ; θυνω, to rush along, to dart along.

Lat., *fumus*, smoke.

Goth., *dauns*, odour. O. H. Germ., *tunst*, storm. Germ., *dunst*, vapour, steam.

Slav., *dunati*, to breathe; *dyma*, smoke.

Throughout the Polynesian dialects this word *kunu, tunu,* has another meaning, which, granted its kindred to the Sanskrit *dhû*, makes the transition of sense from the Greek *θυω,* "to rush, storm," &c., to the Greek *θυω,* "to offer, to sacrifice," intelligible and consistent. That meaning is Haw., "to roast meat on the coals;" Tong., "to singe;" Tah., "to roast or boil;" Sam., "to roast, toast, fry, or boil;" Marqu., "to roast, cook;" N. Zeal., "to roast;" Fiji., *tunu-tunu, adj.* "warm," *v.* "to warm up cold food." If, as Liddell and Scott intimate, after Curtius, the two *θυω* in Greek refer themselves to the Sanskrit *dhû*, the latter must have lost the meaning developed in the Greek *θυω,* "to offer, to sacrifice." They give the earlier sense of *θυω(α)* as "to offer part of a meal as first-fruits to the gods, especially by throwing it on the fire." The Polynesian *kunu, tunu,* has retained the probably older and more material sense of "roasting," "broiling on the coals or embers of the fire."

I am unable, I confess, to apprehend the connection which led our forefathers to invest the conceptions of "to storm, rage," and "to offer sacrifice," or those of "to blow" and "to roast" in the same word, whether *θυω* or *tunu.* I am therefore inclined to think that *θυω,* "to rush along as the wind, to storm," and *kunu,* "to blow softly, to cough," are derived from one root and akin to Sanskrit *dhû,* "to shake, blow as wind," leaving *θυω,* "to offer" by throwing the offering on the fire, and *kunu,* to roast on the coals, though evidently related *inter se,* without a referee in the Sanskrit or other Indo-European tongues, and without a known root so far.

KUPA, *v.* Haw., to dig out, hollow out, as a canoe or a trench; *kupa-paku,* a place deep down in the ground. Tah., *tupa,* to dig out, hollow out, scoop out. Fiji., *cuva,* to stoop, bow down. Mal., *kubur,* grave, tomb. Sunda, *tumpuk,* a hook, a staple.

Sanskr., *kûpa,* a well, a pit; *kûpa-kara,* a well-digger; *kub-ja,* humpbacked, crooked; *kumbha,* a pot, jar. Benfey

(Sansk. Dict.) refers the two latter to a lost verb, *kubh*, with an original signification of "to be crooked." He offers no etymon, however, for *kûpa*, well, pit. The Polynesian reconciles the two. The Sanskrit *kûpa* finds its kindred in the Hawaiian and Tahitian *kupa*, and the Sanskrit *kumbha*, *kub-ja*, and *kubh*, with a primary sense of "to be crooked," refer themselves to the Fijian *cuva*, "to stoop, low down," a sense now lost within the Polynesian dialects proper.

Pers., *kuftan*, *kaftan*, to dig, cleave; *kuft*, *kâf*, fissure. Armen., *kup*, pit, cistern.

Greek, κυπτω, to bend forward, to stoop down; κυφος, humpbacked; κυμβη, a cup, a boat, a wallet; σκυφος, a cup; κυψελη, any hollow vessel.

Lat., *cubo*, lie, recline; *concumbo*, *incumbo; cupa*, a vat, cask.

Goth., *kumbjan*, lie down, recline; *hups*, the hips, loins. A.-Sax., *cop*, a hollow vessel, cup.

Anc. Slav., *kâpona*, a goblet.   Russ., *kopati*, to dig; *kopâni*, a cistern.

Welsh, *cwb* or *cwpan*, a hollow it, expand, b, or cote. Gael., *tubâg*, tub.   expanse,

KUPU, *v.*   Haw., to grow, incr nsic sprout, as plants. Marqu., Tah., *tupu*, id.   Sam., *tupu*, id.; *s.* presiding chief, king.   Fiji., *kubu*, to bud, as flowers or leaves; *tubu*, spring up, increase.   Mangar., *tupua*, high-priest, Polynes. ubique, *tupuna*, *tupuanga*, *tubuna*, ancestors, forefathers, grandparents.   Mal. and Jav., *tumbu*, to grow. Bisayu., *tubu*, id.   Malg., *tuvu-an*, id.

Benfey in his Sansk.-Engl. Dict., *s. v. Çvi*, mentions a "Vedic ptcple. of the red. pf." in *cucuwaṃs*, with the meaning of "large." Benfey calls it "anomalous." No doubt it is anomalous to the verb *çvi* but it indicates the existence at one time of a verb in *çuv*, older than, or at least synonymous with, *çvi*, with the sense of "to increase, grow large."   To the Sanskrit *çvi* Benfey as well as Liddell and Scott refer the Greek κυεω, κυω, κυμα, "to be pregnant, be big, swell of the sea," and their derivatives,

also the Latin *cumulus, cuneus, cavus, caulis, cœlum, cilia,*
&c. How far the family - connection of all these words
with the Sanskrit *çvi* can be proven I do not pretend
to say, but I would be inclined to think that before
Homer's time there may have been a digamma in κυεω
between υ and ε, and that more anciently the word was
κυϝεω, placing it *en rapport* with the Vedic *çuv*, as made
manifest in the still remaining participle *cuçuv-ams.* And
it is further possible that the Latin *cumulus* may come
· from an older form in *cumbulus,* thus establishing for both
of those words their kindred with not only the Sanskrit
çuv, but also the Polynesian *tuvu, kubu, tupu, tumbu.*
The Sanskrit *çopha,* "a swelling," refers itself better, I
think, to the Vedic *çuv,* than to the Sanskrit *çvi.*

LA, *s.* Haw., sun, light, day. N. Zeal., *ra,* sun, day.
Marqu., *a,* id. Sam., *la,* id. Deriv.: Haw., *lae,* be light,
clear, shining; *lai,* shining as the surface of the sea, calm,
still; *laelae* and *lailai,* intens. Sam., *lelei,* something very
good; *l*ɛ'd islanʃhine; *lalangi,* to broil. Fiji., *rai,* to see,
appear, that word iʲ ʲer, a prophet. Teor., *la,* sun. Aru
Islands, *luɪ ˈr·ti, lat* *rie,* bright, shining. Amblaw., *laei,*
sun, day.   ᵣ or·

Irish, *la, lae,* day.
Laghmani (Cabul), *la'e,* day.
Sanskr., *laj, lanj,* to appear, shine; *râj,* to shine. Ved.,
to govern; *s.* a king. If, as Benfey intimates, the Sanskrit
verb *bhrâj,* to shine, to beam, is "probably *abhi-râj,*" an
already Vedic contraction, then the Polynesian root-word
la and *lae* will reappear in several of the West Aryan
dialects. Lat., *flagrare, flamma, flamen.* Greek, φλεγω,
φλοξ. A.-Sax., *blac, blœcan,* &c.
Probably the universal Polynesian *lani, langi, rangi,*
ra'i, lanits (Malg.), designating the upper air, sky, heaven,
and an epithet of chiefs, refers itself to the same original
la, lai, lanj, referred to above, to which may also be
referred
Welsh, *glan,* clean, pure, bright, holy.

Sax., *clœne*, clean, pure.

Swed., *ren*, clean, pure; *grann* (?), fine, elegant.

It may be noted in connection with this word, either as a coincidence or as an instance of ancient connection, that in the old Chaldean the name of the sun and of the Supreme Deity was *Ra*, and that in Egypt the sun was also named *Ra*.

LA², *s.* Haw., Sam., Tong., *ra.* N. Zeal., the sail of a canoe; abbreviated from, or itself an older form of, the Fiji. *laca*, a sail, also the mats from which the sails were made. Sunda., Mal., *layar*, sail. Malg., *laï*, sail, tent, flag.

Sanskr., *láta* (Pictet), a cloth; *latá* (Benfey), a creeper, a plant; *lak-taka*, a rag. As mats and clothing in primitive times were made of bark or flexible plants, the connection between the Sanskrit *latá* and Polynesian *laca*, *la*, becomes intelligible.

Armen., *lôtig*, a mantle.

Lat., *lodix*, a blanket.

Irish, *lothar*, clothing.

LAU, *s.* Haw., to feel for, spread out, expand, be broad, numerous; *s.* leaf of a tree or plant, expanse, place where people dwell, the end, point; *sc.* extension of a thing; the number four hundred; *lau-kua*, to scrape together, to gather up from here and there confusedly; *lau-la*, broad, wide, extension, width; *lau-na*, to associate with, be friendly; *lau-oho* (lit. "leaves of the head"), the hair. Tong., *lau*, *low*, spread out, be broad, exfoliate; *s.* surface, area; *lau-mata*, eyelash; *lo*, a leaf; *lo-gnutu*, the lips (lit. "leaves of the mouth"). N. Zeal. and Mang., *rau*, spread, expand; *raku-raku*, to scratch, scrape. Sam., *lau*, leaf, thatch, lip, brim of a cup, breadth, numeral hundred after the first hundred; *lau-a*, to be in leaf, full-leafed; *laua-ai*, a town, in opposition to the bush; *lau-ulu*, the hair of the head; *launga-tasi*, even, level; *lau-lau*, to lay out, spread out food on a table; *lau-tata*, a level place on a mountain or at its foot; *lau-le-anga*, uneven; *lau-talinga*, the lobe of the ear, a fungus; *lau-tele*, large, wide, common, of people.

Tah., *rau*, a leaf, a hundred; when counting by couples, two hundred; many indefinitely; *rau-rau*, to scratch. Fiji., *lou*, leaves for covering an oven; *longa*, a mat, a bed for planting; *drau*, a leaf; *drau-drau*, leaves on which food is served up, also a hundred. Saparua., *laun*, leaf. Mal., *daun*, id.; *luwas*, broad, extended. Sunda., Rubak., id., Amboyna, *ai-low*, id. Malg., *rav*, *ravin*, leaf; *ravin-tadign*, lobe of the ear; *lava*, long, high, indefinite expression of extension; *lava-lava*, eternal; *lava-tangh*, a spider.

The word *lau*, in the sense of expanse, and hence " the sea, ocean," is not now used in the Polynesian dialects. There remain, however, two compound forms to indicate its former use in that sense: *lau-make*, Haw., lit. the abating or subsiding of water, *i.e.*, drought; *rau-mate*, Tah., to cease from rain, be fair weather; *rau-mate*, N. Zeal., id., hence summer. The other word is *koo-lau*, Haw., *kona-rau*, N. Zeal., *toe-rau*, Tah., on the side of the great ocean, the weather side of an island or group; *toe-lau*, Sam., the north-east trade wind. In Fiji. *lau* is the name of the windward islands generally. In the Malay and pre-Malay dialects that word in that sense still remains under various forms: *laut, lauti, lautan, lauhaha, olat, wolat, medi-laut*, all signifying the sea, on the same principle of derivation as the Latin *æquor*, flat, level, expanse, the sea.

Welsh, *llav*, to extend; *lled*, breadth.

Armor., *blad*, flat, broad.

Lat., *latus*, broad, wide, spacious.

Greek, πλατυς, wide, broad, flat; πλατη, broad surface, blade of an oar; πλακος, broad, flat.

Pers., *lâtû*, blade of an oar, oar.

Lith., *platus*, flat.

Sanskr., *prath*, be extended, to spread.

Goth., *laufs* or *laubs*, a leaf. Icel., *laug*, bath; *lauga*, to bathe; *lögr*, the sea, water, moisture.

Bearing in mind *l* and *n* are convertible in the West Aryan as in the Polynesian dialects, we might refer to the following as original relatives of the Polynesian *lau* :—

Sanskr., *nau*, boat, ship; *snâ*, and its connections, "to bathe."

Greek, *vaω*, to flow, float; *vaω*, *vεω*, to swim, to spin; *vευσις*, *s.* swimming; *vavς*, ship, &c.

Lat., *no-are*, to swim, float; *neo*, to spin; *navis*.

O. H. Germ., *nacha*, a boat. A.-Sax., *naca*, id. O. Norse, *snäcka*, a shell, sobriquet of boats and vessels. Perhaps the Gothic *snaga*, a garment.

Liddell and Scott and also Benfey refer the Greek *vεω* and Latin *neo*, " to spin," to the Sanskrit *nah*, " to bind, tie." With due deference, I would suggest that the underlying sense of "to bind" and " tie " is "to shorten, contract, to knit "—*necto, nodus*—and that the original conception of " to spin " was one of extension, lengthening, as represented in the Polynesian *lau*.

LAHA, *v.* Haw., to spread out, extend laterally, to make broad. With caus. *hoo-laha*, to spread intelligence, to promulgate; *laha-laha*, to open, as the wings of a bird in order to fly; *laha-i* and *lahalahai*, to hover over, fly, light upon, as from a flight. Tong., *lafa*, flat. Sam., *lafa*, a ringworm; *lafa-lafa*, level top of a mountain. N. Zeal., *raha*, to show, exhibit. Tah., *pa-raha*, name of a broad, flat fish. Fiji., *rava-rava*, a spade. Buru (Cajeli), *lehai*, large. Ceram. (Awaya), *ilahe*, id. Matabello, *leleh*, id. Malg., *reff, refi*, a fathom, measure of length.

Sanskr., *rach*, to arrange, prepare, to string, as flowers; *rachanâ*, orderly arrangement, dressing the hair, stringing of flowers, suspending garlands, arrangement of troops; perhaps *drâgh*, to lengthen, extend, stroll.

Lat., *latus*, wide, spacious; *brachium*, the arm. Benfey refers the Latin *locare* to Sanskrit *rach*.

Irish, *legadh*, to lay. Armor., *lacquat*, id.; *raigh* or *brac*, an arm.

Goth., *lagjan*, to lay, put, place; perhaps *lofa*, the palm or flat of the hand. Swed., *lofwe*, wrist. A.-Sax., *laga, lah*, law, statute; *logian*, to place.

Russ., *loju*, place, locus.

LAKA, *v.* Haw., to tame, as a wild animal; *adj.* tame,

well fed, gentle; *pa-laka*, remiss, neglectful. Sam., *lata*, be near, be tame, be at home; *adj.* tame, domesticated. Tah., *rata*, tame. N. Zeal., *rata*, id.

Sanskr., *râdh*, make or be merciful, favourable, gracious, to conciliate.

Greek (according to Benfey), ἱλασκομαι, ἱληκω, to appease, conciliate; ἱλαος, gracious, kind, gentle.

LAKO, *s.* Haw., supply, sufficiency, property, household stuff; *v.* to possess, be supplied; *adj.* rich, prosperous. Tah., *nato-nato* (*n* for *l*), to be well provided. Fiji., *rako*, *v.* to embrace ; *s.* a grasp of the arms.

Sanskr., *râkh*, *lâkh*, to suffice, adorn. Pictet (Orig. Ind.-Eur., ii. 400) refers to Sanskrit *râdha*, " riches," from *râdh*, " prosperari, perfici," and gives the following West Aryan connections :—

Anc. Germ., "*rât*, opes, proventus, fructus. A.-Sax., *ræde*, phaleræ, apparatus. Anc. Sax., *râde*, *ge-rade*, propriété mobilière (Grimm, D. R. A., 566). Mod. Germ., *ge-räthe*, utensils ; *vor-rath*, provision, &c." Whether Pictet be right in referring the above Old German *rât*, &c., to Sanskrit *râdh*, I think the

Greek λαχη, λαχος, an allotted portion; Λαχεσις, goddess of fate ; λαγχανω, obtain by lot, refer themselves better to Sanskrit *râkh*, *lâkh*, than to Sanskrit *râdh*. Liddell and Scott give the root as λαχ; but when we consider that such words as λαχανον, " garden herbs, vegetables, greens ;" λαχνη, " soft, woolly hair, down, nap; " λαχεια, " well tilled, fertile," also claim descent from λαχ, it is hardly possible that the first or earlier conception expressed by λαχ was that of drawing lots or obtaining by lot or by chance. In this dilemma, it seems to me that the Polynesian will give the keynote to the different Western Aryan conceptions, and perhaps the Fijian *rako*, " a grasp of the arms, an armful," embodies by far the older conception, from which the others, as it were, have radiated.

LALA, *s.* Haw., the limb or branch of a tree, or of an animal; in Anc. Haw., a rib of men or animals. Sam., *lala*, small branches ; *v.* to stand out like branches. Tah.,

Mang., *rara*, branch. N. Zeal., *rara*, a rib. Fiji., *rara*, a board. Malg., *raa*, branches. Comp. Tah., *pu-rara*, scattered, dispersed.

Sanskr., *rad*, to split, divide, dig; *rada*, splitting, a tooth. Lat., *radius*, rod, staff, pole; *rado*, to scratch, scrape. Welsh, *rhail*, bar, bolt.

LALO, *adv.* and *prep.* Haw., below, down, under; *adj.* low, base. Sam., *lalo*, id. Tah., N. Zeal., *raro*, id. Marqu., *a'o*, id. Fiji., *ra*, below, west point of heaven, the leeward islands generally. Malg., *lale*, *lalen*, deep, beneath; *tagal*, *lalim*, abyss. Mal., *darah*, *dalam*, deep, depth. Sunda., *djero*, id.

Sanskr., *a-dhas*, underneath, low down; *a-dhara*, lower, inferior.

Goth., *un-dar*, under; *dalath*, down; *dal*, dale, valley, ditch.

LAMA, *s.* Haw., name of a forest tree of hard wood, torch of any material, specially of kukui-nuts, light by night; *malama*, light from sun or moon, a month; *pu-lama*, a torch; *au-lama*, to give light. Sam., *lama*, the candle-nut tree, a torch made of the nuts; *v.* to watch for; *malama*, moon, light, lamp; *v.* to be light. Tong., *mama*, torchlight, sunlight; fig. the world, society at large. Marqu., *ama*, light, the candle-nut tree (*Aleurites*); *maama*, daylight, light. Tah., *rama*, torch; *marama*, the moon, a month; *maramarama*, light. Fiji., *rarama*, light; *rama*, to enlighten, cast light upon, as from a blazing fire. Stewart Islands, *mirima*, moon. Ceram. (Ahliago), *melim*, moon; *matalima*, day. Mal., *malam*, night. Celebes (Bouton), *maromo*, id.

Greek, λαμπας, a torch, a faggot, the name of a nettle; λαμπω, to give light, be bright, shine; λαμπρος, bright, brilliant; ῥαμνος, kind of thorn or prickly shrub.

Lat., *limpidus*, clear, transparent; *lamium*, dead or blind nettle; *ramus*, a bough, branch. According to Professor Mommsen, "*Roma*" or "*Rama*" was equivalent to Anglice "Bush-town," and its oldest inhabitants were the tribe known as *Ramnes*.

Goth., *lauhmoni*, lightning, Sax., *leoma*, ray of light. O. Engl., *leme*, id. Mod. Engl., *gleam*, &c.

Irish, *laom*, flame.

The Rev. W. W. Skeat, in his "Mœso-Gothic Glossary" (London, 1868), refers the word *lauhmoni* to *liuhan*, "enlighten." It is possible, but the Saxon and Irish parallelisms of *leoma* and *laom* would seem to indicate the existence of a radical *m*, although Grimm in his "Teut. Mythol." (vol. i. p. 178) seems to favour a derivation from *lauhatjan*, "to lighten, to shine as lightning."

When we are told that the island of Lemnos (Λῆμνος) in the Ægean Sea was especially sacred to Hephaistos on account of its volcanic fires (Liddell and Scott, *s. v.*), and that it was there he found rest when kicked out of heaven (Il. i. 593), and when we are told that its still older name was *Æthalia* (Αἰθαλη), "the burning or blazing," it is fair to assume that the two names were synonymous, and that λῆμνος in some measure still retained the sense expressed in αἰθαλη, pointing to the same root from which λαμπας sprang, and thus strengthens the position I take of its connection with the Polynesian *lama*.

In tracing this word back to its origin, from light to torch, from torch to faggot, we see that the Polynesian, Greek, and Latin have retained a reminiscence of a once common name for the material of which the faggot was composed, though in after-ages applied to special objects. The development of the idea of light from torches, night-light, and its application to the moon, is peculiar to the Polynesian family, and must have taken place after its separation from the Aryan stock.

LANA, *v.* Haw., to float on the water or in the air, to swing, drift about; in ancient chants, *nana*,—*l* and *n* convertible. It formerly had some now obsolete sense of extension, place, as shown in the compound *lana-nuu*, "the raised *lana*, stage or place," where the idols were set in the *heiau ;* also in *ku-lana*, lit. "stopped floating," a place where many things were collected, a village, a garden; *lana* and *a-lana*, light, floating, easily buoyant. Marqu., *ana* and *aka*, light, not heavy. Tah., *a-raa*, id., to be raised or lightened, as a vessel in the water, Sam., *langa*, to raise up, to rise up, to spring up, as troops from ambush. Fiji., *langa*, lifted up. Mal., *ringan*, light, not heavy.

Another application of this word, and apparently connected with its primary sense, is the Haw. *lana-lana*, also *nana-nana*, the long-legged spider, also a spider's web; *u-lana*, to weave, plait, braid. N. Zeal., *ranga*, id. Tah., *rara'a*, id. Sam., *lalanga*, to weave, braid, also a fine mat.

Probably the Polynesian word for the common house-fly derives from the same original conception of "floating, light, buoyant, agile." Sam., *lango;* Tong., *id.;* Tah., *ra'o;* N. Zeal., *ngaro;* Haw., *nalo;* Marqu., *nao;* N. Celebes, *rango;* Sanguir, *lango*, fly.

Sanskr., *langh*, to jump, step over, surpass, ascend; *laghu* ("*i.e.*, langhu," Benfey), light, not heavy, quick, young; *laghat*, wind.

Greek, λαγως, a hare; ἐλαχυς, small, little, insignificant; ἀραχνης, a spider.

Lat., *aranea*, a spider, cobweb. Perhaps *rana*, a frog, with the underlying conception of "jumping."

LANO, *s.* Sam., a lake; *lalano*, deep, of water. Tong., *ano*, a lake. Tah., *ra'o*, a fleet at sea. Fiji., *drano*, lake or piece of standing water. N. Celebes, *rano*, water. S. Celebes (Bolanghitau), *rano*, id.; *bo-rango*, the sea. Borneo (Dayak-Idaan), *danau*, water. Pulo-Nias, *idano*, water. Mal., *danau*, lake. Malg., *ranu*, the sea. N. Guinea (Motu), *rano*, water; (Kirapuno), *rana*, id.

Sanskr., *dhanv* (Ved.), to run, flow.

I leave to abler hands to determine the possible connection of the compound in such river-names of the Indo-European branches of the Aryan family as *Eri-danus, Rho-danus, Danubis, (Δανουβις),* &c., with the Sanskr. *dhanv.* Whether the Polynesian or the Vedic be the older form, they are evidently related.

LANU, *s.* Sam., colour; *v.* to wash off salt water, to oil the body all over. Fiji., *dranu*, fresh water; *v.* to wash off in fresh after bathing in salt water.

Sanskr., *ran'j*, to dye, to colour.

Greek, ῥαινω, to sprinkle, be sprinkled ; ῥανις, a drop, a spot; ῥαντηριος, sprinkled, spotted, defiled ; perhaps also ῥαξ, a grape, and ῥεγευς, a dyer; λεγνον, the coloured edging or border of a garment.

A.-Sax., *ge-regnan*, to colour.

LAPA, *v.* Haw., to jump, spring about; *s.* a ridge between two depressions, a protuberance; *lapalapa, v.* to rise or stand up, as water-bubbles in boiling, to protrude, as a flame; *s.* flame, blaze, an undulating, rolling country; *adj.* flat or square, where the corners are prominent. Sam., *lapa*, to be flat ; *lalapa*, flat, compressed. Tah., *rapa*, the blade of a paddle or oar; *raparapa, orapa*, any square piece. Fiji., *laba*, to strike or smite, as water against a canoe, as fish with their tails, to kill treacherously. N. Zeal., *raparapa*, the sole of the foot. Malg., *mi-repak*, to creep (ramper), prostrate oneself; *mi-reperip*, volatile, inconstant ; *mi-raverav*, to lean over, to totter, vacillate ; *lavu*, fall, to fall, ready to fall; *lapats*, squint-eyed. Sunda., *lumpu*, lame, limping; *lumpat*, to leap ; *lamboe*, lip.

Lat., *labo*, to totter, be on the point of falling ; *labor*, to slip, glide, fall ; *lapsus*, any quick motion, slip, fall ; *a-lapa*, a slap in the face ; *lambo*, to lap.

Greek, λαπτω, to lap with the tongue ; λαιλαψ, a hurricane with clouds and thick darkness, whirlwind sweeping upwards ; λαιψηρος, light, nimble, swift.

Welsh, *llabiaw*, to slap ; *llab*, a stroke ; *llepiaw*, to lap, lick ; *rhamp*, to rise, reach over, rising up, vaulting.

Sax., *lappian*, to lap, lick ; *rem-pend*, headlong ; *loppe*, a flea ; *ge-limpan*, to happen, befall. Possibly such English words as *flap, slap, slope*, are connected with this family.

Sanskr., *lamb*, to fall, to set as the sun, to hang downward. Perhaps *lâbh*, to throw, to direct ; *reb, rev*, to go by leaps, to flow.

The Sax. *lippa*, Swed. *läpp*, Lat. *labium, labrum*, and the Sunda. *lambee*, lip, probably refer themselves better to the Polynesian *lapa*, "protuberance," than to λαβω, λαμβανω, whether in the sense of "to take" or "receive."

LAPU, s. Haw., ghost, apparition of some one dead, night-monster; *lapu-lapu, v.* to collect together in small heaps, to pick up, as sticks for a faggot; *lapu-wale*, lit. "only a ghost," nothing substantial, foolish, worthless; *akua-lapu*, a spectre. N. Zeal., *rapu*, to seach for. Tah., *rapu, ta-rapu*, to mix together, squeeze, scratch, be in confusion. Fiji., *ravu*, to kill, smash, break.

Sanskr., *ribhu, i.e., rabh-u* (Benfey), name of certain deities; according to Pictet, good spirits in the Vedic mythology; *rabh*, to seize, to take; *rabhas*, zeal.

Lat., *rabies*, rage, frenzy.

Welsh, *rhaib*, fascination; *rheibus*, a sorcerer, a witch.

Touching the Sanskrit *rbhu*, Pictet (Orig. Ind.-Eur., ii. 607), says: "Leur nom comme adjectif, signifie habile, adroit, inventif, et, comme substantif, artisan habile surtout à forger et à construire des chars. Il dérive de la rac. *rabh, temere, ægere*, avec â préf., ordiri, incipere. Cf. *rbhva, rbhvan*, hardi, entreprenant, adroit.

"Lassen, le premier, a rapproché de *rbhu* le grec 'Ορφευς, tout en avouant que les traditions relatives au chantre thrace n'offrent aucun rapport avec celles du *Rigvêda*. Kuhn adopte ce rapprochement, en cherchant dans les Elfes de la Germanie, grands amateurs de musique et de chant, un chaînon qui relie Orphée aux *rbhus* de l'Inde.

"Si l'on part, en effet, d'une forme *arbh = rabh*, dont le dérivé *rbhu* serait un affaiblissement, il devient facile d'y rattacher, avec Kuhn, le scand. *älfr*, ags. *œlf*, anc. all. *alp*, &c., nom d'une classe d'esprits qui tiennent une grande place dans la mythologie du Nord, et les superstitions populaires de l'Allemagne et de l'Angleterre. Leurs attributs sont plus variés que ceux de leurs confrères de l'Inde, et leur sphère d'action est plus étendue. Ils se divisent en plusieurs classes, les blancs, les noirs, les gris, les bruns, suivant leur caractère bon ou malin; les uns beaux et gracieux, les autres laids et difformes. Ces derniers se confondent plus ou moins avec les nains, *dvergar*, qui se rapprochent des *ṛbhus* par leur habileté comme artisans et forgerons. D'un autre côté, les Alfar lumineux qui habitent l'air, et qui se plaisent à la musique et à la danse, ressemblent mieux aux *Maruts* indiens, génies de l'air qui, à leur tour, s'identifient par plusieurs points avec les *ṛbhus.* On voit ainsi qu'un fond commun de croyances, simple à son origine, s'est développé plus tard dans plusieurs directions chez les Indiens et les Germains." And also with the Polynesians.

LATU, *s.* Sam., head-builder, chief constructor; word not found in the other Polynesian dialects. Fiji., *ratu*, equivalent to Master, Sir. Jav., *ratu*, chief, noble. Sulu Isls., *datu*, id. Mal., *datoh*, chief, head-man.

Zend, *ratu*, head, chief. See M. Haug's Essay on the Parsis, p. 175, n. 1.

LAWA, *v.* Haw., to work out, even to the edge or boundary of a land, *i.e*, leave none uncultivated, to fill, suffice, be enough. Sam., *lava*, be enough, to complete; *adv.* indeed, very. Tah., *rava-i*, to suffice. N. Zeal., *rava-kore*, lit. "not full," poor. Fiji., *rawa*, accomplish, obtain, possess.

Sanskr., *labh, lambh*, to obtain, get, acquire, enjoy, undergo, perform; *lábha*, acquisition, gain; *rabh*, to seize, to take.

Lith., *loba*, the work of each day, gain, labour; *lobis*, goods, possessions; *pra-lobti*, become rich; *api-lobe*, after work, *i.e.*, evening.

A. Pictet refers the Lat. *labor*, work, to this same family, as well as the Irish *lobhar* and the Welsh *llafur.* He also, with Bopp and Benfey, refers the Goth. *arbaiths*, labour, work, to the Sanskr. *rabh* = *arb*, as well as the Anc. Slav., *rabu*, a servant. Russ., *rabota*, labour. Gael., *airbhe*, gain, profit, product.

This Polynesian *lawa* is doubtless akin to

LAWE, *v.* Haw., to carry, bear, take from out of; *lawe-lawe*, to wait upon, to attend on, serve, to handle, to feel of; *adj.* pertaining to work. Tah., *rave*, to receive, to take, seize, lay hold of; *s.* work, operation; *rave-rave*, a servant, attendant. Rarot., Paum., *rave*, id. Sam., *lave*, to be of service; *lave-a*, to be removed, of a disease; *lavea'i*, to extricate, to deliver. Fiji., *lave*, to raise, lift up. Malg., *ma-lafa*, to take, seize; *rava*, pillage, destruction. Sunda., *rampok*, theft. Mal., *rampas*, *me-rabut*, take forcibly. Motu (N. Guinea), *law-haia*, to take away.

Sanskr., *labh*, *rabh*, see previous word, "*Lawa.*"

Greek, λαμβανω, ἐλαβον, take hold of, seize, receive, obtain; λημμα, income, gain; λαβη, λαβις, grip, handle.

Lat., *labor*, work, activity; perhaps also *Laverna*, the goddess of gain or profit, the protectress of thieves; *rapio*, *rapax*.

Goth., *raupjan*, to reap, pluck; *raubon*, to reave, rob. Sax., *reafian*, take violently.

Pers., *raftan*, to sweep, clean up; *robodan*, to rób.

Lith., *ruba*, pillage; *rúbina*, thief,

LE'A, *s.* Haw., *le'a-le'a*, gladness, merriment, pleasure, joy; *v.* to delight in, be pleased; as an intensitive, perfectly, thoroughly, very. N. Zeal., *reka*, be gay, joyful. Tah., *re'a-re'a*, id. Marqu., *eka-eka*, id. Sam., *tau-le'a-le'a*, a young man. Tong., *tau-leka-leka*, id., handsome. Fiji., *leca*, good, satisfactory; *vaka-leka*, to be happy. Malg., *reta-reta*, flattering. Mal., *lezat*, pheasant.

Lat., *lœtus*, glad, joyful; *delecto*, *deliciæ*.

Goth., *laikan*, to skip, leap for joy; *laiks*, sport, dance; *ga-leikan*, to please. Sax., *lician*, id. Swed., *leka*, to play, sport.

LEO, *s.* Haw., voice, sound; *leo-leo*, to wail, as for the dead; *leo-leo-a*, to curse, bawl. Sam., *leo*, *s.* voice, sound; *v.* to watch, to guard; *leo-leo*, a watchman; *leo-leo-a*, loud talking, clamour. Marqu., *eo*, voice, speech. Tah., *reo*, id. Tong., *leo*, id. N. Zeal., *reo*, id. Paum., *reko*, id., language.

Greek, ῥεω, ἐρω, to speak, talk; ῥημα, word, saying, &c.; ῥητος, said, spoken.

Lat., *reor*, *ratus*, to believe, think, judge; *prex*, entreaty, prayer; *precor*.

Goth., *rathjan*, to speak, tell; *rodjan*, id.; *redan*, to counsel, provide for, think of. Sax., *ræd*, speech, discourse, counsel; *reord*, speech, language. Perhaps Goth. *laian*, to reprove, revile. A.-Sax., *lean*.

LELO, Haw., also *a-lelo*, *e-lelo*, the tongue; *o-lelo*, to speak, talk. Probably connected with *lale*, the name of a chattering bird. Sam., *a-lelo*, tongue. Tah., *a-rero*. id., small slips, pendant parts of a maro or girdle-cloth; *o-rero*, speech, oration, orator, to speak. N. Zeal., *ko-rero*, speech, rumour. Tong., *elelo*, tongue. Marqu., *'e'o*, id. Fiji., *lali*, a native drum, a bell. Malg., *lela*, tongue; *ma-lela*, orator. Mal., *lidah*, tongue. Sunda. and Jav., *ilat*, id. Macassar, *lelah*, id. Biajau, *delah*, id.

Sanskr., *lal*, *lad*, to sport, dally; *lalana*, lolling the tongue.

Greek, λαλεω, to talk, chat, babble, chirp; λαλη, λαλαξ, &c.

Lat., *lallo*, sing a lullaby.

Welsh, *lloliaw*, to prattle, babble.

Russ., *leleyu*, to dandle, fondle.

LEMU, *v.* Haw., be slow, lag behind; *lemu-lemu*, walk hesitatingly, go slowly; *lemu*, *s.* the buttocks, underpart of a thing. Sam., *lemu*, *adv.* quietly, privately, slowly; *lemu-lemu*, *v.* to draw the finger across the nose, a sign of having had illicit intercourse. Tong., Fiji., *lemu*, the buttocks. N. Zeal., *remu*, the skirt of a garment. Malg., *lamus*, back, loins.

Sanskr., *ram*, to rest, to like to stay, be delighted, rejoice, have sexual intercourse.

Greek, ἠρεμα, gently, quietly, slowly; νω-λεμες, without pause, constantly; νω for νη priv. Benfey refers this to the Sanskr. *ram*.

Goth., *rimis*, rest, quietness.

LENA, *v.* Haw., to bend, strain, as in drawing a bow, to aim, as in shooting. To pull or stretch, as clothes for drying or ironing, to strain the eyes, squint. Sam., *lelena*, to spread out in the sun, smooth down, straighten out, as new siapo (cloth), distend. Marqu., *ena*, id. Tah., *re'a*, a fathom measure.

O. Norse, *glenna,* to distend, in the sense of opening the eyes wide. Swed., *glänt,* half-opened, ajar, as a door. Perhaps Sax. *grinnian,* to grin, show the teeth.

Lat., *ringor,* to open the mouth wide, show the teeth.

LEPA, *s.* Haw., a fringe, something waving, flowing, pendant, a flag; *v.* to roll up the eyes, stand up, as a cock's comb, to move or cut obliquely; *ki-lepa, ka-lepa,* to wave or flutter, as a flag; fig. to peddle, hawk about goods. (In heathen times those who had goods to sell set a flag as a signal.) Another form is *lepe,* a cock's comb; *adj.* diagonally. Tah., *repa,* the edge of a garment; *ta-repa,* to shake, flap; *repe,* the comb of a fowl. Marqu., *epe-epe,* id. Fiji., *reva,* to shake, flap.

Sanskr., *srip,* to creep, to move; *sarpa,* a sliding motion, a snake; *drâpi,* Ved. (vid. Pictet, Orig. Ind.-Eur., ii. 229), mantle, clothing.

Zend, *drafsha,* banner, flag, turban.

Lith., *dribti,* to wave, hang loosely; *drobi,* cloth; *drapanos,* under-garment; *virpu,* to waver.

Greek, ῥεπω, to incline, sink, fall, shift about, to happen; ῥοπη, inclination downwards; ῥοπτρον, the knocker of a door; ῥαβδος, rod, wand, switch; ἑρπω, to creep, crawl; ἑρπετον, a reptile, snake.

Lat., *repo,* to creep, crawl; *serpo,* id.; *serpens,* reptile, worm.

Welsh, *serfu,* to vacillate, have the vertigo; *sarff,* a serpent. Irish, *searpan,* the swan.

LEPO, *s.* Haw., dirt, dust, earth, ground; *v.* to be dirty, defiled, turbid. N. Zeal., *repo,* mud, swamp. Marqu., *epo,* id. Tah., *repo,* earth, dirt, filth. Sam., *lepa,* pond, stagnant water, muddy; *lepu,* to be stirred up, as water. Tong., *lepa,* a well. Fiji., *lobolobo,* soft, muddy; *rebu,* to stir up the water by splashing when fishing. Malg., *lembuk,* gust; *levuh,* corruption; *rhomba,* balsam. Mal., *lumpor,* mud; *lumbut,* soft.

Sanskr., *lip,* to anoint, smear, stain; *lepa,* mortar, plaster, stain, spot.

Greek, λιπα, λιπας, λιπος, grease, fat, tallow; λιπαρος,

fatty, unctuous; λιπαρης· persistent (sticky); ἀλειφω, to anoint with oil, daub, plaster.

Lat., *lippus*, blear-eyed, running, dropping; *liqueo*, be liquid, fluid; *gleba*, a lump of earth, clod, a field.

Welsh, *lupan*, soft, smooth.

Pol., *lep*, glue. Slav., *liepiti*, to glue.

Lith., *limpu*, *lipti*, to stick.

LEWA, *s.* Haw., the upper air, region of clouds; *v.* to swing, float in the air, move back and forth; *hoo-lewa*, to vibrate, float in the air, carry between two persons, as a corpse, a funeral. Tah., *rewa*, the firmament, an abyss; *rewa-rewa*, to fly about, as a flag. Mangr., *rewa*, the overhanging firmament, a tent, a flag. N. Zeal., *rewa*, the eyelid. Marqu., *ewa*, to suspend; *s.* the middle. Sam., *leva* (of time), long since; *v.* be protracted. Fiji., *rewa*, high, height; *vaka-rewa*, to lift up, to hoist, as a sail. Malg., *lifa*, *v.* to fan oneself, *s.* flight; *rafraf*, a fan.

Goth., *luftus*, the air. Sax., *lyfti*, air, arch, vault. O. Engl., *lift*, air.

Lat., *limbus* (?), fringe, flounce.

Sanskr., *dev*, *div*, primarily " jacere, jaculare," according to A. Pictet (Orig. Ind.-Eur., ii. 466), subsequently " to play at dice," play generally. The permutation of *d* and *l* may be observed in the Latin *levir*, brother-in-law (the husband's younger brother) = Sanskr. *devri*, *devara*, id.

If *dev* or *div* has derived the sense of " throwing dice " from an older sense " jacere, jaculare," to throw, to hurl, that sense may be a derivative from a still older one, " to lift up, swing about, be suspended " = the Polynesian *lewa*, *rewa*, " to be suspended, to vibrate." And thus we can also understand the origin of the Goth. *luftus*, the Sax. *lyfte*, the O. Norse *loft*, Swed. *lowera*, *lofwa*, Engl. *luff*.

LI, *v.* Haw., to hang by the neck, to strangle, to furl, as a sail, to see, observe, fear, shrink back with dread; *adj.* trembling, shaking, as from an ague fit; *li-a*, to ponder, think, start suddenly, as a dog at a fly, be cold, shiver; *li-ki*, to gird, tie up tightly, to throng, be troubled, be hustled, as by a crowd, be stiff, as a limb. Sam., *li*, to set firmly together, as the teeth; *s.* a sinnet fastening; *li'a*, a chief's dream; *li'anga*, a giddy height; *li'a-li'a*, to be afraid of; *lia'i*, to whirl round; *lialia'i*, to shake the head. Tah., *ri*, to hang, suspend; *ri-a*, a vision, phantom; *ri'ai*, be seized with fear; *ria-ria*, horror, disgust; *ri-ta*, the spasm or convulsions in lockjaw; *v.* to bite, gnash the teeth; *rita-mata*, to sparkle, glisten, as the eyes in a rage. Tong., *li*, to toss; *li-ti*, throw away; *lia-lia*, disagreeable, abominable. Rarot., *ri-ti*, to tie on. Fiji., *lia-lia*, foolish, crazy. Malg., *man-ri*, to strangle, compress. Mal., *lilit*, to coil, curl.

Greek, ἐιγεω, to shudder with fear, to shiver with cold; ἐιγος, cold, frost; φρισσω, be rough, to bristle, to shiver with cold; φρικη, a rippling as of water, a shivering with fear or cold, cold, frost; φριξ, id.

Lat., *rigeo*, be stiff, hard, benumbed, as with cold; *rigidus; frigeo*, be rigid with cold, benumbed; *frigus*, cold, frost.

Sanskr., *rej*, to tremble (Ved.)

Goth., *reiran*, to tremble; *reiro*, earthquake.

LI'I, *adj.* Haw., obsol.; *li'ili'i*, small, little. Tah., *ri'i*, id. Mangr., *riki*, id. N. Zeal., *riki-riki*, id. Marqu., *'iki'iki*, id. Sam., *li'i*, to be small; *li'ili'i*, ripples; also *ni'ini'i*, small, minute. Sunda., *letik*, small.

Sanskr., *lic*, be small; *leca*, smallness, a little.

Greek, ὀλιγος, small, little, few.

Goth., *leitils*, little. Sax., *lytel*, id.

To the same root, with the sense of "being small, little," refer themselves probably the following:—

LIHA[1], *s.* Haw., a nit, the egg of a louse. Tah., *riha*, id. Sam., Tong., *lia*, id. Tagal., *lisa*, id.

Sanskr., *likshá*, a nit, young louse, a poppy seed; *rikshá*, a nit, a mote in a sunbeam.

Lat., *ricinus*, a tick.

LIHA[2], *v.* Haw., be sick at the stomach, nauseate. Sam., *lifa*, be thin, wasted, as the belly from disease; *malifa-lifa*, a hollow, sunken place in the ground; *faa-lifa*, draw in, as the abdomen, be sloping, as a road. Malg., *mi-lefa*, to flee away, to leave a place.

Sanskr., *rich*, to evacuate, to leave, ptcpl. pf. pass.; *rikka*, empty, purged, free from; *rechana*, purging, evacuation, looseness.

Lat., *linquo*, to leave, forsake; *re-lictus*, *re-liquus*.

Greek, λικμος, λικνον, a winnowing-fan.

Anc. Slav., *riesheti*, to dissolve, to cause to pass away, deliver.

I do not refer to the Greek λειπω or the Gothic *laiba* and *af-lifnan*, which Benfey refers to the Sanskrit *rich*. It may be so; but there is enough without them. The Greek λικ-μος, λικ-νον, have no etymon assigned them in Liddell and Scott.

LIKE, *adj.* Haw., be like, similar, resemble. N. Zeal., *rite*, equal. Rarot., *arite*, id., like. Malay., *litjien*, be even, like.

Goth., *ga-leiks*, like; *ga-leikon*, to liken. Sax., *lic*, like, similar.

LIKO, *v.* Haw., to swell, expand, be fat, shine, glisten; *s.* the shining white in the eyes; *li'o-li'o*, bright, shining; *ma-li'o*, first light of the morning. N. Zeal., *rito*, a bud. Tah, *rito*, to swell, as buds of leaves or flowers. Sam., *li'o*, a circle; *li'o-fingota*, a halo round the moon; *ma-li'o*, a land-crab. Fiji., *liso*, to glisten, be fiery, as of the eyes. Malg., *likouk*, eclat, splendour, glare, brightness.

Sanskr., *rich*, to shine; *riksha*, a star, also a bear. Pali, *ikka*, id. Beng., *rîch*, id. Marath., *rîsa*, id.

Greek, Ἀρκτος, a bear, the constellation Ursa Major, a kind of crab; ἀρκηλος, a young panther.

Lat., *glisco*, to swell, grow fat, increase, spread; *glesum*, amber; *ursus*, a bear; *Ursa*, name of a constellation. French, *lisse*, smooth, glossy.

Goth., *glit-munjan*, to shine, glitter, glisten. Sax., *glite-nan*, *glisnian*, to shine, sparkle.

LIMA, *s.* Haw., arm, hand. Sam., *lima*, id., fore-leg of an animal. Tah., Rarot., *rima*, id. Tonga., *nima*, id. Marqu., *ima*, id.; and through all the Polynesian dialects this word signifies the number "five." Even the New Zealanders, while using the form *ringa* for hand, express the number five with *rima*. Among the Polynesian congeners in the Malay Archipelago, as well as their Malay successors, this word is of universal usage, either as an expression for hand, arm, or for the number five. Celebes, N. and S., *lima, rima,* hand and five. Sanguir, *lima,* id. Sulu Island, *lima,* id. Buru (Cajeli), *limamo,* hand; *lima,* five. Amblau, *lemanatia,* hand; *lima,* five. Amboyna, *lima, rimak,* hand. Saparua, *rimah,* hand. Ceram. (Ahtiago and Tobo), *niman,* hand; *lima,* five. Ceram.(Gah), *numo-niña,* hand; *lim,* five. Ceram. (Wahai), *mimare,* hand; *nima,* five. Teor., *limin,* hand. Goram., *imah-nin,* hand; *liem,* five. Malg., *dimi, limi,* five. Mal. and Jav., *lima,* five.

Some uses of this word occur in the Polynesian which may enable us the better to recognise its West Aryan relations. Thus in Haw., *lima-lima, v.* to handle, employ the hands; *hoo-lima-lima,* to hire, to bargain for work to be done; *lima-lau,* to carry on the hips; *lima-iki,* to fall upon one, as a robber, to assassinate. In Sam., *lima-lima, v.* to do quickly, to be clever at all work; *lima-la'u,* a boaster; *lima-mulu,* slow of hand, stingy; *faa-lima-lima,* snatch covetously at things being distributed. Tah., *rima-haa,* a greedy, dishonest person, one who snatches at everything; *rima-here, rima-io,* a generous, liberal person.

Goth., *niman,* to take, take away, receive; *anda-nem, anda-numts,* a receiver. Sax., *neman,* to take. O. Engl., *nimmer,* a thief; *nimble,* lively, swift, applied chiefly to motions of hands or feet. Probably Sax. *lim,* limb; Icel. *limr;* Swed. *lem,* id.

Greek, νεμω, to deal out, distribute; Mid., to hold, manage; νεμησις, distribution; νεμετωρ, dispenser of rights, avenger; νομευς, a dealer out, distributor; όι νομεις, the ribs of a ship, also the rigging; νομη, division, distribution.

Lat., *numerus,* number, a part of a whole, a member; *numellus,* rigging of a vessel; *numella,* fetters, stocks. Quære *mem-brum,* a limb, member of the body? Benfey

(Sansk.-Engl. Dict.) refers *membrum* to Sanskr. *marman* a vital organ or member, a joint of a limb, and derives *marman* from *mṛi*, to die. It may be so, but I fail to see the application of the idea of death to express, or from which to deduce, the idea of a joint or a limb. Whatever the derivation of *marman*, I hardly think that the Lat. *membrum* originally sprang from the same root; the more so in view of the Ceram. (Wahai) variant—"*mimare*"— of the universal Polynesian *lima*.

Anc. Slav., *su-nimati*, to bring together, congregate. Russ., *s'nimati*, to take away; *vy-nimati*, to seize.

Though apparently one of the ancient forms by which the early Aryans expressed the sense of hand, arm, had become obsolete and superseded by other synonyms before the West Aryans left their primitive abodes, yet traces of the once common word are manifest, in sense and form, in *νεμω, νομευς, numerus, numellus, niman, lim, nimati.* The Greek, the Gothic, and the Slavonic pointing to the hand as "the taker, the distributor," and the sense of the Latin form indicating that the hand was also used as a counter, the "numerator," Mr. A. Pictet refers this family of words to the Sanskrit *nam*, to bow, bend, stoop. Benfey seems to favour the same derivation; but the argument by which Pictet supports his proposition (Orig. Ind.-Eur., ii. 16 and 691) seems to me untenable in view of the direct Polynesian *lima, rima, nima*, of whose existence or application Pictet was apparently ignorant.

If Sanskrit offers no allied word to the Greek, Gothic, Slavonic, Latin, and Polynesian, it may be permissible to look to some of the tribes of the Hindu-Kush, if haply they may have preserved some reminiscence of this word. I find there, in the Gilgit dialect of the Shina, that *lam-oyki* signifies to "take hold;" *oyki* being the infin. inflection, leaves the radical *lam* to express the sense. Whether a corruption of some lost Sanskrit or Zend word, or itself some ancient variation of the primary word of the Gothic, Greek, and Polynesian, I am unable to say.

LIMU, *s.* Haw., sea-weed, sea-grass, moss; *limu, v.* to

turn, change, have various appearances; *limu-limu*, turning, whirling, curling, of the wind, instability of conduct, slippery, tricky; *limu-a*, a long rain, constant flow of water. Sam., *limu*, seaweed, moss; *limu-a*, moss-grown. Tah., *rimu*, seaweed, moss. Marqu., *imu*, id. Malg., *lemuk*, meadow, bottom-land. Sunda., *ha-limun*, moist, damp.

Lat., *limus, s.* slime, mire; *adj.* oblique, slanting.

Greek, λιμνη, salt marsh or firth, pool of standing water; λιμην, harbour, haven, creek; λειμων, moist, grassy place, meadow, holm. Perhaps λημης, humour, gum, rheum.

Sax., *lim*, a viscous substance; *ge-liman*, to glue; *slim*, soft, moist earth.

Pers., *limah*, mud.

Liddell and Scott refer the Greek words quoted above to λειβω, to pour, pour out, shed. I think the Polynesian offers a better reference.

LINA, *adj.* Haw., soft, yielding, tough; *lina-lina*, tough, adhesive, mucous; *s.* wet, clayey land; *v.* to adhere, stick to; *papa-lina*, the cheek. Tong., *linga*, male organ of generation; *talinga*, the ear. Sam., *talinga*, the ear. Tah., *ta-ria*, id.; *papa-ri'a*, the cheek. N. Zeal., *ringa*, the arm, hand; *ta-ringa*, the ear. Marqu., *papa-ika*, the cheek; *pua-ika*, ear. Fiji., *linga*, hand. Malg., *ta-linh*, ear. Pulo Nias, Celebes, *ta-linga*, id. Sulu Islands, Mal., *te-linga*, id. Amboyna (Liang), *te-rina*, id. Ceram. (Wahai), *te-nina-re*, id. Buguis, *un-ka-linai*, to hear. Sunda., *lengen*, arm. Through the Indian Archipelago generally, wax is called *lilin*.

Sanskr., *li*, be viscous, be solvable, to melt, adhere to, cling to; ptcpl. pf. pass., *lina*. As Benfey gives no etymon of the Sanskrit *linga*, a mark, spot, the phallus emblem of *Çiva*, I may be permitted, in view of the above Polynesian relatives, to class them all as descendants of a root, *li* or *lî*, alone retained in the Sanskrit. The Sanskrit *karna*, an ear, a rudder, one of the names of *Çiva*, deserves some attention in this connection. Benfey classes it under a verb, *karn*, to pierce or bore, but intimates by the + that it has no authoritative references. Now, as it is probable that the ear had a name before it. was bored, I would suggest that *karṇa* is a contraction of *ka-rina*, and if so, groups itself with the Polynesian *lina, ta-rina*, and the Sanskrit *linga*.

Greek, ῥινος, the skin of a living person, the hide of a beast; ῥινον, a hide. No etymon or reference given by Liddell and Scott. Λινον, anything made of flax, flax itself, a flaxen cord, fish-line, linen cloth.

Lat., *linum*, flax; *lens*, lentils, pulse; *lentitia*, toughness, flexibility; *lentiscus*, the mastich tree, the resin or oil from it; *lino*, to besmear, daub; *linea*, a thread, line, string.

Probably referring to the same family are the Haw. *lino, v.* to twist, as a string or rope, *s.* a rope; N. Zeal., *rino*, a rope; Marqu., Tah., *nino*, to twist, spin, a rope.

LIPI, LIPI-LIPI, *adv.* Haw., sharp, edge-like, as a mountain ridge or instrument for cutting; *s.* an axe. Sam., *lipi*, to die suddenly. Malg., *lef, lefo, ref*, a pike, an assegay.

Lat., *ripa*, shore, bank; *rupes*, a rock, cliff, crag.

Sax., *rib*, a rib. Icel., *rif*, id.

Russ., *ribro*, a rib.

LIPO, *s.* Haw., the deep water of the sea, also the south and south-west quarter of the heaven; *adj.* deep, shady, blue, black, or dark, as from the depth of the sea or from a cavern or a forest, dark, sombre. Malg., *rivut* (?), storm tempest.

Greek, λιψ, λιβος, the south-west wind. Liddell and Scott (Greek-Engl. Dict.) refer this word " probably from λειβω, because it brought wet." It may be so; but Africa, from the Great Syrtes to Egypt, was called Λιβυη by the Greeks. Now, if Libya was intended by the Greeks to mean the land from which the south-west wind blows, the word is apparently a misnomer, for the Cyrenaica bore from south to south-east of Greece, and not from south to south-west. But to the inhabitants of the Phœnician and Cilician coasts of Asia Minor λιψ would have been a south-west wind, whether it brought wet or dry weather, and those inhabitants, at the time when the Greeks may be supposed to have become acquainted 'with the Mediterranean, were Phœnicians of the Hamitic, Chaldæo-Arabian race, and as they were by all accounts the earliest and the foremost navigators of ancient pre-historic times, it is fair to infer that the name for the south-west point of the compass may have been adopted from them by the early Greeks when they reached the eastern shores of the Mediterranean, as well as by the people occupying the Indian Archipelago, among whom the Cushite navigators introduced so much of their own folk-lore, arts, and probably language. It may not be worth much as a philological argument that the word λιψ as a name for the south-west wind has no relation among the other Aryan branches, and was unknown alike to the Vedic invaders of India, to the Iranians, the Celts, the Teutons, and the Slaves; but it tends to support the presumption that, with both Greeks and Polynesians, it was a foreign word introduced by their early masters and teachers in navigation and commerce. To the Greeks of the southern and western coasts of Asia Minor it pointed across the sea to Libya and the frequent wet winds coming from that direction; to the Polynesians of the Indian Archipelago it pointed to the south-west monsoon and the deep dark-blue unfathomable ocean in that direction.

Of the other meaning of the word *lipo*, viz., " deep water, shady, dark colour," &c., no trace remains in the Greek, if ever any more than the mere technical expression for the south-west wind was adopted by them. If *lipo*, in the sense of " deep water, shady, dark," &c., was an Aryan word, I have found no relative or descendant of it, unless it underlies the sense of the Latin *Libitina*, the goddess presiding over funerals, and in whose temple the mortuary registers were kept. I know not the derivation of her name, but the sombre associations and trappings connected with death and an " iter ad inferos " may well suggest a derivation from a subsequently obsolete word, whose early form and sense corresponded with the Polynesian *lipo*, dark, sombre, &c.

Lo¹, *s.* Haw., a bug. Tah., *ro*, an ant. Tong., *lo*, id. Sam., *lo-ata*, the black ant; *lo-i*, an ant, Paum., *ro-i*, id.

Sanskr., *lû-tâ*, a spider, an ant.

Lo², *v.* Obsol.; *lo-lo, s.* Sam., a flood; *v.* to overflow, be wet, of clothes; *lo-fia*, flooded; *lo-fu*, an obscene term; *lo-i-mata*, tears. Tah., *ro-i-mata*, tears; *ro-tu*, a heavy long rain; *ro-fai*, gust of wind with shower of rain. Fiji., *lo-lo*, a flowing tide.

Sanskr., *ro-ma*, water; *lo-ta*, a tear.

Loha, *s.* Haw., also *a-loha*, love, affection, gratitude, kindness, pity, mercy. Marqu., *aoha*, id. N. Zeal., Tah., *aroha*, id. Rarot., *aroa*, id. Sam., *alofa*, id. Tong., *'ofa*, id. Gilolo (Gablo), *ta-loha*, good.

Sanskr., *lubh*, to court, to desire; *'lobha*, covetousness.

Greek, έ-λευ-θερος, free, gentle (vid. Benfey and Liddell and Scott, έ-λευ-θερος).

Lat., *lubet*, it pleases, is agreeable; *libet, liber, libido*.

Goth., *liubs*, dear, beloved; *ga-laubs*, precious, costly; *ga-lubs*, id.; *lubains*, hope; *lubo*, love. Sax., *lufian, luvian*, to love; *leof*, love. O. Norse, *lofa*, to praise, promise.

Lohi, *v.* Obsol.; *alohi, v.* Haw., *a*, euphon. to shine, be bright, sparkling; *alohi-lohi*, shine bright, as a light or fire. Tong., *alofia*, a volcano.

Sanskr., *rohit*, the sun; *rohita*, red, the colour; *rohini*, lightning, blood; *lohita*, red, blood, saffron; *lohitaka*, red, a ruby, the planet Mars. Probably connected with the verbs *ruch, loch*, to shine; *rochis*, light, flame; *roka*, light; *ruch, s.* light, splendour, beauty.

Lat., *luceo*, shine; *lux*, light, &c.

Greek, λυχνος, light, lamp, illumination; λυγδος, white marble.

A.-Sax., *leoht, lioht*, light. Perhaps also akin to the Lat. *russus, rosa, ruber, rufus*.

Loko, *pr.* Haw., in, within, the inner part of persons and things; in compounds, temper, disposition; also a pond, a collection of water; *loko-ia*, a fish-pond. Tong., *loto*, the centre, middle, what is enclosed, also mind, temper, disposition; *lo-lotu*, deep, depth. N. Zeal., *roto*, within, a pool. Tah., *roto*, id., pond, lagoon. Sam., *loto*, in the midst, a deep hole, the interior, the heart, desire, will; *loto-a*, an enclosure; *loto-i*, be in the middle; *loto-nu'u*, love of country. Marqu., *oto*, within, bottom, interior. Fiji., *loco*, middle joint of the yard of a canoe.

Goth., *ga-lukan*, to lock, shut, enclose. Sax., *loc, loce*, an enclosed place. Swed., *lucka*, has the double sense of a shutter and of a gap, breach, chasm.

LOLE, *v.* Haw., also *loli*, turn over, turn inside out, to flay, skin, as an animal, to change, to alter. N. Zeal., *rori*, id. Tah., *rore*, to wrench or pinch; *rori*, to wash or cleanse; *ta-roria*, twisted about, as branches in a gale of wind. Sam., *lole*, to rub smooth.

Closely connected, if not a mere variant of the foregoing, is the Polynesian Haw., *lule, luli*, to shake, vibrate, overturn; Tah., *rure-rure*, the trembling of the voice in chanting; *ruri*, to change, shift about, pervert.

Sanskr., *lud, lul*, to agitate, shake, trouble; ptcple. of pf. pass., *loḍita*, troubled, agitated; *lola*, shaking, tremulous; *lolâ*, the tongue.

To this family doubtless refer themselves the English, German, and Swedish *roll, rollen, rulla*, as well as *troll, trull, stroll;* but I know not their Gothic or Saxon ancestors.

Welsh, *rholiaw, troliaw*, to roll, troll, whirl; *troll*, a roller; *truliaw*, to drill.

It may be interesting to note that in the Hawaiian, not only *lole, v.* signifies " to flay, to skin, as an animal," but *lole* is also a general name for " clothing, garments." As hogs and dogs are never flayed when cooked for food, and their skins were never employed for the purposes of clothing by any Polynesian tribe in the Pacific, the fact that the expression for flaying an animal was also used to designate clothing, garments, covering of the body, brings us back to the time when the Polynesians lived in places where the skins of animals were employed for clothing; beyond the Pacific, beyond the Malay Archipelago, and probably in a clime where the skins of animals afforded warmth as well as covering for the body.

LOMA, *v.* Haw., be lazy, slow, awkward. Sam., *loma*, be quiet; *luma*, disgrace, reproach. Tah., *roma*, to shrink, become less; *ruma*, gloom, as of evening, sullenness, sadness; *ruma-ruma*, be dark, gloomy, sullen, sad. Fiji., *luma*, ashamed; *druma*, foolish, stupid.

Sanskr., *rumra*, tawny.

Sax., *gloming*, twilight. Engl., *gloom, gloaming, glum.* Dutch, *lommer*, shade; *loom*, dull, heavy, slow. Swed., *loma*, to drag the legs in walking; *glåmig*, wan, languid, lead-coloured, bleak; *glŏmma*, to forget.

LOMI, *v.* Haw., to rub, press, squeeze; *lumi, lulumi*, to gather in a small compass, to crowd, come together with a rush; *s.* a crowd of people. Tong., *lolomi*, to press down, defer, put off. Tah., *rumi*, to press, rub, wring as a cloth, to look away from a person or thing; *romi-romi*, to hide or conceal. Sam., *lomi*, to press on, knead gently, to press under, to suppress. Marqu., *omi*, to press, crush. Fiji., *rombo*, be full, filled.

Lat., *glomus*, a ball; *globus*, any round mass, lump, ball, crowd, as of people; *glomero*. Possibly *lumbus*, loin.

I know not the Gothic or Saxon forms of the English *lump, clump, plump*, though both sense and sound would seem to indicate their connection. But the Sax. *leoma*, utensils, Eng. *lumber*, useless and cumbersome things put away, doubtless refer themselves to the Polynesian *lomi* or some ancient equivalent form in *mb*, like the Fijian *rombo*, and of which the Latin *glomus* and *globus* are but differentiated expressions.

LONO, *v.* Haw., to hear, observe, obey; pass., it is said, reported; *s.* report, fame, tidings. Sam., *longo*, to hear, report; *s.* sound; *longoma*, to hear; *longonoa*, be deaf; *longo-longoa*, be famed, renowned. Tah., *roa*, report, fame, notoriety; *pa-roo*, famous; *tui-roo*, id. Marqu., *ono* or *oko* (*k* for *ng*), sound, to hear. N. Zeal., *rongo*, to hear, to sound, report, news. Tong., *ongo*, sound, tidings. Fiji., *rongo*, id. Iaw., *runu,* to hear. By the usual exchange of *l* and *n,* perhaps the Haw. *nana,* to bark, growl, and the N. Zeal. *nganga,* noise, uproar, refer themselves to this family.

Sanskr., *raṇ,* to shout, to sound; *raṇa,* noise; *raṇa-raṇa,* mosquito.

Pers., *lânah,* cry, noise; *lândan,* to cry, to bark; *ka-rânah,* a raven.

Irish, *lonach,* talkative, a babbler; *lon,* a blackbird; *r'an, ranach,* a cry, roarings.

Lat., *rana,* a frog.

A. Pictet (Orig. Ind.-Eur., i. 474) refers the Greek κορωνη, a crow, a jackdaw, to the Sanskrit *raṇ.* Perhaps the Swedish *röna,* to be aware of, to experience, apprendre, goes back to the Polynesian *lono* or the Sanskrit *raṇ.*

LU, *v.* Haw., to scatter, throw away, as small things, sow, as grain, shake, dive, plunge; *luu,* id., spill out, flow rapidly, rush, overturn; *luai,* to vomit; *lulu,* to shake, scatter; *luku,* destroy, slay, *s.* slaughter. Sam., *lulu,* to shake violently; *lu-e,* id.; *lutu,* to rattle, make a hollow sound in the water with the hand; *lu-ai,* spit out, vomit; *lu-o,* be rough, of the sea, be rainy, be in consternation. Tah., *ru,* to be in a hurry; *ru-ai,* to vomit; *ruru,* to shake, tremble; *rutu,* to beat, as a drum; Mang., *ruku,* to dive; *rutu,* to beat, as a drum. Marqu., *uku,* to dive; *utu,* to beat, strike. N. Zeal., *ruku,* to dive. Fiji., *lu,* to run or leak out; *lu-a,* to vomit; *lutu,* to fall or drop down. Malg., *luai,* vomit. Mal., *luka,* wound.

Sanskr., *lû,* to cut, clip, destroy, wound; *lûni,* harvest, according to Pictet; rice, according to Benfey; *ru* 2, ferire, secare. Vid. A. Pictet, who in " Orig. Ind.-Eur.," ii. 202, refers *lôta* to *lû,* spoils, booty; but Benfey makes no mention of *lôta,* and refers *lotra,* stolen goods, booty, as a corruption of *loptra,* to *lup,* to break, destroy. The probabilities are that the derivatives of *lû* in *lup, lush, lumb,* &c., were formed in analogy with the derivatives of *tu* and similar monosyllabic roots. Thus, in this instance, from *ru,* to hurt, we have *rûksha,* rugged, rough; *ruth,* to strike, to fell; *rudh,* to obstruct, &c.

Greek, λυω, to loosen, unfasten, to dissolve, break up ; λυη, dissolution, separation ; λυτηρ, a deliverer ; λυτρον, price paid, ransom ; λυμη, outrage, ruin, destruction ; ἑυω, ἑυσιον, ἑυσος, &c.

Lat., *luctor*, to wrestle ; *luctamen; lucrum*, gain, profit; *solvo*, to loosen, separate, *so-lutus*; *ruo*, to fall, tumble down, *ruina; ructo*, to spit out, belch out; *ruga*, wrinkle = Sanskr. *rûksha.*

Goth., *laus*, empty ; *lausjan*, loosen ; *fra-lusnan*, to perish.

Irish, *lot*, rapine.

Anc. Slav., *loviti*, to capture.　Pol., *low*, booty.

LUA, *s.*　Haw., a pit, hole, cave; *v.* to dig a hole ; also in ancient times a process of killing a man by breaking his back or bones; *lua-lua*, be flexible, pliant, soft, old garments, a road with many small ravines crossing it ; *lua-u* and *lua-ni*, a parent ; *lua-hine*, an old woman. Mang., *rue-ine*, id.　Sam., *lua*, hole, pit; *lua-o*, an abyss. Tah., *rua*, hole, pit ; *rua-rua*, to slander, to backbite ; *rufa*, worn out, as garments ; *rua-u*, old, stricken in years ; *s.* old man or woman.　Tong., *luo*, hole.　N. Zeal., *rua*, id.　Fiji., *rusa*, decayed, perished.　Malg., *loakh, luaka*, hole, cave, pierced.

Greek, τρυω, τρυχω, to rub down, wear out, waste ; τρυος, toil, labour ; τρυπα, τρυμη, a hole ; τρυπανον, a borer, auger ; τρυχος, a tattered garment, rags ; τρυφη, softness, delicacy ; θρυπτω, break in pieces.　Liddell and Scott refer these words to τειρω, to rub, rub away, as derivatives of it, wear out, and τειρω, to the Sanskrit *tri*, to pass over, hasten, fulfil, &c.　Benfey also concurs in that derivation when he refers τρυμα, a hole, and τρυτανη, the tongue of a balance, to the same *tri*.　With due deference to so great authorities, I would suggest that the above group of Greek words be referred to the Sanskrit *ru, lu*, lædere, secare, with the prefix *t*; and they would thus at once fall into line with their Polynesian relatives, whose development of sense is perfectly analogous to the Greek group, though their development of form has been arrested.　It may be noted, moreover, as distinctive of the two roots, *tri* and *ru*, that while from the former—to pass over frequently, to rub, to smoothen—the idea of "young, fresh, a youth" (*taruṇa*), "soft, delicate" (τερην), "tender, soft, and childhood" (*tener*), were developed, the root *ru, lu*, gave birth to the idea of "old age, weakness, crumpled, flexible, as an old garment;" *lua, lua-u*, τρυχος.

Lat., *trua, trulla*, a tray, ladle, basin; *ruo*, to tumble down, but whose primary sense must have been "to dig," as evidenced in the phrase "*ruta et cæsa*," and in *rutrum*, a spade, mattock. Quære *rus*, country, from *ruo*, to dig, cultivate?

Goth., *riurs*, mortal, corruptible. Scand., *ryc;* Swed., *rycka*, pull up, pluck out.

Anc. Slav., *ryti*, to dig; *ruvati*, to tear away.

Irish, *ruam*, a spade; *rumhar*, a mine; *ruamhar*, labour.

Lu'ɪ, *adj.* Haw., obsol.; *ko-lu'i-lu'i*, indistinct. Tah., *rui*, *adj.* be dark or blind, *s.* night; *a-rui*, id. ; *ta-rui*, be black, as the sky, lowering, Paum., *ruki*, night.

Greek, λυγη, darkness, gloom ; ἡλυγη, shadow, darkness; ἡλυξ, *adj.* id.

Irish, *loch*, dark.

Luhɪ, *adj.* Haw., tiresome ; *v.* be fatigued with labour, oppressed with grief or a burden; *s.* fatigue. Tah., *ruhi*, sleepy, drowsy; *ruhi-ruhia*, aged; *tu-ruhe*, drowsy, sleepy. N. Zeal., *ruruhi*, feeble. Sam., *pulupulusi*, be sick, of a chief. Tong., *puluhi*, id.

Sanskr., *ruj*, to break, to pain, afflict with disease; *s.* pain, sickness; *rujâ*, id.

Greek, λυγρος, sad, gloomy, dismal; λοιγος, ruin, mischief, death ; λευγαλεος, wretched, pitiful.

Lat., *lugeo*, to mourn, be afflicted.

The Polynesian *lu'i* and *luhi* may be variants, as λυγη and λοιγος, of the same root.

Luka, *adj.* Haw., obsol. ; *luka-luka*, the appearance of flourishing, thrifty vegetables; *nuka* (*n* for *l*), full, plump ; *nuka-nuka*, fat, plump, smooth, as young animals or persons. To this probably refers itself the Haw. and Sam.

lu'au, the petals of a plant, the leaves of the taro plant, boiled herbs generally. Perhaps also the Tah. *rutu,* a mountain plantain. I refer this word and its underlying conception to the

Sanskr., *ruch,* to shine, to please, be bright, sweet; *rochana,* splendid, pleasing, the name of several plants; *rochaka,* an onion, a plantain; *lochaka,* a plantain. In " Orig. Ind.-Eur.," i. 299, A. Pictet says : " Dans les langues européennes, c'est la forme *luk* qui domine, comme on le voit par λευκος, luceo ; goth., *liuhath,* lux ; irland., *loiche ;* cymr., *lluch,* id. ; anc. slav., *luc'a,* rayon, &c. Je n'hésite donc pas à rattacher à la même racine que *ro'cana* et *ro'caka,* les noms germaniques et lith. slaves de l'oignon et de l'ail ; ang.-sax., *leac ;* scand., *laukr ;* anc. all., *lauh* (avec mutation regulière du *k* primitif) ; lith., *lu'kai ;* anc. slav. et russe, *luku,* ail, et *lukovitza,* oignon ; pol., *luk,* &c. Le laghmani (du Caboul) *arûkh,* nous ramène à la forme *ruc.* Il est probable que l'oignon a été ainsi nommé de l'éclat caractéristique de ses pellicules."

LULA, *adj.* Haw., calm, as the wind, smooth, as the sea, lazy, indolent ; synon. with, and probably a dialectical variation of, *lulu,* a calm place under lee of an island or precipice. Mang., *ruru ;* Tah., *rurua,* shelter from the wind ; *pa-ruru,* a veil, curtain, to screen. N. Zeal., *ruru,* close, hidden. Fiji., *ruru,* calm ; *drudru,* dull, stupid.

O. Norse, *lura,* lazy, indolent. Swed., *lur,* a nap, light sleep. Engl. (Cumberland), *lurry,* to loiter.

LULU, *s.* Sam., owl. Tong., Fiji., *lulu,* id. Tah., *ruru,* name of albatross, also of a land-bird like the woodpecker. Haw., *nunu* (*n* for *l*), pigeon ; referable perhaps to

Sanskr., *ulûka,* an owl.

Lat., *ulula,* id.

Sax., *ula, ule,* id.

LUPE, *s.* Haw., a kite ; *lupe-a-keke,* the sea-eagle. Sam., Fak., *lupe,* pigeon. Tah., *rupe,* id. ; *rupo-rupo,* be giddy, to reel, stagger. Fiji., *rube,* to hang up, suspend. Sunda., *lumpat,* to flee, to fly. Mal., *rebah,* to fall, to tumble down.

Sanskr., *ropa,* an arrow; *ropanâkâ,* a bird (*Turbus salica*). Benfey refers these to *ruh,* to grow. I think that doubtful.

Greek, ρεμβω, turn round and round; ρεμβη, roving; ρομβος, a spinning, whirling motion. Perhaps κο-λυμβις, a sea-bird, a diver, a grebe. Liddell and Scott give no etymon of this word.

Lat., *co-lumba,* a dove, pigeon; *pa-lumbes,* a wood-pigeon, a ringdove.

For a thorough examination, though with different result, see " Orig. Ind.-Eur.," by A. Pictet, i. 400. The variation in the prefixes *co* and *pa,* whatever their original meanings, evidently shows them to have been merely prefixes. But Pictet, like many others, ignored the Polynesian branch of the Aryan stock in looking for older forms of words.

LUPA, *s.* Not used in other dialects. Tah., *rupa,* a thicket of brushwood, also a thicket of branching coral; *nupa* (*n* for *l*), an impenetrable thicket of underwood or coral. Fiji., *rubu,* a kind of native basket. Perhaps Haw. *a-luka,* to jumble together, mix confusedly (*k* for *p*).

Greek, ρωψ, low shrub, brushwood, brushes; ριψ, wickerwork, plaited osiers or rushes; ριπις, a fan for raising fire; *quære,* like the Haw. *peahi,* made of rushes? τριφος, a fishing-net or basket made of rushes.

MA[1], *prefix.* Haw., implying a sense of fulness, solidity, increase. Sam., *ma,* prefix denoting ability. N. Zeal., *maha,* many, much. In the names of Polynesian places this word still remains in full, as *Maha-pu,* a district in Huahine, Society Group; *Maha-uli-puu,* a land in Koloa, Kauai, Hawaiian group. Malg., *ma, mah, maa, maha,* power, faculty to do or have, a prefix; as a verb to produce, be able, create. Malay. and Sunda., *maha,* great; *mahi,* enough.

Sanskr., *mah,* to grow, increase, be powerful. (Accord-

ing to Benfey, orig. form *magh*); *maha*, great. In South
Indian dialects contracted to *ma*, as *Ma-du* for *Maha-deo*
(Sirwa); *Ma-vali-pura* for *Maha-bali-pura*, the name of
a city.

Lat., *magis, magnus, major*, &c.

Greek, μεγας, great.

Sax., *ma-ra*, more; *ma-est*, most. Goth., *magan*, be
able; *mahts*, might, power.

Irish, *mor*, great.

Pers., *mih*, to grow, increase.

MA², ME, *prep.* and *conj.* Haw., at, by, together, with,
in. Tah., *ma*, and, with, together. Sam., *ma*, for, with,
from, on account of; *mo*, on behalf of. Marqu., *ma, me,
mo*, id. Tong., *ma*, and, with, for; *mo*, id.; *be*, id. N.
Zeal., *ma, me, mo*, and, with, for. Other dialects nearly
similar. In the Kawi, *ma* in compound words means
"with, in possession of," as *ma-gadha*, with a club. Malg.,
a-ma, am, an, with, and, among.

Sanskr., *mith-as*, mutually, reciprocally, with one another; *mith-una*, a couple.

Greek, μετα, in the middle, among, for, with, by aid of,
&c. Dor., πεδα.

Goth., *mith, mid*, with, amongst, together. Sax., *vit*;
Germ., *mit*; Swed., *med*, with, by, &c.

Liddell and Scott, *s. v.* μετα, intimate that the radical
sense was "in the middle." Neither the Gothic nor the
Sanskrit seem to justify that conclusion, although they
are developed forms of a root now alone preserved in the
Polynesian. Neither *mith-as* nor *mith-una* give the
radical sense of "in the middle," but rather the sense of
one thing placed alongside of another, and these words
are therefore later forms of an ancient copulative in *mi*
or *ma*.

MA³, *v.* Haw., to fade, as a leaf, a flower, or colour from
cloth, to blush, as one ashamed, to wilt, wear out. Sam.,
ma, v. to be ashamed, to be all destroyed; *adj.* clean, pure,
bright; *ma-ma*, pale, clear; *s.* shame. Tah., *ma*, clean;
haa-ma, to be ashamed. N. Zeal., *ma*, clean; *whaka-ma*,

bashful. Stewart Isl., *ma*, white. From this we have the following Polynesian derivatives:—Haw., *ma-e*, to blast, to wither; *mae-mae*, be pure, be clean, be dried. Tah., *ma-e*, to be abashed, confounded, thin, lean, withered, fermented, decaying; *ma-e-ma-e*, soft, as fruit or fish, over-ripe. Sam., *ma-e*, to be stale, as fish; *ma-mae*, to wither, fade.

Greek, μασσω, ματτω, to handle, touch, knead, squeeze, wipe; μακτρον, a towel; μαγμος, a wiping, cleaning; ἀποσμαω, to wipe clean off. The Greek composite shows the primary root in μα-ω.

Sanskr., *math*, *manth*, to churn, to agitate, to crush; ptcpl. of pf. pass., *mathita*, churned, stirred, distressed, faded, agitated, destroyed; *mathin*, a churning-stick. The following words, to which Benfey gives no etymon, but which appear to be connected *inter se*, are probably also referable to some older or variant form of *math*, viz., *masi*, ink; *masina*, well ground; *masrina*, soft, unctuous, shining; *masrinita*, polished; *mantha*, the sun.

Lat., *macula*, spot, blot, blemish.

Lith., *minkau*, to pound, beat, thrash.

Slav., *maka*, flour, as pounded up in ancient mortars or ground in ancient querns.

A. Pictet (Orig. Ind.-Eur., ii. 54) sees in the Latin *mane*, the morning, a contraction of a Sanskrit *manthané*, from *math*, *manth*, to churn, thus indicating to a pastoral people the time for making the butter, and he refers the name of the goddess *Matuta*, the goddess of daybreak or morning, to the same Sanskrit *math*. It may be that *mane* is a contraction from *matne*, and that the early Latins identified the morning with the churning-time and called the former by a name derived from the latter. It is a plausible hypothesis until a better is found. To me the Polynesian *ma* and *ma-e* would seem to answer all the requirements of roots to *math*, *macula*, μασσω, and the conjectural μαω in ἀποσμαω; and I am inclined to think that even *mane* and *matuta* derive with better propriety from *ma* and *mae*, in the sense of " blushing, bright, pure, clear, clean," than from the operation of churning.

MA⁴. (Obsolete, only in compounds. An ancient name for the moon.) Haw., *ma-uli*, the day between the old and new moon, in which the moon is not visible; lit. "the dark, obscured moon." By the lunar account it was the first day of the month or moon; by the Hawaiian calendar of thirty days to the month it was the twenty-ninth day. In Sam., *ma-uli* means simply "the moon," but *ma-una* means "the waning moon," from *una*, to pinch off, split off. Hence probably the *ma* in *ma-lama*, Haw., is not *ma* intens., but *ma* the moon, and thus lit. "moonlight;" and also the other Polynesian name for the moon, *ma-hina, ma-sina*, is a composite of a primary but now obsolete *ma*, and *sina, hina*, to shine, be white. This Polynesian *ma*, now only occurring in compounds, brings us in relation with the

Sanskr. *mâ*, to measure; *mâs, mâsa*, the moon, a month, and its numerous West Aryan congeners. Greek, μην; Dor. μαν; Ion. μεις, μηνη (moon). Lat., *mensis*. Goth. *mena*. A.-Sax., *mona*. Lith., *menesis*. Zend, *mâo, mahya*. Pers., *mâh, mâhina*. Kourd, *mah, meh*. Belout, *mâhi*. Afghan, *miashta*. Osset., *mai, mei*. Arm., *amis*. Irish, *mis, mios*. Anc. Slav., *miesetsi*. There appears ·to have been three principal formations in early times upon the root *mâ*, under which the above examples ranged themselves: that in *ma* simply, to which the Zend and Osset. with suffixes *o* and *i* belong; that in *mas*, to which the Sanskr., Pers., Kourd, Belout., Afgh., Armen., Irish, Slav., and Greek (μεις) belong; and that in *mâna* (*i.e.*, mâ + ana, see Benfey), to which the Greek (μην, μαν), Lat., Goth., Lith., A.-Sax. belong. The contradistinction preserved in the Hawaiian and Samoan between the dark and waning moon, *ma-uli, ma-una*, and the bright or shining moon, *ma-sina, ma-hina*, confirms the inference that *ma* was a primary, original name for the moon in Polynesian, and nearest kin to the Zend and Osset. formations. This ancient form in *ma* or *mba* may still be detected in the Gilolo (Gani) *pa-i*, the moon, and the Sulu Island *fa-sina*, **id.**

MA'A[1], s. Haw., a sling; v. to sling, cast, throw away. N. Zeal., *maka*, to throw. Tah., *maa*, a sling, to sling stones, cloven, divided. Tong., *maka*, a stone; *makata*, a sling. Sam., *ma'a*, a stone; *ma'ata*, a sling; *ma'a'a*, hard, strong; *ma'a-i*, sharp, cutting, applied to tools, fire, words; *ma'a-u*, a biting stone, a poisonous stone; *ma'a-ma'a*, small stones, stony. Marq., *maka*, to fight.

Sanskr., *makha*, a warrior, sacrifice, oblation; *makhas-yâmi*, I fight; *maksh*, to divide, to cut.

Greek, μαχη, battle, fight; μαχομαι, to fight, struggle; μαχαιρα, a large dirk or knife; μακελον, an enclosure.

Lat., *macellum*, a place where meat, &c., was sold, shambles, provision market; *maceria*, a wall, enclosure; *macto*, to honour by sacrifice, to appease.

Irish, *machair*, combat.

Goth., *meki*, a sword. Sax., *mâki*, id. A.-Sax., *mece*, *mexe*, id. Scand., *maekir*, id.

Anc. Slav., *meči*, *miči*, glaive. Illyr., *mac*, id. Pol., *miecz*, id.

Pers., *mak*, *muk*, lance, javelin.

MA'A[2], v. Haw., to accustom oneself, gain knowledge by practice; s. experience, manners gained by practice; *maka-u*, ready, prepared; *ma'a-lea*, cunning, crafty. Tah., *mata-u*, be accustomed or used to a thing; *mata-i*, skilful, dexterous. Sam., *mata-u*, to consider, to mark attentively. Fiji., *mata-i*, a mechanic.

Greek, μανθανω, aor. 2, μαθειν, to learn, to acquire a habit, be accustomed to; μαθος, custom; ματος, search; μητις, wisdom, cunning, craft.

Liddell and Scott, after Curtius, refer these Greek words to the Sanskrit *man*; Benfey refers μανθανω, ματος, to Sanskrit *math*, *manth*. The way is somewhat long in both cases. Either may be correct, but I think the Polynesian connection should not be overlooked.

MA'A[3], adj. Haw., going about here and there, loiter-ing, loafing. Tah., *ma'a-ma'a*, foolish, vain, useless. Marqu., *mama'a*, foolish. Fiji., *vaka-mamaka*, proud, buckish.

Greek, ματη, folly, fault; ματαω, be idle, loiter, dally;

ματαιος, foolish, useless, trifling. Liddell and Scott suggest that ματη is derived from μαω, to seek without finding.

MAI, *adv.* Haw., a word of prohibition, "do not," always used imperatively before verbs; *mai-helc, mai-hana,* "do not go," "do not do it." Marqu., *u-moi,* a similar imper. negative, "do not," also simply "not;" *au-ma,* not at all, by no means.

Sanskr., *mâ,* a prohibitive particle, an imper. "do not," a positive "no."

Greek, μη, no, not.

Lat., *ne,* prohib. particle, related to μη and *mâ,* according to Liddell and Scott and Benfey, permut. of *m* and *n.*

MAIA, *s.* Tah., midwife; *maia-a,* animal that has given birth.

Greek, μαια, good mother, nurse, midwife. In Dor., a grandmother. Liddell and Scott give no etymon or reference.

The existence of this word in the Tahitian and Greek seems to indicate that it was once common to the undivided Aryan stock. No other Polynesian, no other Indo-European branch has preserved it, though all have numerous variations of the original theme *ma,* as expressing a parent.

MAITAI, *adj.* Haw., good, beautiful, excellent, proper; *mai-au,* skill, ingenuity, wisdom; *mai-ele,* skill in using words. Tah., *maitai,* be well in any sense, good, holy, happy; *maiere,* to wonder, ponder, be surprised, deliberately, wary. Marqu., *mei-tai.;* Rarot., *mei-taki,* good, handsome, proper. N. Zeal., *pai,* good. Amboyna (Lariki), *mai,* good; (Batumerah), *a-mai-si,* id. Ceram. (Camarian), *mai,* id. Mal., *bai, baik,* id. Malg., *mai-nou,* proper, neat, pure; *ma-mai,* good.

That the root of all these Polynesian and Indonesian forms is *mai* will probably not be contested, but *mai* with that ancient double-consonantal sound of *mb,* of which some of the tribes of the Aryan family retained one, others the other constituent element. Thus, in course of time, the *m* sound prevailed with some, the *b* or its variant *p* with others; and thus the N. Zeal. *pai*, the Mal. *bai*, the Amboy. *mai*, retained in the Haw. and Tah. *mai-tai* and the Rarot. *mei-taki*, are originally one and the same word.

I have found no West Aryan relatives of this word except the

Sanskr. (Ved.), *may-as*, enjoyment; *mayo-bhû*, yielding enjoyment; *mayûkha*, light, splendour, beauty; *mayûra*, a peacock. Benfey gives no etymon.

Lat., *beo, beatus*, may probably connect with this. At least they seem to have no relations with the Indo-European circle.

MA'U[1], MA'U'U, *v.* Haw., to moisten, make wet; *s.* dampness, moisture; also a general name for green herbs, grass, shrubbery, &c. Sam., *ma'u'u*, grass, weeds. Tah., *mauu*, wet, damp; *mou*, coarse grass. Marqu., *mouku*, bulrushes. N. Zeal., *maku*, dampness, moisture; *makuku*, moist, fresh, cool. Malg., *muza*, wave, billow. Sunda., *mi-is*, damp, moist. Gilolo (Gani), *maku-fin*, cool, cold. Sanguir., *matuno*, id.

Sanskr. (Ved.), *mad*, "originally to be wet" (Benfey), to get drunk; *madhu*, sweet, the season of spring, water; *madayitnu*, a cloud; *madhura*, agreeable, tender; *mâdhava*, spring, spirituous liquor, a large creeper (*Gœrtnera racemosa*); *mâdhura*, Arab. jasmine.

Greek, μαδαω, be wet, moist, to run off, as water, fall off, as hair; μαδωνια, the water-lily; μεθη, the drinking of strong drink; μεθυ, wine; μυδος, dampness; μυδαω, be wet, damp, clammy. Liddell and Scott refer μυδος to Sanskr. *mid*, viscidus fio, be unctuous, to liquefy. Its Vedic sense, however, according to Benfey, is "to rejoice," and he connects Sanskrit *mid* with the Greek μειδαω, to smile.

Lat., *madeo*, be wet, moist; *madidus; madulsa*, a drunkard; *mustus*, young, new, fresh; *matula*, a vessel to hold liquor.

A.-Sax., *mædewe*, meadow, low, watery, and grass-covered land; *medu*, mead or wine.

Russ., *motzu*, to wet; *makayu*, to dip, soak.

Illyr., *mas*, new wine.

Pers., *mast*, drunk. '

Welsh, *mwydaw*, to wet.

While nearly all the West Aryan branches in some form or other have retained the sense "wet, moisture, dampness," none, as far as I know, has retained the sense of "green herbs, grass, shrubbery," unless the Sax. *meatta*, Lat. *matta*. Russ., *mat*, a mat, a texture of sedge, rushes, flags, &c., would indicate a connection.

MAU², *v.* Haw., to continue, endure, be firm, remain perpetually, everlasting. Sam., *mau*, be firm, be fast, unwavering, to dwell. Marqu., *mau*, be firm, be assured, a law; *mau-ki*, to hold fast. Fiji., *mau*, sit still, be firm. In Haw., *mau*, *s.* means also the side of a mountain below the naked top, where people may live. In Mangar., *mou*, a hill, a mound. Derivs. Haw., *mau-na*, *s.* a mountain, highland; *adj.* large, swelling, extensive. Sam., *maunga*, a hill, a mountain, a dwelling-place; *mau-alunga*, high, tall, elevated; *mau-lalo*, low, deep; *mau-tu*, stand firm; *mau-mau-a'i*, be firm, unyielding. Tah., *maua*, *moua*, a mountain. N. Zeal., *maunga*, id.

A. Pictet (Orig. Ind.-Eur., i. 127) refers the Latin *mons* and its West Aryan congeners — Irish, *moin*, *muine*, a mountain; Welsh, *mynydd*, *mwnt*, id.; Gael., *monadh*, id.; Armor., *mane*, *mene*, id.; Pers., *man*, a heap, a pile; Lith., *myni-a*, id.—from a root *man*, whence the verb *mânîdan*, *mândan*, to remain in place, to dwell, and the *s.* *mân*, a resting-place, a dwelling, and whence also the Latin *maneo* and the Greek μενω, to stay, remain, stand fast. But Liddell and Scott, after Curtius, refer *maneo* and μενω to a root μαω, with a development into *man* or *men* akin to Sanskrit *man*, to think, that seems to me very bewildering. The Latin *maneo*, the Greek μενω, the Persian *mân*, and Zend *n-mâna*, demeure, dwelling, cannot possibly, with a radical sense of "to stay, remain, be firm," refer themselves to the Sanskrit *man*, to think, or the Greek μαω, which Liddell and Scott see beyond it. I think that there must have been another μαω or μανω, with the sense of "firmness, hardness, endurance," to which the Latin, Greek, Persian, as well as the Polynesian refer themselves.

Maha[1], *s.* Haw., an obsolete general name for fish, now only occurring in compound names of particular kinds of fish, as *maha-e, maha-ha, maha-mea, maha-moe, maha-wela,* all different species of fish. In Sam. the dolphin is called *masi-masi;* in Haw. and Tah., *mahi-mahi.*

Sanskr., *matsya, matsa, maċċha,* fish. Marath., *masa;* Bengal., *mâch;* Singhal., *matsa, masa,* id.

Pers., *mâhi,* fish. Kurd., *mahei;* Afgh., *mahai,* id.

Irish, *meas,* fish.

Maha[2], *v.* Haw., to hide a thing away, to steal; *maha-o,* the pith of a tree or vegetable, a soft or decayed place in the centre or body of a tree, a hole in a tree; *adj.* defective in the centre, rotten, hollow; *maha-oi,* impertinent, bold and immodestly forward. Marqu., *maha-e,* to forget; *maha-ti,* joy; *maho-a,* hidden. Sam., *masa,* be low tide, be sour, offensive, as the smell of putrefying things; *mase-i,* bad conduct, impropriety; *mase-pu,* id. Fiji., *masa,* asleep, as the feet or hands, to be silent; *masa-la,* the ebb-tide; *masa-lai,* corrupt, putrid, sour. Tah., *meho,* be hiding, a hiding-place.

Sanskr., *mach, mañch, much, muñch,* to cheat, be wicked, to boast.

Pers., *mang,* fraud, deception, thief, gambling; *mugh,* a priest.

Greek, μηχος and μηχαρ, means, expedient, remedy; μαγγανον, means for charming and bewitching others; μαγγανεια, jugglery, trickery.

Lat., *mango,* a tricky merchant.

Irish, *mang,* fraud, trickery, ruse.

Lith., *maklote,* a deceiver; *manga,* a prostitute.

Sax., *mangian,* to negotiate.

Liddell and Scott refer the Greek μηχος to the same root as μηδος and μητις, *i.e.,* to μαω, to strive after, desire; and they refer μαγγανον, &c., to μασσω, to handle, touch, squeeze, knead. Under correction, I would suggest that the Polynesian *maha* and the Sanskrit *mach, manch*, offer better etymons than μαω or μασσω. I am aware Benfey and A. Pictet refer the Sanskrit *mâya*, wisdom, a juggler, asura, fraud, deceit, trickery, magic, illusion, to a composite *man + ya*, from *man*, to think, and defend the derivation by referring to *gâya*, woman, from *ǵan, gignere*, and to *âyu*, living, from *an*, spirare ; but apparent analogy is not always proof, as I have frequently experienced in this work, and it is therefore possible that *mâya*, wisdom, is an ancient form of a Sanskrit *machya* or a Polynesian *maha*, before the former became a synonym for the perversion of wisdom, and while the latter designated wisdom as something concealed. Liddell and Scott indicate that the Greek μαγος is from the same root as μεγας = Sanskrit *mah, mahant*, great, powerful, honoured, and the same is intimated by A. Pictet. But the Persian Magi must have been wise before they became great and honoured—they certainly did not become, or were called, wise on account of their greatness. There were wise men in every family and every tribe before there was a college of wise men, a priesthood. Hence I think myself justified in referring the Greek μαγος to the Sanskrit *mâya*, with the primary sense of wisdom, and to the Polynesian *maha*, with the perhaps still older sense of concealing, and to the Sanskrit *mach, manch*, and their kindred, when wisdom had deteriorated into cunning, trickery and fraud.[1]

---

[1] Since writing the above I have read M. François Lenormant's interesting work "La Langue Primitive de la Chaldée," where, apropos of the word μαγος, on p. 367 I find the following : "Enfin doit trouver ici sa place le titre des docteurs chaldéens, *emga* or *imga*, dont la Bible a fait יִצ‎. . . . C'est là le nom dont les Grecs ont fait μαγος quand ils placent des Mages en Chaldée. On a cherché d'abord à ce titre une origine sémitique et on l'a rapporté à la racine עצם‎. Mais dans ce cas il devrait revêtir le plus souvent, sinon constamment, la forme des nominatifs assyriens, en *emgu* pour *emqu*, tandis que, dans le grand nombre d'exemples qu'on en possède, il est invariablement *emga* ou *imga*, présentant le suffixe des dérivés adjectifs en *ga* de l'accadien. C'est en effet certainement un mot de cette dernière langue, *em-ga*, 'glorieux, auguste,' pris très naturellement comme un titre sacerdotal ou doctoral." Thus then this μαγος has neither Sanskrit, Greek, nor Polynesian parentage, but is Accadian, *i.e.*, Turanian. Be it so. The Sanskrit *mach*, the Greek μηχος, still remain to claim kindred with the Polynesian *maha, masa*.

Benfey refers the Greek μεγαρον, μαγαρον, chamber, hall, cave, adytus, and the O. H. Germ. *ga-mah,* New Germ. *ge-mach,* to the Sanskr. *mah,* be great, to adore, honour. Liddell and Scott seem to doubt whether μεγαρον, μαγαρον, refers itself to μεγας, and thence to the Sanskr. *mah.* A. Pictet does not refer at all to it or its probable etymon. In this uncertainty, and in the absence of any Sanskr. descendant of *mah* designating "a chamber, hall, cave, house," &c., it may be permitted to refer the O. H. Germ. *ga-mah* and the Greek μαγαρον to the Polynes. *maha,* to hide, conceal.

MAHI, *v.* Haw., to dig the ground, till, cultivate; *s.* cultivation, planting; *adj.* strong, energetic, as a labourer; *moa-mahi,* a fighting cock. N. Zeal., *mahi,* to work; *kai-mahi,* a servant. Sam., *masi,* the pounded and fermented bread-fruit; *masi-masi,* the smart of a wound. Fiji., *masi,* to rub, to scour; *masi-masi-a,* bread-fruit in a certain state.

Sanskr., *masina, adj.* well-ground; *mas-rina,* soft, polished. No etymon by Benfey.

Greek, μογος, μοχθος, toil, trouble, hard work, distress; μαστιξ, a scourge, plague, whip. Liddell and Scott refer this latter to ἱμας, a leather strap or thong, and that to the Sanskrit *si,* to bind. I fail to see the cause for the elision of the aspirated iota, ἱ, and therefore think that μαστιξ refers itself better to the same root as the Sanskrit *masina* and the Polynesian *mahi, masi.*

Lat., *macer,* lean, emaciated, careworn; *macero,* make soft or tender.

MAKA, *s.* Haw., eye, face, edge, shoot, bud, offspring; *maka-maka,* friend, intimate, relative; *maka* and *hoo-maka,* beginning, commencement. Sam., *mata,* eye, face, point, edge, source, spring; *mata-mata,* to look at; Faa., *mata,* to sharpen, have the appearance of; *'a-mata,* to commence, begin. Tah., *mata,* eye, face, beginning, edge; *haa-mata,* to begin. Tong., *mata,* eye, face, &c.; *ma-mata,* to look. In nearly all the Polynesian dialects the compound *Mata-riki, Mata-ri'i, Mata-li'i,* is a name for the constellation Pleiades, lit. "the small eyes," and in Tahiti the name of a year was *mata-rii,* reckoned from the appearance of those stars above the horizon. Fijian, *mata,* eye, face, presence, origin; *mata-ka,* morning, the dawn. New Guinea (Matu), *mata,* eye.

The different applications of this ancient word in the kindred Asonesian dialects may be seen in the following table:—

Celebes . . .	*mata,* eye; *tau-mata-esen,* male appearance, man; *tau-mata-babine,* woman.	
Sanguir . . .	*mata,* eye.	
Amboyna . .	*mata,* eye ; *meka,* tongue.	
Ceram	*mata, mata-mo, mata-colo,* eye.	
Teor	*matin,* eye ; *matin-olu,* face.	
Biaju	*mata,* eye.	
Saparua . . .	*mata,* eye ; *tu-mata,* man.	
Mentawej Island	*mata,* eye.	
Banjak Island .	*mata,* eye.	
Singkel . . .	*mata,* eye.	
Engano . . .	*bahka,* eye.	
Malay	*mata,* eye ; *muka,* face.	
Sunda and Java	*mata,* eye.	
Malgasse . . .	*mass, massu,* eye.	
Tidore	*moda,* mouth.	
Gilolo (Gani) .	*su-mut,* mouth.	

Corresponding to the Polynesian *mata-ri'i* and *mata-ka,* we find the Sunda *mata-powi,* the Malay *mata-hari,* the Celebes *mata-alo* and *mata-rou,* the Engano *bahka-kaha,* the Banjak Island *mata-bolai,* the Amboyna *ria-mata,* the Malgasse *massu-andru,* also *mas-luk,* all signifying the sun.

Sanskr., *mukha,* face, mouth, front, commencement, ⌐
beak of a bird, tip, point of a thing; *anguli-mukha,* tip of the fingers; *maha-mukha* a crocodile (big-mouth). No etymon given by Benfey.

Lat., *maxilla* (?), chin.

Sax., *muth,* mouth. Goth., *munth.* id.

Examples of relationship are few among the Indo-European branches, and even *mukha, maxilla,* and *muth* have either had no satisfactory etymons assigned them, or have been left standing in the cold awaiting further examination. Among the tribes of the Hindu-Kush, down whose slopes so many ethnic waves have tumbled on the world below, the application of this word in its Sanskrit and Gothic form to the "face" may still be found. The Shinas of Gilgit, and the Narisati and Khowaree of the Chitral Valley use *mūkh* or *mook* for face or cheek; the Chiliss and the Gaware of the Indus Valley use *mūn* for face or cheek; and, following the Sanskrit sense of "front, commencement," they present us with the further derivatives of *pu-muko* (Gilgil), first; *mutoh* (Chiliss), id.; *munsh* (Torwalak), id.; *pa-muk* (Bushgali), before. Even the Malays have adopted this sense in *kota-muka*, "a suburb;" *pangking-muka*, "an antichamber, a verandah."

MAKA'U, *v.* Haw., compound of *ma* intens. and *ka'u*, to fear, dread, tremble, hold in reverence. Sam., *mata'u*, to fear. Tah., *ma-ta'u*, id. N. Zeal., *ma-taku*, be afraid. Fiji., *taku-mogemoge*, to writhe, to struggle, as in pain; *taku-tibi-tibi*, the vibratory motion of light reflected on the water. Marqu., *me-ta'u*, to fear. Tah., *ma-ta'u*, fear, dread. Jav., Mal., *tacut*, fear. Tagal., *tacot*, id. Malg., *tahots*.

Sanskr. (Ved.), *tak*, to start; *tank*, *tang*, to live in distress, to stumble, shake.

Greek, ταχυς, quick, swift, sudden.

MAKE, *v.* Haw., to die, perish, suffer, as a calamity; *s.* death; *adj.* dead, hurt, injured, wounded. Sam., *mate*, to die, be extinct, be benumbed, cramped, to abate, as high wind. Tah., *mate*, to die, be ill, sick, or hurt. Polynes., ubique, *mate*, death. Fiji., *mate*, to die, be sick; *mate-mate*, sickly. Mal., Pulo Nias, Celebes, Aru and Key Isl., *mate*, *mati*, death, dead. Malg., *fati*, id. Jav., *pati*, id. Motu (N. Guinea), *mati*, dead. Allied to this is probably the Haw., Sam., Tah., et al. *ma'i*, sickness, disease, to be sick, ailing. Marqu., Rarot., *maki*, a sore, be wounded.

I know not what may be the Sanskrit equivalent of this word, unless it be *math*, in the sense of "to crush, hurt, kill, distress;" for I think it hardly probable that the concrete sense of "to churn" could have been the original sense of *math*.

Pers., *mat*, confused, astonished; *matkardan*, to make check, in chess-playing.

Goth., *ga-maids*, bruised, maimed. Sax., *ge-maad*, akin to Engl. *mad*. Germ. and Swed., *matt*, weak, feeble, languid. Swed., *smäkta*, to languish; *möda*, trouble, with pain.

The Malgasse and Javanese variants in *fate* and *pati* would seem to indicate a possible connection with the Greek πασχω, παθειν; the Lat. *patior*, to suffer, undergo, perhaps Sanskr. *badh*, to hurt, to trouble; *bi-bhatsa*, disgust, abhorrence, cruel; and the Polynes. *mate*, through some ancient and once common form in *mb*, softened to *f* in the one case, and hardened to *p* in the other.

MAKU, *adj.* Haw., full-grown, firm, hard, full-sized; *maku-a*, full-grown, of full age; *v.* to be large, to grow, to strengthen. Tah., *matu-a*, strong, vigorous, hard, fixed; *matua-u'u*, aged, time-worn; *matua-tua*, be vigorous, as an elderly person, settled. Sam., *matu-a*, full-grown, fit to pluck or dig up, elderly; *adv.* very, exceedingly; marks the superlative degree. Tong., *motu-a*, full-grown, ripe; *matu-a*, an old man. Fiji., *matu-a*, ripe, fit, mature; *adv.* strongly, vigorously. Mal., *tuwah*, old. Balta (Sumatra), *orang-batuah*, an old man.

Lat., *maturus*, ripe, right, proper, seasonable.

MALA[1], *v.* Haw., to swell, grow large, puff up; *s.* a swelling, enlargement, cultivated ground, a garden. Sam., *mala*, *adj.* soft; *s.* a new plantation; *malae*, open space for public meetings. Tah., *marae*, *adj.* cleared of wood, weeds, &c., as a garden; *s.* place of worship. Tong., *malai*, a cleared ground for public purposes. N. Zeal., *mara*, a garden; *marae*, a courtyard. Sunda., *melak, pelak*, to plant.

Sanskr., *mala-ya*, a garden; *mâla*, a field; *mâlâ*, a garland; *mâlati*, a bud; *mâla-kara*, a gardener.

Greek, μηλον; Dor., μαλον, an apple, generally any tree-fruit, a girl's breasts, the cheeks, swellings under the eyes; μαρη, the fist; μαρναμαι, to fight, to box, do battle. Liddell and Scott as well as Benfey refer μαρναμαι to Sanskr. mṛin, to kill, mṛi, death, but give no etymon for μαρη, fist, hand.

Lat., mala, the puffed-out cheek, the jaw; malus, an apple-tree.

MALA[2] and MALAIA, s. Sam., calamity; adj. unfortunate, miserable. Haw., mala-oa, sad, sorrowful; malai-lena, bitter, acid, unpalatable. Tong., mala, misfortune. Tah., mara, an old name for Awa (Piper meth.); mara-mara, bitter, acid. Malg., mara, marats, bitter, sharp. Amboyna, marino, sour. N. Celebes, mansing, id. Fiji., malai, withered.

Greek, μωλος, toil, struggle; μωλυς, feeble, sluggish; μωλυνομαι, be worn out. Liddell and Scott give no etymon or reference to this class of words. Benfey refers them to Sanskr. mai. The Greek μαραινω, to quench, as fire, die out, waste, wither, would seem as nearly related to Sanskr. mlai and Polynes. malaia, as to Sanskr. mṛi, to which Liddell and Scott refer it. In Dravid. (Tamil), mâr is to be confused, be lazy; mâl, to die, to perish.

Sanskr., mlai, grow weary, be faint, languid; mlani, decay, weariness.

Lat., a-marus, bitter, harsh, sharp; marceo, to wither, be faint, feeble; mœreo, to mourn, be afflicted; mora, delay, hindrance.

Goth., mournan, to mourn, be troubled.

MALALA, s. Sam., charcoal; malala-ola, live coals. Tah., mara-ia, black, dark colour, a dark native cloth, a negro or black man. Haw., mala-o, obsol.; malao-lao, twilight, between day and night.

To this word probably refers itself the Polynes. colour-expression, viz., Haw., mele, yellow; Sam., melo-melo, red; Tong., melo, yellow, brown, tawny; Amboyna, mala, blue; Ceram., marah, blue, merah, red; Mal. and Biajon, merah, red; Celebes, *merai*, red, *moro-no*, blue, *moro-nago*, yellow, &c.

Sanskr., *mala*, dirt, filth, defilement; sin. *malina*, dirty, black, obscure, bad; *mâlin-ya*, blackness; *marâla*, cloud, lamp-black.

Greek, μελας, originally any dark colour, dark-red, dark-blue, swarthy, murky; μολυνω, to stain, sully, defile; μορον, the black mulberry.

Lat., *malus*, bad, &c.; *morus*, dark-coloured, black, a mulberry; *merula*, a blackbird.

Sax., *mœl*, *màl*; Germ., *mahl*, spot, mark, stain. Swed., *mälm*, a cloud; *mulen*, cloudy, dark, sad.

MALI, *v.* Haw., also *mali-mali*, to beseech, beg, flatter, soothe; *malie*, still, quiet, soft, gentle. Tong., Sam., *malie*, well, agreeable, satisfied. Tah., *marie*, be silent. Fiji., *mamari*, apologise, excuse, flatter.

Sanskr., *mrij*, to rub, stroke, wipe, cleanse; *mârj*, id.

Greek, αμελγω, to milk, squeeze, press out; αμεργω, to pluck, pull out; ομοργνυμι, to wipe off.

Lat., *mulceo*, stroke, touch gently; *mulgeo*, to milk; *mulier*, a woman; *lac* (for *mlac*), milk.

Goth., *miluks*, milk. Sax., *meoluk*, id.

Lith., *milszti*, to rub with the hands.

MALO[1], *s.* Haw., a strip of kapa or cloth tied around the loins of men to hide the sexual organs. Polynesian, ubique, *malo*, *maro*, id., ceinture, girdle-cloth, breech-cloth.

Sanskr., *mal*, *mall*, to hold; *malla*, a cup; *maltaka*, a leaf to wrap up something, a cup; *malâ-mallaka*, a piece of cloth worn over the privities.

Greek, μηρνομαι; Dor., μαρνομαι, to draw up, furl, wind round. No etymon in Liddell and Scott.

MALO[2], *v.* Haw., to dry up, as water in pools or rivers, be dry, as land, in opposition to water, to wither, as vegetables drying up; *maloo*, id., dry, barren. Tah., *maro*, dry, not wet; *marohi*, dry, withered. A later application of this word in a derivative sense is probably the Sam. *malo*, to be hard, be strong; *malosi*, strong; the Marqu.

mao, firm, solid ; ·N. Zeal., *maroke,* dry ; Rarot., Mang., *maro,* dry and hard, as land.

Sanskr., *mṛi,* to die·; *maru,* a desert, a mountain ; *marut,* the deities of wind ; *marka,* a body ; *markara,* a barren woman ; *mart-ya,* a mortar, the earth ; *mîra,* ocean.

For the argument by which A. Pictet connects *maru* and *mira* with *mṛi,* see " Orig. Ind.-Eur," i. 110–111. It is doubtless correct. But in that case " to die " could hardly have been the primary sense or conception of *mṛi.* To the early Aryans the desert, the *maru,* which approached their abodes on the west, must have presented itself primarily under the aspect of " dry, arid, sterile, barren," a sense still retained in the Polynesian *maro.* Hence the sense of " to wither, to die," is a secondary one. Again, those ancient Aryans called the deity of the wind the *Marut ;* and if that word, as it probably does, refers itself to the root or stem *mṛi,* the primary sense of that word was certainly not " to die," for the winds are not necessarily " killing," but they are " drying," and that is probably the original sense of their name.

Lat., *morior, mors,* &c.

Sax., *mor,* Eng., *moor,* equivalent to the Sanskr. *maru.*

MALU, *s.* Haw., a shade, the shadow of anything that keeps off the sun ; peace, quiet, secret, unlawfully. Sam., *matu,* shade, shelter ; *adj.* cool, soft, gentle ; *malu-malu,* overcast, cloudy. Tah., *maru,* shade, covert, soft, gentle, easy. Marqu., *mau,* shade, shelter. Mang., *moru,* secret. Fiji., *malu-malu,* shade ; *malua,* gently. Malg., *malu, maluts,* obscure, in the shade. Amblaw, *maloh,* soft. Amboyna, Saparua, Ceram, *malu, maru,* soft.

Greek, μαλη, the armpit; " ὑπο μαλης," under the armpit, secretly, furtively. Liddell and Scott give no reference; its etymon unknown. But it combines in a remarkable degree the two principal senses of the Polynesian *malu,* " shade and softness." Probably μηρος, the upper part, of the thigh, the ham, is akin to μαλη, the conditions of that portion of the thigh corresponding to those of the armpit.

Lat., *ala*, armpit, shoulder, wing. According to Liddell and Scott = $\mu\alpha\lambda\eta$, "the μ thrown off."

MAMO, *s.* Haw., children, descendants, posterity. Tah., Marqu., *mamo*, race, lineage. N. Zeal., *momo*, id.

Goth., *mammo*, flesh.

Sanskr., *mâṁsa* (?), flesh. No reference in Benfey's Sansk. Dict.

MANA[1], *v.* Haw., chew food for infants; *s.* a mouthful. Sam., *manga*, a mouthful of chewed awa; *faa-manga*, open the mouth, to gape. Tong., Marqu., *mana*, *manga*, chewed food. Tah., *maa* (*n* elided), food, provisions. Pulo Nias, *manga*, to eat. Celebes, *monga*, id.

Lat., *mando-ere*, to chew, masticate. Benfey refers *mando* to Sanskrit *mad*, originally "to be wet," then "to be drunk." It is possible, but is it so ? Does the Sanskrit *mandura*, a stable, the Greek $\mu\alpha\nu\delta\rho\alpha$, stable, fold, byre, enclosure for animals, and the Latin *mandra*, id., derive from the same root as the Latin *mandere*, to chew ?

MANA[2], *s.* Haw., branch of a tree, limb of a body, the cross piece of a cross; *v.* to branch out, be divided; *mana-mana*, branching, projecting, fingers or toes, as coupled with *lima* or *vavae; manea*, the hoof of a beast, the nail of fingers or toes, the claw of beast or bird, the ball of a man's foot; *mana-halo*, stretch the arms and legs in swimming. Marqu., *menana*, fins of fish. Tong., *manga*, anything forked or straddling, barbed. N. Zeal., *manga*, a branch. Sam., *manga*, a branch, anything forked or curved; *manga-manga*, branched, forked. Tah., *maa*, cloven, divided; *mani-ao*, foot or toes. Amblaw, *wangan* (*w* for *m*), finger. Engano, *minu-afa*, finger (*afa*, hand).

Lat., *manus*, hand. Benfey refers this to Sanskrit *mâ*, to measure. But as neither the Sanskrit itself nor any other West Aryan dialect has retained any application of this ancient *mâ* to the hand, *manus*, as "the measurer," it may be permitted to seek a relative for the Latin *manus* in the Polynesian *mana*.

MANA[3], *s.* Haw., power, energy, authority, intelligence; *manana*, be angry, displeased; *hoo-mana*, to worship, reverence; *hoo-mana-mana,* use magical incantations, sorcery. Sam., *mana,* supernatural power; *mana-mana,* bear in mind, remember; *mana-tu,* to think; *mana-mea,* to love, desire. Tah., *mana,* power, might; *mana-a,* manageable. Tong., *mana,* thunder, omen. Fiji., *mana,* sign, wonder, miracle. Also used when addressing a deity or at the close of a prayer, equivalent to " Amen, so be it." Malg., *minai, mineh,* insane.

To the stem of this word or its root doubtless refers itself another series of Polynesian derivatives, viz. : Haw., *manawa, s.* feelings, affection, sympathy; the soft place in the heads of infants. Tong., *manawa,* breath, feelings, disposition. Sam., *manawa, v.* to breathe, to throb, pulsate; *s.* the belly, the anterior fontanelle of children; *manawa-si,* fearful. Tah., *manawa,* the belly, the interior of man; *manawa-fate,* be in bitterness of grief of mind; *mana-wa-nawa,* to think, to ponder; *manawa-rû,* eager desire. Marqu., *menawa,* belly, breathing, breath. N. Zeal., *manawa,* to breathe. Mangar., *manawa,* belly, disposition, temper.

Within the Polynesian area proper I have not found any derivative of this family used to express the sense of " man " or " mankind." The Asonesian, Sunda, Malay, Goram, Matabello, Sanguir, Ceram., *manusia, manusa, manesh,* evidently refer to later Sanskrit or Sanskritoid sources.

Sanskr., *man,* to think, consider, desire, respect; *manas,* mind, intellect; *manu, manus,* man = " the thinker;" *mantri,* a wise man; *mân,* to honour, respect; *mântrika,* a scorcerer; *mantra,* holy sayings, prayer; *manava,* human, mankind, a boy; *mânin, manavant,* proud; *mnâ,* remember.

Zend, *manthra,* magic formula, incantation.

Greek, μαντις, a seer, a diviner, one who utters oracles; μηνις, Dor. μανις, wrath, divine wrath; μαινομαι; μενος, might, force, strength, courage, temper; μνημη, memory.

Lat., *mens,* mind; *memini,* remember; *mentior,* to lie; *moneo,* to remind; *monstro,* point out, show; *monstrum,* an unlucky omen, strange, &c. Perhaps *vates*, a prophet, seer (*v* for *m*).

Goth., *man*, I think; *manna*, man; *minan*, *munan*, think, consider; *muns*, mind, meaning. A.-Sax., *manian*, *munan*. O. H. Germ., *minnia*, love; *manen*, to put in mind; *meina*, meaning. Swed., *minne*, memory, mind; *munter*, cheerful.

Irish, *manadh*, incantation, divination, omen; *menar*, to think; *menone*, soul, mind.

Lith., *moniti*, to bewitch; *minti*, think; *pra-mona*, invention.

A. Pictet (Orig. Ind.-Eur., ii. 546) says, "D'après toutes les analogies connues, le sens primitif de ces racines" (the abstract idea of thinking, reflection, mind, &c.) "doit avoir été plus ou moins matériel, mais il est souvent difficile à reconnaître." If the primitive material sense has been lost in the Sanskrit *man* and its West Aryan congeners (the Latin *manus* excepted), may not the Polynesian *mana*, limbs of body, claws of birds or beasts, &c., supply the missing link, and furnish that primitive material sense from which those of power, energy, will, feeling, thought, &c., were the facile and secondary developments?

MANAI, *s.* Haw., instrument for stringing flowers for wreaths. Sam., *manaia*, handsome, good-looking; *faa-manaia*, to adorn; *manongi*, fragrant. Rarat., *manea*. Marqu., *mainai*, handsome. Tong., *aka-manea*, to adorn. Tah., *monoi*, sweet-scented oil. Celebes (Bouton), *minak*, oil. Biajon, *mange*, id. Mal. and Sunda., *minyak*, id.; *ka-minian*, frankincense. Sula Isl., *mina*, sweet. Amblaw, *mina*, id. Teor., *minek*, id. Buru (Waiapo), *du-mina*, id. Mal. and Biajon, *manis*, id. Engano, *moneh-moneh*, id. Singkel Isl., *monde*, handsome.

Sanskr., *mangh*, *mank*, to adorn; *mangala*, lucky, propitious, burnt-offering, turmeric; *mankura*, a mirror; *mani*, precious stone, a jewel, fleshy processes hanging from the neck of a goat; *manîvaka*, a flower; *manava*, a necklace of sixteen strings.

Pers., *man-gôsh*, ear-jewel.

Anc. Irish, *maini*, precious.   Armor., *maneag*, necklace.

Greek, μανος and μαννος, a necklace; μανιακης, a brace-let.   Liddell and Scott refer this to μανος, porous, loose, evidently for want of a better etymon.

Lat., *monile*, necklace, collar; *mon-edula*, jackdaw (de-vourer of jewels); *manis* and *manus*, O. Lat. for *bonus*, good, gentle.

A.-Sax., *menas*, *pl.* collars; *hals-mene*, necklace.   Anc. Germ., *menni*, *manili*, id.

Anc. Slav., *monisto*, necklace.

In " India, What can it Teach us ?" pp. 135, 136, Prof. Max Müller refutes the assumption that *mana* was a Babylonian word borrowed by the old Vedic bards in " Rig-Veda," viii. 78, 2.   If *mana* itself does not occur again in the " Rig-Veda," its derivatives doubtless show themselves in the Greek, Latin, Irish, Saxon, and Slave above quoted.   The Polynesian evidently only retains a derivative sense.

MANO[1], *adj.* Haw., numerous, many; *s.* the number four thousand; *mano-mano*, many-fold, many, thick to-gether.   Sam., *mano*, a myriad, a great number.   Tah., *mano*, many, numerous, one thousand.   Tong., *mano*, ten thousand.   Marqu., id., numerous.

Goth., *manags*, many, much; *managei*, a crowd, multi-tude; *managnan*, to abound.   Sax., *mœneg*, many.

Russ., *mnogei*, many; *mnoju*, to multiply.

MANO[2], *s.* Haw., fountain-head of a stream of water; *mano-wai*, channel of a brook or stream.   The material heart, whence issues the blood as from a fountain; *ku-mano*, the head of a watercourse, a brook, or stream.   N. Zeal., *manga*, a brook.   Tah., *manu*, to float, be afloat, be adrift.

Sanskr., *mangh*, move swiftly; *mangiri*, a boat.

Lat., *mano-are*, to flow, to run.

MANO[3], *s.* Haw., a shark.   Sam., *mangō*, id.   Tah., *mao*, id.   Marqu., *makō*, *mangō*, id.

Sanskr., *mâni-kya*, the house-lizard; *mona*, a crocodile. Hind. (Malabar), *mani*, crocodile, alligator.

MEKI, *s.* Haw., an ancient name for iron; the modern name is *hao*. Only found in Hawaiian dialect.

Hind. (Khol), *medh*, iron.

Slav., *miedi*, bronze.

That the Polynesians were acquainted with iron, and had names for it, before its introduction among them by Europeans in the seventeenth and eighteenth centuries, I believe is now admitted by competent Polynesian scholars. Among these names the Hawaiian *meki* calls our attention as one of widespread connections and great antiquity.

I think philologists will not now question the fact that, in naming and defining the various phenomena of nature, mankind commenced by giving general names to substances of the same nature before it distinguished the specific differences between those substances by particular names. Thus all metals probably received one or more generic names before their differences were noted by specific individual names. Thus with colours; thus with animals; thus with the body or the most prominent parts of the body; thus with trees and fruits, &c. Thus language grew from vague and general terms to specific and more definite, and as mankind dispersed in tribes and families, they carried with them these generic terms, subject to dialectical differences and phonetic corruption, and added to them or dropped from them such concrete and definite terms as their mental development and the circumstances of their new positions might require. And thus, in course of time, many or most of the originally generic and synonymous words became specific appellations with various tribes. Thus only can I account for the singular fact that in different sections or tribes of the same race the same word frequently signifies different objects or ideas, although, where a close analysis is possible, those objects will generally be found to have been, or were deemed to be, generically related.

Applying the foregoing observations to the word now

under consideration, it seems obvious to me that this word, under some ancient form,—whose nearest relative I will not presume to determine,—originally signified metal in general, without any specific reference to iron, gold, copper, silver, &c.

The following list will show its varied application :—
Hind. (Khol), *medh*, iron. Slav., *miedi*, bronze. Haw., *meki*, iron. Jav. and Mal,. *mas*, gold;' *besi* (for *mbesi*), iron. Amboyna, *pisi-putih*, silver. Malg., *vih*, iron; *vi-futsi*, tin. Ceram. *masa*, gold. Sula Isl., *fa-maka*, gold. Scand., *messing* (*t* and *s* convertible), brass. Germ., *messer* (the metal instrument), knife.

Similarly we find the various applications of another ancient word, whose first and general sense doubtless was metal of any kind, then specialised to indicate this or that metal. That word is the Sanskrit *ayas*, metal generally, then applied specifically to iron, copper, and gold. . Zend., *ayô*, iron, copper. Pers., *ayan*, iron. Lat., *æs,* copper. Goth., *aiz*, copper.

No Polynesian relative proper now exists among the Pacific groups, but among the Asonesian groups we still find the following :—Celebes (Bouton), *ase*, iron ; (Menado), *wassy*, iron. Sanguir, *wasi*, iron. Sunda, *wadja*, steel. Malay, *tambadja*, copper; *badja*, steel.

I have purposely omitted the Greek μεταλλον and its apparent kindred in Latin, Welsh, and Irish, as its etymology seems not to be well established. Pott and Liddell and Scott refer it to the compound μετα-ἀλλον; A. Pictet, following Gesenius, thinks it is an Arab word, " *matala*, Hebrew *matal*, cudit, maxime ferrum," and that it was brought by the Phenicians to Greece. The μετ-ἀλλα theory is ingenious. It may be correct, but sounds too artificial, and does not satisfactorily explain the difference in sense between the Latin *metallum*, metal generally, gold and silver principally, and the Greek μεταλλον, a mine, trench, ditch, for any purpose, from a salt-pit to a gold-mine, with the specific object generally attached; ἁλος μεταλλον, a salt-pit; χρυσεα μεταλλα, gold-mines; μαρμαρον μεταλλον, a marble quarry. Mr. A. Pictet considers the Slavic *miedi*, bronze, copper, to be related to the Sanskrit *madhuka*, tin. If so, it only confirms my proposition that, whatever may have been the earliest form of the word, its primary sense was that of metal generally. That proposition I think still further corroborated from the compound terms which meet us in the Amboyna *pisē-putih*, silver, lit. " white iron or metal," and the Malgasse *vih-futsi*, tin, lit. " white iron."

Among the Southern Polynesians iron was also known before its introduction by Europeans. The Raratongans called it *kurima*, but I am not positive as to its relationship. It may refer to the Gilolo word *kurachi*, the name for gold as well as for yellow. If, as I think, *achi* and *kur-achi* is a dialectical variation of the Celebes term *ase*, then the first syllable, *kura*, is a Polynesian and pre-Malay word for red, bright, yellow ; and thus the compound word *kur-achi* becomes analogous to the Amboyna *pisi-putih*, and would signify " the red or yellow iron or metal."

When Bougainville visited Tahiti in 1768, he found the natives acquainted with iron, and says that they called it *a-ouri*. That *ouri* or *uri* and the Rarotongan *kuri* in *kurima* are but dialectical variations of the same word.

In the Samoan group *u'a-mea*, in the Tongan *uku-mea*, and in the Fijian *ka-uka-mea*, mean primarily metal of any kind, and conventionally iron ; for when the Tongans speak of copper, they add the adjective *kula*, red, thus calling it " the red metal or iron ;" and when they speak of silver they add *hina-hina*, thus making it " the white metal or iron." I know not whence this *uka*, the kernel or root of the above names for metal or iron, is derived or how related. It may refer to the Sanskrit *uchh*, to shine, and to the Pulo Nias *a-uso*, yellow.

The same manner of compounding is observable in the West Aryan branches. The Greek ἀργυρος, silver, comes from ἀργος or its root ἀργ, and the Aryan *ira*, *era*, earth= the white earth, ore, or metal.

MELE, *s.* Haw., song, chant; *v.* to sing, recite, chant. Tah., *mere, mere-mere*, the grief of parents at the loss of a child. Fiji., *mela, me-mela*, sounding, ringing, as metal when struck. Celebes (Gorontalo), *moloija*, to speak.

Greek, μελος, song, strain, melody; μελπω, to sing and dance. No etymon by Liddell and Scott.

Old Norse, *mal*, song, recitation. Swed., *măl*, speech, languages; *an-măla*, announce, mention. Goth., *merjan*, announce, proclaim; *meritha*, fame, report.

Liddell and Scott and Benfey refer the Greek μεριμνα, μερμηρα, thought, care, trouble, as well as Gothic *merjan* and Latin *mora*, to Sanskrit *smri, smarati*. I think *merjan* and its kindred *mal* and *an-mălan* refer themselves better to the Greek μελος and the Polynesian *mele, mere*, while μεριμνα, &c., fall better in line with the Sanskrit *mlai* and the Polynesian *mala*[2] (*vide* p. 222). The Sanskrit *smri* has doubtless its kindred in the Sax. *smeortan*, Engl. *smart*, Swed. *smărta*, if, judging from the prosth. *s.*, they do not all come under the *mlai* and *mala* just referred to. It will be well to bear in mind the peculiar characteristics of the Old Norse *mal* and the Hawaiian *mele-inoa*. They both recited in metric form the power and glory of dead ancestors as well as of living heroes. As neither Norse nor Polynesian have borrowed from each other, that custom, and its name, of chanting the exploits of ancestors, must have been a common Aryan trait before even the first separation.

MELU, *adj.* Haw., soft, as fish long kept, swelling up, bad. Fiji., *midra*, rotten, bad. Sunda and Mal., *mura-ati*, soft-hearted, mild.

Greek, ἀ-μαλος, soft, weak, feeble; μαλακος, soft, meek; μελι, honey; μαλθα, mixture of wax and pitch; μαλθακος, βλαξ, βλακος, slack, stupid, lazy.

Lat., *mollis*, soft, weak, delicate; *mel*, honey. Liddell and Scott refer *mollis* and *mulco* to μαλακος, and *mulsum* to μελι. They were probably one family of words in the beginning.

Welsh, *mall*, soft, melting, insipid; *s.* malady, evil.

Goth., *milditha*, mildness; *milith*, honey.

I know not the etymology of the Latin *muli-er*, woman, but it may possibly refer to this family, and have its nearest kindred in the Sundan *mura-ati*. The Sanskrit *mallâ*, a woman, the Arabian jasmine, does not certainly refer to *mal* or *mall*, to hold, but refers itself better to the Greek *à-μαλος* and *μαλακος*. Probably all of these are akin to the Polynesian *malu*, q.v., p. 224. If so, the Hawaiian *melu*, soft, derivatively applied to spoiled fish, would indicate an adaptation or borrowing from the Marquesan or Tongan dialects, where the original *a* sound is not unfrequently changed to *e*.

MENE, *v.* Haw., to shrink, settle down, pucker up; *adj.* blunt, dull; *mene-mene*, to contract, shrink, to fear, have compassion; *adj.* fearful of, solicitous for; *menui*, contracted, blunted, shortened; *mino*, *mimino*, to wrinkle, curl up, fade, wither. Sam., *mene-mene*, small, of the breasts; *min-gi*, curly; *mingo-mingoi*, to wriggle about. Marqu., *mene*, blunt, dull. Tah., *mene-mene*, round, globular; *mimio*, wrinkled, furrowed; *mio-mio*, id. Mal., *memindik*, to shorten, to lessen.

Lat., *minuo*, diminish; *minor*, less; *minimus;* quære *minister* as opposed to *magister ?*

Greek, *μινυθω*, to make smaller, to lessen, to curtail; *μινυνθα*, little, very little; *μειων*, less.

Goth., *mins*, less. Sax., *minsian*, diminish.

Welsh, *main*. Irish, *min*, *mion*, small, fine.

Sanskr., *mî*, *minâ*, *minî*, to hurt; *a-mî*, to scrape off; *pra-mî*, to diminish.

MI, MIMI, *v.* Polynes., ubique, to make water, void urine. Haw., *mi-a*, id. Sam., *mianga*, urine. Malg., *min-min*, foggy; *maman*, urine.

Sanskr., *mih*, to sprinkle, to urinate; *meha*, urine; *megha*, a cloud.

Lat., *mingo*, *meio*, to urinate.

Greek, *ò-μιχεω*, to make water, urinate; *ò-μιχλη*, mist, fog; *ò-μιχμα*, urine.

Lith., *myzu*, make water; *migla*, mist.

Goth., *maîhstus*, a dunghill. Sax., *miox*, *meox*, dung, excrement. Germ., *mist*, id., also fog. Engl., *mist*.

Benfey refers μιαινω to stain, defile, and μιαρος and μιασμα to Sanskrit *mih*.

MIO, *v.* Haw., be pinched up, cramped, tumble about in water; sink out of sight, to move softly, noiselessly; to leer; *s.* pass or narrow channel where water passes through rapidly; *mio-mio*, to dive, swim, puff, breathe hard, as in swimming. Sam., *mio*, to wander about; *mimio*, be confused, as a current at sea; behave coldly to another.

Sanskr., *mish* 2, to wink, contract the eyelids, look angrily, contend, resist.

Lat., *mico*, to quiver, beat, palpitate.

Benfey refers the Latin *miser* and the Greek μισος to Sanskrit *mish*.

MIKI, *s.* Haw., a pinch, what can be taken by the fingers; *v.* to pinch, snatch, hurry; *miki-miki*, to pinch, nibble as a fish. Sam., *miti*, to suck, sip, sniff; *mimiti*, to suck a wound, draw in, as a current. Tah., *miti*, to lick, lap as a dog. Marqu., *miti*, id., to touch, fumble.

Greek, μικος, μικκος, and μικρος, and σμικρος, small, little, petty.

Lat., *mica*, small bit, crumb, morsel.

MIKO, *v.* Haw., be seasoned, salted, entangled, mixed; *adj.* seasoned with salt, savory; *miko-miko*, tasteful, pungent, relishable. Tah., Mangar., *miti*, the salt water, sea, sauce. Amboyna, *mit, met*, the sea, salt water. Timor Laut, *meti*, sea.

Sanskr., *miçra* ("*i.e.*, *miç* + *ra*, perhaps for *miksh*, desider. of *mih*, without red," Benfey, Sansk.-Engl. Dict., *s. v.*), mixed, mixings.

Greek, μιγνυμι, pf. μεμιχα, μισγω, to mix, mix up, mingle; μιγας, promiscuously; μικτος, mixed, compounded.

Lat., *misceo*, mix.

Sax., *miscan*, mix.

Benfey, referring the Sanskrit *miçra* to a desider. of *mih*, seems to me rather forced. It is a derivative no doubt, but its root or primitive form might be found more readily in the Hawaiian *miko*, did the *amour propre* of Indo-European philologists permit them to seek for lost roots outside the orthodox Indo-European boundary.

MILI, *v.* Haw., to feel of, handle, carry, look at, examine; *mili-mili, s.* a curiosity, a thing to be looked at; *adj.* desirable to be looked at, admirable. Sam., *mili*, to rub, rub in, as an ointment; *mili-pa'u*, to fondle, caress. Tah., *miri*, to embalm a corpse; *miri-miri*, to handle and examine a thing. Marqu., *mii*, to look at, admire. Mang., *miri-miri*, to view, handle, examine. Tong., *mili*, to rub, smoothe, stroke.

Lat., *miror*, to wonder, be astonished; *mirus*, wonderful, strange.

Corn., *miras*, to look.

Russ., *miryu*, to stop, allay, pacify; *za-mirayu*, be astonished.

MOE, *v.* Haw., to lie down, fall prostrate, lean forward, lie down in sleep, to sleep, to dream. Sam., *moe*, to sleep, be congealed, to roost, to cohabit; *adv.* uselessly, in vain; *moenga*, sleeping-place, a hen's nest, cohabiting. Tah., *moe*, to sleep, lie down, to loose, forget. Tong., *mohe*, sleep; Rotumah, *mose*, sleep. Fiji., *moce*, sleep. Malg., *moket*, tired, weary.

Sanskr., *muh*, be faint, lose consciousness, fail, be perplexed, confused, stupid; caus. *mohaya*, to perplex, to stupefy; *pra-mohita*, insensible; *mogha*, vain, useless; *moha*, fainting, loss of consciousness; *mohin*, bewildering, infatuating.

Irish, *muich, much*, stupor, fainting. Amor., *môch* (obsolete or not found, but existing in compounds, as *roz-môch*, a poppy, lit. the rose of sleep or of stupor; vid. A. Pictet, " Orig. Ind.-Eur.," i. 293).

Lith., *mēgote, mēgmi* (pres.), to sleep; *mēgo-zole*, the poppy, lit. the herb of sleep; *mēgas*, sleep.

Anc. Ger., *mâgo*, poppy. Ger., *mohn*, id.; quære *mühe*, pain, trouble? Swed., *wall-mo*, poppy.

In Dravidian, Tamil, *mug-ir*, to fold up, as a flower its

petals; Canar., *much-ch-u* (mug), to cover up, shut in. In Tamil and Anc. Canar., *mugil*, a cloud (Caldwell's Drav. Gram.)

Mo'o, *s.* Haw., general name for all kinds of lizards. Tah., *mo'o*, lizard. Sam, *mo'o*, lizard; *v.* to be surprised.

Sanskr., *mush*, to steal, rob, plunder; *muçali*, a house-lizard; *músha*, rat, mouse; *mosha*, robbing.

Zend, *múska;* Pers. and Bokhara, *músh;* Kurd., *meshk;* Afghan, *mukhak;* Arm., *mugn;* Osset, *misht*, rat, mouse.

Greek, μυς, a mouse.

Lat., *mus*, mouse, rat, marten, sable.

A.-Sax., O. H. Germ., Scand., *mûs*, mouse.

Anc. Slav., *myshi;* Illyr., *misc*, mouse.

Moko, *v.* Haw., to pound with the fist, to fight, box. Sam., *moto*, strike with the fist. Marqu., *moto*, to compress, squeeze. Fiji., *moko*, to embrace, clasp round with the arms.

Greek, μοθος, battle, turmoil of battle.

Goth., *motjan*, to meet; Swed., *möta*, to meet, fall in with; *mot*, against, contrary, opposed to; *mota*, to stop, hinder.

Liddell and Scott refer the Greek μοθος to the Sanskrit *math*, to agitate, crush, kill, churn; and A. Pictet is of the same opinion. The Scandinavian *mot, mota*, would seem to offer an equally good, if not better, connection for the Greek μοθος; the more so as they evidently refer themselves with better sense to the Polynesian *moto*, in what was probably its primary meaning of "pressing together, to clasp, embrace," than they would to the Sanskrit *math*.

Mola, *v.* Haw., to turn, be unstable, spin round. Only found in the Hawaiian among the Pacific Polynesians. Possibly akin to the Haw., Sam., *milo*, and N. Zeal. *miro*, to twist, as a string or rope, to make twine; *mi-milo*, a whirlpool. Fiji., *mulo*, to twist. Malg., *ma-mule*, to spin; *fa-mule*, a twisted string, twine.

Greek, μυλη, a mill; μυλλω, have sexual intercourse; μυλλας, prostitute.

Lat., *mola*, a mill; *molo*, to grind.

Goth., *malan*, to grind. A.-Sax., *mylen*, *myll*, mill.

Lith., *malti*, to grind; *malunas*, mill.

Russ., *melinitsa*, mill.

Welsh, *malu*, to grind; *melin*, mill.

Irish, *meilim*, to grind; *muillion*, mill.

A. Pictet refers the Indo-European forms to a lost Sanskrit root, *mal*, "a secondary form of *mar*, *mr*, in its active sense of destroying, killing, crushing" (Orig. Ind.-Eur., ii. 119). But all the Indo-European references mentioned by Pictet imply a primary sense of twisting, turning round, whirling, as found in the Polynesian *mola*, *milo*, *mulo*, and not necessarily an underlying sense of destruction, killing, crushing. Until the Sanskrit root *mal* is found, perhaps the Polynesian *mola*, *milo*, will suffice.

MOLE, *s.* Haw., tap-root of a tree, bottom of a pit or sea, foundation, cause; fig. offspring, descendants from a root. So far as I am aware, only found in the Hawaiian dialect.

Sanskr., *mûla*, root of a tree, the lowest part, origin, cause, commencement, near, proximate; *pâda-mûla*, sole of the foot.

Lat., *moles*, a mass, lump, heap, foundation, a dam.

Benfey refers the Sanskrit *mûla* to a "vb. *mah*," whose original form again was *magh*, to be great, powerful. I know not the process of such a derivation, but think it faulty in view of the Polynesian *mole* and the Latin *moles*.

MOLIA, *v.* Haw., to devote, to give up to good or bad, to bless or to curse, according to the prayer of the priest, to pray for, be sanctified, to worship, sacrifice, to curse. "*Molia mai e ola*," bless him, let him live; "*Molia mai e make*," curse him, let him die. Tah., *moria*, name of a religious ceremony after restoration from sickness; *mori-mori*, prayer at do. Sam., *molia-molia*, be disappointed, deceived. Marqu., *moi;* Fiji., *moli*, thanks. Sunda., *mulija;* Mal., *mulieja*, dignified, illustrious.

Anc. Slav., *moliti*, to pray; *moliva*, prayer.

Pol., *modlic*, to pray ; *modla*, prayer.

Lith., *malda*, prayer.

Irish, *molaim*, to praise ; *moladh*, praise. Welsh, *mali*, to adore ; *mawl*, *molud*, praise.

A. Pictet (Orig. Ind.-Eur., ii. 701) refers the above West Aryan forms to the "Sanskrit *mad*, petere, rogare, in Vedic (Westerz), prop. exhilare," though Benfey (Sansk. Dict.) says that the original meaning of *mad* was "to be wet," and that in the Vedas it means "to get drunk." And Pictet considers the *l* in the Anc. Slav. and Irish and Welsh as an exchange for an original *d* or *dl* as preserved in the Polish. We have no remains of Ancient Polish with which to compare the Ancient Slave or the Irish and Welsh ; and I think, therefore, that the Polynesian offers a simpler and a better reference.

In Haug's "Essays on the Sacred Songs of the Parsis," p. 175, n. 2, he states that "for blessing and cursing one and the same word is used" in the Avesta—*âfrênâmî*—which thus corresponded to the old Hebrew word *berek*, "to give a blessing and to curse." It strengthens the West Aryan connections shown above of the Polynesian *molia* to find that the ancient Iranians also used a word expressing the same double sense.

MU¹, *v.* Haw., to shut the lips, hold the mouth full of water, make an indistinct sound, to hum, be silent ; *mu-mu*, id. ; *mumule*, be dumb, silent, out of one's head ; *mu-a*, to mumble food with the lips ; *mua-mua*, drinking water and spitting it out again ; *mui*, collect, assemble ; *mu-i-mu-i*, id. ; *mu-o*, to bud ; *mu-o-mu-o*, to swell out, as the bud of a flower, original sense, to pout with the lips ; *mu-u*, to collect, lay up in store ; *mu-ki*, apply the lips or mouth to a thing, to kiss. After the introduction of tobacco, to light a pipe, take a whiff, to squirt water through the teeth ; *mu*, *s.* a small black bug, a moth. Sam., *mu-i*, to murmur ; *mu-mu*, be in swarms, as flies, small fish, or children ; *mu-su*, be unwilling, indolent ; *musu-musu*, to whisper. Tah., *mu*, a buzz or confused noise ; *v.* to buzz, make noise or din ; *mu-hu*, noise, din of talking ; *mu-mu*, same as *mu, mu-i*, to tie up, collect; *muta-muta*, to mutter without speaking out, generally of discontent. Marqu., *moto*, to compress, to shut; *mutu*, dumb, stupid. Rarat., *mu-teki, mu-rare*, silent, dumb. Fiji., *mu-mu*, to swarm, as flies or mosquitoes. Malg., *mu-a*, dumb, foolish; *muk, mok*, mosquitoes. Ceram. (Wahai), *mumun*, fly. Mal., *nya-mok*, mosquito.

Sanskr., *mû*, to bind, compress; *mûka*, dumb; *s.* a fish; *maukya*, dumbness.

Greek, μυ, a muttering sound made with the lips; μυαω, to compress the lips in sign of displeasure; μυω, to close or shut, of the eyes or mouth; μυζω, to murmur; μυγμος, moaning, muttering; μυεω, initiate into mysteries; μυια, house-fly; μυνδος, dumb; μυδος, μυττος, id.; μυ-ωψ, blinking, short-sighted.

Lat., *mu*=μυ, *v.* supra; *musca*, a fly; *musso*, to murmur, mutter; *mussito*, be silent, speak softly; *mutio*, murmur, mumble; *mutus*, mute, dumb, silent.

O. H. Germ., *mucca;* Sax., *myge*, midge, gnat.

A. Pictet (*l. c.*, i. 421) refers the Greek, Latin, Old German, and Saxon names for "fly," as well as the corresponding Slavoid names—Russ., *mucha;* Bahem., *maucha;* Illyr., *muha;* Lith., *musse*—to the Sanskrit root *mac*, to sound, to be irritated, and its relative *maksh*, whence the Sanskrit forms *makshikâ*, a fly; *macaka*, a gnat, a mosquito. Under correction, I would suggest the Polynesian *mu* as a better reference; or, if everything must be referred to the Sanskrit as a test of linguistic kindred, there are the Sanskrit, Greek, and Latin *mu*, with their derivatives of μυζω, *musso*, &c.

Mu[2], *v.* Sam., to burn, to glow, to redden; *mu-mu*, to burn brightly, as a fire; *adj.* red; *faa-mu*, to kindle a fire; *mu-litini*, fiercely hot, of the sun. Haw., *mu-kole*, red, sore inflamed of the eyes. Ceram. (Wahai), *mulai*, hot.

Greek, μυδρος, any red-hot mass, especially of iron. No etymon given by Liddell and Scott.

Muku, *v.* Haw., to cut short, cut off, to cease, to stop, as a sickness; *moku, v.* nearly identical in sense, to divide in two, cut off, break asunder; *s.* a part of a country, a district, division, an island, a ship supposed to be floating islands, a piece of anything broken off. ˉTong., *mutu*, to break, separate; *motu*, small island. N. Zeal., *muku*, to break off, cease, fail, as a crop. Marqu., *motu*, to tear, break off; *s.* an island. Tah., *motu*, to tear, break; *s.* a low island; *motu-u*, to be stranded, as a rope; fig. mental weariness; *mutu*, be gone, vanished. Sam., *mutu*, to cut off, be defective; *motu*, be broken, severed, snapped asunder; *s.* an islet, a district. Fiji., *mudu*, to cut off, cause to cease; *musu*, cut crosswise, break off; *mucu*, blunt, of the edge. Mal., *mukim*, district.

Sanskr., *mus*, *mush*, to break to pieces; *musala*, *muçala*, a pestle, club. Perhaps *much*, to let loose, dismiss, to leave, abandon, take away. Perhaps also—

Greek, μυκης, a mushroom, any knobbed, round body, the chape or cap of a sword's scabbard, the stump of a tree; μυτιλος, curtailed, maimed.

Lat., *mutilus*, maimed, mutilated.

MULI, *prep.* Haw., after, behind, in time or place; *s.* a successor, the last of a series, hindmost, the younger child of two; *muli-wai*, lit. the last of the water, the mouth of a river, a firth. Sam., *muli*, the end, the hindpart, bottom, rump; *adj.* the young, of men and trees; *muli-muli*, to follow after; *muli-a'i*, the last; *muli-vae*, the heel; *muli-vai*, mouth of a river. Tah., *muri*, behind, afterwards; *muri-a-pape*, the mouth of a river. Marqu., *imui*, after. N. Zeal., *muri*, behind, after, younger, tip end. Tong., *muli*, behind, abaft, foreign, strange; *mui*, young. Fiji., *muri*, to follow, go behind; *muri-muri*, the last. Sunda., *mulih*, to go behind. Mal., *burit*, the hinder-parts. Jav., *buri*, the last.

Liddell and Scott consider the Greek μυριος, numerous, infinite, incessant, &c., and the Latin *multus*, much, numerous, frequent, &c., are related, but give no etymon for either. I am induced to think that a still earlier sense of μυριος and *multus* was that of frequency, sequence, succession, and thus would bring them within the family lines of the Polynesian *muli, muri.* Such expressions as *multo die,* late in the day; *multa nocte,* late in the night; *multum esse,* to be prolix, tedious, also to be frequent, of common occurrence, seem to be, based upon an earlier conception, when the word indicated sequence, succession, one thing following another, which doubtless was the radical sense of the Polynesian *muli.*

On p. 223, s. v. *Mali,* I have followed Benfey in referring the Latin *mulier* to the Sanskrit *mṛij,* and the Latin *mulgeo,* analogous to Sanskrit *duhitṛi.* I now think it more appropriate to refer *muli-er,* woman, to the Polynesian *muli,* she "who follows, comes after" the man.

NA[1], *art.* Haw., plur. prefix, they; *na hale,* the houses. In some South Polynesian dialects, *nga,* id.; *nga-lima,* the hands. Tagal., *ma-na,* they.

Sanskr., *nânâ,* various, different.

Irish, *na,* they; *na-lamha,* the hands. For an analysis of the Sanskrit *nânâ,* in connection with the Polynesian and Irish *na,* see Fr. Bopp, "Über die Verwandtschaft der Mal. Polynes. Spr. mit d. Ind.-Eur.," p. 98.

NA[2], NANA. Fiji., word used by children when addressing their mother; correlative to *ta* and *tata* for father; a familiar word for mother; *ngane,* a male's sister or a female's brother. Within the Polynesian area proper, *nana* is obsolete, and *ngane* or *nane* only remains in compounds, as *tua-ngane,* a woman's brother. Sam., *kai-ku-nane,* id. Haw., within the Indonesian circle of Polynesian relatives the word is still found. Celebes (Bouton), *i-nana,* mother; (Menado), *i-nany,* id. Sumatra (Singkel), *i-nanga,* id. Banjak Isls., *nenne,* id. Ceram. (Gah) and Matabello, *nina,* id. Buru., *neina,* id. Sunda, *neenee,* grandmother. Ke Isls., *nen,* mother.

Greek, νεννος or ναννας, a mother's or father's brother, an uncle; ναννα, aunt; νιννη, grandmother or mother-in-law. "*Nanâ* = mother, is cited from the Rig-Veda by Aufrecht."—Liddell and Scott, *s. v.*

NAE, *adv.* Haw., truly, indeed; but Tong., *nai,* perhaps, may be. N. Zeal., *nake*, but. Mang., *anake.* Tah., *anae*, only, merely, together, entirely.

Greek, ναι, yea, verily.

Lat., *nae*, truly, indeed.

NA'O, *v.* Haw., to thrust in, as the hand or fingers into some unknown receptacle, to penetrate, as the mind, to think deeply; *na'o-na'o*, to thrust in the hand, to seize, steal, look earnestly at, contemplate; *adj.* deep down, as a pit; *ma-na'o*, to think, call to mind; *s.* thought, idea. Sam., *nga'o*, diligent, industrious; *na'o-na'o*, to feel for, as for fishes in holes by introducing the arm; *ma-na'o*, desire, wish. Tah., *nao*, to take up little by little, as food; *nanao*, to thrust the hand into a hole or aperture; *s.* the tattooed marks on the skin; *ma-nao*, to think, reflect; *pu-naonao*, take out of a bag or basket, to steal; *ti-nao*, put the hand in a hole. N. Zeal., Rarot., *ma-nako*, think, hope, remember. Sumatra (Singkel), *me-nangko*, to steal. Pulo Nias, *me-nago*, id. Sunda, Mal., *ing-ngat-an*, to remember, memory.

Probably related to this family of words are the Haw., *noo, noo-noo*, seek, search after, reflect; *no-i*, to beg, entreat, ask for; *no-ii*, to glean, gather up, as small things, collect one's thoughts; *noi-au*, wisdom, knowledge. Sam., *no, no-no*, to borrow; *no'o-i*, to answer back. N. Zeal., Rarot., *i-noi*, to beg, entreat. Tah., *no-u-no-u*, to desire, covet.

Sanskr., *jñâ*, to know, be intelligent, recognise, search, investigate; *jñâta*, known, thought; *jña*, knowing. Zend, *jnâ*, to know.

Greek, γιγνωσκω, inf. γνωναι, to perceive, mark, know; γνωσις, investigation, knowledge; νοος, νους, mind, thought, sense; νοεω, to perceive, observe, think.

Lat., *nosco*, to know; *cognosco; notus; gnarus; gnavus.*

Goth., *kunnau*, to know. O. H. Germ., *knau*, to know. Sax., *cnawan*, to know.

Anc. Slav., *znati.* Lith., *zinoti.* Russ., *znayu*, to know.

Irish, *na*, soul, intellect; *gno*, known, famous; *gnas*, custom, habit.

The material and probably original sense seems to have been retained only by the Polynesian branches.

NAU, *v.* Haw., to chew, gnash the teeth, hold in the breath; *nau-nau*, to bite, as bitter plants; to chew, mince, to move the lips ᐧ as in chewing, mumbling. N. Zeal., *ngau*, to bite. Tong., *ngau-ngau*, a talker, a braggart. Sam., *ngau*, to break, chew sugar-cane; *ngau-ngau*, to fold up. Tah., *a-nau*, to grieve, as a parent for his child. Allied to this is probably the Haw. and Marqu. *nahu*, to bite, snatch at, to gnaw, to bite off, to file, to rasp; *s.* pain of biting, colic, inward pains.

Greek, κναω, κναιω, to scrape, scratch, tickle, itch; κνηκος, a kind of thistle.

Sax., *gnagan*, to gnaw, scrape, bite little by little. O. Norse, *naga*, id.; *nagga*, a quarrel. Possibly also Sax. *knægan*, to neigh as a horse, to whinny.

Irish, *cnaoidhim*, to gnaw, consume; *cnagh*, *cnaoi*, consumption; *cnuigh*, a maggot.

NAUA, *s.* Haw., noon; *adj.* cold, distant, angry, celebrating a chief's birth or residence. " *Owai kou naua ?* " was often asked in olden times of unknown or doubtful pretenders to nobility, equivalent to " Where were you born ? who were your ancestors? " So far as I know, this word only occurs with these meanings in the Hawaiian. In the Samoan we find *na'ua*, exceedingly, very; *nau-nau*, to be very great, to exceed. Tah., *nau-anei*, to-day. The primary sense of this word probably still lingers in the expressions " exceedingly," " distant," associating it on one side with the conceptions of zenith and noon, and on the other side with the birthplace of chiefs, who were considered not only as πορφυρο-γεννητοι, but also as διοσδοτοι, thus marking the distance (socially) between themselves and the commoners. Among the West Aryan relatives of this word probably the nearest is—

Welsh, *nawn*, noon, properly the summit of a thing, from *naw*, up, ultimate, what limits.

Sanskr., *nabhas*, sky, atmosphere, ether; *nabhas-vant*, wind.

Greek, νεφος, νεφελη, cloud.

Lat., *nubes*, a cloud; *nebula*, mist, vapour.

A.-Sax., *ge-nip*, a cloud. O. H. Germ., *nibul*, mist, fog.
O. Norse, *nifle*, id.; *Nifle-heim*, the Scandinavian Tartarus.

Anc. Slav., *Nebo*, heaven.

NAKA, *v.* Haw., to tremble, shake, be unsteady, be fearful. Probably *nake-ke*, to move back and forth; to rattle, rustle, as paper in the wind or as new kapa; to shake to and fro. Sam., *ngata*, a snake; *ngate-to*, to shake, tremble, be troubled. Marqu., *nganga*, *kaka*, the large house-lizard. Buru (Wayapo), *niha*, snake.

Sax., *snaca*, snake. O. H. Germ., *sneccho*, snail; *snachan*, to crawl.

Irish, *sna'gaim*, to crawl.

Sanskr., *nâga*, a serpent. Hind., *nag*, id. Cinghal., *nayâ*, id.

Does the Gothic *snaga*, a garment, belong to this family of words, from the trailing, shaking, fluttering of a garment?

A. Pictet refers the Sanskrit *nâga* to a primary compound, *nâ + ga*, what does not walk, " qui ne marche pas." With due deference, I think the earlier sense of *gâ*, *gam*, is to go, to move, irrespective of the manner of going or moving. Hence the compound *na-ga*, which Benfey interprets as " immovable, a mountain, a tree." It is probable, therefore, that *nâga* is a word of so old adoption that its etymon and origin had been lost within the Sanskrit language. The Polynesian *naka* certainly offers a more reasonable explanation than the self-contradictory *nâ-ga* of Pictet.

NALU, NANU (*l* and *n* convertible), *s.* Haw., surf, sea, wave, the slimy fluid on a new-born child; *adj.* roaring, surging. Sam., Tong., *ngalu*, a wave, a breaker; *v.* to break heavy, of the sea. Tah., *nanu*, the slimy matter on new-born infants; *nanu-miti*, flood-tide; *pa-nanu*, to flow as the tide; *nanu-nanu*, make a noise like a pigeon; Timor Laut, *noar*, river.

Sanskr., *nad*, to sound, to roar; *nada*, a river; *nard*, to roar; *nâra*, *nîra*, water.

Greek, ϝαρος, νηρος, flowing, liquid, wet, damp.

Welsh, *nadu*, to cry.   Irish, *naodhan*, spring, fountain.

Sax., *snora*, a snoring.

Tribes of Hindu-Kush (Torwalak), *nâd*, a river; (Narisati), *neudi*, id.; (Bushgali), *nunni*, id.

Liddell and Scott refer ϝαρος, νηρος, &c., to the Sanskrit *snâ*, to bathe; and so does Benfey. Such etymon may have been plausible while the Polynesian *nalu* was unknown, even were the *s* in *snâ* not a prosthetic.

NAMU, *v.* Haw., to speak rapidly and unintelligibly, to mock by imitating another, to nibble, as a fish at bait; *s.* unmeaning talk, a person of foreign language, a rapid motion of the jaws. N. Zeal., *namu*, to grumble, murmur. Sam., *namu*, mosquito; *nanu*, to stammer, pronounce wrongly. Mangar., *nanu*, to curse. Tong., Tah., *namu*, mosquito. Fiji., *namu*, to chew.

Sanskr., *nam*, to sound.

NANI, *s.* Haw., glory, beauty, splendour; *nanea*, pleasant, easy, cheerful, joy, comfort. Tah., *nani*, rich, having great possessions; *nani-nani*, well furnished, as a house. Marqu., *nani*, brilliant. Sam., *nanea*, be sufficient for a purpose.

Sanskr., *nand*, be pleased, rejoice; *nandi*, joy; *nandana*, gladdening.

NAPA, *v.* Haw., to writhe, to spring, as timber, to bend, be tremulous, as the air under a hot sun; *adj.* crooked; *napai*, bent, warped, as a board; *napana*, the joints of limbs, as wrists, elbows, knees; *napa-napa*, to bend, to arch, be bright, shining; *nape, nape-nape*, to bend, yield, be flexible, vibrate rapidly. Sam., *ngape*, be broken, fragile. Tah., *anapa*, flash of lightning; *nape-nape*, active, vigilant.

Sanskr., *nabh*, to burst, split, injure; *nâbhe*, navel, nave for a wheel, centre.

Zend, *nafa*, *nâfô*, navel, nave, centre.

Greek, ἀμβων, ἀμβη, (Ion.) ἀμβιξ, anything rising, projecting, as a hill, lip, edge; ὀμφαλος, navel, button, knob, centre.

Lat., *umbo*, the boss of a shield, the elbow, cape, projection; *umbilicus*, navel; *napus*, turnip.

Sax., *nafa*, nave, hub of a wheel; *nafela*, navel; *hnepan*, to lean, nod. Goth., *hnuipan*, pf. *hnaup*, to knap, break. O. H. Germ., *naba*, *nabulo*, navel. O. Norse, *nabhi*, head; *knappr*, a rocky projection; *snapr*, a point, beak; *knefi*, the fist. Engl., *nape*, joint of the neck; *nap*, short sleep, a nodding; *snap*, to break short.

Irish, *cnap*, a round body; *neip*, a turnip.

NATU, *v.* Marqu., to mix, to wash clothes. Mangar., *natu*, to dip, soak. Tong., *natu*, to mix, to knead. Tah., *natu*, to scratch, pinch, press repeatedly, mash, mix. Haw., *naku*, to stir up, as water, to trouble, give pain, to root, as a hog, seek, search. N. Zeal., *ngatu*, to scratch, scrape. Sam., *ngatu*, the stick used in rubbing for fire.

Greek, *νασσω*, Att. *ναττω*, to press, to squeeze close, stamp down; *νακος*, a fleece; *νοτεω*, be wet, damp, drip; *νοτος*, south wind.

Goth., *natjan*, to wet, wash. Germ., *netzen*, to moisten, to soak, steep; *nass*, wet, humid, moist. Dutch, *nat*, id.

NE'E, *v.* Haw., to move along horizontally, hitch along by degrees; *ne'e-ne'e*, id., draw near, approach, crawl; *nei*, similar to *nee*, but with more energy. N. Zeal., *neke*, to move along. Tah., *ne'e*, to move, to crawl; *ne'e-ne'e*, move repeatedly; *a-nee*, to spread, extend. Marqu., *neke-neke*, approach, draw near. Sam., *ne'e*, to bear up, as a boat lifted up by the water.

Sanskr., *naç*[1], *naksh*, to approach, to attain, to reach to.

Lat., *nanciscor*, *nactus*, to obtain, reach.

The Greek *νεω*—*β* (Liddell and Scott), to swim, inasmuch as it expresses a horizontal motion, would seem to ally itself better to the Polynesian *ne'e*, *neke*, than to the Sanskrit *snu*, to flow, distil, pour forth.

NEO, NEA, *adj.* Haw., desolate, empty; *v.* be desolate, still, silent; *v.a.* sweep off everything, to destroy; *nea-nea*, lonely, desolate; *neko*, filthy, bad-smelling. Rarot., *nea*, lonely, desolate. Tah., *neo-neo*, offensive in smell, putrid. Sam., *ngao-ngao*, deserted, empty, forsaken. Marqu., *neo*, the hiccough. Fiji., *neke*, empty, of crabs after spawning.

Sanskr., *naç*[2], be lost, disappear, perish; *naça*, loss, destruction, death; *naçin*, perishable; *nashti*, ruin.

Zend, *naçu*, corpse, cadavre.

Greek, νεκυς, νεκρος, dead body, corpse; νοσος, disease, sickness, distress.

Lat., *nex*, death, murder; *neco*, to kill, destroy; *noceo*, to harm, hurt, injure; *noxius; per-nicies.*

Goth., *naus*, a corpse; *nawis*, dead; *nauths*, need, necessity; *nauthjan*, to force, compel, constrain. Sax., *nead*, *neod*, need, want; *ge-neadan*, to compel.

In further correlation to the Sanskrit *naç* we have the Sam. *ngase, adj.* palsied, languid, lifeless; *v.* be languid, wane, as the moon, to die; Haw., *nahe*, soft, slow, weak, gentle; *nahe-nahe*, empty, as the bowels from fasting or sickness.

Ni'o, *v.* Haw., to sleep sitting and nod the head; *nio-lo*, sleep, drowsiness. Tah., *ni-nito*, to stretch, as when waking from sleep or when feeling weary.

Lat., *nico*, wink, make signs with the eyes. The Samoan *nengo* expresses exactly the same sense as the Latin *nico;* but in the absence of the ordinarily intermediate North Marquesan form, I will not venture to connect the Samoan with the Hawaiian or Tahitian.

Liddell and Scott, following Curtius, refer the above Latin *nico, nicto*, as well as *nuo, nuto, numen, con-niveo*, and the Greek νευω, to nod, beckon; νευμα, nod, sign; νυσταζω, to nod in sleep, to slumber, as relatives to an assumed root, νευ. There is no possibility of calculating the permutations of the West Aryan vowels, but while a Polynesian *ni'o, nito*, is to be had, it may be as well to separate the Latin *nico, nicto, con-niveo, -nixi*, from whatever root may have given birth to *nuo, nuto*, νευω, &c. To such a root I would refer the Polynes. Sam., *ngulu*, to sleep; Marqu., *nou*, to wink the eyes; Fiji., *nu*, be stunned or asleep, as the head or feet; Sunda, *nun-du-tau*, to nod, be sleepy; perhaps Engano, *pa-nuko*, to sleep.

NIHA, *adj.* Haw., rude, rough, harsh, wild, unsocial. Tah., *nifa-nifa*, spotted, variegated. Sam., *lifa* (*l* for *n*), thin, wasted. Malg., *manidz*, cold. Ceram. (Wahai), *lifie*, cold. Biadju, *jer-nih*, cold.

Sanskr., *niç*, *niça*, night; *nîla*, "*i.e.*, *niç-la*" (Benfey), black or dark-blue; *nîhâra*, fog, frost, rime.

Greek, νιφω, to snow; νιφας, snowflake, snowstorm; νυξ, night.

Lat., *niger* ("quasi *niç-va*," Benfey), black, dark, unlucky, ominous; *nix*, snow.

Zend, *çniz* or *çnij*, to snow.

Lith., *snigti*, to snow; *snegas*, snow. Anc. Slav., *sniegu;* Bohem., *snih*, to snow.

Goth., *snaiws*, snow. Sax., *snaw*, id.; *niht*, night. O. Norse, *nithing*, a villain, dastard, outlaw; *sniar*, to snow.

In confirmation of the above etymology, a similar formation may be observed in some of the pre-Malay dialects of the Indian Archipelago. Thus in Teor, night is called *po-gara-gara*, "the rough, rude, harsh night," while in the Ceram. (Gah) dialect night is simply called *gara-gara*, "the wild, the rough, unpleasant," scil. night; while the Ceram. (Awaija) *pepeta*, cold, meets us again in the Sunda, *petting*, night. Following the same analogy, the Sanskrit *nakta;* Vedic *nas* or *nak*, night, and its West Aryan relatives, *naths*, *nox*, &c., are generally derived from the Sanskrit *naç*, be lost, disappear, destroy. The Old Norse *nithing*, from *nith*, brings back the original sense of this word; and the Sanskrit *nîhâra* seems also to be in accord with the Polynesian *niha*.

NIHI, *v.* Haw., turn sideways on entering a house; *nihi-nihi*, *s.* anything standing on the edge, edgewise, the sharp ridge of a mountain; the corner of a table or square piece of timber; *adj.* difficult, strait, narrow, edged. Sam., *ma-nifi*, thin. Tah., *ma-nihi*, to slip or slide, as in climbing smooth trees. Tong., *ma-nifi*, thin, narrow. Malg., *ma-nifi*, thin, slender. Mal., *nipies*, thin.

Welsh, *nig*, straight, narrow.

Judging from analogy and the idiomatic character of

the language, there can be little doubt that the Polynesian *niho, nifo,* tooth—also in Tah. horn, projection, and in Haw. *niho-niho,* rough, projecting, proturberance, teethed like a saw or a shark's mouth—is a dialectical variation of *nihi,* peculiar to the Pacific branch of the Polynesian family. Among its pre-Malay congeners in the Indian Archipelago both forms occur, signifying tooth; *ex. gr.,* Saparua, *nio;* Matabello, *nifoa;* Ceram. (Teluti), *lilico* (*l* for *n*), (Ahtiago), *nifau;* Celebes (Bolangh), *do-gnito;* (Buton) *nichi;* (Menado),*ngisi;* Sulu Isl.,*nihi;* Buru,*nisi;* Amboyna,*niki.* Teor., *nifin;* Sanguir. Isl., *isi;* Malg., *nij, nifi;* Timor Laut, *nifat.*

I am inclined to believe that the Icelandic *nef,* Saxon *neb,* nib, bill, beak, and perhaps the Greek νυσσω, to prick with a sharp point, νυσσα, the turning-post at a race-course, originally refer themselves to the same root-word as the Polynesian *nihi, nifi, niho, nifo.*

NIKI, *v.,* also NAKI. Haw., to tie, knot, bind, fasten, confine; *niki-niki,* a sheath, what confines. Tah., *nati,* to tie, bind; *na-nati, nati-nati,* id.; *niti-niti,* niggardly, close-fisted.

Sanskr., *nah* ("for orig. *nadh,*" Benfey), to tie, bind, fasten; *naddhi,* cord; *naha,* obstruction.

Lat., *necto,* knit, bind, join; *nexus, nodus,* knot; *nux,* nut.

Goth., *nati,* a net; *nethla,* a needle. Sax., *cynthan,* to knit, tie, fasten. O. H. Germ., *nahan, nawan,* to sew; *nat,* seam.

Welsh, *noden;* Arm., *neûd;* Irish, *snadh,* threads; cnotadh, a knot; *cnudh, cnô,* a nut.

NU, *v.* Haw., to sound, roar, groan, grunt; *s. nu–nu,* a dove; *adj.* moaning, grunting, cooing, sullen, dumb; *nunulu,* to chirp, as birds, to grunt, growl. Sam., *ngu,* to growl, murmur; *ngu-ngu,* dumb; *nunu,* be silent from anger. Tong., *ta-nguru,* to snore. Rarot., *nguru-nguru,* to groan, growl; *ma-ngu-ngu,* thunder. Paum., *nguru-nguru,* to grunt; *s.* a hog; Marqu., *nunu,* dumb.

Sanskr., *nu, nû,* to shout. Ved., *nâu,* voice (Pictet).

Pers., *nuwâ, nawâ,* cry, sound, voice.

NUKU, *s.* Haw., the bill of a bird, the snout of an animal, mouth, nose of a pitcher or person; *nuku-nuku, v.*

to find fault, complain, scold; *adv.* on end, edgeways. Sam., *ngutu*, the mouth of men, animals, bottles, &c., the beak of a bird; *ngutu-a*, talk impudently; *ngutu-ngutu*, to promise and not perform. Tah., *utu*, the lip, bill of a bird, edge of a thing, the long snout of some fishes; *utu-taa*, forward, perverse. Marqu., *ngutu*, *kutu*, bill, beak, mouth. N. Zeal., *ngutu*, id. Tong., *ngutu*, face, mouth; *lo-ngutu*, the lips. Gilolo (Gari), *us-nut*, nose. Kaioa Isl., *us-nod*, id. Ternati, *nunu*, id. Saparua, *nuku*, mouth. Mentawej Isl., *ngungu*, mouth. Buru (Cajeli), *nuum*, id. Engano, *oku*, id.

This word, so common among the eastern branches, has so far as I can learn, only two representatives in the west: the Persian *nôk*, *nawk*, point, angle, beak, and the English *snout*, the Dutch *snuite*, Swedish *snut*, *snyte*.

PA, *s.* Haw., anything with a flat surface, as a board, plank, table, smooth rock, a wall, fence, enclosure; *v.* to fence, enclose; *pa-pa*, smooth, flat, a board, plank, a row, rank, a company sitting or standing in a row, a storey in a building; *papa-lina*, the cheeks of the face; *pa-pohaku*, a stone fence; *pa-pa*, *v.* to erect a screen or shade to prevent the light or heat of the sun; fig. to prohibit, forbid. Tah., *pa*, a fence, hedge, enclosed place; *pa-pa*, board, seat, flat rock, stratum of rocks, shoulder-blade; *pa-ti*, rank of people standing in a row, range of mountains; *pati-a*, fence of upright sticks. Sam., *pa*, a wall; *pa-pa*, a rock, a floor-mat, a board; *adj.* plain, level, flat; *pa-o*, to stop, check, forbid, correct. Marqu., *pa*, fence, wall; *po-pa-hi*, to command under penalty. Fiji., *ba*, a fence to enclose fish; *ba-i*, a garden fence or village fence. Malg., *fa-fan*, a plank; *fahets*, stockade, fence.

Sanskr., *pâ²*, to guard, preserve, protect, to govern; *pâ-tri*, a protector. Benfey (Sansk. Dict.) says that "the link between the signification of *pâ¹*, to drink, and *pâ²*, to protect, is formed by the signification to nourish," and he refers to the Greek παομαι, to get, acquire; πωμα, a lid or cover; A.-Sax., *foda*; Goth., *fodjan*, to feed; Lat., *pasco,* &c. Under correction, it seems to me that the Polynesian conception of *pa* as a wall, fence, enclosure, and perhaps the still older conception of board, plank, flat rock, row, scil. of rocks or stakes as a fence, is as good, if not a better, origin of the Sanskrit *pâ*, to guard, protect. This primary sense of the Sanskrit *pâ* occurs again—and there only, I believe—in its derivative *pâli*, a line, row, bank, dike, boundary, to which I shall refer again under the Polynesian *pali.*

PA'A[1], *v.* Haw., be fast, make fast, take hold of, hold on to, confirm, establish, secure, to finish as a work, to fix, hold back, detain, retain in memory, assert ; *pa'a-kai,* salt, lit. hard, solid water ; *pa'a-hao,* prisoner, lit. ironbound. Marqu., *pa'a,* ripe, as fruit, mature ; *pa'a-kaikai,* retain by heat, know ; *paka,* circle, reunion ; *patia,* to fasten, attach to. N. Zeal., *pa'a-tütü,* hatchet, on account of its hardness. Tah., *pa'a-na,* strong, vigorous, healthy ; *pa'a-ora,* a conqueror.

Sanskr., *pac,* to bind ; *pâça,* a tie, string, fetter, noose, net ; *paçu,* cattle.

Lat., *pango,* to fasten, fix, drive into ; *paciscor,* agree, contract ; *pactum, pax,* &c. ; *com-pesco,* keep in check, bridle, confine ; *pagus,* village ; *pecu, pecus,* cattle ; *fascis, fascia.*

Goth., *fahan,* to catch, apprehend ; *faihu,* cattle, property ; *fatha,* a hedge ; *fastan,* to hold fast, keep, observe ; *faths*[2], a leader, a chief. A.-Sax., *feoh,* cattle. Dutch, *pak,* a bundle. Engl., *pack,* to pack.

Lith., *pecku,* cattle.

Greek, πηγνυμι, επαγον, to make fast, fix, make solid, construct, make hard, freeze ; πηγος, firm, strong, solid ; παχνη, hoar-frost ; παχυς, thick, large, stout ; παγος, a firm-set rock, a peak, rocky hill ; πωϋ, flock of sheep ; ποιμην, a herdsman.[1]

---

[1] As an instance of idiomatic similarity, it may be interesting to notice that both Greeks and Polynesians formed their name for crabs or such shell-fish upon the root of this word. The Greeks called crabs by the general name of παγ-ουρος, lit. hard-tailed, hard-shelled. The Polynesians, Tah., call a small crab *pa'a-iea;* Sam., *pa'a,* general name for crabs ; Haw., *papai,* crabs.

PA'A[2], PA'A-PA'A, v. Haw., to burn, scorch, consume by fire; adj. scorched, burnt; s. dryness, thirst. N. Zeal., paka, anything dried in the sun. Rarot., paka-paka, burnt, scorched. Tah., pa'a, crust of bread-fruit, scales 'on the skin. Sam., pa'a-a, crisp, dry, as leaves. Marqu., paka, thirst.

Sanskr., pach[1], to cook, bake, roast, ripen; pak-tri, cooking, a cook; pâka, cooking, burning, baking, food.

Zend, pach, to cook. Pers., pagî-dan, id.; pêcha, fire; pochton, to cook. Affghan, pachaval, to cook. Arm. (k for p), khoh, kitchen. Osset., fichin, to cook. Shina (Gilgit), puch-oyki, be ripe. Khowaree (in Chitrat Valley), pećhi, heat; petch, hot.

Anc. Slav., peka, heat; pekari, baker; pectle, to cook. Lith., peczus, oven, fireplace; kepti, kepa (by inversion), to cook, roast.

Lat., coquo (c for p), to cook; culina (for cuc-lina), kitchen; papina, restaurant, eating-house.

Greek, πεπτω, πεττω, to cook, dress, bake; πεπων, sun-ripe, mellow; ποπανον, cake for sacrifices; πεμμα, pastry.

PA'I, PAKI (both forms), v. Haw., to strike with the palm of the hand, smite, spatter, dash; pai-o, to strive, contend, scold, strike to and fro. Sam., pai, to touch, reach to, arrive at; pati, to clasp the hands. Tong., pati, id. Tah., pai-pai, to drive evil spirits out of one possessed, done by clapping of hands and striking around wildly; pai-o, to arrange or adjust an affair in dispute; pati, start suddenly, jump, leap. Marqu., pai-o, dispute, quarrel.

Greek, παιω, to strike, smite, whether with the hand or a weapon, drive away, strike upon, correct, as a child; παραπαιω, strike on one side, strike falsely, fly off from, wander.

Lat., pavio, strike, beat, stamp, pave.

PAINA, v. Haw., to eat, to feed; to ring, squeak, sound, as in tearing or breaking a thing; s. a part separated or broken off, a meal, an eating. Tah., paina, a crashing noise, like the breaking of a stick.

Greek, παιω, to eat. Liddell and Scott consider this

word as a "modification in sense" of παιω, "to strike,"
and I think correctly so. The primary sense of "crashing,
tearing, breaking," evidently here underlies the conception
of "eating." The similar "modification in sense" of the
Polynesian *pai-na*, from the root *pai*, strengthens the relation of the Greek and Polynesian.

PAU, *v.* Haw., be all, entire, complete, finished, ended,
consumed, past. Sam., *pa'u*, to fall down, to set, as the
sun; *pa-pa'u*, shallow, as the sea. Tah., *pau*, consumed,
expended; *pau*, a shallow place of water; *pau-pau-te-aho*,
be out of breath, short-winded. Marqu., *pau*, be all,
ended.

Greek, παυω, to bring to an end, to cease, have done;
παυλα, pause, rest, end; παυρος, little, small, few; φαυλος,
slight, mean, trivial.

Lat., *paucus, paulus*, few, little, small; *pauper*, poor,
needy.

Goth., *faus, faws*, few; *fawizo-haban*, to lack, be short
of. A.-Sax., *feava*, few.

Welsh, *peus*, place of rest, country.

Related to the above Polynesian *pau*, as root, are the
following derivations:—

Haw., *pauku*, fraction, portion; *poko*, short, small; *pokole*,
id. N. Zeal., *poto*, short. Sam., *poto-poto*, a small portion.
Tah., *poto*, id. Vide s. v. *Pokii*.

PAHI, *s.* Haw., any cutting instrument, as reed, shell,
knife, or stones; *v.* to cut thin, to stand up on edge. N.
Zeal., *ta-pahi*, to cut. Tah., *ta-pahi*, a cleaver with which
to split bread-fruit; *v.* to split, divide. Sam., *fasi*, to break,
kill, split; *s.* a piece; *fasi-fasi*, split in pieces; *ta-fasi*, to
split open, break off. Fiji., *vasi*, a shell or knife to scrape
yams with. Buguis, *behi*, adze. Celebes (Menado), *pahegy*,
knife. Malg., *bassi*, hatchet.

Sanskr., *bash, vash*, to hurt or kill; *vas* (s. Benfey), to
cut. No Sanskrit derivatives from either form appear to
exist, at least I find none quoted by Benfey.

PAKA, *v.* Haw., to strike, as large drops of rain on dry
leaves, making a noise, to strike, fight, make war, cut,

pare, fend off, slide; *paka-paka, v.* to drop, as large rain-drops; *s.* a heavy rain-shower, a pattering noise. N. Zeal., *pata,* a drop; *pakanga,* battle.. Tong., *pata,* rough, coarse. Sam., *pata,* coarse, be lumpy, swollen, as the skin from bites of insects; *adj.* blustering, bullying; *papata,* any-thing done quickly.

Greek, πασσω, παττω (Att.), to sprinkle; πατασσω, to beat, knock; πατατος, clatter, crashing, sharp loud noise made by the collision of two bodies, the plash of waves, the rattling of wind.

Welsh, *fat,* a blow; *fatiaw,* to strike lightly.

Engl., *to pat, to patter, to spatter,* whose Gothic or Saxon ancestors are unknown to me.

PAKAU, *s.* N. Zeal., wing of a fowl. Tong., *ta-pakau,* id. Sam., *a-pa'au,* id. Marqu., *pako,* a kite; *pekehu,* wing. Rarot., *peau,* id. Haw., *peheu, eheu,* wing of a bird, fin of a shark, flipper of a turtle, brim of a hat. Tah., *pehau,* fin of a fish. Gilolo (Gani), *ni-fako,* wing. Mysal., *ku-feu,* id. Tagal., *pac-pac,* id.

Sanskr., *paksha,* a wing, the feather of an arrow, a flank, side; *pakshi,* a bird; *pakshin,* winged, a bird; *pakshman,* an eyelash.

PALA, *adj.* Haw., soft, ripe, rotten; *v.* to daub, besmear, blot out; *pala-a,* any dark colour, as brown, purple, &c.; *pala-i,* blush, shamefacedness; *pala-hea,* daub, stain, be dirty, defiled; *pala-kai,* to wither, droop, be barren, fade, fail; *o-pala,* dirt, filth, refuse; *ka-pala, ha-pala,* stain, spot, mark, print; *pala-pala,* to paint, spot, stamp, as in painting, or printing the kapa cloth. Tah., *para,* ripe, as fruit, and other vegetables, manure, dung; *para-i,* to daub, blot, efface. Sam., *pala,* ripe, rotten, muddy, a black mud used for dyeing; *pala-ie,* old rotten cloth; *pala-pala,* mud, blood; *pala-si,* drop as ripe fruit, fall down. Mang., *para-u,* worn out. Sunda, *balah,* dirt, foulness. Allied to this is probably the Haw. *palu-palu,* Tah. *paru-paru,* weak, feeble, diseased.

Sanskr., *palala,* mire, mud; *pallala,* a small pond.

Greek, παλαι, long ago, of old; παλαιος, old, weak;

παλεω, be disabled; παλυνω, to strew, sprinkle, besmear; πελος, dark-coloured, dusky; πελιος, dark, livid; πηλος, clay, earth, mud, mire.

Lat., *pullus*, black, dark-coloured; *fulvus*, deep yellow, reddish; *fuligo*, soot; *palus*, marsh, swamp, bog.

Goth., *fuls*, foul, stinking. Sax., *falu*, *fealo*, pale yellow, fawn colour; *pol*, pool.

In Dravid. (Tamil), *paru* means old, become ripe; *param*, a ripe fruit.

PALAOA, s. Haw., name of an ivory ornament made of the sperm whale's teeth, worn by chiefs; ivory, a whale. N. Zeal. and Mangar., *paraoa*, id. Marqu., *paaoa*, id. Tah., *para-u*, the shell of the pearl-oyster; *niho parau*, white teeth.

Greek, φαλος, white, shining; φαλιος, φαλαρος, φαλαρις, φαλακρος, bald-headed; φαλη or φαλλη, and φαλλαινα, a whale. Liddell and Scott refer φαλος to φαος, light, and φαω, to shine. It may be so; but, under correction, it seems to me like deriving cheese from chalk because both are white and shining. Liddell and Scott offer no etymon for φαλλη or φαλλαινα, but consider them akin to Latin *balena* and Scandinavian *hval*, whale. To me the Greek φαλος and φαλλη, as well as the Polynesian *pala-oa* and *para-u*, refer themselves to some common primitive root, now lost, of which the Polynesian *pala*, in some of its meanings, the Sanskrit *palita*, grey, grey-haired, the Greek πολιος, grey, grisly, the Latin *palleo*, are the scattered but nearly related descendants.

PALE, v. Haw., to refuse, stand in the way, hinder, fend off, parry, resist; s. what defends, a sheath, garment, curtain, covering; *palena*, a border, boundary; *papale*, hat. Tah., *pare*, a fort, place of refuge; *pare-pare*, to defend, guard, entreat the deities for favours; *pare-u*, a garment worn around the loins. Sam., *pale*, a head-dress, frontlet; *faa-pale*, to bear patiently, be exempt from work. Marqu., *pae*, head-dress, a veil.

Cognate to this is probably the Haw. *pole*, *pole-pole*, to ward off, fend off, separate. Fiji., *bore*, to scrape or wash the dirt off; to brighten up. Sam., *pole-pole-wale*, to palpitate, as the heart, be distressed in mind. ,

Greek, φαρος, a large cloth, cloak, or mantle, shroud; παλλω, to sway, swing, poise, toss; παλμη, a shield; παλμος, a quivering motion, vibration, palpitation; πελτη, a small shield; πελεμιζω, shake, make to quiver, drive away.

Lat., *pello*, to strike, beat, put in motion, to thrust away, push back, expel; *parma*, a shield; *palpo*, to tap, to stroke gently; *palpito; palla, pallium,* a covering, outer garment.

Armor., *pallen*, a covering, cloak.

Pers., *par*, a turban. Beluch, *phall*, id.

Liddell and Scott give no root, but refer φαρος to *palla, pallium*, as of probably same root. That reference, however, brings to light the connection of φαρος and *palla* with παλλω and *pello*, and their derivatives, as well as with Polynesian *pale* and *pole*. From these premises I am led to the conclusion that the Greek φαρετρα, a quiver, also belongs to this family, and not to φερω, to bear, as Liddell and Scott intimate. And though these gentlemen refer βλεφαρον, the eyelid, and βλεφαρις, the eyelash, to the verb βλεπω, to see, look, I would, in view of the foregoing *pale*, παλλω, *pello*, and their derivatives, consider these words as composite rather than as derivatives of βλεπω, and formed from βλεπω or βλεμμα, and φαρος, originally perhaps βλεπ (or βλεω-) φαρος = the covering of the eye.

A. Pictet (Orig. Ind-Eur., ii. 223) mentions that Kuhn refers the Sanskrit *phala, phalaka*, shield, to Sanskrit *phal*, to burst, findi, the primitive form having been *spal*, and from this derives the Greek σφελας, a footstool, and the Gothic *spilda*, a tablet, &c. While admitting the possibility of a similar derivation for παλμη and πελτη, Mr. Pictet adds :—" Tout fois, on trouve, en sanscrit, védique une rac., *spar*, sauver, proteger (cf. ang.-sax. *sparian*, scand. *spara*, anc. all. *sparôn*, favere, parcere), qui donnerait pour le bouclier un sens bien approprié, et à laquelle παρμη pour σπαρμη se relierait mieux qu'à *phal*."

It would ill become me to argue with so eminent men as the foregoing authorities, but I may be permitted to suggest that the Polynesian *pale* comprises both the senses of *phal* or *spal*, findi, and *spar*, sauver, proteger, and this is the older form, from which the others have diverged by affixing prosthetic letters, the better to define the particular sense intended.

PALI, *s.* Haw., a cliff, precipice; *adj.* precipitous, rugged, full of ravines. Tah., *pari*, perpendicular cliffs by the seaside; *v.* to square or shape a piece of timber. N. Zeal., *pari*, precipice.

Sanskr., *pâli*, the tip of the ear, edge of a sword, a line, row, raised bank or dike, boundary, margin.

Pers., *barin*, lofty, elevated, high in office.

Welsh, *par*, what shoots to a point, a spear; *yspar*, id.; *bær*, a spear, spit.

Icel., *fiall, fell*, a mountain. Germ., *fels*.

PANA, *v.* Haw., to shoot, as an arrow, to snap, as with the fingers, spread out, open, excite, throw, to give a name (nickname); *s.* a bow; *pana-i, v.* to put one thing in place of another, substitute, redeem, fit, stitch together, graft; *s.* ransom, price, surety, substitute; *adj.* closing up an entrance, filling up a place, wanting; *pani, v.* with nearly similar meanings to *pana-i; s.* a door, shutter, gate, stopple. N. Zeal., *pana*, to push. Sam., *fana*, to shoot; *fanga*, a bag, a fish-trap; *au-fana*, a bow; *pa-pani*, the cross-poles of a scaffolding. Tong., *fana*, a bow, the prow of a vessel. Tah., *fana*, a bow; *pani, pa-pani*, to close, shut up, hide. Rarot., *panaki*, to repair, substitute. Marqu., *pana*, to buoy up, wave, shoot at; *s.* a bow. Fiji., *vana*, to shoot with a bow, to pierce. Sunda, *panah*, a bow; *panto*, a door. Malg., *fanank*, a bow.

Sanskr., *pañch, pach*, to spread out, make evident, state fully; *pañchâ*, spreading; *pañchan*, the number five; *pañkti*, five, also a line, row, multitude.

Pers., *panghah*, the spread-out hand, the spread-out talons of a bird, also hook, net, string; *pangh*, five.

Sax., *fang*, a tusk, talon, claw; *fengan*, to catch.

Under the sense of "extending, spreading," may be referred the Gothic *fana*, a cloth, flag. Sax., *panna*, any broad and somewhat hollow surface. O. Norse, *panna*, forehead; *spannan*, to span, as a measure from one thing to another; perhaps *spinnan*, to spin. Lat., *pando-ere*, to spread, throw open, &c., display; *vannus*, a winnowing machine, a fan; *pannus*. Greek, πηνος, πηνη, the thread on the bobbin in the shuttle, the woof; *pl.* the web; πηνιζομαι, to wind off a reel.

Under the sense of "shooting, throwing, exciting with violence," may be referred the Greek φενω, to slay; φονος, φονη, murder, slaughter. Goth., *banja*, wound, sore. Sax., *bana*, a murderer. Pers., *ban, banu*, reaping, harvest. Irish, *banaim*, throw down, carry off, pillage; *beanaim*, to reap, harvest.

Under the sense of "replacing, substituting, ransom, price," may be referred the Latin *venus, venum*, sale; *vendo* (*venum-do*), to sell. Probably also *pando-ere*, in the sense of unfolding, displaying, scil. the goods for sale.

Of the sense of "closing, shutting," and, by inference, "concealing," I have found no trace or reference in the other Aryan branches, unless it be the *Panis* mentioned in Vedic mythology, who were demons of the night, and stole the golden-haired cattle of Indra, and drove them to a hiding-place near the eastern horizon, and whose name may have had an etymological reference to this Polynesian *pani*, though its mythical application may be of later origin. If so, its primary sense would be "the hiders, the concealers," scil. of Indra's cattle, "those who shut out the rays of the sun."

In "Orig. Ind.-Eur.," ii. 69–70, Mr. A. Pictet seems to refer the *panis* to the Sanskrit word *pani*, a merchant, for derivation and *raison d'être*. I think the philo-Sanskritism of Mr. Pictet has led him into error. If in the Vedic myths the *Panis* were analogues and synonyms of *Vrtra*, their etymology must be traced higher up than the Sanskrit *pani*, a merchant; and as the older meanings of that word seem to be lost in the Sanskrit, the Polynesian fortunately retains them, and enables us to find the correct rendering of the *Paṇis* as another term of *Vṛtra*. The Greek version of the myth, referred to by Pictet, could therefore evidently only have arisen after the original sense of *paṇi* had become obsolete and forgotten.

PANI, *v.* Tonga., N. Zeal, to besmear, plaster over. Marqu, *pani*, cocoanut-oil for ointment. Sam., *pani*, to dye the hair with the juice of the *pani* tree. Haw., *pani-o*, to spot, paint in spots; *pani-ki*, colouring matter, a dye. Fiji., *pani*, to anoint the head.

Sanskr.. *pánka*, mud, mire, clay, ointment. No root in Benfey's Sansk. Dict.

Allied to this is probably the Samoan *panu-panu*, be smeared over, be daubed; *pa-panu*, be daubed with mud or with colouring matter. Marqu., *panu*, tarnished, dull, blue. Haw., *pano*, black, dark-coloured, thick, dense; *poni*, besmear, anoint. Tah., *pao-pao*, be bespattered with mud; *haa-pao-pao*, to make brownish or dark. Mangar., *pangu*, black, dark-coloured. N. Zeal., *mangu*, id.

PAPA, *s.* Haw., an ancestor some generations back, a race, a family. Sam., *papa*, a general name for titles of high chiefs. Tah., *pa*, term of reverence, used by children in addressing their father, and common people their chief; *pa-tea*, term of respect addressed to a mother or a woman of rank. Mang., *paum*, *papa*, id. Gilolo, Tidore, Jav., Mal., *bapa*, *baba*, father. Suls. Isl., *ni-baba*, id. Amboyna (Batumerah), *ko-papa*, id. Malg., *baba*, id. N. Zeal, *paapaa*, father.

Greek, παππας, father; παππος, grandfather.

Lat., *pappas*, foster-father, tutor, guardian.

PAWA, *s.* Haw., the blue sky, expanse of heaven, the dawn, breaking of daylight, a watch, period of time; also *pewa*, the dawn. Fiji., *bewa-bewa*, scud, light clouds. Sunda, *powi*, day. Gilolo (Gani), *fowe*, sun. Pulo Nias, Banjak Isl., *bawa*, the moon. Malg., *ava*, rainbow.

This word probably refers to Sanskrit *bhá*, to shine; *s.* light, splendour, the sun; *vi-bhata*, daybreak. Greek, φοιβος, pure, bright, radiant; a form approaching the

Polynesian *pawa, powi, fowe,* an epithet of the sun-god. Liddell and Scott refer ἥβη, Dor. ἄβα, youth, and ἀβρός, graceful, beauteous, splendid, to the same root, and *s. v.* φοῖβος remark that Kaune considers φοῖβος connected with ἥβη. If the aspirate indicates a lost digamma, F, the original form of ἄβα would have been Fαβα = Polynesian *pawa.*

PE, *adj.* Marqu., bad, impudent, naked. Tah., *pe,* rotten, decayed. Sam., *pe,* be dead, as trees, extinguished, as fire, dried up, as water. Haw., *pe,* to crush, pound fine; *pepe,* broken, bruised, pliable, rotten, soft; *u-pepe,* weak, feeble, dry. Fiji., *be,* impudent, irreverent.

Benfey (Sansk. Dict.) refers the Latin *pejor, pessimus, pecco,* to a Sanskrit word, *pâpa,* evil, wicked, sinful. The Polynesian *pe* apparently offers a better and more direct root for *pejor, pecco,* &c. Benfey gives no root or etymon of *pâpa,* nor, if derived from *pâ,* to protect, to guard, how the transition is made to wickedness, crime, sin. Here, as in so many other instances, the Polynesian supplies the missing-link in the Hawaiian verb *papa,* "to prohibit, forbid, rebuke, reprove," a derivative or duplicate of *pa,* "to fence, enclose, restrict." And thus the transition from the Polynesian *papa,* prohibited, forbidden, to the Sanskrit *pâpa,* sinful, wicked, becomes easy and intelligible.

PELA, *s.* Haw., putrid flesh, burnt bones, offal, filth; *v.* be unclean, to stink; *pela-pela,* id. Tong., *pela,* corruption. Tah., *pera,* filth, dirt, cadaver. Fiji., *vela-vela,* filthy, disgusting.

Sanskr., *phela,* orts, leavings, droppings.

PENA, *v.* Marqu., to create, work, make, prepare. Sam., *pena,* to cut up, as a pig, to snare. Tah., *pena, penapena,* to bring up the rear of an army, to cover, protect the helpless.

Greek, πενομαι, to work, toil, prepare; πενεστης, a labourer, workman; πενης, id., a poor man; πονος, work, toil, drudgery; πονεω, work hard, to toil, suffer.

It may be for want of better etymology that the Latin *pœne, pene,* near by, almost; *penula,* a cloak, covering, outer garment, refer themselves to this family of words, in some forgotten sense analogous to the Tahitian *pena*.

In the West Aryan branches, the derivative sense of "pain, suffering, want," was developed from the primary idea of "working, working hard," and found expression in words like—Greek, πενια, πεινα, ἠπανια, &c.; Lat., *penuria, pœna, punio;* Sax., *pine;* Slav., *pina;* but seems to have been unknown to the Polynesians.

PENU, *s.* Paumotu, head. Tah., *penu*, a stone pestle.

Welsh, *pen*, head, summit. Gael., *ben*, id., top of mountains.

PI, *v.* Haw., to sprinkle, as water; to throw water with the hand; *pi-pi, ka-pi,* id. Sam., *pi*, to splash, slap, as fish in a trap; *ta-pi,* rinse with fresh water; *pisi*, to splash with water. Tah., *pi-pi*, sprinkle with water.

Sanskr., *pi = pâ*, to drink; *piv*, id.; *pinu*, to sprinkle; *pitha*, a drink, water; *pipâsâ*, thirst.

Greek, πινω, to drink; πιστρα, a drinking trough, drink, water; πιπισκω, give to drink; πωμα, drink, liquor, &c.

Lat., *bibo*, to drink; *bibulus, potus.*

Slav., *pi, piti, pivati,* to drink.

The transition from the sense conveyed in the Poly nesian to that in the West Aryan tongues will be intelligible to those who have observed the manner of drinking which probably obtained before cups or containers were used, and which is still very common among the Polynesians when travelling; it is by "throwing the water with the hand" from the spring or river to the mouth. That primary sense seems to have survived in the Sanskrit *pinu*, to sprinkle.

PIA-PIA, *adj.* Haw., the thick white liquid from sore eyes, dirty, watery, as the eyes; *pie, piepie,* slimy, slippery. Marqu., *pia,* blear-eyed. Tah., *pia-a,* fat, fleshy; *pia-pia,* the sweet gum in the banana blossoms, coagulated blood; *pie-e,* fat. Sam., *pia-pia,* the froth of the sea or of a pot boiling.

Sanskr., *pyai* ("developed out of Vedic *pî*," Benfey), pf. pass.; *pyâna, pîna,* fat, bulky; *pînatâ,* fatness; *pîvân,* fat, large; *pînasa*, cold in the nose, catarrh, cough. Benfey thinks the last is "probably *apinas*." Under correction, the Vedic *pî*, with the sense retained in the Polynes. Haw. *pia-pia*, explains the compound *pi-nasa*, vulg. "snotty nose," much better than *apinasa*, "by, on, or with the nose." Benfey refers *pichchhila*, slimy, lubricous, to the Greek πισσα and the Latin *pix*—Perhaps.

Greek, πιαν, fat, plump; πιαρ, any fatty substance, oil, thick juice, cream; πιμελη, soft fat, grease, adeps; πισσα, pitch, pine-gum.

Lat., *pinguis*, fat, corpulent; *s.* oily fat in the flesh; *pix*, pitch, tar.

Pers., *pî, pîh, pêd*, grease. Osset., *fiû*, id.

Irish, *bith, bioth*, resin, gum.

A.-Sax., *faeth;* O. H. Germ, *feist*, fat.

Pi'ı, *v.* Haw., to strike upon or extend, as the shadow on the ground or on a wall; to ascend, go up. N. Zeal., *piki*, to ascend. Sam., *pi'i*, to cling to, to climb. Marqu., *piki*, to climb, ascend; *piki-a*, steps, acclivity. Tong., *piki*, to adhere to, to climb, ascend. Fiji., *bici-bici*, a peculiar kind of marking on native cloth.

Sanskr., *pin'j*, to dye or colour; *pin'jara*, yellow, tawny.

Lat., *pingo*, to paint, represent, embroider.

The marking out or tracing a shadow on the ground or on a wall was probably the primary attempt at painting. In the Hawaiian alone the sense of an ascent, compared to the lengthening of the shadows, has been retained. As the sun descended the shadows were thought to ascend or creep up the mountain-side. The sense of "marking, tracing," seems only to have been retained in the Fijian, where so much other archaic Polynesian lore has been retained, and thus brings this word in connection with the Sanskrit and Latin.

Pi'o, *v.* Haw., to bend, to curve, be vanquished, as an enemy, extinguished, quenched, as fire; *s.* captive, prisoner. Sam., *pi'o*, crooked, wrong, in a moral sense. Tah., *pi'o*, crooked, bent, wrong. Tong., *piko*, to bend, curve.

Sanskr. (Ved.), *pîy*, to hate, hurt, destroy ; *pîyu, pîyant*, enemy, rascal ; quoted by Pictet (Orig. Ind.-Eur., ii. 201), but not found in Benfey's Sansk. Dict. Pictet refers to Aufrecht, and connects with this word the

Goth. *fijan*, to hate ; *fijand*, enemy ; *fajan*, find fault with, blame ; *fijathwa*, hatred. Sax., *figan, feon*, to hate ; *feond*, enemy.

Irish, *fi*, bad ; *fiamh*, horrible ; *fiamhan*, crime.

To this Sanskrit *pîy* Aufrecht and Pictet refer the Latin *pejor, pessimus*, which Benfey refers to Sanskrit *pâpa*, and which I have referred to the Polynesian *pe*, vide p. 260, *s. v.*

PIKO, *s.* Haw., end, extremity, top, tip, navel ; *piko-piko*, dotted, spotted, variegated, like calm spots in the sea ; probably allied to *piki*, to cut off, to shorten ; *piki-piki*, be rough, as a chopped sea ; *piki-piki-o*, rough, lumpy, as the water in a cross-sea. Sam., *pito*, the end of any-thing, only used in compounds ; *pito-pito*, the anus. Marqu., *pito*, the navel. Tah., *pito*, id. ; *pito-a*, spotted ; *pito-pito*, a button. Tong., *pito*, navel, also full, *i.e.*, filled to the top, brimful. Fiji., *vico-vico*, the navel.

Lat., *apex*, point, top ; *a-picatus*, mitred as a priest ; *spica*, ear of corn ; *picus*, woodpecker ; *pica*, a magpie ; *pug-nus*, fist ; *pungo, pupugi*, to prick ; *pugio*, a short sword, dagger ; *pugil*, a boxer ; *pugna*, fight.

Greek, πυξ, with the clenched fist ; πυγων, the elbow ; πυγμη, a fist ; πυγη, the rump, buttocks ; πυκτης, a boxer ; πυγμαιος, dwarfish.

Sax., *peac*, peak, top, point, end of anything ; *piic*, beak, bill, nib, anything ending in a point ; *fyst*, fist ; *feothan*, to fight. O. Norse, *fikta*, fight.

Pers., *paykân*, lance, pike.

Sanskr., *pika*, the Indian cuckoo ; *pichchha*, a tail, feather of a tail, a crest.

Probably the Greek πιθος, a large wine-jar ; Lat. *fidelia*, id. ; πιτυς, a pine-tree, and πευκη, the fir ; Lat. *picea;* also πικρος, pointed, sharp, are related to this family of words.

Liddell and Scott (Greek Lex., *s. v.* Πευκη) say, " Butt-man makes it probable that the radical notion of πευκη is not that of bitterness, but of sharp-pointedness, the fir being so called either from its pointed shape or from its spines. The same root appears in πικρος, Lat. *pungo*, *pupugi*, our *pike*, *peak*. . . . With πευκη come πισσα, πιττα, as the production of the tree, Lat. *pix*, Germ. *pech*, our *pitch*." The same authorities say of πυγη, πυγων, πυξ, that "the root is probably the same as the Sanskr. *bhuǵ*, Germ. *beugen*, to bow or bend," and to this they refer also the Lat. *pugnus*, *pugil*, and the O. H. Germ. *fust*, fist. A. Pictet (Orig. Ind.-Eur., i. 231–233) refers the Lat. *picea*, as a deriv. of *prix*, from the Sanskr. *pic̣ = pish*, conterere, grind, pound, and the Greek πευκη, to the Sanskr. *pú*, purificare, and the Greek πιτυς to the Sanskr. *pîta*, yellow.

In this uncertainty I may be excused for venturing to ally *pix* and πισσα, *picea* and πευκη, πιτυς and πικρος, to Polynesian words that offer as good, or better, an explanation of both the probably archaic meanings and forms of these words.

As regards the Greek πυγη, πυγμη, &c., which Liddell and Scott refer to the Sanskrit *bhuǵ*, and the Latin *pungo*, *pupugi*, which they refer to the same root as *picea*, πικρος, peak, I think the Polynesian *pito*, *piko-piko*, are better relatives to fall back upon for an etymological pedigree, inasmuch as they satisfactorily explain all the divergences of sense and sound which the West Aryan forms present for inquiry and solution. I fail to see wherein *pungo*, *pupugi*, *pugio*, differ from *pugnus*, *pugno*, *pugil;* yet the former are referred to the same root as *pike*, *picea*, πευκη, and the latter to *bhuǵ*.

Pili, *v.* Haw., to coincide, agree with, adhere to, belong to, be attached to; *s.* name for the thatching grass, general name of the belongings of a person, such as his property, children, family; *pili-alo* (lit. attached to the bosom), a friend; *pili-hua* (lit. words that stick, &c., to the mouth), wonder, sadness, trouble; *pili-kia* (lit. crowded posts), difficulty, trouble, want of room or want of means; *pili-koko*, blood-relations; *pili*, adj., joining, things adhering or coming in contact that ought not; hence, topsy-turvy,

helter-skelter, destitute, poor; *ka-pili*, to fit different substances together, repair what is broken, to plaster, besmear;
o-pili, draw up, contract oneself, as with cold or with
cramp. Tah., *piri*, adhere, stick to, be squeezed, confined,
close; *adj.* adhesive, glutinous, narrow, confined; *s.* a
wonder, a curiosity, a puzzle; *piri-ati, piri-rua*, a twin;
piri-taa, a relation by consanguinity; *pipiri*, stingy, close;
piri-oi, a cripple, lame; *ta-piri*, join things together; *o-piri*,
confused, bashful; *o-piri-piri*, dribbling, as water, drop
by drop; *piri-a*, the groin. Sam., *pili-pili*, be near, approach to; *pili-a*, be caught, be entangled, as trees falling
together; *pipili*, a cripple; *pili*, a class of lizards; *faa-pili*,
to bring near, to decoy; *ta-pili*, to fan the fire; *s. a.* fan.
Doubtless a dialectical variation of this is the Samoan
and Tongan *fili*, to choose, select, deliberate, be involved,
intricate, search, guess, contend; *s.* an enemy, the chosen
opponent in battle or in play. Tong., *fili-hi*, overturn
topsy-turvy. N. Zeal., Rarot., Mangar., *piri*, adhere, stick
to, close, near. Fakaafo, *pili*, near, adjoining. Malg.,
fili, choice, selection; *fili-mpuri*, the buttocks; *mi-fili*, or
mi-fidi, to choose, select. Jav., Mal., *pilih;* Tagal., *pili*,
to choose.

Greek, πιλεω, to press close, press wool or hair into felt;
πιλος, felt, a ball, a globe; πιλναω, to bring near; πιλοω,
to contract, as by cold; πελας, near by, close to; οἱ πελας
(ὀντες), neighbours; φιλος, φιλιος, friendly, dear, beloved;
φιλεω.

Lat., *pilus*, hair; *pileus*, a felt hat; *pilosus*, hairy; *pris*,
obsol. pos. of *prior, primus*, and root of *pridem, pristinus*,
&c., former, previous, in time and order, with the sense of
"next, last," as *priore œstate* last summer; *prius vinum*,
last year's wine or vintage; *pristina nox*, last night just
past; *prima nocte*, at the approach of night; *priores*, ancestors, forefathers; *priscus, pristinus*, old, former; *pridie*,
on the day before. All these varying terms indicate a
primary sense of closeness, nearness, proximity. To the
f variety of form refer themselves *filius, filia*, son, daughter,
and probably *filix*, fern.

Sax., *filian, fylgan,* to follow; *freond,* friend. Goth., *frijon,* to love ; *frijonds,* friend ; *frithus,* peace. O. H. Germ., *filz,* felt. Swed., *pilt,* a boy ; *flicka,* a girl (?).

Sanskr., *pri* 3 (Benfey), be pleased with; *a-pri,* be attached to; *pria,* beloved, dear; *pri,* to please, be satisfied, to assent; *prîti,* joy, gratification.

Zend, *fri,* to love ; *friathva,* love.

Cymric, *priawd,* a husband, conjux.

Po'o, *s.* Haw., name of a place under the sand; *po'o-po'o, adj.* deep, as a hole dug in the ground, a pit, sunken in, as the eyes; *v.* be deep, be lower down, sunk in ; *ka-po'o,* to enter into, as a spirit, to sink, as in water, to set, as the sun; *s.* the armpit; *na-po'o,* to sink, set, as the sun. Tah., *poo-poo,* deep, as a hole, sunken, depressed; *popo'o,* be indented, hollow, sunken; *a-po'o,* a pit, hole, grave ; *a-poo-ihu,* the nostrils. Mangar., *poko-poko,* deep, dug out. N. Zeal., *ta-poko,* to enter into. Fiji., *boto,* bottom, or under part ; *boto-ni-kete,* the abdomen, belly. Gilolo (Galela), *poko,* belly ; *biaju, butah,* id.

Sanskr., *budh,* to fathom, to penetrate, to understand, know ; *budh-na* (Ved.), depth, ground; *pota, potaka,* the site, foundation of a house. (No etymon in Benfey for *pota.*)

Sax., *botm, bytne,* bottom. O. H. Germ., *boden.*

Greek, πυθμην, the bottom or foundation of a thing, bottom, depth of the sea, the bottom, stock, root of a tree ; πυνδαξ, the bottom of a vessel; πυματος, the hindmost, undermost, last ; βυθος, depth, especially of the sea, a hole or pit dug in the ground, hole, hollow.

Lat., *puteus,* a pit, well, cistern ; *fodio,* to dig ; *fodina,* a pit; *fossa,* ditch ; *fundus,* the bottom of anything, ground.

Parsee, *bunda,* root, bottom.

Irish, *bun,* foundation.

So far as regards the material sense of this word, the Polynesian forms of *poko, poto, po'o, boto, butah,* correspond to the West Aryan forms *bot-, but-, budh-, put-, pynd-, fod-, fund-,* with remarkable precision in form and sense. But to the united Aryan mind the material sense of "fathoming, penetrating, digging into a thing," had already suggested the moral sense of " experience, knowledge, wisdom," which have found expression along the whole line. In the Polynesian, the Sam. *poto, v.* be wise; *s.* wisdom, also a hard-working man, a man sc. of experience; *poto-poto*, to assemble, to gather together; Tong., *poto*, wise, shrewd, cunning; N. Zeal., *tu-poto*, suspicious; Tah., *a-po'o, v.* to assemble for consultation; *s.* a council; *a-poo-raa*, a council, assembly; Malg., *vokato*, be honest, worthy; *voto*, promise, vow; Mal., *budi*, wisdom;—in these we find the same development of thought as in the Sanskrit *budh*, to understand, know; *budha*, wise; *budhi*, mind, intellect, reflection. Greek, πευθομαι, πυνθανομαι, to ask, inquire, learn; πευσις, inquiry, information. Lat., *fundo, -are*, to found, consolidate; *puto*, to count, adjust, judge, consider. Goth., *bindan*, to bid, command, instruct. Sax., *beodan*, command; *bod*, an order; *boda*, a messenger. Irish, *budh*, intelligent, wise. Lith., *bundu*, inf. *busti*, to watch.

PoHA, *v.* Haw., to burst forth, as sound, to thunder, to break, as a boil, to break in upon, as sudden light in a dark place, to come in sight, to open, as a bud or a seed-pod. Marqu., *poha*, similar meanings, also to hatch. Sam., *foa*, to chip, as a hole in an egg-shell, to break; *fo-foa*, to hatch. Mal., *puchah*, to break.

Sanskr., *push*, to nourish, thrive, prosper, unfold; *pushta*, pcl. pass. nourished, eminent, loud; *push-pa*, a flower, the menses; *push-kara*, a drum; *posha*, nourishing, thriving.

I have followed the order of meanings as indicated in Benfey's Sansk. Dict.; but, judging from the Polynesian relatives *poha* or *foa*, I should say that to " unfold" was the primary sense in Sanskrit from which " thriving, nourishing," &c., were developed. In *pushtā*, " loud," the Sanskrit has also preserved one of the primary senses of *push*, " bursting with a noise;" for " loud " is certainly not a developed or derivative sense of " to nourish," but a natural and usual accompaniment of the sense of " bursting, breaking." Moreover, there can be no possible association of ideas between a flower, *push-pa*, and a drum, *push-kara,* unless the former refers to the "bursting, breaking, opening" of the flower-pod, and the latter refers to the peculiarly "bursting, thundering, loud" noise of the drum. The Polynesian word and sense give the key to these two different meanings. That a primary sense of Sanskr. *push* was "to burst, break open," is evident from the Mal. *puchah,* which indicates a Sanskrit origin rather than a Polynesian.

POKI'I, *s.* Haw., the youngest member of a family. N. Zeal., *potiki,* id. Tah., *potii,* a girl; *potiti,* diminutive, small. Marqu., *poti'i,* an infant.

Sanskr., *pota,* the young of any animals or plants.

Lat., *putus, pusus,* a boy, a lad.

I am inclined to look upon the Polynesian as a compound word, *pot* or *pok,* with whatever may have been its final vowel, and *iki* or *iti,* small. Benfey gives no etymon for *pota,* and it hardly refers itself to *putra,* a son—*pu-tra*—according to Benfey, Pictet, and others; while the Latin *pu-tus* can hardly be related to *pu-ter,* of which *puer* is a contraction, according to Pictet, both of which, *pu-tra* and *pu-er,* probably refer to Sanskrit *pû,* to purify.

On p. 265, I have referred to the Polynesian *poko, poto,* short, small, as a possible corruption of *pauku,* and allied to *pau.* But *poto* may be an independent word, and in conjunction with *iki* form the Polynesian N. Zeal. *pot-iki.*

POLI[1], *s.* Haw., lower part of the belly, the lap, bosom, space between the breasts, hollow, cavity; *poli-wawae,* hollow of the foot, instep. Tong., *foli,* encircling, round about. Fiji., *voli,* go round, about.

Lat., *vola,* hollow of the hand or foot.

Greek, γυαλον, hollow, the hollow of a vessel, rock, or ground, cave, grotto, dale.

Sax., *bolla.* Engl., *bowl,* drinking vessel. Sanskr., *bholi,* a camel. No reference by Benfey. The original camel known to the Aryans was the Bactrian camel, with two humps. *Bholi* might thus signify the hollow between the two humps, the animal with such a hollow back. A.

Pictet (Orig. Ind.-Eur., i. 384, &c.) analyses the Anc. Slav. *veli-badu* and the Gothic *ul-bandus*, names for camel, and concludes that they derive from the Sanskrit *vala* or *bala*, "fort, puissant," and the Sanskrit *bandha*, "corps, l'animal du corps puissant et robuste." Whatever the value of the compounds *badu* and *bandus*, it may be just as possible that *veli* and *ul* refer themselves through the Sanskrit *bholi*, the Latin *vola*, to the primary sense of "hollow, cavity," as found in the Polynesian *poli*.

POLI², *s.* Haw., a soft, porous stone, duplicate form of *poli-poli*, generally used; *v.* to soften, as a stone in the art of making stone-adzes; *poli-e*, a shining substance, a bright gleam.

Lat., *polio,* to polish, make smooth, furbish; *pollis, pollen*, fine flour, meal; *polenta*, pearl barley.

Welsh, *ca-boli*, to polish.

Sanskr., *báluka*, sand, powder, camphor. No etymon in Benfey.

POLU, *polu-polu*, *adj.* Haw., thick, fat, fleshy, gross. Tah., *pori*, *s.* bulk, size, excessive fatness; *pori-a*, fat, fleshy, of man or beast; *haa-pori*, to fatten. Fiji., *vora*, grow fat, stout; *vore,* a pig; *voroka*, large, bulky. Ceram. (Ahtiago), *war*, pig. Matabello, *boör*, id.

Sanskr., *bala*, strength, bulkiness, the body; *balin, adj.* strong; *s.* a bull, a camel, a hog; *varâhu, varâha*, a hog.

Lat., *verres*, a boar; *porcus,* a hog, pig. Umbr., *purka*, id.

Greek, πορκος, a hog.

Sax., *fearh.* O. H. Germ., *farah*, hog, pig. Germ., *ferkel*, sucking-pig. Engl., *farrow*, litter of pigs.

Lith., *parszas*, hog.

Liddell and Scott (Greek Dict.), following Curtius, refer the Greek, Latin, German, and Lithuanian forms of this word to the Sanskrit *prishat*, "the porcine deer," from *prish*, "to sprinkle," as etymon. The step from *prish* to *pork* may not be so difficult materially and mentally, but as it is only a hypothesis, I prefer to connect the *pork* family, through the sense of "bulk, strength, fatness," with the Sanskrit *bala, balin, varâha,* Latin *verres,* Polynesian *pori, vora, vore.*

Mr. A. Pictet (Orig. Ind.-Eur., i. 335) refers the Latin *verres* to the Sanskrit *vrish,* "to rain, moisten, engender," whence *vrisha,* a bull, a cat, a peacock's tail; *vrishan,* a bull, a horse; *vrishni,* a ram; *vrishana,* the testicles or scrotum. Thus *verres* would stand for *verses.* It is plausible, and perhaps is so, though Benfey refers *verres* to *varâha.* But Mr. Pictet's analysis of *varâha* (ib. p. 371), to which he refers the A.-Sax. *beorgh,* a hog, O. Germ. *barch, parh,* Mod. Germ. *borg,* a gelded hog, Engl. *barrow,* as derived from the Sanskrit *rah,* "to leave, abandon, be deprived of," on the analogy of the French *sanglier,* being derived from the Latin *singularis,* the characteristic of the animal being "loneliness, solitude," seems to me more ingenious than correct.

PONA, *s.* Haw., joints, as of the spine or of the fingers, space between the joints of bones; joints of sugar-cane or bamboo; *v.* to divide into joints or pieces, to show spots differently variegated. N. Zeal., *pona,* ankle-joints, knots. Tah., *pona,* joint of finger or toe, a knot, tie; *pona-turi,* the knee-joint. Sam., *pona,* knot, joint, a lump, a fault; *pona-ata, pona-ua,* the Adam's apple in the throat; *pona-pona-vae,* the ankle. Marqu., *pona,* joints. Fiji., *vono,* joints or pieces; *adj.* inlaid with pearl or ivory. Malg., *vaneh,* joints of cane or bamboo.

Sanskr., *venu,* a bamboo, reed, flute, pipe; *vamça,* id.

PU[1], *s.* Haw., a shell, the trumpet-shell, a wind-instrument made by twisting the ti-leaf; *puhi, v.* to blow, as the wind, to puff, breathe hard; *puha,* to breathe like a turtle, snort, hawk; *pu-eo,* an owl. Tah., *pu,* a conch-shell, trumpet; *puo,* to blow, as wind; *puha,* to blow, as the turtle or whale; *puhi-puhi,* blow, as the wind, to fan, as a fire; *puki-aru,* mist arising from the sea breaking over a reef. Sam., *pu,* trumpet-shell; *pu-alii,* sonorous, deep-sounding voice; *pusa,* to send up smoke, spray, dust, vapour. Marqu., *pu,* trumpet-shell; *pu-aina,* the ear, to be attentive; *pu-aka,* pillow, bed; *pua-pua,* foam, froth;

puhi, blow, smoke, blow on a shell. Fiji., *vu*, to cough; *vuso*, to foam, froth. Celebes (Menado), *pupusy*, smoke. Saparua, *poho*, smoke.

Sanskr., *phut*, *pût*, imitative sound of blowing; *phut-kara*, blowing, hissing; *pupphusa*, the lungs; perhaps *bukk*, to sound, to bark.

Greek, βυζω, to hoot; βυας, the owl; βυκανη, trumpet; βυκτης, a wind, hurricane; φυσα, bellows, breath, wind; φυσαω, to blow, puff; φυσητηρ, blow-pipe, wind-instrument, spiracle.

Lat., *bucina*, trumpet, bugle; *pustula*, blister, bladder; *bucca*, inflated cheek.

Welsh, *buchiaw*, to bellow, low.

Anc. Slav., *boucati*, to bellow, roar. Illyr., *buciti*, be sonorous; *bukka*, noise.

Pu², *s.* Sam., a hole, the anus, the vagina; *pui-pui*, a door, partition; *v.* to shut, shut off; *pui talinga*, the earhole; *puta*, stomach; *pute*, navel; *pute pute*, the centre of the waistcloth. Tah., *pu*, middle, centre; *pu-taria*, earhole; *puta*, hole, aperture; *v.* to be pierced. Marqu., *pu-ava*, a hole in the rocks; *puta*, hole, aperture; *v.* to enter or go out; *putoe*, belly; *putuna*, bowels, intestines. Haw., *puka*, to enter, pass through, utter, publish; *s.* a doorway, entrance, hole; *pu-ai*, the gullet. Fiji., *buca*, space between two mountains, a valley, a gorge. Mal., *pusat*, centre; *putus*, to pass through.

Sanskr., *bhûka*, a hole, head of a fountain, darkness; *bukka*, the heart; *puta*, concavity, cup, vessel, hollow of the hand, a funnel; *put*, a hell for children.

Pers., *putah*, *butah*, cavity, vessel.

Irish, *puite*, vase, cavity, cunnus.

Arm., *pos*. Alban., *pus*, a pit, a hole.

Pu³, *v.* Haw., to come forth from, come out of, draw out, move off. Tah., *pu*, to be obtained, gratified, completed. Marqu., *pu*, come forth, go off, issue. Sam., *pu-pu*, give out heat, as from an aperture, show anger, rinse the mouth rinse off a curse. From this derive Haw., *pu-a*, blossom, flower, sheaf of grain or grass, a flock, a herd, descendants, children. Tong., Sam., *fua*, fruit, flowers. Tah., *pua*, blossom. Fiji., *vua*, fruit, produce, gr. child. Buru., *fuan*, fruit. Ceram. (Ahtiago), *vuan*, id. Malg., *vua*, id. Mal., *buwah*, id.

Sanskr., *bhû*, to become, exist, to be, spring up; *bhûti*, production, birth, wealth.

Greek, φυω, to bring forth, to put forth, shoots, spring up, come into being, grow, with its numerous derivatives; φυσις, nature, result of growth; φυας, shoot, sucker; φυη, growth, stature; φυλον, race, tribe; φυλλον, a leaf; φυμα, growth, produce; φυτον, plant, tree, descendants, pupil, child; φυτωρ, begetter, father.

Lat., *fui, futurus, futus, spuo, spuma.* Benfey as well as Liddell and Scott consider the Latin *spuo*, the Greek πτυω, and Gothic *speiwan*, as related to each other, and to the Sanskrit *shthiv*, to spit; and Liddell and Scott give a root of πτυ or πυτ. That root is probably correct, in view of the other form πυτιζω, and πτυω must have been a later transposition of an older πυτω that goes back to an original *pu*, as we find it in the Polynesian, and as, considering *s* as prosthetic, we find it in the Latin *s-puo*. The transition from *pu*, πυτ or πτυ, to Sanskrit *shthiv* seems rather violent, and I am not called on to defend it.

Pu'u, *s.* Haw., any round protuberance belonging to a larger body, a hill, a peak, a wart, the knuckles, Adam's apple in the throat, the throat itself, a heap, the heart; *puku-puku, v.* to wrinkle the forehead, draw down the eyebrows, frown; *puku-i*, to sit doubled up, be bent up, fold the arms together; *puu-lima*, the wrists; *o-pu'u*, bud, protuberance, bunch, a whale's tooth, spur of a young cock; *v.* to bend, as trees or plants; *adj.* swelling high, as the surf before breaking; *o-puu-puu*, rough, uneven, bulging, swelling out, convex. N. Zeal., *puku*, the stomach; *puku-waewae*, the ankle. Tong., *to-pu-wae*, sole of the foot, shoe, sandal. Marqu., *puku*, to swell, puff out the cheeks of the face, fruit, bunch, bundle; *pu'u-na*, produce; *puutike*, protuberance, tumours; *ta-pu-wae*, sole of the foot. Mang., *papa-puku*, the buttocks. Sam., *pu'u, pu'u-pu'u*, short, squat; *ta-pu-wae*, the ankle, foot from the ankle. Tah., *pu'u*, ball, protuberance; *puupuu*, rough, uneven; *putu*, to clasp the hands. Fiji., *buku*, the peaked end of a thing, a tail, a knot; *buku-buku-ni-linga*, the elbow; *buku-buku-ni-yawa*, the heel; *buku-ni-kesu*, the back of the head, occiput.

Sanskr., *bhuj*, to bend, make crooked; *bhuja*, the arm, hand, proboscis of an elephant, bending; *bhujaga*, a snake; *bhujantara*, the breast.

Pers., *bukan*, stomach.

Goth., *biugan, baug, bugum*, to bow, to bend. Sax., *bugan*, to bend; *boga*, a bow; *eln-boga*, elbow; *bi-bugan*, to flee away. O. H. Germ., *buh, buoc;* Mod. Germ., *bucht, buckel, bucken, bug, beugen;* Swed., *buk*, the belly; *bugt*, a bend; *puckel*, a hump, bunch.

Greek, φυγη, flight; φευγω, to flee; φυξις, place of refuge. Liddell and Scott also refer πυξ, πυγη, πυγων, to the Sanskrit *bhuj;* but see remarks s. v. *Piko*, p. 263.

Lat., *fuga*, flight; *fugax*.

Slav., *bega*, to flee; *bugti*, to frighten.

Welsh, *bvg*, a swelling; *bog*, id.; *boc*, the cheek; *bogel*, navel.

PULA[1], *v.* Sam., to shine, be yellow, as fruit; *puba*, the eyes; *pula-pula*, to shine a little, as the eyes on recovery from sickness; *s.* the shining appearance at the bottom of the sea; *papula*, to shine. Tah., *pura*, to blaze up, as fire, to sparkle, be luminous, as the sea; *s.* a spark or flash of fire; *pura-rea*, sallow, sickly, pale. Fiji., *vula*, the moon; *vula-vula*, white. N. Celebes (Bolanghitan), *puro*, fire; *wura*, moon; (Ratahan), *ma-wuroh*, white. Amblaw, *purini*, white; *bular*, moon. Gilolo (Gani), *wulan*, white. Rotti, *fula*, white. Solor, *burang*, id. Mentawey Isl., *me-bulan*, white. Malg., *vula*, moon, month, metal, silver. Mal., *bulan*, moon. Jav., *wulan*, id. Buru, *fhulan*, id. Matabello, *wulan*, id.; *wuli-wulan*, yellow.

Greek, πυρ, fire (funereal, sacrificial, and on the hearth), lightning, blaze; πυρετος, fiery heat, fever; πυριδιον, a spark; πυρσος, πυρρος, flame-coloured, yellowish, tawny, red.

Lat., *pruna*, live-coal. Umbr., *pir*, fire. Sax., *fyr*, fire. Norse, *fur*, id.; *fudra*, to flame.

Bohem., *pyr*, embers.

Liddell and Scott (*s. v. Πυρ*) give no root or Sanskrit reference to the above West Aryan equivalents of the Polynesian *pura*. Benfey refers *πυρ* and *fyr* to the Sanskrit *pû*, to purify, to clean. A. Pictet does not refer to *πυρ* in his "Orig. Ind.-Eur."

PULA², *s.* Haw., small particles of anything, as dust, motes, leaves of the hala tree used in fishing; *pula-pula*, sugar-cane tops used for planting. N. Zeal., *pura-pura*, seeds. Stewart Isl., *bura*, thatching material. Fiji., *vura-vura*, reeds, shoots, or suckers.

Lat., *pulvis*, dust, powder, perhaps *far* and *farina*.

Greek, *πυρος*, wheat, grain generally. Liddell and Scott say, "Deriv. uncertain; in Sanskrit *pura* is some kind of grain." Pictet, "Orig. Ind.-Eur.," i. 266, refers this and several West Aryan terms for grain of different kinds, as well as the Sanskrit *pûra*, *pûrika*, a cake, to the Sanskrit *pri*, *pûr*, to fill, collect, satisfy. The primary sense is probably found in the Polynesian *pula* and the Latin *pulvis*.

PULU, *v.* Haw., be wet, wash, bathe; *pulu-pulu*, id., be soft, as that which is soaked in water, wet, as clothes. Sam., Tong., *fufulu*, to rub, wash, wipe; *pulu*, the husk of the cocoa-nut. Tah., *puru*, id. Fiji., *vulu-vulu*, to wash the hands.

Sanskr., *plu*, to swim, navigate; *pluta*, bathed, wet; *â-plu*, to bathe, wash; *â-pluta*, wet; *plava*, swimming, a boat; *plush*, be wet, to sprinkle.

Greek, *πλεω*, *πλωω*, to sail, swim, float; *πλοιον*, a floating vessel; *πλυνω*, wash clean, as clothes; *πλυτος*, washed; *πλυνος*.

Lat., *pluo*, to rain; *pluvia*; *fluo*, to flow; *fluvius*, river; *fluxus*.

Goth., *flodus*, flood, river. A.-Sax., *fleowan*, to flow.

Slav., *plova*, inf. *plouti*, to navigate. Lith., *plauti*, *plowiti*, to wash; *pluditi*, to float.

PUNA, *s.* Haw., a source or spring of water, wells,

cavern, pit; *ma-puna*, boiling up, flowing off, as water in a spring. N. Zeal., *puna*, spring of water. Tah., *wai-puna*, spring water, bubbling water; Sam., *puna*, spring up, boil up, bubble; *s.* spring of water. Tong., Marqu., *puna*, id. Tagal., *ma-punga*, liquid.

Lat., *fundo, -ere*, to pour out, to spill, of liquids; *fons*, spring, source, fountain.

Welsh, *fwn, fynnon*, source, fountain.

As a general rule, the letter *s* is replaced in most of the Polynesian dialects by the letter *h*, or it is omitted; but there are a few words in the Samoan beginning with *s* which have West Aryan relations, and which are not found, or have become obsolete, in the other Polynesian dialects. Such as—

SA, *adj.* Sam., sacred, holy, forbidden; *s.* sign, portent, omen; *faa-sa*, to prohibit, to consecrate. Fakaafo, *sa*, id.

Lat., *sacer*, consecrated, sacred, execrated, cursed.

Greek, ἀγος, religious awe, curse, pollution; ἀγνος, filled with awe, hallowed, sacred; ἀγιος, devoted to the gods, holy, accursed, execrable; ἀζω, to be awe-struck, to dread.

Liddell and Scott, as well as Benfey, refer ἀγιος to Sanskrit *yaj*, to sacrifice, to worship. A. Pictet also refers to *yaj*, and suggests that the aspirate in ἀγιος is a substitute for the Sanskrit *y*, as in ἡμερος it is of the Sanskrit *y* in *yam*, to tame, govern. It may be so; at any rate, it is a substitute for *s* in the Latin *sacer*. Benfey refers the Latin *sacer* to Sanskrit *sach*, to follow, obey; Greek, ἐπομαι. Neither *yaj* nor *sach* seem to me to answer so fully to the requirements of the Greek ἀγιος, ἀζω, and Latin *sacer*, as the Polynesian *sa, sa-sa*, of whose existence I hardly suppose that those authors were cognisant.

SAMI, *s.* Sam., the sea, salt water, a strong, decaying cocoa-nut; *adj.* brackish, strong tasting. N. Celebes (Bholaugh), *simuto*, salt.

Sanskr., *samîcha*, the ocean. Benfey refers this word to *sama-añcha*, " going with, accompanying, common, uniform." Such analysis seems rather laboured in face of the Polynesian *sami*.

Perhaps the Greek ψαμμος, ψαμαθος, sand, the sand of the sea-shore, is connected with *sami* and *samîcha*, though Liddell and Scott give it a far-away root of ψαω, to rub, to smoothe. If we bear in mind that in primitive times, within the Aryan linguistic lines, as well as within those of other races, there must have existed an original complex sound of *mb* or *mp* which in course of time lost its complex character, and with this or that branch of the family assumed the simpler form of either *m*, *b*, or *p;* bearing this in mind, it is possible that the Latin *sabulum, sabuna* = *sabulum, samburra,* may connect themselves with the Greek ψαμμος, the Polynesian *sami,* and the Sanskrit *samîcha*.

SOLI, *v.* Sam., to tread on, to trample on; *soli-soli,* prostration, putting the soles of a chief's feet against the palms of the hands and the 'cheeks.

Lat., *solum,* the lowest part of anything, the bottom, ground; *solea,* the sole of a shoe or sandal; *solidus.*

WA, *s.* Haw., space between two objects, as between two rafters or posts, space between two points of time, a definite period of time, private talk or gossip; *v.* to reflect, to think. Sam., N. Zeal., Tah., Marqu., *wa,* space between, with similar applications as above.

Mang., *wa,* talk, gossip. Rarot., *wa,* to wonder. Among the derivations of this root we may note—Haw., *wa-e,* to break and separate, to select, assort; *s.* the knee, sidetimbers in a boat; *waena,* a space enclosed by boundarylines, a field, a garden; *adv.* in the middle of, between; *wa-wae,* the leg of a man or beast, the foot; *waa* and *waha,* opening generally, mouth, ditch, mouth of a person, mouth of a bag, pit, cavern; *wahi,* a word, a saying. Sam., *wae,* the leg of an animal, a stool; *v.* to divide; *waenga,* a division; *wae-wae,* divide, cut up in parts; *ma-wae,* to split, crack open; *s.* a fissure; *wa-i-masina,* space of time between the old and new moon, the night with no moon; *wa-i-palolo,* the time of the palolo-fishing, the wet season;

wa-nu, valley, ravine, chasm. Tah., *wa-e,* to share out, divide; *s.* the timbers of a boat, rafters of a small house; *wae-wae,* leg, foot; *a-wae,* id., also the moon; *waha,* mouth; *waha-iti,* a whisperer, mischief-maker; *waha-pape,* a flatterer; *waha-waha,* contempt, disregard. Marqu., *wa-e,* foot, leg; *wa-wena,* middle, between, centre. Tong., *waha,* space between two objects; *wahi,* divide, separate. Rarot., Mangar., *wa-wa,* rent, split; *waa,* mouth. N. Zeal., *waha,* mouth; *wae-wae,* leg, foot; *whaka-wa,* to consider, to judge. Fiji., *wase,* to divide; *vosa,* to speak, talk; *s.* word, speech. Malg., *vak, vakt,* to split, break; *vaki,* crack, fissure. Timor·Laut., *wahad,* the face. Kawi, *basa,* speech, language. Mal., *waktu,* time.

The above are some of the most prominent derivations of the root *wa,* primarily signifying the space between two objects. I do not find that the root itself has been retained in any of the West Aryan dialects, either in form or sense. Some of their derivations, however, seem to acknowledge the existence of such a root as the Polynesian *wa,* with such a primary meaning as here given. I find thus in the

Sanskr., *vaka,* a crane; *vakra,* crooked, bent; *van'k,* to go tortuously, be crooked; *van'ka,* the bend of a river; *van'kri,* a rib, the ribs of a building; *van'kshana,* the groin. Another series of derivations is found in *vajra,* cross, forked, a thunderbolt; *vâja,* a wing, a sound; *vaktra,* the mouth; *vach,* to speak, say; *vachas,* speech, word; *vacha,* a parrot; also *vahsa,* a year, and the breast. No Sanskrit root will act as a solvent, phonetic or otherwise, of all the above words. There is apparently nothing in common between *vâja,* sound, and *van'kri,* a rib, or between *vajra,* a thunderbolt, and *vaktra,* mouth, and we look in vain to the Sanskrit or its West Aryan congeners for an explanation. The Polynesian, however, by preserving the root *wa,* with its primary meaning, and a number of derivations running parallel to those of the Sanskrit, furnishes a bond of union between its apparently discrepant and incongruous descendants.

Lat., *vaco*, be empty, void; *vacuus, vacious; vacillo*, to bother, waver = Sanskr., *van'k; vagor-ari*, to ramble about = Sanskr., *vaj; vox*, voice; *voco*, to call; *vagio*, to cry, squall = Sanskr., *vach; vetus*, old.

Goth., *wagjan*, to wag, shake; *wegs*, wagging, raging, tempest; *wegas*, pl. waves. Sax., *wang*, the jaw, jawbone; *waeg*, ware; *waecg*, a wedge. O. H. Germ., *waga*, cradle; *wankon*, unstable, vacillating; *ga-wahan*, to remind, mention.

Greek, ἔπος for ϝέπος, word; εἶπον for ϝεϝεπον, vide Benfey; ὄψ, voice, word; ὄσσα, rumour, fame, voice, sound; ἔτος for ϝέτος, a year; βάζω, to speak, say; βαβάζω, to dance; βαβάκτης, a chatterer, also a dancer, a reveller.

Here again the Polynesian *wa* and its derivatives furnish the key wherewith to find the connection between such words as ἔτος, a year, and ἔπος, a word, βάζω, to speak, and its duplicate, βαβάζω, to dance; between the Saxon *waeg*, wave, and the Old High German *ga-wahan*, to mention; between the Latin *vaco*, be empty, *vagio*, to cry, and *vetus*, old.

WA'A, *s.* Haw., canoe, boat, vessel. Sam., *wa'a*, id. Tah., *wa'a*, id. N. Zeal., Tong., Rarot., Marqu., Mangar., *waka*, id., a raft. Fiji., *waqa*, id., also the shrine of a god, the case or cover of a thing; *waqa-waqa*, the region of the ribs, the ribs. Malg., *vatha*, chest, box. Bura and Amblaw, *waa, waga*, boat. Ceram. (Tobo), *waha*, id. Flores (Mangarai), *wangka*, id. Pulo Nias and Banjak Isl., *wongie*, cause. Singket (Sumatra), *bungke*, id. Arn. Isl. (Wammer), *bokka*, id. Amboyna, *haka*, id.

Sanskr., *vaha*, vehicle of any kind; *vaha-na*, vehicle, raft, boat; root, *vah*, to carry, to bear. Zend, *vaca*, cart.

Lat., *vas*, pl. *vasa*, vessel, a vase; *veho*, to carry, to bear; *vehiculum*, carriage, waggon, vessel, ship; *via*, road, way.

Greek, ὄχος, a carriage, anything that bears; ὄχη, prop, support; ὄχεω, to sustain, to carry, &c. (Liddell and Scott); ἄχθος, load, burden (Benfey); αὐχήν, the neck, throat.

I am aware that both Liddell and Scott and Benfey refer the Greek ἄμαξα, a car, waggon, to the Greek ἄξων and the Sanskrit *akshas*, the axle of a wheel, a car; but neither of these authorities account for the prefix *aω*, if so be that this word refers itself to *ἀξων* or *akshas.* It cannot well be a syncope of *ava*, for in that case we would have had *ἀμμαξα* and not *ἀμαξα.* If it is the copulative *ά*, answering to an original *ἀμα*, that copulative, I believe, has never assumed the form of *ἀω* or *ἀμ*, though A. Pictet, in "Orig. Ind.-Eur.," ii. 112, assumes so *faute de mieux.* I am forced to believe, therefore, that *ἀμαξα* does not refer to *ἀξων*, but is composed of *a* euphon and *μαξα*, and that *μαξα* is another instance of the permutation of *v* and *m* which we find in the Greek *μαλλος* for the Latin *vellus*, wool, both from Sanskrit *var*, to cover, and in the Greek *μαντις* for the Latin *vates*, according to Liddell and Scott's own suggestion. This ancient *μαξα*, or perhaps still older *Fαξα*, I think refers itself to the Zend *vaça*, the Sanskr. *vaha*, the Lith. *wazis*, the Anc. Slav. *vozn*, the Sax. *waegn*, *wæn*, the Irish *feghum*, *fe'un*, the Welsh *gwain*, all signifying a waggon, a car, a vehicle. Assuming this to be correct, we can explain the otherwise singular circumstance that the constellation Ursa Major has received the identical appellation in sound and sense in so widely different branches of the Aryan race as are the Northmen of Iceland and the Polynesians of New Zealand. The Icelanders called it the "*wagn*," the English Saxons called it the "*waenes thisla*" or the "*waen;*" with the Greeks in Homer's time *ἀμαξα* was the ancient and vulgar name for the Ursa Major; in New Zealand it was called *waka.* This correspondence in sense and sound, as regards the Polynesians, points to a time when the Polynesian *waka* bore the larger sense of any vehicle, terrestrial or marine, while yet the Polynesians were a continental people, and before their oceanic life had narrowed down the sense of this word to the only vehicle that remained available to them, the canoe.

WAI, *s.* Haw., water (fresh, in contradistinction from *kai*, salt water, ocean water, brackish water). In the Polynesian dialects proper, North and South, *wai* is the special name for fresh drinking-water, and for liquids generally, as *wai-u,* milk, lit. breast-water; *wai-maka,* tears, lit. eye-water. In Fiji., *wai* is water generally; *wai-dranu,* fresh water; *wai-tui,* salt water, the sea. In Buru and Amb-law, *wai,* water; Ceram. (Ahtiago), *wai,* id.; Salibabo, *wai,* id.; Saparua, *wai,* id.; Solor, *wai,* id.; Kayoa, *woya,* id.; Gilolo (Gani), *waiyr,* id.; Amboyna, *weyl, wehl,* and *wehr,* id.; Arn. Isls., *wajar,* id.; Mal. *ayer,* id.; Flores (Man-garai), *wai-tasik,* the sea; Biajan, *boi,* water.

To judge from the formation of this word in some of the Indonesian dialects, I am inclined to think that the Polynesian form in *wai* is an abrasion of an older form in *waki* or *wati.* We find in the N. Celebes (Ratahan), in Sangvir, in Tidore, in Gilolo (Galela), the form of *aki,* and in N. Celebes (Menado and Bantek) the form of *akei,* signifying water; these having lost the initial *w,* as the former have lost the middle *k.* To an original form of *wati, waki,* corresponds the

Sanskr., *vadhu, badhu,* river. Zend, *vaidhi,* id. Vide Pictet, " Orig. Ind.-Eur.," i. 140.

Armor., *gwaz,* watercourse, rivulet.

Goth., *wato.* Swed., *watten.* Germ., *wasser.* Engl. and Dutch, *water.* O. H. Germ., *wazar.*

Benfey thinks the Gothic *wato,* "base, *watan,* represents the organic form of the verb *und,* viz., *vad.*" · I am not competent to discuss the derivation of *und* from *vad;* but the existence of a root or stem in *vad* seems highly probable in view of the Sanskrit derivation *vadhu* and the Zend *vaidhi;* and I think the connection of *wato* may be dismissed as not proven, though perhaps probable, there being sufficient evidence to establish the connection of the Polynesian *wai, waki, aki,* with the Sanskrit, Zend, and Armorican *vadhu, vaidhi, gwaz.* As Curtius " will not connect" ὕδωρ with ὕω (Liddell and Scott), it may possibly stand for a more ancient Fυδωρ, and thus establish its connection with *vadhu,* &c.

It is strange, however, to find among the dialects spoken by the " tribes of the Hindu-Kush," as related by Major Biddulph, such terms for " water" as *woi,* Gilgit dialect of the Shina; *woy*, Chiliss dialect of the Indus Valley. If these are not corruptions of some Sanskrit word for water unknown to me, they may possibly be remnants of some pre-Vedic period of Aryan speech still lingering in the fastnesses of the Hindu-Kush. Compare with that the Kaioa *woya*, the Biajan *boi*, and the Polynesian *wai*.

WAUKE, *s.* Haw., name of a shrub or bush, from the bark of which "kapa" (cloth) is made; a species of mulberry. Tah., *aute;* Marqu., *ute*, id. (Morus papyrifera). Sam., *aute*, Hibiscus, Rosa-sinensis.

Zend, *vaêti*, willow. Vide A. Pictet, "Orig. Ind.-Eur.," i. 253: "Spiegel l'a traduit d'abord par saule, à cause de l'analogie du persan *bêd;* mais plus tard il a trouvé dans le Mino Khired une forme *bît* que Nerio sengh rend en sanskrit par *phala*, fruit. Il ne saurait donc ici être question du saule, et Spiegel incline à comparer le latin *vitis*, tout en restant en doute sur l'identité complète de signification."

Greek, οἰσος, οἰσυα, an osier; according to Liddell and Scott related to ἰτεα, a willow, to Lat. *vitis*, a vine, *vitex;* to O. H. Germ. *wida*, *weida*, Sax. *withig*, Engl. *withe*, *withy*, "probably from Sanskrit *ve*," to weave.

Sanskr., *vetas*, ratan, reed; *vaitasa*, a sort of cane, Chlamus fasciculatus.

A. Pictet, *l. c.*, refers the Greek, German, and Zend words to the Sanskrit *vat*, a form of *vrit*, to surround, to tie; *vata*, a string, a rope, the Indian fig-tree; *vatara*, a mat; *vîtika*, the betel plant, a tie; *vita*, a branch, and its shoot. I do not assume to decide between these two authorities, but simply claim a *locus standi* for the Polynesian *wauke*, *aute*, in primary family of speech from which the Zend *vaêti*, the Latin *vitis*, and the Greek ἰτεα and οἰσος derived their being.

WAHA[1], *v.* Haw., to carry on the back, to bear. Sam., Tong., *fafa*, id. N. Zeal., *waha*, id.

Sanskr., *vah*, to carry, conduct, bear.

Zend, *vaz*, to carry, to lead.

Greek, ὀχεω, to bear, carry.

Lat., *veho*, to carry, &c.

Lith., *vesti*, to carry.

See p. 278, s. v. *Wa'a*. Of the two forms, *waka*, canoe, vessel, and *waha*, to bear, carry, the former is, in my opinion, a denominative of the latter, and originally bore the same relation to *waha* as the Latin *vec-tabulum* to *veho*, as the Sanskrit *vaha*, *vahana*, to *vah*, as the Zend *vaca* to *vaz*. The Fijian forms and meanings show this plainly.

WAHA[2], *s.* Tonga., the sea. Sam., *wasa*, the sea, the ocean, specially between two distant points.

Fiji., *wasa*, sea, ocean.

Sanskr., *vasu*, water, kind of salt; *vasuka*, sea-salt; *vaçira*, id.

WAHI[1], *s.* Haw., place, space, situation; *wahi-noho*, a residence, dwelling-place. Tah., Marqu., *wahi*, id. Sam., *fasi*, a piece, a place.

Sanskr., *vas* (1), to dwell; *vasati*, a dwelling; *vasana*, id.

Irish, *fosra, fois*, habitation; *fos, fosadh*, repose; *foisim*, to dwell. Goth., *wisan*. A.-Sax., *wessan*, remain. O. Norse, *wist*, dwelling. O. H. Germ., *heim-vist*, domicile.

Lith., *weisle*, family, race.

Greek, ἑστια for Ϝεστια, hearth, home.

Lat., *vesta*, *vestibulum*.

WAHI[2], *s.* Haw. (accent on ult.), a covering, wrapper *v.* to cover, wrap up, surround. Marqu., *fafi*, to clothe, clothing, bundle.

Sanskr. *vas* (3), to wear, as clothes, put on; *vasi, vasana*, covering, clothes.

Lat., *vestis*, garment; *vagina*, sheath, husk.

Greek, ἑσθης, dress, clothing; ἑννυμι, to clothe; ἑανος, fit to wear, ἑ for Ϝε; εἱμα, dress.

Goth., *wasjan*, to clothe, to wear; *waste*, cloth.

WAHINE, *s.* Haw., female, woman, wife. Marqu., *vehine*, id. Tah., *vahine*, id. Sam., *fafine*, id. Tong., *fefine*, id. Rarot., *vaine*, id. N. Zeal. and Paum., *wahine*, id. Salebabo, *babine*, woman, wife. S. Celebes, *bawine, baine*, id. Buru, *fine, ge-fine*, id. Saparua, *pipi-na*, id. Gilolo (Gani), *mapin*, id. Amboyna, *mahina*, id. Teor, *mawina*, woman; *mewina*, wife. Madura, *bahine*, woman. Malay, *bini*, wife.

Ceram. (Teluti), *ihina,* woman; *nihina,* wife. Ceram. (Ahtiago), *vina,* woman; *invina,* wife. Savu, Amblaw, *ina,* mother. Rotti, Timor, *ena,* id. Goram Isl., *wawima,* woman, wife.

From a general survey of the Polynesian and Indonesian dialects above quoted, it becomes tolerably certain that this is a compound word, the first constituent being an ancient form in *wa, ba,* or *ma,* with a primary meaning of breast, bosom, an attribute and designation of a female, as retained in the Æolian and Doric forms of μᾶ, which Liddell and Scott call a shortened form of ματης, but which may be the original in μα-ζος, one of the breasts, especially of women; in μη-τρα, womb, matrix; in Lat. *mamma,* breast; in Goth. *wamba,* Germ. *wamme,* Scot. *wame,* womb, belly; in Sanskr., *vâma,* udder; *vâmâ,* a woman; *vâmê,* a mare; and in such compounds perhaps as Lat. *femina,* woman = Sanskr. *vâ-mâ, femur,* thigh; *fetus, feo, fetare,* as Sax. *wif-man,* woman. The second constituent, *hina, hine, ina, ena, ine,* must have been a very early term used to express the female gender, and which in time became the terminal form in several dialects, and, its original sense lost, it remained as an indicator of the feminine gender of the particular word to which it was attached. In the Gothic dialects we find such words as (Germ.) *koenig, koenig-inn, held, held-inn, gott, gött-inn,* (Swed.) *gud, gud-inna, fruste, frust-inna, hjelte, hjelt-inna,* &c.; in Lat., *leo, leæna, rex, reg-ina, tutor, tutel-ina;* in Greek, ἥρω, ἥρω-ινη, et al. Probably the Zend *ca-ine,* a girl, and *zen,* a woman, refer to the same formation and ancient female designation.

WAHO, *prepos.* Haw., out, outside, outward. Sam., *fafo;* Rarot., Mangar., *wao;* Tah., *waho;* Marqu., *waho;* N. Zeal., *waho,* id.

Sanskr., *vakis,* outward, outside. Benfey thinks "perhaps from *aradhi,*" i.e., *ara-dhâ,* limit, end. The Polynesian offers the better, and probably surer, etymon or reference.

WALA, *v.* Haw., to excite; *wala-wala,* be excited, make a great noise, to shout; *wala-au,* to speak in a boisterous manner, to cry out. Sam., *wala-au,* to call to, to invite.

Rarot., *warakau,* to cry out. Tah., *waro-waro,* a voice heard without seeing the person, the vibration of sound on the ear or of scents on the organ of smelling.

Sanskr., *varvara,* a barbarian, an outcast, the clash of weapons. According to Benfey "probably borrowed from βαρβαρος;" but not so according to Curtius; *vide* Liddell and Scott, *s. v.*

Pers., *barbar,* cry, murmur, a madman, a quarreller; *bala,* cry, clamour.

Lat., *balbus,* stammering, stuttering; *balo,* to bleat, speak foolishly.

Welsh, *ballaw,* to bark.

Russ., *swara,* quarrel.

Greek, βαρβαρος, a name for all with whom the Greek was not the native speech. No etymon given. The Polynesian *wala* seems to me a satisfactory reference.

WALI, *v.* Haw., to grind to powder, mince fine, to mix; *adj.* fine, soft, like paste. Tah., *wari,* paste, mud, dirt. Sam., *wali,* paint, plaster; *v.* to paint.

Sanskr., *val,* to move to and fro, to turn, surround; *val-ana,* turning, agitation.

Greek, ἀλεω, to grind, bruise, pound; ἀλετης, grinding ἀλευρον, wheaten flour; ἀλως and ἀλωη, threshing-floor.

Lat., *volvo,* to roll, turn, wind round; *volvæ,* folding doors; *valgus,* bow-legged.

Goth., *walwjan,* to roll, wallow; *walugjan,* to reel about. Sax., *wæltan,* to welter, roll about. Germ., *walzen.*

A. Pictet, "Orig. Ind.-Eur.," ii. 119, intimates, after Ahrens, that ἀλεα and ἀλευρον have an initial μ omitted. Liddell and Scott seem to concur in the opinion that these, with many other kindred words, were once digammated; and if they are akin to *volvo* and *walwjan,* they certainly must have been. I have on page 117 referred the words that are of undoubted kindred to ἐιλω to the Polynesian *hili, fili,* and see therefore no object in placing *walwjan, volvo,* and ἀλεω (for Ϝαλεω), in the same category as ειλω, ιλλω, ἐλιξ, &c., while the Sanskrit *val* and the Polynesian *vali* stand ready to receive them.

WANA, *v.* Haw. (for *wa-ana*), to appear, come in sight, approach ; *waana-ao*, early dawn, first light of day. Tah., *fa*, appear, come in sight. This word I consider related to Sanskr., *bhâ*, to shine, appear ; *s.* light, sun ; *bhâna*, appearance ; *bhâta*, bright, morning.

Greek, φαω, give light, shine ; φαινω, come to light, appear; φανσις, an appearance, &c. *Vide* p. 97, s. v. *Haoa*, and p. 107, s. v. *Hana*².

WANANA, *v.* Haw., to prophesy, foretell future events (a probable syncope of *wana-ana*) ; *hawa-na*, to whisper, speak in a low voice. Tong., *fe-fana-fana*, to whisper ; *fananga*, a fable ; *wana*, curse, malediction. Sam., *fangono*, a tale intermingled with song. Tah., *wanaa*, an orator, fluent of words, oration, counsel. Marqu., *wanana*, a song, singing.

Sanskr. *van* 1, to sound ; *van* 2, to ask, to beg (Benfey) ; *bhan*, to speak, sound ; *bhand*, to upbraid, reprove, to speak.

Sax., *bannan*, *a-bannan*, to proclaim. Swed., *banna*, to rebuke, revile ; *for-banna*, to curse, damn. Engl., *ban*, *banish*. Perhaps Goth. *wenjan*, to hope, expect ; *wens*, expectation, hope. A. Pictet refers these to Sanskr. *badh*, *bandh*, to punish, orig. to tie, ligare.

Liddell and Scott assume φα = Sanskr. *bhâ*, as the root of φημη, φατις, φανη, &c., as well as of Lat. *fari*, *fama*, *fabula*, *fas*, and refer to *bhash* and *bhan* as derivative forms of *bhâ*. They say that this root φα " has two main branches : 1. Expressing light as seen by the eye ; φαω, φαινω, &c. 2. Expressing light as reaching the mind ; φημι, φασκω, &c. Benfey refers φημι, &c., to *bhâsh*, and thinks that *bhâsh* is probably related to *bhâ*." Whatever eventually may be decided on as to the root or roots of these two classes of words, the Polynesian relationship cannot well, I think, be ignored.

WELA, *v.* HAW., be on fire, to burn, be warm, hot, physically and mentally, hence to rage, be angry ; *s.* heat of fire or of the sun ; N. Zeal., Mangar., Tah., *wera*, id., to burn. Sam., *wela*, id., to be cooked ; *wewela*, be hot. Marqu., *wea*, heat, burning. Fiji., *weweli*, bright, shining.

Sanskr., *jval*, to blaze, shine, burn, be red-hot; *jvar*, be feverish; *jvâla*, flame; *ulkâ*, for *jvalka* (Benfey), a fire-brand.

Pars., *war*, heat; *waragh*, flame.

Anc. Slav., *varu*, heat.

Irish, *gualaim*, I burn; *gual*, a coal.

Goth., *wulan*, to well up, boil, be fervent. A.-Sax. *wellain*, id.; *well*, spring, fountain.

Lat., *bullo, bullio*, to boil, bubble. Benfey refers ζαλη, the surging of the sea, surge, spray, to the Sanskrit *jval*. Liddell and Scott suggest a root ζα, and intimate that ζαλη is akin to σαλος and the Latin *salum*. I am inclined to Benfey's opinion on the strength of the derivative of ζαλη, viz., ζαλευκος, very white, which strongly calls to mind the English expression " a white heat," and thus unites in one the sense of hot as well as of shining.

Connected with the Polynesian branch of this word, and derived from the sense of " bright, shining, flaming," are Haw., *wea* and *weo*, flesh-coloured, reddish, spotted with red. N. Zeal., *whero*, id. Tah., *wea*, burning, conflagration ; *weo*, copper or brass (from its colour). Marqu., *weakiki*, of a bright red colour. Mangar., *werowero*, flame of fire. Fiji., *veloreloa*, yellow. In the Indonesian dialects we find *biadjon, bea*, white. Sangvir, *ma-wera*, id. Salibabo, *ma-wira*, id. Celebes (Menado), *ma-bida*, id. The only corresponding word in the West Aryan dialects that I know of is the

Slav., *bela*, white.

A. Pictet, " Orig. Ind.-Eur.," ii. 678, derives the Sanskrit *ulka* from *valka*, and this form *val*, " circumdare, tegere, la flamme qui enveloppe." Benfey derives *valka* from *jval*, *vide supra*. Benfey's derivation seems to me the most correct, as it accounts better, and in a more natural way, for the different derivative meanings in the various Aryan branches.

WELI, *v.* Haw., to branch out, as roots of a tree, to take root; *s.* a shoot, a scion, a sucker, the phosphorescent light in the sea, the light from sparks of fire; *weli* or

welina and *walina*, a form of salutation = " Health to you,"
" May you prosper." Tah., *weri-weria*, abundance of
food; *weri-weri-hiwa*, many coloured. Fiji., *veli*, a curl,
curled.

Lat., *ver*, the spring; *vernus*.

Greek, ἔαρ, ἤρ, for ϝεαρ, ϝηρ, spring of the year, young,
fresh, prime; ἐαρινος.

Old Norse, *vår;* Swed. *war*, spring. To these Latin,
Greek, and Norse terms Benfey and Liddell and Scott refer

Slav., *vesna*, spring.

Lith., *vasara*, summer.

Sanskr., *vasanta*, the season of spring; and they may
have added *vasa*, sweet, day, a ray of light, the sun, wealth,
gold; *vasna*, price, wages, wealth, assuming probably that
these Sanskrit, Slavonic, and Lithuanian terms go back to
Sanskrit *vas 2* (Benfey), to shine, "the original form of
ust;" *vide* Benfey. If so, the Latin, Greek, and Norse are
probably the older formations, inasmuch as, by retaining
the *r*, they seem to conform better to that oldest form of
Aryan speech so frequently found in the Polynesian
before the *r* began to change to *s*.

WELO, *v.* Haw., to float or stream in the wind; to
flutter or shake in the wind, *s.* the setting of the sun, or
the appearance of it floating on the ocean; *welo-welo*,
colours or cloth streaming in the wind, a tail, as of a kite,
light streaming from a brand of fire thrown into the air in
the dark; *hoku-welo-welo*, a comet, a meteor; *ko-welo*, to
drag behind, as the trail of a garment, to stream, as a flag
or pennant. Sam., Tong., *welo*, to dart, cast a spear or
dart. Tah., *wero*, to dart, throw a spear; *s.* storm, tempest,
fig. great rage; *wero-wero*, to twinkle, as the stars. Marqu.,
weo, a tail. Mangar., *wero*, a lance, spear.

Greek, βαλλω, ἐβαλον, to throw, cast, hurl, of missiles,
throw out, let fall, push forward; βελος, a missile, a dart;
βελεμνον, id.; βολη, a throw, a stroke; βολος, anything
thrown, missile, javelin, a cast of the dice.

Sanskr., *pal*, to go, to move. To this Benfey refers
the Lat. *pello*, Greek παλλω, O. H. Germ. *fallan*, A.-Sax.

feallan. Liddell and Scott are silent on these connections, but see p. 256, s. v. *Pale.*

WI, *adj.* Haw., destitute, suffering, starving; *s.* starvation, famine; *wiwi*, lean, meagre; *hoo-wiwi*, to lessen, diminish. Marqu., *wiwi*, poor, feeble; *wiwi-i*, solitude. Tah., *veve*, poor, destitute, bare; *v.* to be in want.

Sanskr., *vi*, *prep.* "compounded with verbs and nouns it implies: 1. separation; 2. privation; 3. wrongness, baseness," &c. (Benfey); as *vi-deha*, without body; *vi-dhará*, without man, a widow; *vi-dhantá*, poverty, without wealth.

Lat., *ve* or *vi*, in compound words, as *ve-cors*, without reason, frantic; *ve-grandis*, not large, small; *ve-sanus*, out of the senses, raving unsound; *vi-duus*, *vi-dua*, without husband or wife, widower, widow. Of other things, empty, void, without.

Goth., *widuwo*, A.-Sax., *wuduwa*, widow.

Benfey (Sansk. Dict., *s. v.*) leads one to infer that *vi* is but an aphærsis of *dui*. It seems to me that the natural inference, and the natural turn of men's thoughts, would be that *dui*, two, implied addition rather than diminution. It is possible that the Sanskrit *dui* may have been "worn down," as Professor Sayce calls it, to a preposition or mere affix, not only in the Sanskrit, but also in the Gothic and Latin; but with a substantial Polynesian *wi* still alive indicating destitution, deprivation, diminution, I incline to consider the latter as the base of, and proper relative to, the Sanskrit, Gothic, and Latin preposition or affix.

WIKI, *v.* Haw., to hasten, be quick; *adv.* quickly, in haste; *a-wiki*, *a-wiwi*, id.

Zend, *vi*, rapid; also fish.

Sanskr., *vij*, to tremble, to fear; *vega*, i.e., *vij-a* (Benfey), speed, flight of an arrow, impetus; *vegin*, *vegita*, speed, haste, quickly.

Anc. Slav., *viej-di*, the eyelids. Benfey refers ἀίσσω, to move with a quick shooting motion, to shoot, dart, to the Sanskrit *vij*. Liddell and Scott think it "perhaps akin to ἀω, ἀημι."

ADDENDA.

JUST as I had finished my own foregoing work, I received
" Samoa, a Hundred Years Ago, and Long Before, &c., by
George Turner, LL.D., of the London Missionary Society,
with a preface by E. B. Tylor, F.R.S., London, 1884." It
may be late, but not too late, for me to add my mite
of acknowledgment and honour to Rev. Mr. Turner for
this seasonable publication of what he has gathered and
preserved of Samoan folk-lore and of Samoan heathen
life and customs—a section of Polynesian studies which
has hitherto been a comparative blank. There can no
longer be any doubt that the Samoans came to their present group from the Fijis, that last rendezvous of the
Polynesian tribes after their exodus from the Asiatic
Archipelago, and before their dispersion in the East
Pacific. The references to that fact, as gathered from
their own traditions, are too many and too plain to be
called in question any longer. The traditions also give
glimpses of lands beyond the Fijis, in the west, to which
the spirits of the dead returned to join their ancestors—
that famous *Pulo-tu*, the seat of the gods and the ancestors
of the Tonga Islands, and which the Fijians adopted with
so much other Polynesian lore.

The cosmogery of the Samoans is hazy and varied, like
most of the other southern groups, and shows the mani-
pulation of older and common materials, and their local
adaptation by later priests, bards, or island philosophers.
As in their language, so in their myths the Samoans
betray the impress of that great inter-migratory wave

which swept the Eastern Pacific groups some seven or eight hundred years ago, and to which I have frequently referred in the first and second volumes of this work. Savea, the first of the Maliatoas, according to the genealogy presented by Mr. Turner, falls in twenty-four generations before A.D. 1878, or about 1150 A.D. Before him thirteen generations are recorded, including Pili, the son of the god Tangaloa; from Pili back to the beginning of things are quoted seven more generations, thus making a total of forty-four generations, viz., twenty-four purely historical, thirteen semi-mythical, and seven mythic, or, at best, eponymic. But forty-four generations of Samoan existence bring us to the middle or beginning of the sixth century A.D., at which period the expulsion from, or the abandonment of, the Fijis must have already commenced; for, by properly sifting the Hawaiian traditions, we find that the Hawaiian group was being settled about one or two generations later. Thus the one chronology in a measure supports the other.

As to the origin of the name " Samoa," Mr. Turner gives three different traditions; but they all indicate that later existence of national life when, the true origin of the name, either historical or linguistic, having been forgotten, men sought in fanciful combinations to give a *raison d'être* for what had escaped the memory of themselves or their forefathers.

As in the other Polynesian principal groups, the Samoans located the place of departure of the spirits of their dead on the west end of the westernmost of their islands, at Fale-a-Lupo on Sawaii, from which the spirits started on their journey to Pulo-tu, thus confirming that universal sentiment of a Western origin which pervaded the members of the other groups. In this ancestral home of Pulo-tu the Samoans also located that famous spring, or "life-giving water," *Wai-ola*, which was such a prominent element in the ancient creed of all the Polynesians.

At the close of the book Mr. Turner gives a table of "One hundred and thirty-two words in fifty-nine

Polynesian dialects." I know not what Mr. Turner's defi-
nition of "Polynesian" may be, but it seems to me to be
unwarrantably catholic and expansive when such dialects
as Bau, Aneitum, Eromanga, New Caledonian, Moreton
Bay, Mysol, and Dorey are included as "Polynesian." Of
the one hundred and thirty-two words referred to in Mr.
Turner's table, seventy-one are missing in no less than
thirty-five of the fifty-nine dialects enumerated—an omis-
sion that rather impairs the value of the table. I regret
that so many evident misprints of words should have passed
unnoticed in the table. Of incorrect renderings of the
meaning of certain words there are not a few. I cannot
take up all such, but feel in duty bound to quote a small
number.

In the Hawaiian dialect, then, "*lawaia*" is not "fish,"
but means "to fish," *i'a* being the name of fish. "*Manu*"
does not mean "fowl," but birds in general, *moa* being
the name of a "fowl." "*Laokoa*" is not "day," *la*
being the name for that, and *la-okoa* meaning the entire
day, the whole day. "*Hoahanau kane*" and "*hoahanau
wahine*" are not Hawaiian for "brother" and "sister."
Hoahanau certainly means "born of same parents, lit.
fellow-births," but is of a common gender, and never used
with the suffixes *kane* or *wahine*. "*N'uku*" is never used
to express "the mouth" of human beings, except in
derision or in scolding, the proper word being *waha*.
There is no such verb as "*maka*," "to see," although
as a noun it means "eye." "*Umiumi*" is not "a hundred," but means "beard;" the Hawaiians did not count
by "hundreds" until after contact with Europeans, but
counted by "forties." In the Marquesan, "*akau*" is
not a "tree," but *kaau* is the word; "*ko*" is not an
"ant," but *heoo.;* "*koniu*" is not an "arrow," but *taa;*
"*vaiei*" is not to "give," but *taiona*. In the Malay proper, "*tasek*" is not the "sea," but *laut;* "*nior*" is not
"cocoa-nut," but *klapa;* "*minchit*" or "*mintjiet*" no
doubt means "rat," but nineteen out of twenty Malays
would employ the word *tikus* in preference. "*Buruk*"

may mean " bad," but W. E. Maxwell (Manual of Malay Language), and A. de Wilde and T. Raorda (Neder-duitsch-Maleisch en Soendasch Woordenboek "), ignore the word, and use *jahat, mara, gusar*, instead to express the sense of " bad, evil, wicked, not good." " *Mentua* " is not " mother," but " mother-in-law," while *ma, mak, ibu, bonda*, signify the natural mother. " *Damang* " may be " chief " for all I know, but *datu* is the more common and accepted word.

Barring a few blemishes like these, Mr. Turner's work is of the greatest value to the Polynesian ethnologist. It fills in a great measure a lacuna that no one yet had attempted to fill, and will enable future writers to tread the mazes of Polynesian migrations and Polynesian myths with steps more sure and eyes more clear than we have hitherto been able to do.

PRINTED BY BALLANTYNE, HANSON AND CO
EDINBURGH AND LONDON.

Made in United States
North Haven, CT
27 March 2023

34584098R00170